Cut By: _____

Scanned By: _____

Scanned By

Tales & Novels by Maria Edgeworth

Volume II (of II)

Maria Edgeworth was born at Black Bourton, Oxfordshire on January 1st 1768. Her early years were with her mother's family in England. Sadly, her mother died when Maria was five.

Maria was educated at Mrs Lattafière's school in Derby in 1775. There she studied dancing, French and other subjects. Maria transferred to Mrs Devis's school in Upper Wimpole Street, London. Her father began to focus more attention on Maria in 1781 when she nearly lost her sight to an eye infection.

She returned home to Ireland at 14 and took charge of her younger siblings. She herself was home-tutored by her father in Irish economics and politics, science, literature and law. Despite her youth literature was in her blood. Maria also became her father's assistant in managing the family's large Edgeworthstown estate.

Maria first published 1795 with 'Letters for Literary Ladies'. That same year 'An Essay on the Noble Science of Self-Justification', written for a female audience, advised women on how to obtain better rights in general and specifically from their husbands.

'Practical Education' (1798) is a progressive work on education. Maria's ambition was to create an independent thinker who understands the consequences of his or her actions.

Her first novel, 'Castle Rackrent' was published anonymously in 1800 without her father's knowledge. It was an immediate success and firmly established Maria's appeal to the public.

Her father married four times and the last of these to Frances, a year younger and a confidante of Maria, who pushed them to travel more widely: London, Britain and Europe were all now visited.

The second series of 'Tales of Fashionable Life' (1812) did so well that she was now the most commercially successful novelist of her age.

She particularly worked hard to improve the living standards of the poor in Edgeworthstown and to provide schools for the local children of all and any denomination.

After a visit to see her relations Maria had severe chest pains and died suddenly of a heart attack in Edgeworthstown on 22nd May 1849. She was 81.

Index of Contents

LAME JERVAS

CHAPTER I

Some years ago, a lad of the name of William Jervas, or, as he was called from his lameness, Lame Jervas, whose business it was to tend the horses in one of the Cornwall tin-mines, was missing. He was left one night in a little hut, at one end of the mine, where he always slept; but in the morning, he could no where be found; and this his sudden disappearance gave rise to a number of strange and ridiculous stories among the miners. The most rational, however, concluded that the lad, tired of his situation, had made his escape during the night. It was certainly rather surprising that he could no where be traced; but after the neighbours had wondered and talked for some time about it, the circumstance was by degrees forgotten. The name of William Jervas was scarcely remembered by any, except two or three of the oldest miners, when, twenty years afterward, there came a party of gentlemen and ladies to see the mines! and, as the guide was showing the curiosities of the place, one among the company, a gentleman of about six-and-thirty years of age, pointed to some letters that were carved on the rock, and asked, "Whose name was written there?" "Only the name of one William Jervas," answered the guide; "a poor lad, who ran away from the mines a great long while ago." "Are you sure that he ran away?" said the gentleman. "Yes," answered the guide, "sure and certain I am of that." "Not at all sure and certain of any such thing," cried one of the oldest of the miners, who interrupted the guide, and then related all that he knew, all that he had heard, and all that he imagined and believed concerning the sudden disappearance of Jervas; concluding by positively assuring the stranger that the ghost of the said Jervas was often seen to walk, slowly, in the long west gallery of the mine, with a blue taper in his hand.—"I will take my Bible oath," added the man, "that about a month after he was missing, I saw the ghost just as the clock struck twelve, walking slowly, with the light in one hand, and a chain dragging after him in t'other; and he was coming straight towards me, and I ran away into the stables to the horses; and from that time forth I've taken special good care never to go late in the evening to that there gallery, or near it: for I never was so frightened, above or under ground, in all my born days."

The stranger, upon hearing this story, burst into a loud fit of laughter; and, on recovering himself, he desired the ghost-seer to look stedfastly in his face, and to tell whether he bore any resemblance to the ghost that walked with the blue taper in the west gallery. The miner stared for some minutes, and answered, "No; he that walks in the gallery is clear another guess sort of a person; in a white jacket, a leather apron, and ragged cap, like what Jervas used to wear in his lifetime; and, moreover, he limps in his gait, as Lame Jervas always did, I remember well." The gentleman walked on, and the miners observed, what had before escaped their notice, that he limped a little; and, when he came again to the light, the guide, after considering him very attentively, said, "If I was not afraid of affronting the like of a gentleman such as your honour, I should make bold for to say that you be very much—only a deal darker complexioned—you be very much of the same sort of person as our Lame Jervas used for to be." "Not at all like our Lame Jervas," cried the old miner, who professed to have seen the ghost; "no more like to him than Black Jack to Blue John." The by-standers laughed at this comparison; and the guide, provoked at being laughed at, sturdily maintained that not a man that wore a head in Cornwall should laugh him out of his senses. Each party now growing violent in support of his opinion, from words they were just coming to blows, when the stranger at once put an end to the dispute, by declaring that he was the very man. "Jervas!" exclaimed they all at once, "Jervas alive!—our Lame Jervas turned gentleman!"

The miners could scarcely believe their eyes, or their ears, especially when, upon following him out of the mine, they saw him get into a handsome coach, and drive toward the mansion of one of the principal gentlemen of the neighbourhood, who was a proprietor of the mine.

The next day, all the head miners were invited to dine in tents, pitched in a field near this gentleman's house. It was fine weather, and harvest time; the guests assembled, and in the tents found abundance of good cheer provided for them.

After dinner, Mr. R—, the master of the house, appeared, accompanied by Lame Jervas, dressed in his miner's old jacket and cap. Even the ghost-seer acknowledged that he now looked wonderful like himself. Mr. R—, the master of the house, filled a glass, and drank—"Welcome home to our friend, Mr. Jervas; and may good faith always meet with good fortune." The toast went round, each drank, and repeated, "Welcome home to our friend Mr. Jervas; and may good faith always meet good fortune." Indeed, what was meant by the good faith, or the good fortune, none could guess; and many in whispers, and some aloud, made bold to ask for an explanation of the toast.

Mr. Jervas, on whom all eyes were fixed, after thanking the company for their welcome home, took his seat at the table; and in compliance with Mr. R—'s request, and the wishes of all present, related to them his story nearly in the following manner:

"Where I was born, or who were my parents, I do not well know myself; nor can I recollect who was my nurse, or whether I was ever nursed at all: but, luckily, these circumstances are not of much importance to the world. The first thing which I can distinctly remember is the being set, along with a number of children of my own age, to pick and wash loose ore of tin mixed with the earth, which in those days we used to call shoad, or squad—I don't know what you call it now."

"We call it squad to this day, master," interrupted one of the miners.

"I might be at this time, I suppose," continued the gentleman, "about five or six years old; and from that time till I was thirteen I worked in the mine where we were yesterday. From the bottom of my heart I rejoice that the times are bettered for youngsters since then; for I know I had a hard life of it.

"My good master, here, never knew any thing of the matter but I was cruelly used by those under him. First, the oldwoman—Betty Morgan, I think, was her name—who set us our tasks of picking and washing the squad, was as cross as the rheumatism could make her. She never picked an ounce herself, but made us do her heap for her among us; and I being the youngest, it was shoved down to me. Often and often my day's wages were kept back, not having done this woman's task; and I did not dare to tell my master the truth, lest she should beat me. But, God rest her soul! she was an angel of light in comparison with the trap-door keeper, who was my next tyrant.

"It was our business to open and shut certain doors, that were placed in the mine for letting in air to the different galleries: but my young tyrant left them every one to me to take care of; and I was made to run to and fro, till I had scarcely breath in my body, while every miner in turn was swearing at me for the idlest little fellow upon the surface of the earth; though the surface of the earth, alas! was a place on which I had never yet, to my knowledge, set my foot.

"In my own defence, I made all the excuses I could think of; and, from excuses, I went on to all kinds of deceit: for tyranny and injustice always produce cunning and falsehood.

"One day, having shut all the doors on my side of the mine, I left three open on my companion's side. The men, I thought, would not go to work on that side of the mine for a day or two: but in this I was mistaken; and about noon I was alarmed by the report of a man having been killed in one of the galleries for want of fresh air.

"The door-keepers were summoned before the overseer; or, as you call him, the viewer. I was the youngest, and the blame was all laid upon me. The man, who had only swooned, recovered; but I was thrashed and thrashed for the neglect of another person, till the viewer was tired.

"A weary life I led afterwards with my friend the door-keeper, who was enraged against me for having told the truth.

"In process of time, as I grew stronger and bigger, I was set to other work. First, I was employed at the barrow; and then a pick-axe and a gad were put into my hands; and I thought myself a great man.—It was my fate to fall among the idlest set in the mine. I observed that those men who worked by task, and who had the luck to hit upon easy beds of the rock, were not obliged to work more than three or four hours a day: they got high wages with little labour; and they spent their money jollily above-ground in the ale-houses, as I heard. I did not know that these jolly fellows often left their wives and families starving while they were getting drunk.

[Footnote: A gad is a tool used in mines; it resembles a smith's punch.]

"I longed for the time when I should be a man, and do as I saw others do. I longed for the days when I should be able to drink and be idle; and, in the mean time, I set all my wits to work to baffle and overreach the viewer.

"I was now about fourteen, and, had I grown up with these notions and habits, I must have spent my life in wretchedness, and I should probably have ended my days in a workhouse; but fortunately for me, an accident happened, which made as great a change in my mind as in my body.

"One of my companions bribed me, with a strong dram, to go down into a hole in the mine to search for his gad; which he, being half intoxicated, had dropped. My head could not stand the strength of the dram which he made me swallow to give me courage: and being quite insensible to the danger, I took a leap down a precipice which I should have shuddered to look at, if I had not lost my recollection.

"I soon came to my senses, for I broke my leg; and it is wonderful I did not break my neck by my fall. I was drawn up by cords, and was carried to a hut in the mine, near the stables, where I lay in great pain.

"My master was in the mine at the time the accident happened; and, hearing where I was, he had the goodness to come directly to me himself, to let me know that he had sent for a surgeon.

"The surgeon, who lived in the neighbourhood, was not at home; but there was then upon a visit at my master's a Mr. Y—, an old gentleman who had been a surgeon; and, though he had for many years left off practice, he no sooner heard of the accident that had happened to me than he had the goodness to come down into the mine, to set my leg.

"After the operation was over, my master returned to tell me that I should want for nothing. Never shall I forget the humanity with which he treated me. I do not remember that I had ever heard him speak to me before this time; but now his voice and manner were so full of compassion and kindness, that I looked up to him as to a new sort of being.

"His goodness wakened and warmed me to a sense of gratitude—the first virtuous emotion I was conscious of having ever felt.

"I was attended with the greatest care, during my illness, by the benevolent surgeon, Mr. Y—. The circumstance of my having been intoxicated, when I took the leap, had been concealed by the man who gave me the dram; who declared that I had fallen by accident, as I was looking down the hole for a gad that I had dropped. I did not join in this falsehood: for, the moment my master spoke to me with so much goodness about my mishap, my heart opened to him, and I told him just how the thing happened.

"Mr. Y— also heard the truth from me, and I had no reason to repent having told it, for this gave him, as he said, hopes that I might turn out well, and was the cause of his taking some pains to instruct me. He observed to me, that it was a pity a lad like me should so early in my days take to dram-drinking; and he explained the consequences of intemperance, of which I had never before heard or thought.

"While I was confined to my bed, I had leisure for many reflections. The drunken and brutal among the miners, with whom I formerly associated, never came near me in my illness; but the better sort used to come and see me often, and I began to take a liking to their ways, and to wish to imitate them.

"As they stood talking over their own affairs in my hut, I learned how they laid out their time and their money; and I now began to desire to have, as they had, a little garden, and property of my own, for which I knew I must work hard. So I rose from my bed with very different views from those which I had when I was laid down upon it; and from this time forward I kept company with the sober and industrious as much as I could. I saw things with different eyes: formerly I used, like my companions, to be ready enough to take any advantage that lay in my way of my employer; but my gratitude to him who had befriended me in my helpless state wrought such a change in me, that I now took part with my master on all occasions, and could not bear to see him wronged—so gratitude first made me honest.

"My master would not let the viewer turn me out of the work, as he wanted to do, because I was lame and weak, and not able to do much.—'Let him have the care of my horses in the stable,' said my master: 'he can do something. I don't want to make money of poor Lame Jervas. So, as long as he is willing to work, he shall not be turned out to starve.'—These were his very words; and when I heard them I said in my heart, 'God bless him!' And, from that time forth, I could, as I thought, have fought with the stoutest man in the mine that said a word to his disparagement.

"Perhaps my feeling of attachment to him was the stronger, because he was, I may say, the first person then in the world who had ever shown me any tenderness, and the only one from whom I felt sure of meeting with justice.

"About this time, as I was busied in the stable, unperceived by them, I saw through a window a party of the miners, amongst whom were several of my old associates, at work opposite to me. Suddenly, one of them gave a shout—then all was hushed—they threw down their tools, huddled together, and I judged by the keenness of their looks that they knew they had made some valuable discovery. I further observed, that, instead of beginning to work the vein, they covered it up immediately with rubbish, and defaced the country with their pick-axes; so that, to look at, no one could have suspected there was any load to be found near. I also saw them secrete a lump of spar, in which they had reason to guess there were Cornish diamonds, as they call them, and they carefully hid the bits of kellus, which they had picked out, lest the viewer should notice them and suspect the truth.

[Footnote: Kellus is the miner's name for a substance like a white soft stone, which lies above the floor or spar, near to a vein.]

"From all this, the whispering that went on, and the pains they took to chase or entice the overseer away from this spot, I conjectured they meant to keep their discovery a secret, that they might turn it to their own advantage.

"There was a passage out of the mine, known only to themselves, as they thought, through which they intended to convey all the newly-found ore. This passage, I should observe, led through an old gallery in the mine, along the side of the mountain, immediately up to the surface of the earth; so that you could by this way come in and out of the mine without the assistance of the gin, by which people and ore are usually let down or drawn up.

"I made myself sure of my facts by searching this passage, in which I found plenty of their purloined treasure. I then went up to one of the party, whose name was Clarke, and, drawing him aside, ventured to expostulate with him. Clarke cursed me for a spy, and then knocked me down, and returned to tell his associates what I had been saying, and how he had served me. They one and all swore that they would be revenged upon me, if I gave the least hint of what I had seen to our master.

"From this time they watched me, whenever he came down amongst us, lest I should have an opportunity of speaking to him; and they never, on any account, would suffer me to go out of the mine. Under pretence that the horses must be looked after, and that no one tended them so well as I did, they contrived to keep me prisoner night and day; hinting to me pretty plainly, that if I ever again complained of being thus shut up, I should not long be buried alive.

"Whether they would have gone the lengths they threatened I know not: perhaps they threw out these hints only with a design to intimidate me, and so to preserve their secret. I confess I was alarmed; but there was something in the thought of showing my good master how much I was attached to his interests, that continually prevailed over my fears; and my spirits rose with the reflection that I, a poor insignificant lad; I, that was often the scoff and laughing-stock of the miners; I, that went by the name of Lame Jervas; I, who they thought could be bullied to any thing by their threats, might do a nobler action than any man amongst them would have the courage to do in my place. Then the kindness of my master, and the words he said about me to the viewer, came into my memory; and I was so worked up, that I resolved, let the consequence be what it might, I would, living or dying, be faithful to my benefactor.

"I now waited anxiously for an opportunity to speak to him; and if I did but hear the sound of his voice at a distance, my heart beat violently. 'You little know,' thought I, 'that there is one here whom perhaps you quite forget, who is ready to hazard his life to do you a service.'

"One day, as he was coming near the place where I was at work, rubbing down a horse, he took notice that I fixed my eyes very earnestly upon him; and he came closer to me, saying, 'I am glad to see you better, Jervas:—do you want any thing?' 'I want for nothing, thank you, sir,—but,'—and as I said but, I looked round, to see who was near. Instantly Clarke, one of the gang, who had his eyes upon us, called me, and despatched me, on some errand, to a distant part of the mine. As I was coming back, however, it was my good fortune to meet my master by himself in one of the galleries. I told him my secret and my fears. He answered me only with a nod, and these words, 'Thank you—trust to me—make haste back to those that sent you.'

"I did so; but I fancy there was something unusual in my manner or countenance which gave alarm; for, at the close of the day, I saw Clarke and the gang whispering together; and I observed that they refrained from going to their secret treasure the whole of the day. I was in great fear that they suspected me, and that they would take immediate and perhaps bloody revenge.

"These fears increased when I found myself left alone in my hut at night; and, as I lay quite still, but broad awake in my bed, I listened to every sound, and once or twice started up on hearing some noise near me; but it was only the horses moving in the stable, which was close to my hut. I lay down again, laughing at my own fears, and endeavoured to compose myself to sleep, reflecting that I had never, in my life, more reason to sleep with a safe conscience.

"I then turned round, and fell into a sweet sound sleep; but from this I was suddenly roused by a noise at the door of my hut. 'It is only the horses again,' thought I; but, opening my eyes, I saw a light under the door. I rubbed my eyes, hoping I had been in a dream: the light disappeared, and I thought it was my fancy. As I kept my eyes, however, turned towards the door, I saw the light again through the key-hole, and the latch was pulled up; the door was then softly pushed inwards, and I saw on the wall the large shadow of a man with a pistol in his hand. My heart sunk within me, and I gave myself up for lost. The man came in: he was muffled up in a thick coat, his hat was slouched, and a lantern in his hand. Which of the gang it was I did not know, but I took it for granted that it was one of them come with intent to murder me. Terror at this instant left me; and starting upright in my bed, I exclaimed—'I'm ready to die! I die in a good cause! Give me five minutes to say my prayers!' and I fell upon my knees. The man standing silent beside the bed, with one hand upon me, as if afraid I should escape from him.

"When I had finished my short prayer, I looked up towards my murderer, expecting the stroke: but, what was my surprise and joy, when, as he held the lantern up to his face, I beheld—the countenance of my master, smiling upon me with the most encouraging benevolence. 'Awake, Jervas,' said he, 'and try if you can find out the difference between a friend and an enemy. Put on your clothes as fast as you can, and show me the way to this new vein.'

"No one ever was sooner dressed than I was. I led the way to the spot, which was covered up with rubbish, so that I was some time clearing out an opening, my master assisting me all the while: for, as he said, he was impatient to get me out of the mine safe, as he did not think my apprehensions wholly without foundation. The light of our lantern was scarcely sufficient for our purpose; but, when we came to the vein, my master saw enough to be certain that I was in the right. We covered up the place as before, and he noted the situation, so that he could be sure to find it again. Then I showed him the way to the secret passage; but this passage he knew already, for by it he had descended into the mine this night.

"As we passed along, I pointed out the heaps of ore which lay ready to be carried off. 'It is enough, Jervas,' said he, clapping his hand upon my shoulder; 'you have given me proof sufficient of your fidelity. Since you were so ready to die in a good cause, and that cause mine, it is my business to take care you shall live by it: so follow me out of this place directly; and I will take good care of you, my honest lad.'

"I followed him with quick steps, and a joyful heart: he took me home with him to his own house, where he said I might sleep for the rest of the night secure from all fear of murderers: and so, showing me into a small closet within his own bedchamber, he wished me a good night; desiring me, if I waked early, not to open the window-shutters of my room, nor go to the window, lest some of his people should see me.

"I lay down, for the first time in my life, upon a feather-bed; but, whether it was from the unusual feeling of the soft bed, or from the hurry of mind in which I had been kept, and the sudden change of my circumstances, I could not sleep a wink all the remainder of the night.

"Before daybreak, my master came into my room, and bid me rise, put on the clothes which he brought me, and follow him without making any noise. I followed him out of the house before any body else was awake; and he took me across the fields towards the high road. At this place we waited till we heard the tinkling of the bells of a team of horses. 'Here comes the waggon,' said he, 'in which you are to go. I have taken every possible precaution to prevent any of the miners or people in the neighbourhood from tracing you; and you will be in safety at Exeter, with my friend Mr. Y—; to whom I am going to send you. Take this,' continued he, putting a letter directed to Mr. Y— into my hand; 'and here are five guineas for you. I shall desire Mr. Y— to pay you an annuity of ten guineas out of the profits of the new vein, provided it turns out well, and you do not turn out ill. So fare you well, Jervas. I shall hear how you go on; and I only hope you will serve your next master, whoever he may be, as faithfully as you have served me.'

"'I shall never find so good a master,' was all I could say for the soul of me; for I was quite overcome by his goodness and by sorrow at parting with him, as I then thought, for ever."

CHAPTER II

"The morning clouds began to clear away; I could see my master at some distance, and I kept looking after him, as the waggon went on slowly, and as he walked fast away over the fields; but, when I had lost sight of him, my thoughts were forcibly turned to other things. I seemed to awake to quite a new scene, and new feelings. Buried underground in a mine, as I had been from my infancy, the face of nature was totally unknown to me.

"'We shall have a brave fine day of it, I hope and trust,' said the waggoner, pointing with his long whip to the rising sun.

"He went on whistling, whilst I, to whom the rising sun was a spectacle wholly surprising, started up in astonishment! I know not what exclamations I uttered, as I gazed upon it; but I remember the waggoner burst out into a loud laugh. 'Lud a marcy,' said he, holding his sides, 'to hear un, and look at un, a body would think the oaf had never seen the sun rise afore in all his born days!'

"Upon this hint, which was nearer the truth than he imagined, recollecting that we were still in Cornwall, and not out of the reach of my enemies, I drew myself back into the waggon, lest any of the miners, passing the road to their morning's work, might chance to spy me out.

"It was well for me that I took this precaution; for we had not gone much farther when we met a party of the miners; and, as I sat wedged up in a corner behind a heap of parcels, I heard the voice of Clarke, who asked the waggoner as he passed us, 'What o'clock it might be?' I kept myself quite snug till he was out of sight; nay, long afterwards, I was content to sit within the waggon, rather than venture out; and I amused myself with listening to the bells of the team, which jingled continually.

"On our second day's journey, however, I ventured out of my hiding-place; I walked with the waggoner up and down the hills, enjoying the fresh air, the singing of the birds, and the delightful smell of the honey-suckles and the dog-roses in the hedges. All these wild flowers, and even the weeds on the banks by the way-side, were to me matters of wonder and admiration. At every step, almost, I paused to observe something that was new to me; and I could not help feeling surprised at the insensibility of my fellow-traveller, who plodded on, seldom interrupting his whistling, except to cry, 'Gee, Blackbird, aw, woa;' or, 'How now, Smiler;' and certain other words or sounds of menace and encouragement, addressed to his horses in a language which seemed intelligible to them and to him, though utterly incomprehensible to me.

"Once, as I was in admiration of a plant, whose stem was about two feet high, and which had a round, shining, pale purple, beautiful flower, the waggoner, with a look of extreme scorn, exclaimed, 'Help thee, lad, does not thee know 'tis a common thistle? Didst thee not know that a thistle would prick thee?' continued he, laughing at the face I made when I touched the prickly leaves; 'why my horse Dobbin has more sense by half! he is not like an ass hunting for thistles.'

"After this, the waggoner seemed to look upon me as very nearly an idiot. Just as we were going into the town of Plymouth, he eyed me from head to foot, and muttered, 'The lad's beside himself, sure enough.' In truth, I believe I was a droll figure; for my hat was stuck full of weeds, and of all sorts of wild flowers; and both my coat and waistcoat pockets were stuffed out with pebbles and funguses.

"Such an effect, however, had the waggoner's contemptuous look upon me, that I pulled the weeds out of my hat, and threw down all my treasure of pebbles before we entered the town. Nay, so much was I overawed, and in such dread was I of passing for an idiot, that when we came within view of the sea, in the fine harbour of Plymouth, I did not utter a single exclamation; although I was struck prodigiously at this, my first sight of the ocean, as much almost as I had been at the spectacle of the rising sun. I just ventured, however, to ask my companion some questions about the vessels which I beheld sailing on the sea, and the shipping with which the bay was filled. But he answered coldly, 'They be nothing in life but the boats and ships, man: them that see them for the first time are often struck all on a heap, as I've noticed, in passing by here: but I've seen it all a many and a many times.' So he turned away, went on chewing a straw, and seemed not a whit more moved with admiration than he had been at the sight of my thistle.

"I conceived a high opinion of a man who had seen so much that he could admire nothing; and he preserved and increased my respect for him by the profound silence which he maintained, during the five succeeding days of our journey: he seldom or never opened his lips except to inform me of the names of the towns through which we passed. I have since reflected that it was fortunate for me that I had such a supercilious fellow-traveller on my first journey; for he made me at once thoroughly sensible of my own ignorance, and extremely anxious to supply my deficiencies, and to find one who would give some other answer to my questions than a smile of contempt, or, 'I do na knaw, I say.'

"We arrived at Exeter at last; and, with much ado, I found my way to Mr. Y—'s house. It was evening when I got there; and the servant to whom I gave the letter said he supposed Mr. Y— would not see me that night, as he liked to have his evenings to himself; but he took the letter, and in a few minutes returned, desiring me to follow him up stairs.

"I found the good old gentleman and some of his friends in his study, with his grand-children about him; one little chap on his knee, another climbing on the arm of his chair; and two bigger lads were busy looking at a glass tube which he was showing them when I came in. It does not become me to repeat the handsome things he said to me, upon reading over my good master's letter; but he was very gracious to me, and told me that he would look out for some place or employment that would suit me; and in the mean time, that I should be welcome to stay in his house, where I should meet with the good treatment (which he was pleased to say) I deserved. Then, observing that I was overcome with bashfulness, at being looked at by so many strangers, he kindly dismissed me.

"The next day he sent for me again to his study, when he was alone; and asked me several questions, seeming pleased with the openness and simplicity of my answers. He saw that I gazed with vast curiosity at several objects in the room, which were new to me: and pointing to the glass tube, which he had been showing the boys when I first came in, he asked me if they had such things as that in our mines; and if I knew the use of it? I told him I had seen something like it in our overseer's hands; but that I had never known its use. It was a thermometer. Mr. Y— took great pains to show me how, and on what occasions, this instrument might be useful.

"I saw I had now to do with a person who was somewhat different from my friend the waggoner; and I cannot express the surprise and gratitude I felt, when I found that he did not think me quite a fool. Instead of looking at me with scorn, as one very nearly an idiot, he answered my questions with condescension; and sometimes was so good as to add, 'That's a sensible question, my lad.'

"While we were looking at the thermometer, he found out that I could not read the words temperate, freezing point, boiling water heat, &c. which were written upon the ivory scale, in small characters. He took that occasion to point out to me the use and advantages of knowing how to read and write; and he told me that, as I wished to learn, he would desire the writing-master, who came to attend his young grandson, to teach me.

"I shall not detain you with a journal of my progress through my spelling-book and copy-books: it is enough to say that I applied with diligence, and soon could write my name in rather more intelligible characters than those in which the name of Jervas is cut on the rock that we were looking at yesterday.

"My eagerness to read the books which he put into my hands, and the attention which I paid to his lessons, pleased my writing-master so much, that he took a pride, as he said, 'in bringing me forward as fast as possible.'

"And here, I must confess, he was rather imprudent in the warmth of his commendations; my head could not stand them; as much as I was humbled and mortified by the waggoner's calling me an idiot, so much was I elated by my writing-master's calling me a genius. I wrote some very bad lines in praise of a thistle, which I thought prodigiously fine, because my writing-master looked surprised, when I showed them to him; and because he told me that, having given a copy of them to some gentlemen in Exeter, they agreed that the rhymes were wonderful for me.

"I was at this period very nearly spoiled for life: but fortunately my friend Mr. Y— saw my danger, and cured me of my conceit, without damping my ardour to acquire knowledge. He took me to the books in his study, and showed me many volumes of fine poems; pointing out some passages to me that greatly diminished my admiration of my own lines on the thistle The vast distance which I perceived between myself and these writers threw me into despair. Mr. Y— seeing me thoroughly abashed, observed that he was glad to find I saw the difference between bad and good poetry; and pointed out to me, it was not likely, if I turned my industry to writing verses, that I should ever either earn my bread, or equal those who had enjoyed greater advantages of leisure and education. 'But, Jervas,' continued he, 'I commend you for your application and quickness in learning to write and read, in so short a time: you will find both these qualifications of great advantage to you. Now, I advise you, turn your thoughts to something that may make you useful to other people. You have your bread to earn, and this you can only do by making yourself useful in some way or other. Look about you, and you will see that I tell you truth. You may perceive that the servants in my house are all useful to me, and that I pay them for their services. The cook who can dress my dinner, the baker who bakes bread for me, the smith who knows how to shoe my horses, the writing-master who undertakes to teach my children to write, can all earn money for themselves, and make themselves independent.—And you may remark that, of all those I have mentioned, the writing-master is the most respected, and the best paid. There are some kinds of knowledge, and some kinds of labour, that are more highly paid for than others. But I have said enough to you, Jervas, for the present: I do not want to lecture you, but to serve you.—You are a young lad, and have had no experience; I am an old man, and have had a great deal: so perhaps my advice may be of some use to you.'

"His advice was indeed of the greatest use to me: every word he said sunk into my mind. I wish those who give advice to young people, especially to those in a lower station than themselves, would follow this gentleman's example; and, instead of haranguing with the haughtiness of superior knowledge, would speak with such kindness as to persuade at the same time that they convince.

"The very day that Mr. Y— spoke to me in this manner, he called me in, that I might tell his eldest grandson the names which we miners give to certain fossils that had been sent him from Cornwall; and, after observing to the boy that this knowledge would be useful to him, he begged me to tell him exactly how the mine, in which I had been employed, was worked. This I did, as well as I was able; and imperfect as my description was, it entertained the boys so much that I determined to try to make a sort of model of the tin-mine for their amusement.

"But this I found no easy task; my remembrance, even of the place in which I had lived all my life, was not sufficiently exact to serve me, as to the length, height, breadth, &c. of the different parts; and though Mr. Y— had a good collection of fossils, I was at a loss, for want of materials, to represent properly the different strata and veins; or, as we call it, the country.

"My temper, naturally enthusiastic, was not on this occasion to be daunted by any difficulties. I was roused by the notion that I should be able to complete something that would be really useful to my kind benefactor's family; and I anticipated with rapture, the moment when I should produce my model complete, and justify Mr. Y—'s opinion of my diligence and capacity. I thought of nothing else from the moment these ideas came into my head. The measures, plans, and specimens of earths and ore which were wanting, I knew could only be obtained from the mine; and such was my ardour to accomplish my little project, that I determined at all hazards to return into Cornwall, and to ask my good master's permission to revisit the mine in the night time.

"Accordingly, without a moment's delay, I set out upon this expedition. Part of the journey I performed on foot; but wherever I could, I got a set down, because I was impatient to get near the Land's End. I concluded that the wonder excited by my sudden disappearance had subsided by this time; that I was too insignificant to make it worth while to continue a search after me for more than a few days; and that, in all likelihood, my master had dismissed from his work the gang who had been concerned in the plot, and who were the only persons whose revenge I had reason to fear.

"However, as I drew near the mine, I had the prudence not to expose myself unnecessarily; and I watched my opportunity so well, that I contrived to meet my master, in his walk homeward, when no one was with him. I hastily gave him a letter from Mr. Y—, as a certificate of my good conduct since my leaving him; then explained the reason of my return, and asked permission to examine the mines that night.

"He expressed a good deal of surprise, but no displeasure, at my boldness in returning: he willingly granted my request; but, at the same time, warned me that some of my enemies were still in the neighbourhood; and that, though he had dismissed them from his works, and though several had left the country in search of employment elsewhere, yet he was informed that two or three of the gang, and Clarke among the number, were seen lurking about the country: that they had sworn vengeance against me for betraying them, as they called it; and had been indefatigably active in their search after me.

"My master consequently advised me to stay only the ensuing night, and to depart before daybreak: he also cautioned me not to wake the man who now slept in my hut in the mine.

"I did not like to spoil the only good suit of clothes of which I was possessed; so, before I went down into the mine, I got from my master my old jacket, apron, and cap, in which being equipped, and furnished with a lantern, and rod for measuring, I descended into the mine.

"I went to work as quietly as possible, surveyed the place exactly, and remembered what I had heard Mr. Y— observe, 'that people can never make their knowledge useful, if they have not been at the pains to make it exact.' I was determined to give him a proof of my exactness: accordingly I measured and minuted down every thing with the most cautious accuracy; and, so intent was my mind upon my work, the thoughts of Clarke and his associates never came across me for a moment. Nay, I absolutely forgot the man in the hut, and am astonished he was not sooner waked.

"What roused him at last was, I believe, the noise I made in loosening some earth and stones for specimens. A great stone came tumbling down, and immediately afterwards I heard one of the horses neigh, which showed me I had waked them at least; and I betook myself to a hiding-place, in the western gallery, where I kept quiet, for I believe a quarter of an hour, in order to give the horses and the man, if he were awake, time to go to sleep again.

"I ventured out of my hiding-place too soon; for, just as I left my nook, I saw the man at the end of the gallery. Instantly, upon the sight of me, he put both his hands before his face, gave a loud shriek, turned his back, and took to his heels with the greatest precipitation. I guessed that, as he said yesterday, he took me for the ghost of myself; and that his terror made him mistake my lantern for a blue taper. I had no chain; but that I had a rod in my hand is most certain: and it is also true that I took advantage of his fears, to drive him out of my way; for the moment he began to run, I shook my rod as fast and as loud as I could against the tin top of my lantern; and I trampled with my feet as if I was pursuing him.

"As soon as the coast was clear, I hastened back for my specimens; which I packed up in my basket, and then decamped as fast as I could. This is the only time I ever walked in the western gallery with a blue taper in my hand, dragging a chain after me, whatever the ghost-seer may report to the contrary.

"I was heartily glad to get away, and to have thus happily accomplished the object of my journey. I carried my basket on my back for some miles, till I got to the place where a waggon put up; and in this I travelled safely back to Exeter.

"I determined not to show my model to Mr. Y—, or the boys, till it should be as complete as I could make it. I got a good ingenious carpenter, who had been in the habit of working for the toy-shops, to help me; and laid out the best part of my worldly treasure upon this my grand first project. I had new models made of the sieves for lueing, the box and trough, the buddle, wreck, and tool, beside some dozen of wooden workmen, wheelbarrows, &c,; with which the carpenter, by my directions, furnished my mine. I paid a smith and tinman, moreover, for models of our stamps, and blowing-house, and an iron grate for my box: besides, I had a lion rampant [Footnote: A lion rampant is stamped on the block tin which is brought thence.], and other small matters, from the pewterer; also a pair of bellows, finished by the glover; for all which articles, as they were out of the common way, I was charged high.

[Footnote: The names of vessels and machines used in the Cornish tin-mines.]

"It was some time, even when all this was ready, before we could contrive to make our puppets do their business properly: but patience accomplishes every thing. At last we got our wooden miners to obey us, and to perform their several tasks at the word of command; that is to say, at the pulling of certain strings and wires, which we fastened to their legs, arms, heads, and shoulders: which wires, being slender and black, were at a little distance invisible to the spectators. When the skeletons were perfect, we fell to work to dress and paint them; and I never shall forget the delight with which I contemplated our whole company of puppets: men, women, and children, fresh painted and dizened out, all in their proper colours. The carpenter could scarcely prevent me from spoiling them: I was so impatient to set them at work that I could not wait till their clothes were dry; and I was every half hour rubbing my fingers upon their cheeks, to try whether the red paint was yet hard enough.

"With some pride, I announced my intended exhibition to Mr. Y—; and he appointed that evening for seeing it, saying that none but his own boys should be present at the first representation. It was for them alone it was originally designed; but I was so charmed with my newly-finished work, that I would gladly have had all Exeter present at the exhibition. However, before night, I was convinced of my friend Mr. Y—'s superior prudence: the whole thing, as the carpenter said, went off pretty well; but several disasters happened which I had not foreseen. There was one stiff old fellow, whose arms, twitch them which way I would, I could never get to bend: and an obstinate old woman, who would never do any thing else but curtsy, when I wanted her to kneel down and to do her work. My children sorted their heaps of rubbish and ore very dexterously; excepting one unlucky little chap, who, from the beginning, had his head, somehow or other, turned the wrong way upon his shoulders; and I could never manage, all the night, to set it right again: it was in vain I flattered myself that his wry neck would escape observation; for, as he was one of the wheelbarrow boys, he was a conspicuous figure in the piece; and, whenever he appeared, wheeling or emptying his barrow, I to my mortification heard repeated peals of laughter from the spectators, in which even my patron, notwithstanding his good-natured struggles against it for some time, was at last compelled to join.

"I, all the while, was wiping my forehead behind my show-box; for I never was in such a bath of heat in my life: not the hardest day's work I ever wrought in the mine made me one half so hot as setting these puppets to work.

"When my exhibition was over, good Mr. Y— came to me, and consoled me for all disasters, by the praises he bestowed upon my patience and ingenuity: he showed me that he knew the difficulties with which I had to contend: and he mentioned the defects to me in the kindest manner, and how they might be remedied. 'I see,' said he, smiling, 'that you have endeavoured to make something useful for the entertainment of my boys; and I will take pains to make it turn out advantageously to you.'

"The next morning I went to look at my show-box, which Mr. Y— had desired me to leave in his study; and I was surprised to see the front of the box, which I had left open for the spectators, filled up with boards, and having a circular glass in the middle. The eldest boy, who stood by enjoying my surprise, bid me look in, and tell him what I saw. What was my astonishment, when I first looked through this glass— 'As large as the life!—As large as the life!' cried I, in admiration—'I see the puppets, the wheelbarrows, every thing as large as life!'

"Mr. Y— then told me, that it was by his grandson's directions that this glass, which he said was called a magnifying-glass, or convex-lens, was added to my show-box. 'He makes you a present of it; and now,' added he, smiling, 'get all your little performers into order, and prepare for a second representation: I will send for a clock-maker in this town, who is an ingenious man, and will show you how to manage properly the motions of your puppets; and then we will get a good painter to paint them for you."

"There was at this time, in Exeter, a society of literary gentlemen, who met once a week at each other's houses. Mr. Y— was one of these; and several of the principal families in Exeter, especially those who had children, came on the appointed evening to see the model of the Cornwall tin-mine, which, with the assistance of the clock-maker and painter, was now become really a show worth looking at. I made but few blunders this time, and the company were indulgent enough to pardon these, and to express themselves well pleased with my little exhibition. They gave me, indeed, solid marks of their satisfaction, which were quite unexpected: after the exhibition, Mr. Y—'s youngest grandchild, in the name of the rest of the company, presented me with a purse, containing the contributions which had been made for me.

"After repaying all my expenses for my journey and machinery, I found I had six guineas and a crown to spare. So I thought myself a rich man; and, having never seen so much money together in my life before, as six golden guineas and a crown, I should, most probably, like the generality of people who come into the possession of unexpected wealth, have become extravagant, had it not been for the timely advice of my kind monitor, Mr. Y—. When I showed him a pair of Chinese tumblers, which I had bought from a pedlar for twice as much as they were worth, merely because they pleased my fancy, he shook his head, and observed that I might, before my death, want this very money to buy a loaf of bread. 'If you spend your money as fast as you get it, Jervas,' said he, 'no matter how ingenious or industrious you are, you will always be poor. Remember the good proverb that says, Industry is Fortune's right hand, and Frugality her left;' a proverb which has been worth ten times more to me than all my little purse contained: so true it is, that those do not always give most who give money."

"I had soon reason to rejoice at having thrown away no more money on baubles, as I had occasion for my whole stock to fit myself out for a new way of life. 'Jervas,' said Mr. Y— to me, 'I have at last found an occupation, which I hope will suit you.'—Unknown to me, he had been, ever since he first saw my little model, intent upon turning it to my lasting advantage. Among the gentlemen of the society which I have before mentioned, there was one who had formed a design of sending some well-informed lecturer through England, to exhibit models of the machines used in manufactories: Mr. Y— purposely invited this gentleman the evening that I exhibited my tin-mine, and proposed to him that I should be permitted to accompany his lecturer. To this he agreed. Mr. Y— told me that although the person who was fixed upon as lecturer was not exactly the sort of man he should have chosen, yet as he was a relation of the gentleman who set the business on foot, no objection could well be made to him.

"I was rather daunted by the cold and haughty look with which my new master, the lecturer, received me when I was presented to him. Mr. Y—, observing this, whispered to me at parting. 'Make yourself useful, and you will soon be agreeable to him. We must not expect to find friends ready made wherever we go in the world: we often have to make friends for ourselves with great pains and care.' It cost me both pains and care, I know, to make this lecturer my friend. He was what is called born a gentleman; and he began by treating me as a low-born upstart, who, being perfectly ignorant, wanted to pass for a self-taught genius. That I was low-born, I did not attempt to conceal; nor did I perceive that I had any reason to be ashamed of my birth, or of having raised myself by honest means to a station above that in which I was born. I was proud of this circumstance, and therefore it was no torment to me to hear the continual hints which my well-born master threw out upon this subject. I moreover never pretended to any knowledge which I had not; so that, by degrees, notwithstanding his prejudices, he began to feel that I had neither the presumption of an upstart, nor of a self-taught genius. I kept in mind the counsel given to me by Mr. Y—, to endeavour to make myself useful to my employer; but it was no easy matter to do this at first, because he had such a dread of my awkwardness that he would never let me touch any of his apparatus. I was always left to stand like a cipher beside him whilst he lectured; and I had regularly the mortification of hearing him conclude his lecture with, 'Now, gentlemen and ladies, I will not detain you any longer from what, I am sensible, is much better worth your attention than any thing I can offer—Mr. Jervas's puppet-show.'

"It happened one day that he sent me with a shilling, as he thought, to pay a hostler for the feeding of his horse; as I rubbed the money between my finger and thumb, I perceived that the white surface came off, and the piece looked yellow: I recollected that my master had the day before been showing some experiments with quicksilver and gold, and that he had covered a guinea with quicksilver: so I immediately took the money back, and my master, for the first time in his life, thanked me very cordially; for this was in reality a guinea, and not a shilling. He was also surprised at my directly mentioning the experiment he had shown.

"The next day that he lectured, he omitted the offensive conclusion about Mr. Jervas's puppet-show. I observed, farther, to my infinite satisfaction, that after this affair of the guinea, he was not so suspicious of my honesty as he used to appear to be: he now yielded more to his natural indolence, and suffered me to pack up his things for him, and to do a hundred little services which formerly he used roughly to refuse at my hands; saying, 'I had rather do it myself, sir,' or, 'I don't like to have any body meddle with my things, Mr. Jervas.' But his tone changed, and it was now, 'Jervas, I'll leave you to put up these things, whilst I go and read;'—or, 'Jervas, will you see that I leave none of my goods behind me, there's a good lad?'—In truth, he was rather apt to leave his goods behind him: he was the most absent and forgetful man alive. During the first half year we travelled together, whilst he attempted to take care of his own things, I counted that he lost two pair and a half of slippers, one boot, three night-caps, one shirt, and fifteen pocket-handkerchiefs. Many of these losses, I make no doubt, were set down in his imagination to my account whilst he had no opinion of my honesty; but I am satisfied that he was afterwards thoroughly convinced of the injustice of his suspicions, as, from the time that I had the charge of his goods, as he called them, to the day we parted, including a space of above four years and a half, he never lost any thing but one red nightcap, which, to the best of my belief, he sent in his wig one Sunday morning to the barber's, but which never came back again, and an old ragged blue pocket-handkerchief, which he said he put under his pillow, or into his boot, when he went to bed at night. He had an odd way of sticking his pocket-handkerchief into his boot, 'that he might be sure to find it in the morning.' I suspect the handkerchief was carried down in the boot when it was taken to be cleaned. He was, however, perfectly certain that these two losses were not to be imputed to any carelessness of mine. He often said he was obliged to me for the attention I paid to his interests; he treated me now very civilly, and would sometimes condescend to explain to me in private what I did not understand in his public lectures.

"I was presently advanced to the dignity of his secretary. He wrote a miserably bad hand: and his manuscripts were so scratched and interlined, that it was with the utmost difficulty he could decipher his own writing, when he was obliged to have recourse to his notes in lecturing. He was, moreover, extremely near-sighted; and he had a strange trick of wrinkling up the skin on the bridge of his nose when he was perplexed: altogether, his look was so comical when he began to pore over these papers of his, that few of the younger part of our audiences could resist their inclination to laugh. This disconcerted him beyond measure; and he was truly glad to accept my offer of copying out his scrawls fairly in a good bold round hand. I could now write, if I may say it without vanity, an excellent hand, and could go over his calculations as far as the first four rules of arithmetic were concerned; so that I became quite his factotum: and I thought myself rewarded for all my pains, by having opportunities of gaining every day some fresh piece of knowledge from the perusal of the notes which I transcribed.

"It was now that I felt most thoroughly the advantage of having learned to read and write: stores of useful information were opened to me, and my curiosity and desire to inform myself were insatiable. I often sat up half the night reading and writing: I had free access now to all my fellow-traveller's books, and I thought I could never study them enough.

"At the commencement of my studies, my master often praised my diligence, and would show me where to look for what I wanted in his books, or explain difficulties: I looked up to him as a miracle of science and learning; nay, I was actually growing fond of him, but this did not last long. In process of time, he grew shy of explaining things to me; he scolded me for thumbing his books, though, God knows, my thumbs were always cleaner than his own, and he thwarted me continually upon some pretence or other. I could not for some time conceive the cause of this change in my master's behaviour: indeed it was hard for me to guess or believe that he was become jealous of the talents and knowledge of a poor lad, whose ignorance he, but a few years before, had so much despised and derided. I was the more surprised at this new turn of his mind, because I was conscious that, instead of becoming more conceited, I had of late become more humble; but this humility was, by my suspicious master, attributed to artifice, and tended more than any thing to confirm him in his notion that I had formed a plan to supplant him in his office of lecturer, a scheme which had never entered into my head. I was thunderstruck when he one day said to me, 'You need not study so hard, Mr. Jervas; for I promise you that, even with Mr. Y—'s assistance, and all your art, you will not be able to supplant me, clever as, with all affected humility, you think yourself.'

"The truth lightened upon me at once. Had he been a judge of the human countenance, he must have seen my innocence in my looks: but he was so fixed in his opinion, that I knew any protestations I could make of my never having thought of the scheme he imputed to me, would serve only to confirm him in his idea of my dissimulation. I contented myself with returning to him his books and his manuscripts, and thenceforward withdrew my attention from his lectures, to which I had always till now been one of the most eager auditors; by these proceedings I hoped to quiet his suspicions. I no longer applied myself to any studies in which he was engaged, to show him that all competition with him was far from my thoughts; and I have since reflected that this fit of jealousy of his, which I at the time looked upon as a misfortune, because it stopped me short in pursuits which were highly agreeable to my taste, was in fact of essential service to me. My reading had been too general; and I had endeavoured to master so many things, that I was not likely to make myself thoroughly skilled in any. As a blacksmith said once to me, when he was asked why he was not both blacksmith and whitesmith, 'The smith that will meddle with all things may go shoe the goslings;' an old proverb, which, from its mixture of drollery and good sense, became ever after a favourite of mine.

"Having returned my master's books, I had only such to read as I could purchase or borrow for myself, and I became very careful in my choice: I also took every opportunity of learning all I could from the conversation of sensible people, wherever we went; and I found that one piece of knowledge helped me to another often when I least expected it. And this I may add, for the encouragement of others, that every thing which I learned accurately was, at some time or other of my life, of use to me.

"After having made a progress through England, my fellow-traveller determined to try his fortune in the metropolis, and to give lectures there to young people during the winter season. Accordingly, we proceeded towards London, taking Woolwich in our way, where we exhibited before the young gentlemen of the military academy. My master, who, since he had withdrawn his notes from my hands, had no one to copy them fairly, found himself, during his lecture, in some perplexity; and, as he exhibited his usual odd contortions upon this occasion, the young gentlemen could not restrain their laughter: he also prolonged his lecture more than his audience liked, and several yawned terribly, and made signs of an impatient desire to see what was in my box, as a relief from their fatigue. This my master quickly perceived, and, being extremely provoked, he spoke to me with a degree of harshness and insolence which, as I bore it with temper, prepossessed the young company in my favour. He concluded his lecture with the old sentence: 'Gentlemen, I shall no longer detain you from what I am sure is much better worthy of your attention than any thing I can offer, viz. Mr. Jervas's puppet-show.' This was an unlucky speech on the present occasion, for it happened that every body, after having seen what he called my puppet-show, was precisely of this opinion. My master grew more and more impatient, and wanted to hurry me away, but one spirited young man most warmly took me and my tin-mine under his protection: I stood my ground, insisting upon my right to finish my exhibition, as my master had been allowed full time to finish his. The young gentleman who supported me was as well pleased by my present firmness as he had been by my former patience. At parting he made a handsome collection for me, which I refused to accept, taking only the regular price. 'Well,' said he, 'you shall be no loser by this. You are going to town; my father is in London; here is his direction. I'll mention you to him the next time I write home, and you'll not be the worse for that.'

"As soon as we got to London, I went according to my direction. The young gentleman had been more punctual in writing home than young gentlemen sometimes are. I was appointed to come with my models the next evening, when a number of young people were collected, beside the children of the family. The young spectators gathered round me at one end of a large saloon, asking me innumerable questions after the exhibition was over; whilst the master of the house, who was an East India director, was walking up and down the room, conversing with a gentleman in an officer's uniform. They were, as I afterwards understood, talking about the casting of some guns at Woolwich for the East India Company. 'Charles,' said the director, coming to the place where we were standing, and tapping one of his sons on the shoulder, 'do you recollect what your brother told us about the proportion of tin which is used in casting brass cannon at Woolwich?' The young gentleman answered that he could not recollect, but referred his father to me; adding, that his brother told him I was the person from whom he had the information. My memory served me exactly; and I had reason to rejoice that I had not neglected the opportunity of gaining this knowledge, during our short stay at Woolwich. The East India director, pleased with my answering his first question accurately, condescended, in compliance with his children's entreaties, to examine my models, and questioned me upon a variety of subjects: at length he observed to the gentleman with whom he had been conversing, that I explained myself well, that I knew all I did know accurately, and that I had the art of captivating the attention of young people. 'I do think,' concluded he, 'that he would answer Dr. Bell's description better than any person I have seen.' He then inquired particularly into my history and connexions, all of which I told him exactly. He took down the direction to Mr. Y—, and my good master (as I shall always call Mr. R—), and to several other gentlemen, at whose houses I had been during the last three or four years, telling me that he would write to them about me; and that if he found my accounts of myself were as exact as my knowledge upon other subjects, he thought he could place me in a very eligible situation. The answers to these letters were all perfectly satisfactory: he gave me the letter from Mr. R—, saying 'you had better keep this letter, and take care of it; for it will be a recommendation to you in any part of the world where courage and fidelity are held in esteem.' Upon looking into this letter, I found that my good master had related, in the handsomest manner, the whole of my conduct about the discovery of the vein in his mine.

"The director now informed me that, if I had no objection to go to India, I should be appointed to go out to Madras as an assistant to Dr. Bell, one of the directors of the asylum for the instruction of orphans; an establishment which is immediately under the auspices of the East India Company, and which does them honour.

[Footnote: Vide a small pamphlet, printed for Cadell and Davies, entitled, "An Experiment in Education, made at the Male Asylum of Madras, by the Rev. Dr. A. Bell."]

"The salary which was offered me was munificent beyond my utmost expectations; and the account of the institution, which was put into my hands, charmed me. I speedily settled all my concerns with the lecturer, who was in great astonishment that this appointment had not fallen upon him. To console him for the last time, I showed him a passage in Dr. Bell's pamphlet, in which it is said that the doctor prefers to all others, for teaching at his school, youths who have no fixed habits as tutors, and who will implicitly follow his directions. I was at this time but nineteen: my master was somewhat appeased by this view of the affair, and we parted, as I wished, upon civil terms; though I could not feel much regret at leaving him. I had no pleasure in living with one who would not let me become attached to him; for, having early met with two excellent friends and masters, the agreeable feelings of gratitude and affection were in a manner necessary to my happiness.

"Before I left England, I received new proofs of Mr. R—'s goodness: he wrote to me to say that, as I was going to a distant country, to which a small annuity of ten guineas a year could not easily be remitted, he had determined to lay out a sum equal to the value of the annuity he had promised me, in a manner which he hoped would be advantageous: he further said, that as the vein of the mine with which I had made him acquainted turned out better than he expected, he had added the value of fifty guineas more than my annuity; and that if I would go to Mr. Ramsden's, mathematical instrument maker, in Piccadilly, I should receive all he had ordered to be ready for me. At Mr. Ramsden's I found ready to be packed up for me two small globes, siphons, prisms, an air-gun and an air-pump, a speaking trumpet, a small apparatus for showing the gases, and an apparatus for freezing water. Mr. Ramsden informed me that these were not all the things Mr. R— had bespoken; that he had ordered a small balloon, and a portable telegraph, in form of an umbrella, which would be sent home, as he expected, in the course of the next week. Mr. Ramsden also had directions to furnish me with a set of mathematical instruments of his own making. 'But,' added he with a smile, 'you will be lucky if you get them soon enough out of my hands.' In fact, I believe I called a hundred times in the course of a fortnight upon Ramsden, and it was only the day before the fleet sailed that they were finished and delivered to me.

"I cannot here omit to mention an incident that happened in one of my walks to Ramsden's: I was rather late, and was pushing my way hastily through a crowd that was gathered at the turning of a street, when a hawker by accident flapped a bundle of wet hand-bills in my eyes, and at the same instant screamed in my ears, 'The last dying speech and confession of Jonathan Clarke, who was executed on Monday, the 11th instant.'—Jonathan Clarke! The name struck my ears suddenly, and the words I shocked me so much that I stood fixed to the spot; and it was I not till the hawker had passed by me some yards, and was beginning with 'The last dying speech and confession of Jonathan Clarke, the Cornwall miner,' that I recollected myself enough to speak: I called after the hawker in vain: he was bawling too loud to hear me, and I was forced to run the whole length of the street before I could overtake him, and get one of the hand-bills. On reading it, I could have no doubt that it was really the last dying speech of my old enemy Clarke. His birth, parentage, and every circumstance, convinced me of the truth. Amongst other things in his confession, I came to a plan he had laid to murder a poor lad in the tin-mine, where he formerly worked; 'and he thanked God that this plan was never executed, as the boy providentially disappeared the very night on which the murder was to have been perpetrated. He further set forth that, after being turned away by his master, and obliged to fly from Cornwall, he came up to London, and worked as a coal-heaver for a little while, but soon became what is called a mud-lark; that is, a plunderer of the ships' cargoes that unload in the Thames. He plied this abominable trade for some time, drinking every day to the value of what he stole, till, in a quarrel at an ale-house about the division of some articles to be sold to a receiver of stolen goods, he struck the woman of the house a blow, of which she died; and, as it was proved that he had long-borne her malice for some old dispute, Clarke was on his trial brought in guilty of wilful murder, and sentenced to be hanged.

"I shuddered whilst I read all this.—To such an end, after the utmost his cunning could do, was this villain brought at last! How thankful I was that I did not continue his associate I in my boyish days! My gratitude to my good master increased upon the reflection that it was his humanity which had raised me from vice and misery, to virtue and happiness. We sailed from the Downs the 20th of March, one thousand seven hundred and.... But why I tell you this I do not know; except it be in compliance with the custom of all voyagers, who think that it is important to the world to know on what day they sailed from this or that port. I shall not, however, imitate them in giving you a journal of the wind, or a copy of the ship's log-book. Suffice it to say, that we arrived safely at Madras, after a voyage of about the usual number of months and days, during all which I am sorry that I have not for your entertainment any escape or imminent danger of shipwreck to relate; nor even any description of a storm or a water-spout.

"You will, I am afraid, be much disappointed to find that, upon my arrival in India, where doubtless you expected that I should like others have wonderful adventures, I began to live at Dr. Bell's asylum in Madras a quiet regular life; in which for years I may safely say, that every day in the week was extremely like that which preceded it. This regularity was nowise irksome to me, notwithstanding that I had for some years, in England, been so much used to a roving way of life. I had never any taste for rambling; and under Dr. Bell, who treated me with strict justice, as far as the business of the asylum was concerned, and with distinguished kindness in all other circumstances, I enjoyed as much freedom as I desired. I never had those absurd vague notions of liberty, which render men uneasy under the necessary restraints of all civilized society, and which do not make them the more fit to live with savages. The young people who were under my care gradually became attached to me, and I to them. I obeyed Dr. Bell's directions exactly in all things; and he was pleased to say, after I had been with him for some time, that he never had any assistant who was so entirely agreeable to him. When the business of the day was over, I often amused myself, and the elder boys, with my apparatus for preparing the gases, my speaking-trumpet, air-gun, &c.

"One day, I think it was in the fourth year of my residence at Madras, Dr. Bell sent for me into his closet, and asked me if I had ever heard of a scholar of his, of the name of William Smith, a youth of seventeen years of age; who, in the year 1794, attended the embassy to Tippoo Sultan, when the hostage princes were restored; and who went through a course of experiments in natural philosophy, in the presence of the sultan. I answered Dr. Bell that, before I left England, I had read, in his account of the asylum, extracts from this William Smith's letters, whilst he was at the sultan's court; and that I remembered all the experiments he had exhibited perfectly well; and also that he was detained, by the sultan's order, nineteen days after the embassy had taken leave, for the purpose of instructing two aruzbegs, or lords, in the use of an extensive and elegant mathematical apparatus, presented to Tippoo by the government at Madras.

[Footnote: *Extracts from William Smith's Letters to Dr. Bell, (vide the Pamphlet before mentioned.)*

'Devanelli Fort, April 8, 1792.

'REVEREND SIR,

'I take the liberty of informing you that we arrived here the 28th ult. without any particular occurrence in the way. The day after our arrival we made our first visit to the sultan; and he entertained us at his court for upwards of three hours.

'On the 1st instant Captain Dovetoun sent me an order to open the boxes, and lay out the machines, to show them to the sultan. Accordingly, on the third, I was sent for, and I exhibited the following experiments; viz. head and wig; dancing images; electric stool; cotton fired; small receiver and stand; hemispheres; Archimedes' screw; siphon; Tantalus's cup; water-pump; condensing engine, &c. Captain Dovetoun was present, and explained, as I went on, to the sultan, who has given us an instance of his being acquainted with some of these experiments. He has shown us a condensing engine made by himself, which spouted water higher than ours. He desired me to teach two men, his aruzbegs.

'I can assure you that Tippoo Sultan was mightily pleased with the electric machine. He was prepared for every experiment I exhibited, except the firing of the inflammable air.

'It did cost me several minutes before the firing of the inflammable air proved successful; during which time he was in a very impatient emotion; and, when that was done, it did indeed surprise him. He desired me to go over it three times.

'I take the liberty to write for your information the familiar discourse Tippoo Sultan was pleased to enter into with me, that took place at the close of the experiments.

'There were some silver trumpets, newly made, brought in to him for his inspection, and which he desired the trumpeters to sound hauw and jauw; i.e. come and go; after which, he asked me if they were like those I saw at Madras. I answered, Yes; but those at Madras are made of copper. He asked me again whether the tune was any thing like what I had ever heard. I answered, No. How then? says he; and presently ordering the instrument to be put into my hands, desired me to blow. I told him, very civilly, that I could not blow. No! says he: you could; what are you afraid of? I told him again that I spoke truth; and that I was brought up in a school where my master informed me what lying was, and always punished those boys that spoke untruths.

'June 11th. After this the sultan arose (five hours being elapsed) to quit the court, and desired the present (of a hundred rupees) to be delivered into my hands, with these words: "This is given you as a present for the trouble you took in performing those experiments, which verily pleased me;" and a command that I am to stay in the fort ten days; "after which," he continued, "I will send you to Kistnagherry, with two hircarrahs, in order to conduct you safely through my country." I returned the compliment with a salam, in the manner I was instructed; saying that I thankfully accepted his present, and am willing to obey his commands. The language which the sultan used was the Carnatic Malabar. Mine very little differed from his. Poornbia was the interpreter of such terms as the sultan did not understand.']

"Well,' said Dr. Bell, 'since that time Tippoo Sultan has been at war, and has had no leisure, I suppose, for the study of philosophy, or mathematics; but now that he has just made peace, and wants something to amuse him, he has sent to the government at Madras, to request that I will permit some of my scholars to pay a second visit at his court to refresh the memory of the aruzbegs, and, I presume, to exhibit some new wonders for Tippoo's entertainment.'

"Dr. B. proposed to me to go on this embassy: accordingly, I prepared all my apparatus, and, having carefully remarked what experiments Tippoo had already seen, I selected such as would be new to him. I packed up my speaking-trumpet, my apparatus for freezing water, and that for exhibiting the gases, my balloon and telegraph, and with these and my model of the tin-mine, which I took by Dr. Bell's advice, I set out with two of his eldest scholars upon our expedition. We were met on the entrance of Tippoo's dominions by four hircarrahs or soldiers, whom the sultan sent as a guard to conduct us safely through his dominions. He received us at court the day after our arrival. Unaccustomed as I was to Asiatic magnificence, I confess that my eyes were at first so dazzled by the display of oriental pomp that, as I prostrated myself at the foot of the sultan's throne, I considered him as a personage high as human veneration could look upon. After having made my salam, or salutation, according to the custom of his court, as I was instructed to do, the sultan commanded me, by his interpreter, to display my knowledge of the arts and sciences, for the instruction and amusement of his court.

"My boxes and machines had all been previously opened, and laid out: I was prepared to show my apparatus for freezing, but Tippoo's eye was fixed upon the painted silk balloon; and with prodigious eagerness he interrupted me several times with questions about that great empty bag. I endeavoured to make him understand as well as I could, by my interpreter and his own, that this great empty bag was to be filled with a species of air lighter than the common air; and that, when filled, the bag which I informed him was in our country called a balloon, would mount far above his palace. No sooner was this repeated to him, by the interpreter, than the sultan commanded me instantly to fill the balloon; and when I replied that it could not be done instantly, and that I was not prepared to exhibit it on this day, Tippoo gave signs of the most childish impatience. He signified to me, that since I could not show him what he wanted to see, the sultan would not see what I wanted to show. I replied, through his interpreter, in the most respectful but firm manner, that no one would be so presumptuous as to show to Tippoo Sultan, in his own court, any thing which he did not desire to see: that it was in compliance with his wishes that I came to his court, from which, in obedience to his commands, I should at any time be ready to withdraw. A youth, who stood at the right hand of Tippoo's throne, seemed much to approve of this answer, and the sultan, assuming a more composed and dignified aspect, signified to me that he was satisfied to await for the sight of the filling of the great bag till the next day; and that he should, in the mean time, be well pleased to see what I was now prepared to show.

"The apparatus for freezing, which we then exhibited, seemed to please him; but I observed that he was, during a great part of the time whilst I was explaining it, intent upon something else; and no sooner had I done speaking than he caused to be produced the condensing engines, made by himself, which he formerly showed to William Smith, and which he said spouted water higher than any of ours. The sultan, I perceived, was much more intent upon displaying his small stock of mechanical knowledge than upon increasing it; and the mixture of vanity and ignorance, which he displayed upon this and many subsequent occasions, considerably lessened the awe which his external magnificence at first excited in my mind. Sometimes he would put himself in competition with me, to show his courtiers his superiority; but failing in these attempts, he would then treat me as a species of mechanic juggler, who was fit only to exhibit for the amusement of his court. When he saw my speaking-trumpet, which was made of copper, he at first looked at it with great scorn, and ordered his trumpeters to show me theirs, which were made of silver. As he had formerly done when my predecessor was at his court, he desired his trumpeters to sound through these trumpets the words hauw and jauw, i.e. come and go: but, upon trial, mine was found to be far superior to the sultan's: and I received intimation, through one of his courtiers, that it would be prudent to offer it immediately to Tippoo. This I accordingly did, and he accepted it with the eagerness of a child who has begged and obtained a new play-thing."

CHAPTER IV

"The next day, Tippoo and his whole court assembled to see my balloon. Tippoo was seated in a splendid pavilion, and his principal courtiers stood in a semicircle on each side of him: the youth, whom I formerly observed, was again on his right hand, and his eyes were immovably fixed upon my balloon, which had been previously filled and fastened down by cords. I had the curiosity to ask who this youth was: I was informed he was the sultan's eldest son, Prince Abdul Calie. I had not time to make any farther inquiries, for Tippoo now ordered a signal to be given, as had been previously agreed upon. I instantly cut the cords which held the balloon, and it ascended with a rapid but graceful motion, to the unspeakable astonishment and delight of all the spectators. Some clapped their hands and shouted, others looked up in speechless ecstasy, and in the general emotion all ranks for an instant were confounded: even Tippoo Sultan seemed at this interval to be forgotten, and to forget himself, in the admiration of this new wonder.

"As soon as the balloon was out of sight, the court returned to their usual places, the noise subsided, and the sultan, as if desirous to fix the public attention upon himself, and to show his own superior magnificence, issued orders immediately to his treasurer to present me, as a token of his royal approbation, with two hundred star pagodas. When I approached to make my salam and compliment of thanks, as I was instructed, the sultan, who observed that some of the courtiers already began to regard me with envy, as if my reward had been too great, determined to divert himself with their spleen, and to astonish me with his generosity: he took from his finger a diamond ring, which he presented to me by one of his officers. The young prince, Abdul Calie, whispered to his father whilst I was withdrawing, and I soon afterwards received a message from the sultan, requesting, or, in other words, ordering me to remain some time at his court, to instruct the young prince, his son, in the use of my European machines, for which they had in their language no names.

"This command proved a source of real pleasure to me; for I found Prince Abdul Calie not only a youth of quick apprehension, but of a most amiable disposition, unlike the imperious and capricious temper which I had remarked in his father. Prince Abdul Calie had been, when he was about twelve years old, one of the hostage princes left with Lord Cornwallis at Seringapatam. With that politeness which is seldom to be found in the sons of eastern despots, this prince, after my first introduction, ordered the magnificent palanquin, given to him by Lord Cornwallis, to be shown to me; then pointing to the enamelled snakes which support the panels, and on which the sun at that instant happened to shine, Prince Abdul Calie was pleased to say, 'The remembrance of your noble countryman's kindness to me is as fresh and lively in my soul as those colours now appear to my eye.'

"Another thing gave me a good opinion of this young prince; he did not seem to value presents merely by their costliness; whether he gave or received, he considered the feelings of others; and I know that he often excited in my mind more gratitude by the gift of a mere trifle, by a word or a look, than his ostentatious father could by the most valuable donations. Tippoo, though he ordered his treasurer to pay me fifty rupees per day, whilst I was in his service, yet treated me with a species of insolence; which, having some of the feelings of a free-born Briton about me, I found it difficult to endure with patience. His son, on the contrary, showed that he felt obliged to me for the little instruction I was able to give him; and never appeared to think that, as a prince, he could pay for all the kindness, as well as the service of his inferiors, by pagodas or rupees: so true it is that attachment cannot be bought; and those who wish to have friends, as well as servants, should keep this truth constantly in mind. My English spirit of independence induced me to make these and many more such reflections whilst I was at Tippoo's court.

"Every day afforded me fresh occasion to form comparisons between the sultan and his son; and my attachment to my pupil every day increased. My pupil! It was with astonishment I sometimes reflected that a young prince was actually my pupil. Thus an obscure individual, in a country like England, where arts, sciences, and literature are open to all ranks, may obtain a degree of knowledge which an eastern despot, in all his pride, would gladly purchase with ingots of his purest gold.

"One evening, after the business of the day was over, Tippoo Sultan came into his son's apartment, whilst I was explaining to the young prince the use of some of the mathematical instruments in my pocket-case. 'We are well acquainted with these things,' said the sultan in a haughty tone: 'the government of Madras sent us such things as those, with others, which are now in the possession of some of my aruzbegs, who have doubtless explained them sufficiently to the prince my son.' Prince Abdul Calie modestly replied, 'that he had never before been made to understand them; for that the aruzbeg, who had formerly attempted to explain them, had not the art of making things so clear to him as I had done.'

"I felt a glow of pleasure at this compliment, and at the consciousness that I deserved it. How little did I imagine, when I used to sit up at nights studying my old master's books, that one of them would be the means of procuring me such honour.

[Footnote: Jervas here alludes to a book entitled, "A Description of Pocket and Magazine Cases of Drawing Instruments: in which is explained the use of each instrument, and particularly of the sector and plain scale, Gunter's scale, &c. By J. Barrow, private teacher of mathematics."]

"'What is contained in that box?' said the sultan, pointing to the box which held the model of the tin-mine. 'I do not remember to have seen it opened in my presence.'

"I replied that it had not been opened, because I feared that it was not worthy to be shown to him. But he commanded that it should instantly be exhibited; and, to my great surprise, it seemed to delight him excessively: he examined every part, moved the wires of the puppets, and asked innumerable questions concerning our tin-mines. I was the more astonished at this, because I had imagined he would have considered every object of commerce as beneath the notice of a sultan. Nor could I guess why he should be peculiarly interested in this subject: but he soon explained this to me, by saying that he had, in his dominions, certain mines of tin, which he had a notion would, if properly managed, bring a considerable revenue to the royal treasury; but that at present, through negligence or fraud, these mines were rather burdensome than profitable.

"He inquired from me how my model came into my possession; and, when his interpreter told him that I made it myself, he caused the question and answer to be repeated twice, before he would believe that he understood me rightly. He next inquired whether I was acquainted with the art of mining; and how I came by my information: in short, he commanded me to relate my history. I replied that it was a long story, concerning only an obscure individual, and unworthy the attention of a great monarch: but he seemed this evening to have nothing to do but to gratify his curiosity, which my apology only served to increase. He again commanded me to relate my adventures, and I then told him the history of my early life. I was much flattered by the interest which the young prince took in my escape from the mine, and by the praises he bestowed on my fidelity to my master.

"The sultan, on the contrary, heard me at first with curiosity, but afterwards with an air of incredulity. Upon observing this, I produced the letter from my good master to the East India director, which gave a full account of the whole affair. I put this letter into the hands of the interpreter, and with some difficulty he translated it into the Carnatic Malabar, which was the language the sultan used in speaking to me.

"The letter, which had the counter-signatures of some of the East India Company's servants resident at Madras, whose names were well known to Tippoo, failed not to make a great impression in favour of my integrity: of my knowledge he had before a high opinion. He stood musing for some time, with his eyes fixed upon the model of the tin-mine; and, after consulting with the young prince, as I guessed by their tones and looks, he bade his interpreter tell me that, if I would undertake to visit the tin-mines in his dominions, to instruct his miners how to work them, and to manage the ore according to the English fashion, I should receive from the royal treasury a reward more than proportioned to my services, and suitable to the generosity of a sultan.

"Some days were given me to consider of this proposal. Though tempted by the idea that I might realize, in a short time, a sum that would make me independent for the rest of my life, yet my suspicions of the capricious and tyrannical temper of Tippoo made me dread to have him for a master; and, above all, I resolved to do nothing without the express permission of Dr. Bell, to whom I immediately wrote. He seemed, by his answer, to think that such an opportunity of making my fortune was not to be neglected: my hopes, therefore, prevailed over my fears, and I accepted the proposal.

"The presents which he had made me, and the salary allowed me during six weeks that I had attended the young prince, amounted to a considerable sum; 500 star pagodas and 500 rupees: all which I left, together with my ring, in the care of a great Gentoo merchant of the name of Omychund, who had shown me many civilities. With proper guides, and full powers from the sultan, I proceeded on my journey, and devoted myself with the greatest ardour to my undertaking. A very laborious and difficult undertaking it proved: for in no country are prejudices in favour of their own customs more inveterate, amongst workmen of every description, than in India; and although I was empowered to inflict what punishment I thought proper on those who disobeyed, or even hesitated to fulfil my orders, yet, thank God! I could never bring myself to have a poor slave tortured, or put to death, because he roasted ore in a manner which I did not think so good as my own method; nor even because he was not so well convinced as I was of the advantages of our Cornwall smelting-furnace.

"My moderation was of more service to me, in the minds of the people, than the utmost violence I could have employed to enforce obedience. As I got by degrees some little knowledge of their language, I grew more and more acceptable to them; and some few, who tried methods of my proposing, and found that they succeeded, were, by my directions, rewarded with the entire possession of the difference of profit between the old and new modes. This bounty enticed others; and in time that change was accomplished by gentle means, which I had at first almost despaired of ever effecting.

"When the works were in proper train, I despatched a messenger to the sultan's court, to request that he would be pleased to appoint some confidential person to visit the mines, in order to be an eye-witness of what had been done; and I further begged, as I had now accomplished the object of the sultan's wishes, that I might be recalled, after deputing whomsoever he should think proper to superintend and manage the mines in my stead. I moreover offered, before I withdrew, to instruct the person who should be appointed. My messenger, after a long delay, returned to me, with a command from Tippoo Sultan to remain where I was till his further orders. For these I waited three months, and then, concluding that I was forgotten, I determined to set out to refresh Tippoo's memory.

"I found him at Devanelli Fort, thinking of nothing less than of me or my tin-mines: he was busily engaged in making preparations for a war with some Soubha or other, whose name I forget, and all his ideas were bent on conquests and vengeance. He scarcely deigned to see, much less to listen to me: his treasurer gave me to understand that too much had already been lavished upon me, a stranger as I was; and that Tippoo's resources, at all events, would be now employed in carrying on schemes of war, not petty projects of commerce. Thus insulted, and denied all my promised reward, I could not but reflect upon the hard fate of those who attempt to serve capricious despots.

"I prepared as fast as possible to depart from Tippoo's court. The Hindoo merchant with whom I had lodged the pagodas and rupees promised to transmit them to me at Madras; and he delivered to me the diamond ring which Tippoo had given to me during his fit of generosity, or of ostentation. The sultan, who cared no more what became of me, made no opposition to my departure: but I was obliged to wait a day or two for a guard, as the hircarrahs who formerly conducted me were now out upon some expedition.

"Whilst I waited impatiently for their return, Prince Abdul Calie, who had not been during all this time at Devanelli Fort, arrived; and when I went to take leave of him, he inquired into the reason of my sudden departure. In language as respectful as I could use, and with as much delicacy as I thought myself bound to observe, in speaking to a son of his father, I related the truth. The prince's countenance showed what he felt. He paused, and seemed to be lost in thought, for a few minutes: he then said to me, 'The sultan, my father, is at this time so intent upon preparations for war, that even I should despair of being listened to on any other subject. But you have in your possession, as I recollect, what might be useful to him either in war or peace; and, if you desire it, I will speak of this machine to the sultan.'

"I did not immediately know to what machine of mine the prince alluded; but he explained to me that he meant my portable telegraph, which would be of infinite use to Tippoo in conveying orders of intelligence across the deserts. I left the matter entirely to the prince, after returning him my very sincere thanks for being thus interested in my concerns.

"A few hours after this conversation, I was summoned into the sultan's presence. His impatience to make trial of the telegraphs was excessive; and I, who but the day before had been almost trampled upon by the officers and lords of his court, instantly became a person of the greatest importance. The trial of the telegraphs succeeded beyond even my expectations; and the sultan was in a species of ecstasy on the occasion.

"I cannot omit to notice an instance of the violence of his temper, and its sudden changes from joy to rage. One of his blacks, a gentle Hindoo lad, of the name of Saheb, was set to manage a telegraph at one of the stations, a few yards distant from the sultan. I had previously instructed Saheb in what he was to do; but, from want of practice, he made some mistake, which threw Tippoo into such a transport of passion, that he instantly ordered the slave's head to be cut off! a sentence which would infallibly have been executed, if I had not represented that it would be expedient to suffer his head to remain on his shoulders till the message was delivered by his telegraph; because there was no one present who could immediately supply his place. Saheb then read off his message without making any new blunder; and the moment the exhibition was over, I threw myself at the feet of the sultan, and implored him to pardon Saheb. I was not likely at this moment to be refused such a trifle! Saheb was pardoned.

"An order upon the treasurer for five hundred star pagodas, to reward my services at the royal tin-mines, was given to me; and upon my presenting to Tippoo Sultan the portable telegraphs, on which his ardent wishes were fixed, he exclaimed: 'Ask any favour in the wide-extended power of Tippoo Sultan to confer, and it shall be granted."

"I concluded that this was merely an oriental figure of speech; but I resolved to run the hazard of a refusal. I did not ask for a province, though this was in the wide-extended power of Tippoo Sultan to confer; but as I had a great curiosity to see the diamond mines of Golconda, of which both in Europe and in India I had heard so much, I requested the sultan's permission to visit those which belonged to him. He hesitated; but after saying some words to an officer near him, he bade his interpreter tell me that he granted my request.

"Accordingly, after lodging my pagodas and rupees along with the rest in the hands of Omychund, the Gentoo merchant, who was a man of great wealth and credit, I set out in company with some diamond merchants who were going to Golconda. My curiosity was amply gratified by the sight of these celebrated mines; and I determined that, when I returned to Europe, I would write a description of them. This description, however, I shall spare you for the present, and proceed with my story.

"The diamond merchants with whom I travelled had a great deal of business to transact at various places; and this was the cause of much delay to me, which I could scarcely bear with patience; for now that I had gratified my curiosity, I was extremely desirous to return to Madras with my little treasure. The five years' salary due to me by the East India Company, which I had never used, I had put out at interest at Madras, where sometimes the rate was as high as twelve per cent.; and if you knew (said Mr. Jervas, addressing himself to the miners at Mr. R—'s table) any thing of the nature of compound interest, you would perceive that I was in a fair way to get rich: for, in the course of fourteen or fifteen years, any sum that is put out at compound interest, even in England, where the rate of legal interest is five per cent., becomes double; that is, one hundred pounds put out at compound interest, in fourteen years, becomes two hundred. But few people have the patience, or the prudence, to make this use of their money. I was, however, determined to employ all my capital in this manner; and I calculated that, in seven years, I should have accumulated a sum fully sufficient to support me all the rest of my life in ease and affluence.

"Full of these hopes and calculations, I pursued my journey along with the merchants. Arrived at Devanelli Fort, I learned that the Soubha, with whom the sultan had been going to war, had given up the territory in dispute, and had pacified Tippoo by submissions and presents. Whether he chose peace or war was indifferent to me: I was intent on my private affairs, and I went immediately to Omychund, my banker, to settle them. I had taken my diamond ring with me to the mines, that I might compare it with others, and learn its value; and I found that it was worth nearly treble what I had been offered for it. Omychund congratulated me upon this discovery, and we were just going to settle our accounts, when an officer came in, and, after asking whether I was not the young Englishman who had lately visited the mines of Golconda, summoned me immediately to appear before the sultan. I was terrified, for I imagined I was perhaps suspected of having purloined some of the diamonds; but I followed the officer without hesitation, conscious of my innocence.

"Tippoo Sultan, contrary to my expectations, received me with a smiling countenance; and, pointing to the officer who accompanied me, asked me whether I recollected to have ever seen his face before? I replied, No: but the sultan then informed me that this officer, who was one of his own guards, had attended me in disguise during my whole visit to the diamond mines; and that he was perfectly satisfied of my honourable conduct. Then, after making a signal to the officer and all present to withdraw, he bade me approach nearer to him; paid some compliments to my abilities, and proceeded to explain to me that he stood in farther need of my services; and that, if I served him with fidelity, I should have no reason to complain, on my return to my own country, of his want of generosity.

"All thoughts of war being now, as he told me, out of his mind, he had leisure for other projects to enrich himself; and he was determined to begin by reforming certain abuses, which had long tended to impoverish the royal treasury. I was at a loss to know whither this preamble would lead: at length, having exhausted his oriental pomp of words, he concluded by informing me that he had reason to believe he was terribly cheated in the management of his mines at Golconda; that they were rented from him by a Feulinga Brahmin, as he called him, whose agreement with the adventurers in the mines was, that all the stones they found under a pago in weight were to be their own; and all above this weight were to be his, for the sultan's use. Now it seems that this agreement was never honestly fulfilled by any of the parties: the slaves cheating the merchants, the merchants cheating the Feulinga Brahmin, and he, in his turn, defrauding the sultan; so that, Tippoo assured me, he had often purchased, from diamond merchants, stones of a larger spread and finer water than any he could get directly from his own mines; and that he had been frequently obliged to reward these merchants with rich vests, or fine horses, in order to encourage others to offer their diamonds for sale.

[Footnote: *Philosophical Transactions*, vol. ii. p.472.]

"I could not but observe, whilst Tippoo related all this, the great agitation of his looks and voice, which showed me the strong hold the passion for diamonds had upon his soul; on which I should perhaps have made some wise reflections, but that people have seldom leisure or inclination to make wise reflections when standing in the presence of a prince as powerful and as despotic as Tippoo Sultan.

"The service that he required from me was a very dangerous one; no less than to visit the mines secretly by night, to search those small cisterns in which the workmen leave the diamonds mixed with the sand, gravelly stuff, and red earth, to sink and drain off during their absence. I by no means relished this undertaking: besides that it would expose me to imminent danger, it was odious to my feelings to become a spy and an informer. This I stated to the sultan, but he gave no credit to this motive; and, attributing my reluctance wholly to fear, he promised that he would take effectual measures to secure my safety; and that, after I had executed this commission, he would immediately send a guard with me to Madras. I saw that a dark frown lowered on his brow, when I persisted in declining this office; but I fortunately bethought myself at this moment of a method of escaping the effects of his anger, without giving up my own principles.

"I represented to him that the seizure of the diamonds in the cisterns, which he proposed, even should it afford him any convincing proofs of the dishonesty of the slaves and diamond merchants, and even if he could in future take effectual precautions to secure himself from their frauds, would not be a source of wealth to him equal to one which I could propose. His avarice fixed his attention, and he eagerly commanded me to proceed. I then explained to him that one of his richest diamond-mines had been for some time abandoned; because the workmen, having dug till they came to water, were then forced to stop for want of engines such as are known in Europe. Now, having observed that there was a rapid current at the foot of the mountain, on which I could erect a water-mill, I offered to clear this valuable mine."

CHAPTER V

"The sultan was pleased with the proposal; but, recollecting how apt he was to change his humour, and how ill he received me when I returned from his tin-mines, I had the precaution to represent that, as this undertaking would be attended with considerable expense, it would be necessary that a year's salary should be advanced to me before my departure for Golconda; and that, if the payments were not in future regularly made, I should be at liberty to resign my employment, and return to Madras. Prince Abdul Calie was present when the sultan pledged his word to this, and gave me full powers to employ certain of his artificers and workmen.

"I shall not trouble you with a history of all my difficulties, delays, and disappointments, in the execution of my undertaking; however interesting they were to me, the relation would be tiresome to those who have no diamond-mines to drain. It is enough for you to know that at length my engines were set a-going properly, and did their business so effectually, that the place was by degrees cleared of water, and the workmen were able to open fresh and valuable veins. During all this time, including a period of three years, my salary was regularly paid to the Gentoo merchant, Omychund, in whose hands I left all my money, upon his promising to pay me as high interest as what I could obtain at Madras. I drew upon him only for such small sums as were absolutely necessary; as I was resolved to live with the utmost economy, that I might the sooner be enabled to return in affluence to my native country.

"And here I must pause to praise myself, or rather to rejoice from the bottom of my soul, that I did not, when power was in my hands, make use of it for the purposes of extortion. The condition of the poor slaves, who were employed by me, was envied by all the others: and I have reason to know that, even in the most debased and miserable state of existence, the human heart can be wakened by kind treatment to feelings of affection and gratitude. These slaves became so much attached to me that, although the governor of the mines, and certain diamond merchants, were lying in wait continually to get rid of me some way or other, they never could effect their purposes. I was always apprised of my danger in time by some of these trusty slaves; who, with astonishing sagacity and fidelity, guarded me while I lived amongst them.

"A life of daily suspicion and danger was, however, terrible; and my influence extended but a little way in making others happy. I might, for a short season, lessen the suffering of these slaves; but still they were slaves, and most of them were treated scarcely as if they were human beings, by the rapacious adventurers for whom they laboured.

"These poor wretches generally work almost naked; they dare not wear a coat, lest the governor should say they have thriven much, are rich, and so increase his demands upon them. The wisest, when they find a great stone, conceal it till they have an opportunity; and then, with wife and children, run all away into the Visiapore country, where they are secure and well used.

[Footnote: Philosophical Transactions.]

"My heart sickened at the daily sight of so much misery; and nothing but my hopes of finally prevailing on the sultan to better their condition, by showing him how much he would be the gainer by it, could have induced me to remain so long in this situation. Repeatedly Tippoo promised me that the first diamond of twenty pagos weight which I should bring to him, he would grant me all I asked in favour of the slaves under my care. I imparted to them this promise, which excited them to great exertions. At last we were fortunate enough to find a diamond above the weight required. It was a well-spread stone, of a beautiful pale rose-colour, and of an adamantine hardness. I am sure that the sight of that famous stone, which is known by the name of the Pitt diamond, never gave its possessor such heartfelt joy as I experienced when I beheld this. I looked upon it as the pledge of future happiness, not only to myself, but to hundreds of my fellow-creatures.

"I set out immediately for Tippoo Sultan's court. It was too late in the evening, when I arrived, to see the sultan that night; so I went to Omychund, the Hindoo merchant, to settle my affairs with him. He received me with open arms, saying that he had thriven much upon my pagodas and rupees, and that he was ready to account with me for my salary; also for the interest which he owed me; for all which he gave me an order upon an English merchant at Madras, with whom I was well acquainted.

"This being settled to my satisfaction, I told him the business which now brought me to Tippoo's court, and showed him my rose-coloured diamond. His eyes opened at the sight with a prodigious expression of avaricious eagerness. 'Trust me,' said he, 'keep this diamond. I know Tippoo better than you do; he will not grant those privileges to the slaves that you talk about; and, after all, what concern are they of yours? They are used to the life they lead. They are not Europeans. What concern are they of yours? Once in your native country, you will dream of them no more. You will think only of enjoying the wealth you shall have brought from India. Trust me, keep the diamond. Fly this night towards Madras. I have a slave who perfectly knows the road across the country: you will be in no danger of pursuit, for the sultan will suppose you to be still at Golconda. No one could inform him of the truth but myself; and you must see, by the advice I now give you, that I am your firm friend.'

"As he finished these words, he clapped his hands, to summon one of his slaves, as he said, to give instant orders for my flight. He looked upon me with incredulous surprise, when I coolly told him that the flight which he proposed was far from my thoughts; and that it was my determination to give the sultan the diamond that belonged to him.

"Seeing that I was in earnest, Omychund suddenly changed his countenance; and in a tone of raillery, asked me whether I could believe that his proposal was serious. Indeed I was left in doubt whether he had been in earnest or not; and, at all events, I gave him to understand that I was incapable of betraying him to the sultan.

"The next morning, as early as I could, I presented myself before the sultan, who singled me from the crowd, and took me with him into the apartment of Prince Abdul Calie.

"I proceeded cautiously: Tippoo was all impatience to hear news of his diamond mine, and repeatedly interrupted me in my account of what had been done there, by asking whether we had yet come to any diamonds? I produced first one of a violet colour, which I had reserved as a present for Prince Abdul Calie; it was a fine stone, but nothing equal to our rose-coloured diamond. Tippoo admired this, however, so much, that I was certain he would be in raptures with that which I had in store for him. Before I showed it to him, in speaking of the weight of that which I had designed to present to the prince, I reminded him of his royal promise with respect to the slaves. 'True,' cried the sultan: 'but is this diamond twenty pagos weight? when you bring me one of that value, you may depend upon having all you ask.' I instantly produced the rose-coloured diamond, weighed it in his presence, and, as the scale in which it was put descended, Tippoo burst forth into an exclamation of joy. I seized the favourable moment; he nodded as I knelt before him, and bade me rise, saying my request was granted; though why I should ask favours for a parcel of mean slaves, he observed, was incomprehensible.

"Prince Abdul Calie did not appear to be of this opinion; he at this instant cast upon me a look full of benevolence; and whilst his father was absorbed in the contemplation of his rose-coloured diamond, which he weighed, I believe, a hundred times, the generous young prince presented to me that violet-coloured diamond which I brought for him. A princely gift made in a princely manner.

"Tippoo's secretary made out for me the necessary order to the governor of the mines, by which a certain share of the profits of his labour was, by the sultan's command, to belong to each slave; and all those who had been employed in my service were, as a reward for their good conduct, to be emancipated. A number of petty exactions were by this order abolished; and the property acquired in land, dress, &c. by the slaves, was secured to them. Most gladly did I see the sultan's signet affixed to this paper; and when it was delivered into my hands, my heart bounded with joy. I resolved to be the bearer of these good tidings myself. Although my passport was made out for Madras, and two hircarrahs, by the sultan's orders, were actually ready to attend me thither, yet I could not refuse myself the pleasure of beholding the joy of the slaves, at this change in their condition; and, to the latest hour of my life, I shall rejoice that I returned to Golconda the messenger of happiness. Never shall I forget the scene to which I was there a witness; never will the expressions of joy and gratitude be effaced from my memory, which lighted up the dark faces of these poor creatures! who, say what we will, have as much sensibility, perhaps more, than we have ourselves.

"No sooner was I awake, the morning after my arrival, than I heard them singing songs under my window, in which my own name was frequently repeated. They received me with a shout of joy when I went out amongst them; and, crowding round me, they pressed me to accept of some little tokens of their gratitude and good-will, which I had not the heart to refuse. The very children, by their caresses, seemed to beg me not to reject these little offerings. I determined, if ever I reached Europe, to give all of them to you, sir, my good master, as the best present I could make to one of your way of thinking.

"The day after my arrival was spent in rejoicings. All the slaves, who had worked under my inspection, had saved some little matters, with which they had purchased for their wives and for themselves coloured cottons, and handkerchiefs for their heads. Now that they were not in dread of being robbed or persecuted by the governor of the mines, they ventured to produce them in open day. These cottons of Malabar are dyed of remarkably bright and gaudy colours; and, when the slaves appeared decked in them, it was to me one of the gayest spectacles I ever beheld. They were dancing with a degree of animation of which, till then, I never had an idea.

"I stood under the shade of a large banyan tree, enjoying the sight; when suddenly I felt from behind a blow on my head which stunned me. I fell to the ground; and when I came to my senses, found myself in the hands of four armed soldiers, and a Hindoo, who was pulling my diamond ring from my finger. They were carrying me away amid the cries and lamentations of the slaves, who followed us. 'Stand off'! it is in vain you shriek,' said one of the soldiers to the surrounding crowd; 'what we do is by order of the sultan. Thus he punishes traitors.'

"Without further explanation, I was thrown into a dungeon belonging to the governor of the mines, who stood by with insulting joy to see me chained to a large stone in my horrid prison. I knew him to be my enemy: but what was my astonishment when I recollected in the countenance of the Hindoo, who was fastening my chains and loading me with curses, that very Saheb, whose life I had formerly saved! To all my questions no answer was given, but, 'It is the will of the sultan;' or, 'Thus the sultan avenges himself upon traitors.'

"The door of my dungeon was then locked and barred, and I was left alone in perfect darkness. Is this, thought I, the reward of all my faithful services? Bitterly did I regret that I was not in my native country, where no man, at the will of a sultan, can be thrown into a dungeon, without knowing his crime or his accusers. I cannot attempt to describe to you what I felt, during this most miserable day of my existence. Feeble at last, for want of food, I stretched myself out, as well as my chains would allow me, and tried to compose myself to sleep. I sunk into a state of insensibility, in which I must have remained for several hours, for it was midnight when I was roused by the unbarring of my prison door. It was Saheb who entered, carrying in one hand a torch, and in the other some food, which he set before me in silence. I cast upon him a look of scorn, and was about to reproach him with his ingratitude, when he threw himself at my feet, and burst into tears. 'Is it possible,' said he to me, 'that you are not sure of the heart of Saheb? You saved my life; I am come to save yours. But eat, master,' continued he; 'eat whilst I speak, for we have no time to lose. To-morrow's sun must see us far from hence. You cannot support the fatigues you have to undergo without taking food.'

"I yielded to his entreaties, and, whilst I ate, Saheb informed me that my imprisonment was owing to the treacherous Hindoo merchant, Omychund; who, in hopes, I suppose, of possessing himself in quiet of all the wealth which I had intrusted to his care, went to the sultan, and accused me of having secreted certain diamonds of great value, which he pretended I had shown to him in confidence. Tippoo, enraged at this, despatched immediate orders to four of his soldiers to go in search of me, seize, imprison, and torture me, till I should confess where these diamonds were concealed. Saheb was in the sultan's apartment when this order was given, and immediately hastened to Prince Abdul Calie, whom he knew to be my friend, and informed him of what had happened. The prince sent for Omychund, and, after carefully questioning him, was convinced, by his contradictory answers, and by his confusion, that the charge against me was wholly unfounded: he dismissed Omychund, however, without letting him know his opinion, and then sent Saheb for the four soldiers who were setting out in search of me. In their presence he gave Saheb orders aloud to take charge of me the moment I should be found, and secretly commissioned him to favour my escape. The soldiers thought that in obeying the prince they obeyed the sultan; and, consequently, when I was taken and lodged in my dungeon, the keys of it were delivered to Saheb.

"When he had finished telling me all this, he restored to me my ring, which he said he snatched from my finger, as soon as I was seized, that I might not be robbed of it by the governor, or some of the soldiers.

"The grateful Saheb now struck off my chains; and my own anxiety for my escape was scarcely equal to his. He had swift horses belonging to the soldiers in readiness; and we pursued our course all night without interruption. He was well acquainted with the country, having accompanied the sultan on several expeditions. When we thought ourselves beyond the reach of all pursuers, Saheb permitted me to rest; but I never rested at my ease till I was out of Tippoo Sultan's dominions, and once more in safety at Madras. Dr. Bell received me with great kindness, heard my story, and congratulated me on my escape from Tippoo's power.

"I was now rich beyond my hopes; for I had Omychund's order upon the Madras merchant safe in my pocket, and the whole sum was punctually paid to me. My ring I sold to the governor of Madras for more even than I expected.

"I had the satisfaction to learn, before I left Madras, that Omychund's treachery was made known to the sultan, by means of Prince Abdul Calie, whose memory will ever be dear to me. Tippoo, as I have been informed, in speaking of me, was heard to regret that he could not recall to his service such an honest Englishman.

"I was eager to reward the faithful Saheb, but he absolutely refused the money which I offered him, saying, 'that he would not be paid for saving the life of one who had saved his.' He expressed a great desire to accompany me to my native country, from the moment that I told him we had no slaves there;

and that as soon as any slave touched the English shore, by our laws, he obtained his freedom. He pressed me so earnestly to take him along with me as my servant, that I could not refuse; so he sailed with me for Europe. As the wind filled the sails of our vessel, much did I rejoice that the gales which blew me from the shores of India were not tainted with the curses of any of my fellow-creatures. Here I am, thank Heaven! once more in free and happy England, with a good fortune, clean hands, and a pure conscience, not unworthy to present myself to my first good master, to him whose humanity and generosity were the cause of—"

Here Mr. R— interrupted his own praises, by saying to those of the miners who had not fallen fast asleep, "My good friends, you now know the meaning of the toast which you all drank after dinner; let us drink it again before we part 'Welcome home to our friend, Mr. Jervas, and may good faith always meet with good fortune!'"

October, 1799.

THE WILL

CHAPTER I

Mr. Pearson, a wealthy Lincolnshire farmer, who had always been esteemed a prudent sensible man, though something of a humourist, made the following will:

"I, John Pearson, of The Wold in Lincolnshire, farmer, being of sound mind and body, do make this my last will and testament, &c.

"I give and bequeath my farm of West Woldland to my eldest nephew, Grimes Goodenough; my farm of Holland Fen to my dear nephew, John Wright, and my farm of Clover-hill to my youngest nephew, Pierce Marvel.

"I farther will and desire that the sum of ten thousand pounds, which is now in the hands of William Constantine, gentleman, my executor, may by him, immediately after my decease, be put out to interest for ten years: and I will and desire that, at the end of the said ten years, the said sum of ten thousand pounds, and the interest so accumulated thereon, be given to whichsoever of my aforesaid nephews shall at that time be the richest.

"And I trust that the said William Constantine, gentleman, my executor and very good friend, being a clear-headed honest man, will understand and execute this my last will and testament, according to the plain meaning of my words; though it should happen that this my will should not be drawn up in due legal form, of which I know little or nothing."

Mr. Constantine, the executor, being, as described, a clear-headed honest man, found no difficulty either in understanding or executing this trust: the ten thousand pounds were, immediately upon Pearson's decease, placed out upon interest; and the three nephews were put into possession of their farms. These were of very different value. Goodenough's wanted improvement, but would pay richly for any that should be judiciously made; Wright's farm was by far the worst of the three; and Marvel's the best.

The Lincolnshire world was much divided in opinion concerning these young men; and many bets were laid relating to the legacy. People judged according to their own characters; the enterprising declared for Marvel, the prudent for Wright, the timid for Goodenough.

The nephews had scarcely been in possession of their farms a week when, one evening, as they were all supping together at Wright's house, Marvel suddenly turned to Goodenough, and exclaimed, "When do you begin your improvements, cousin Goodenough?"

"Never, cousin Marvel."

"Then you'll never touch the ten thousand, my boy. What! will you do nothing to your marsh? Nothing to your common? Nothing to your plantations? Do not you mean ever to make any improvements?"

"I mean not to make any improvements."

"Well, you'll let me make some for you."

"Not I."

"No! Won't you let me cut down some of those trees for you, that are spoiling one another in your wood?"

"Not a tree shall be cut down. Not a stick shall be stirred. Not a change shall be made, I say."

"Not a change for the better, cousin Goodenough?" said Wright.

"Not a change can be for the better, to my mind; I shall plough, and sow, and reap, as our forefathers did, and that's enough for me."

"What! will you not even try the new plough?" said Marvel.

"Not I; no new ploughs for me. No plough can be so good as the old one."

"How do you know, as you never tried it, or would see it tried?" said Wright: "I find it better than the old one."

"No matter; the old one will do well enough for me, as it did for my father before me." After having repeated these words in precisely the same tone several times, he went on slowly eating his supper, whilst Marvel, in detestation of his obstinate stupidity, turned his back upon him, and began to enumerate to Wright sundry of his own ingenious projects.

"My dear Wright," said he, "you are worth talking to, and you shall hear all my schemes."

"Willingly; but I do not promise to approve of them all."

"Oh! you will, you will, the moment you hear them; and I will let you have a share in some of them. In the first place, there's that fine rabbit-warren near Clover-hill. The true silver grey rabbits—silver sprigs, they call them—do you know that the skins of those silver sprigs are worth any money?"

"Any money! what money?"

"Pooh! I don't know exactly: but I mean to buy that warren."

"Before you know what it is worth! Let us consider; each dozen of skins is worth, say, from ten to fifteen shillings."

"You need not trouble yourself to calculate now," interrupted Marvel, "for I have determined to have the warren. With the money that I shall get for my silver sprigs, I will next year make a decoy, and supply the London market with wild-fowl. Don't you remember the day that we met Simon Stubbs, the carrier, loaded with game and wild-fowl, he said that a decoy in Lincolnshire must be a fortune to any man. I'll have the best decoy not only in Lincolnshire but in all England. By-the-bye, there's another thing I must do, Wright; I'll exchange any part of Clover-hill you please with you, for as much land in Holland Fen."

"Take him at his word, cousin Wright," said Goodenough.

"No, no," replied Wright; "I know the value of land, and the difference between Clover-hill and Holland Fen, better than he does: I would not take him at his word, for that would be taking him in."

"I would not take anybody in," said Goodenough; "but if another man is a fool, that's no reason I should be one. Now, if a man offers me a good bargain, why should not I close with him, and say—Done?" "Then say done," cried Marvel, "and you shall have the bargain, Goodenough. You have an undrained marsh of your own: I'll exchange with you, and welcome, ten acres of the marsh for five of Clover-hill."

"Done," said Goodenough.

"Done. I shall stock it with geese, and you'll see what the quills and feathers alone will bring me in. I've engaged with one already to sell them for me. But, Wright, here's another scheme I have. Wildmore common, you know, is covered with those huge thistles, which prick the noses of the sheep so as to hinder them from feeding and fattening: I will take that common into my own hands."

"Ay," said Goodenough; "exchange the rest of Clover-hill for it:—that's like you!"

"And I will mow the thistles," pursued Marvel, without deigning to reply to Goodenough. "I will mow the thistles; their down I can contrive to work up into cotton, and the stalks into cordage: and, with the profit I shall make of these thistles, and of my decoy, and of my goose-quills and feathers, and of my silver sprig rabbits, I will buy jackets for my sheep, for my sheep shall all have jackets after shearing. Why should not Lincolnshire sheep, if they have jackets, become as valuable as the Leicestershire breed? You'll see my sheep will be the finest in the whole county; and, with the profit I shall make of them, I will set up a fishery in Fen-lake; and with the profits of the fishery—now comes my grand scheme—I shall be the richest of you all! with the profits of the fishery, and the decoy, and the sheep, and the silver sprigs, and the quills and feathers, geese and thistles, I will purchase that fine heronry, near Spalding."

At these words, Goodenough laid down his knife and fork; and, sticking his arms a-kimbo, laughed contemptuously, if not heartily.

"So, then, the end of all this turmoil is to purchase a heronry! Much good may it do you, cousin Marvel. You understand your own affair best: you will make great improvements, I grant, and no doubt will be the richest of us all. The ten thousand pounds will be yours for certain: for, as we all know, cousin Marvel, you are a genius!—But why a genius should set his fancy upon a heronry, of all things in this mortal world, is more than I can pretend to tell, being no genius myself."

"Look here, Wright," continued Marvel, still without vouchsafing any direct reply to Goodenough: "here's a description, in this last newspaper, of the fine present that the grand seignior has made to his majesty. The plume of herons' feathers alone is estimated at a thousand guineas! Think of what I shall make by my heronry! At the end of ten years, I shall be so rich that it will hardly be worth my while," said Marvel, laughing, "to accept of my uncle's legacy. I will give it to you, Wright; for you are a generous fellow, and I am sure you will deserve it."

In return for this liberal promise, Wright endeavoured to convince Marvel, that if he attempted such a variety of schemes at once, they would probably all fail; and that to ensure success, it would be necessary to calculate, and to make himself master of the business, before he should undertake to conduct it. Marvel, however, was of too sanguine and presumptuous a temper to listen to this sage advice: he was piqued by the sneers of his cousin Goodenough, and determined to prove the superiority of his own spirit and intellect. He plunged at once into the midst of a business which he did not understand. He took a rabbit-warren of two hundred and fifty acres into his hands; stocked ten acres of marsh land with geese; and exchanged some of the best part of Clover-hill for a share in a common covered with thistles. He planted a considerable tract of land, with a degree of expedition that astonished all the neighbourhood: but it was remarked that the fences were not quite sufficient; especially as the young trees were in a dangerous situation, being surrounded by land stocked with sheep and horned cattle. Wright warned him of the danger; but he had no time this year, he said, to complete the fences: the men who tended his sheep might easily keep them from the plantation for this season, and the next spring he purposed to dig such a ditch round the whole as should secure it for ever. He was now extremely busy, making jackets for his sheep, providing willows for his decoy, and gorse and corn for his geese: the geese, of which he had a prodigious flock, were not yet turned into their fen, because a new scheme had occurred to Marvel, relative to some reeds with which a part of this fen was covered; on these reeds myriads of starlings were accustomed to roost, who broke them down with their weight. Now Marvel knew that such reeds would be valuable for thatching, and with this view he determined to drive away the starlings; but the measures necessary for this purpose would frighten his friends, the geese, and therefore he was obliged to protect and feed them in his farm-yard, at a considerable expense, whilst he was carrying on the war with the starlings. He fired guns at them morning and evening, he sent up rockets and kites with fiery tails, and at last he banished them; but half his geese, in the mean time, died for want of food; and the women and children, who plucked them, stole one quarter of the feathers, and one half of the quills, whilst Marvel was absent letting up rockets in the fen.

The rabbit-warren was, however, to make up for all other losses: a furrier had engaged to take as many silver sprigs from him as he pleased, at sixteen shillings a dozen, provided he should send them properly dressed, and in time to be shipped for China, where these silver grey rabbit skins sold to the best advantage. As winter came on, it was necessary to supply the warren with winter food: and Marvel was much astonished at the multitude of unforeseen expenses into which his rabbits led him. The banks of the warren wanted repair, and the warrener's house was not habitable in bad weather: these appeared but slight circumstances when Marvel made the purchase; but, alas! he had reason to change his opinion in the course of a few months. The first week in November, there was a heavy fall of snow; and the warren walls should have been immediately cleared of snow, to have kept the rabbits within their bounds: but Marvel happened this week to be on a visit in Yorkshire, and he was obliged to leave the care of the warren entirely to the warrener, who was obliged to quit his house during the snow, and to take shelter with a neighbour: he neglected to clear the walls; and Marvel upon his return home, found that his silver sprigs had strayed into a neighbouring warren. The second week in November is the time when the rabbits are usually killed, as the skins are then in full prime: it was in vain that Marvel raised a hue and cry after his silver sprigs; a fortnight passed away before one-third of them could be recovered. The season was lost, and the furrier sued him for breach of contract; and what was worse, Goodenough laughed at his misfortunes. The next year he expected to retrieve his loss: he repaired the warrener's house, new faced the banks, and capped them with furze; but the common grey rabbit had been introduced into the warren, by the stragglers of the preceding year; and as these grey rabbits are of a much more hardy race than the silver sprigs, they soon obtained and kept possession of the land. Marvel now pronounced rabbits to be the most useless and vexatious animals upon earth; and, in one quarter of an hour, thoroughly convinced himself that tillage was far more profitable than rabbits. He ploughed up his warren, and sowed it with corn; but, unluckily, his attention had been so much taken up by the fishery, the decoy, the geese, the thistles, and the hopes of the heronry, that he totally forgot his intention of making the best of all possible ditches round his plantation. When he went to visit this plantation, he beheld a miserable spectacle: the rabbits which had strayed beyond their bounds during the great snow, and those which had been hunted from their burrows, when the warren was ploughed up, had all taken shelter in this spot; and these refugees supported themselves, for some months, upon the bark and roots of the finest young trees.

Marvel's loss was great, but his mortification still greater; for his cousin Goodenough laughed at him without mercy. Something must be done, he saw, to retrieve his credit: ad the heronry was his resource.

"What will signify a few trees, more or less," thought he, "or the loss of a few silver sprigs, or the death of a few geese, or the waste of a few quills and feathers? My sheep will sell well, my thistles will bring me up again; and as soon as I have sold my sheep at Partney fair, and manufactured my thistles, I will set out with my money in my pocket for Spalding, and make my bargain for the heronry. A plume of herons' feathers is worth a thousand guineas! My fortune will be made when I get possession of the Spalding heronry."

So intent was Marvel upon the thoughts of the Spalding heronry, that he neglected every thing else. About a week before the fair of Partney, he bethought himself of his sheep, which he had left to the care of a shepherd boy: he now ordered the boy to drive them home, that he might see them. Their jackets hung upon them like bags: the poor animals had fallen away in the most deplorable manner. Marvel could scarcely believe that these were his sheep; or that these were the sheep which he had expected to be the pride of Lincolnshire, and which he had hoped would set the fashion of jackets. Behold, they were dying of the rot!

"What an unfortunate man I am!" exclaimed Marvel, turning to his cousin Wright, whom he had summoned along with Goodenough, in the pride of his heart, to view, value, and admire his sheep. "All your sheep, Wright, are fat and sound: mine were finer than yours when I bought them: how comes it that I am so unlucky?"

"Jack of all trades, and master of none!" said Goodenough, with a sneer.

"You forgot, I am afraid, what I told you, when first you bought these sheep," said Wright, "that you should always keep them in fold, every morning, till the dew was off: if you had done so, they would now be as well and thriving as mine. Do not you remember my telling you that?"

"Yes; and I charged this boy always to keep them in fold till the dew was off," replied Marvel, turning with an angry countenance to the shepherd boy.

"I never heard nothing of it till this minute, I am sure, master," said the boy.

Marvel now recollected that, at the very moment when he was going to give this order to the boy, his attention had been drawn away by the sight of a new decoy in the fields adjoining to his sheep pasture. In his haste to examine the decoy, he forgot to give that order to his shepherd, on which the safety of his fine flock of sheep depended.

[Footnote: A General View of the Agriculture of the County of Lincoln, p. 330. "It well deserves noting that a shepherd, who, when young, was shepherd's boy to an old man, who lived at Netlam, near Lincoln, a place famous for the rot, told Mr. Neve that he was persuaded sheep took the rot only of a morning, before the dew was well off. At that time they folded, being open field: his master's shepherd kept his flock in fold always till the dew was gone; and, with no other attention, his sheep were kept sound, when all the neighbours lost their flocks."]

Such are the negligences and blunders of those who endeavour to do half a dozen things at once.

The failure of one undertaking never discouraged Marvel from beginning another; and it is a pity, that, with so much spirit and activity, he had so little steadiness and prudence. His sheep died, and he set out for Spalding full of the thoughts of the heronry. Now this heronry belonged to Sir Plantagenet Mowbray, an elderly gentleman, who was almost distracted with family pride: he valued himself upon never having parted with one inch of the landed property that had descended to him, through a long line of ancestors, from the Plantagenets. He looked down upon the whole race of farmers and traders as beings of a different species from himself; and the indignation with which he heard, from a Lincolnshire farmer, a proposal to purchase his heronry, may perhaps be imagined, but cannot be described. It was in vain that Marvel rose in his offers; it was in vain that he declared he was ready to give any price that Sir Plantagenet would set upon the heronry. Sir Plantagenet sent word, by his steward, that not a feather of his birds should be touched; that he was astonished at the insolence of such a proposal; and that he advised Marvel to keep out of the way of his people, lest they should revenge the insult that had been offered to their master.

This haughty answer, and the disappointment of all his hopes and schemes respecting the heronry, threw Marvel into a degree of rage scarcely inferior to what was felt by Sir Plantagenet. As he was galloping down the avenue from Plantagenet-hall, he overtook a young man, of a shabby appearance, who was mounted upon a very fine horse. At first Marvel took it for granted that he was one of Sir Plantagenet's people, and he was riding past him, when he heard the stranger say, in a friendly tone, "Your horse gallops well, sir: but have a care; there's a carrion a little way farther on that may startle him."

Marvel pulled in his horse; the stranger rode up beside him, and they entered into conversation. "That carrion, sir," said he, pointing to the dead horse, which had just been shot for the baronet's son's hounds, "that carrion, sir, was in my opinion the best horse Sir Plantagenet, or his son either, were possessed of. 'Tis a shame for any man, who pretends to be a gentleman, and who talks this way and that so high of his family, should be so stingy in the article of horseflesh."

Marvel was not unwilling at this instant to hear the haughty baronet blamed and ridiculed; and his companion exactly fell in with his humour, by telling a variety of anecdotes to prove Sir Plantagenet to be every thing that was odious and contemptible. The history of his insolence about the heronry was now related by Marvel; and the stranger seemed to sympathize so much in his feelings, that, from a stranger, he began to consider him as a friend. Insensibly the conversation returned to the point at which it commenced; and his new friend observed that it was in vain to expect any thing good from any gentleman, or indeed from any man, who was stingy in the article of horseflesh.

A new sense of honour and of shame began to rise in our hero's mind; and he sat uneasy in his saddle, whilst he reflected that the horse upon which he was mounted, was perhaps as deservedly an object of contempt as any of Sir Plantagenet's stud. His new friend, without seeming to notice his embarrassment, continued his conversation, and drew a tempting picture of the pleasures and glories of a horse-race: he said, "he was just training a horse for the York races, and a finer animal never was crossed. Sir Plantagenet's eldest son would have been the proudest and happiest of men, if his father would but have bought the horse for him: but he had refused, and the youth himself had not the price, or half the price, at his command."

Our hero was no judge of horses, but he was ambitious to prove that his spirit was superior to that of the haughty baronet; and that something good might be expected from him, as he was not stingy in horseflesh. Besides, he was worked up to a high degree of curiosity to see the York races; and his companion assured him that he could not appear there without being well mounted. In short, the hour was not at an end before he had offered a hundred guineas for the finest horse that ever was crossed. He was charmed with the idea that he should meet Sir Plantagenet Mowbray's son and heir at the York races, and should show him that he was able and willing to pay for the horse, which his arrogant father could not afford to purchase.

From the anecdote of the heronry, his companion perceived that Marvel was a man fond of projects; and he proposed to him a scheme, which caught his fancy so much that it consoled him for his disappointment. It was the fault of our enterprizing hero's character always to think the last scheme for making a fortune the best. As soon as he reached home he was in haste to abandon some of his old projects, which now appeared to him flat, stale, and unprofitable. About a score of his flock, though tainted with the rot, were not yet dead; he was eager to sell them, but no one would buy sheep of such a wretched appearance. At last Wright took them off his hands. "I will throw the threescore jackets into the bargain," said Marvel; "for you are a generous fellow, to offer so handsomely for my poor sheep, and you deserve to be treated as you treat others. If I come in at the end of the ten years for the legacy, I shall remember you, as I told you before: as to my cousin Goodenough here, he thinks so much of himself, that there is no occasion for others to think of him. I asked him to join me in a bond, yesterday, for a hundred pounds, just to try him, and he refused me. When I come in for the legacy, I will cut him off with a shilling,—I will give him fair notice."

"Cut me off with what you will," said Goodenough, sullenly, "not a farthing of my money shall ever be lent to one that has a project for every day in the year. Get into what difficulties you may, I will never join you in any bond, I promise you. It is enough for me to take care of myself."

"Don't flatter yourself that I am getting into any difficulties," replied Marvel. "I wanted the hundred guineas only to pay for a horse; and the friend who sold him to me will wait my convenience."

"The friend" said Wright; "do you mean that man who rode home with you from Spalding?—I advise you not to make a friend of him, for he is a notorious jockey." "He will not take me in, though," said Marvel; "I am as sharp as he is, and he sees that: so we understand one another very well. To my certain knowledge, a hundred and twenty guineas could be had to-morrow for the horse I bought from him; yet he let me have him for a hundred."

"And how can a man of your sense, cousin Marvel," said Wright, "believe that a person, who never saw you till within these three days, would be so much your friend as to make you a present of twenty guineas?"

"A present!"

"Yes; if he lets you have a horse for a hundred, which you can sell for a hundred and twenty, does not he make you a present of twenty guineas?"

"Well, but I can tell you the reason for all that: he wants me to enter into a scheme with him, for breeding horses on the common here: and so he would not, at first setting out, stand to higgle with me for the price of a horse."

"And would you for twenty guineas, cousin Marvel, run the hazard of joining in any scheme with a man of his character? Pray inquire in the country and in York, where you are going, what sort of a character this man bears. Take my advice, pay him for his horse, and have nothing more to do with him."

"But I have not the ready cash to pay him for his horse, that's one thing," said Marvel.

"Let that be no difficulty," replied Wright; "for I have a hundred guineas here, just brought home from Partney fair, and they are heartily at your service."

Goodenough twitched Wright's elbow three times as he uttered these words: but Wright finished his sentence, and put the money into Marvel's hands immediately upon his promising to pay for the horse, break off all connexion with his friend the jockey, if he should find upon inquiry that he was not a person of good character, and at all events to suspend any treaty with him till after his return from York.

"Whilst you are gone," said Wright, "I will make inquiries about the profit of breeding of horses on the commons. I have an acquaintance, a sensible old man, who has kept accounts of what he has done in that way himself; and he will show us his accounts, from which we shall be able to judge."

CHAPTER II

Wright heard nothing more of him for about a fortnight; he then received the following letter:

"DER COUSIN WRIGHT,

"It is a very great pity that you could not be persuaded to come along with me to York races, where I have seen more of life, and of the world, in a week, than ever I did in all my life before.—York is a surprising fine town; and has a handsome cathedral, and assembly-room: but I am not in the humour, just now, to describe them: so I shall proceed to what is much better worth thinking of.

"You must know, cousin Wright, that I am in love, and never was I so happy or so miserable in my days. If I was not a farmer there would be some hopes for me; but, to be sure, it is not to be expected that such a lady as she is should think of a mere country booby; in which light, indeed, she was pleased to say, as I heard from good authority, she did not consider me; though my manners wanted polish. These were her own words. I shall spare nothing to please her, if possible, and am not wholly without hope, though I have a powerful rival; no less a person than the eldest son and heir of Sir Plantagenet Mowbray, Bart. But her virtue will never, I am persuaded, suffer her to listen to such addresses as his. Now mine are honourable, and pure as her soul; the purity of which no one could doubt, who had seen her last night, as I did, in the character of the Fair Penitent. She was universally admired: and another night sung and danced like an angel. But I can give you no idea of her by pen and ink; so I beseech you to come and see her, and give your advice to me candidly, for I have the highest opinion of your judgment and good-nature.

"I find you were quite right about that scoundrel who rode with me from Spalding! He has arrested me for a hundred guineas; and is, without exception, the shabbiest dog I ever met with: but I am out of his clutches, and have better friends. I will tell you the whole story when we meet, and pay you your hundred with many thanks. Pray set out as soon as you receive this, for every moment is an age to me: and I won't declare myself, more than I have done, if possible, till you come; for I have a great opinion of your judgment; yet hope you won't put on your severe face, nor be prejudiced against her, because of her being on the stage. Leave such illiberality to cousin Goodenough: it would be quite beneath you! Pray bring with you that volume of old plays that is at the top of my bed, under the bag of thistles; or in the basket of reeds that I was making; or in the out-house, where I keep the goose-quills and feathers. I don't find my memory so clear, since my head is so full of this charming Alicia Barton. Pray make no delay, as you value the peace of mind of your

"Affectionate cousin and friend,
"PIERCE MARVEL.

"P. S. Mr. Barton, her brother, is the most generous of men, and the cleverest. He is not averse to the match. Sir Plantagenet Mowbray's son and heir, who is as insolent as his father, may find that a Lincolnshire farmer is not a person to be despised. I have thoughts of selling my farm of Clover-hill, and of going into another way of life; for which, as Mr. Barton said, and Alicia hinted, nay, as I am inclined to believe too, I am much better suited than for farming. Of this more when we meet. Pray set out as soon as you receive this. Alicia has dark eyes, and yet a fair complexion. I am sure you will like her."

Far from feeling sure that he should like Miss Alicia Barton, Wright was so much alarmed for his cousin, on the perusal of this letter, that he resolved to set out immediately for York, lest the sale of Clover-hill should be concluded before his arrival. A new project and a new love were, indeed, powerful temptations to one of Marvel's character.

As Goodenough was plodding at his accustomed pace in his morning's work, he met Wright on horseback, who asked him if he had any commissions that he could execute in York, whither he was going.

"None, thank Heaven!" said Goodenough. "So I see it is as I always knew it would be! Marvel is 'ticing you into his own ways, and will make you just such another as his self. Ay, you must go to York races! Well, so much the better for me. Much pleasure to you at the races."

"I am not going to the races; I am going to do Marvel a service."

"Charity begins at home: that's my maxim," replied Goodenough.

"It is quite fitting that charity should begin at home," said Wright; "but then it should not end at home; for those that help nobody will find none to help them in time of need."

"Those that help nobody will not be so apt to come to need," replied Goodenough. "But yonder's my men standing idle. If I but turn my head, that's the way of them. Good morrow to you, cousin Wright; I can't stand argufying here about charity, which won't plough my ground, nor bring me a jot nearer to the ten thousand pounds' legacy: so good morrow to you. My service to cousin Marvel."

Goodenough proceeded to his men, who were in truth standing idle, as it was their custom to do when their master's eye was not, as they thought, upon them; for he kept them so hard at work, when he was present, that not a labouring man in the country would hire himself to Goodenough, when he could get employment elsewhere. Goodenough's partizans, however, observed that he got his money's worth out of every man he employed; and that this was the way to grow rich. The question, said they, is not which of the three nephews will be the best beloved, but which will be the richest at the end of ten years; and, on this ground, who can dispute that Goodenough's maxim is the best, "Charity begins at home?" Wright's friends looked rather alarmed when they heard of this journey to York; and Marvel's advocates, though they put a good face upon the matter, heartily wished him safe home.

Upon Wright's arrival in York, he found it no easy matter to discover his cousin Marvel; for he had forgotten to date his letter, and no direction was given to inn or lodging: at last, after inquiring at all the public-houses without success, Wright bethought himself of asking where Miss Alicia Barton, the actress, lodged; for there he would probably meet her lover. Mr. Harrison, an eminent dyer, to whom he applied for information, very civilly offered to show him to the house. Wright had gained this dyer's good opinion by the punctuality with which he had, for three years past, supplied him, at the day and hour appointed, with the quantity of woad for which he had agreed. Punctuality never fails to gain the good opinion of men of business.

As the dyer walked with Wright to Miss Barton's lodgings, they entered into conversation about her; and Wright asked what character she bore. "I know nothing of her character for my own share," said Harrison, "not being in that line of business; but I think I could put you into a way of seeing her in her true colours, whatever they may be; for she is very intimate with a milliner, whom my wife (though not with my good-will entirely) visits. In return for which, I shall be glad that you will do my business along with your own; and let me know if any thing is going wrong."

The dyer introduced Wright to the milliner as a gentleman farmer, who wanted to take home with him a fashionable cap and bonnet, or two, for some ladies in Lincolnshire. The milliner ordered down some dusty bandboxes, which she protested and vowed were just arrived from London with the newest fashions; and, whilst she was displaying these, Wright talked of the races, and the players, and Miss Alicia Barton.

"Is she as handsome as they say? I have a huge cur'osity to see her," said Wright, feigning more rusticity of manner and more simplicity than was natural to him. "I have, truly, a woundy cur'osity to see her, I've heard so much of her, even down in Lincolnshire."

"If you go to see the play, sir, you can't fail to have your curiosity gratified, for Miss Barton plays to-night—(Jenny! reach me a play-bill)—for her own benefit, and appears in her very best character, the Romp."

"The Romp!—Odds! Is that her best character? Why, now, to my notion, bad's the best, if that be the best of her characters. The Romp!—Odds so! What would our grandmothers say to that?"

"Oh, sir, times are changed, as well as fashions, since our grandmothers' days," said the milliner. "Put up this bonnet for the gentleman, Jenny.—I am sure I don't pretend to say any thing in favour of the times, whatever I may of the fashions. But, as to fashion, to be sure no one can be more fashionable, here in York, than Miss Barton. All our gentlemen are dying for her."

"Odds my life, I'll keep out of her way! And yet I've a huge cur'osity to set my eyes upon her. Pray, now, could I any way get to the sight or speech of her in a room, or so? for seeing a woman on the stage is one thing, and seeing her off, as I take it, is another."

"I take it so too, sir. Jenny, put up the cap for the gentleman, and make out a bill."

"No, no; the bonnet's all I want, which I'll pay for on the nail."

Wright took out a long purse full of guineas: then put it up again, and opened a pocket-book full of bank-notes. The milliner's respect for him obviously increased. "Jenny! Do run and see who's within there. Miss Barton was trying on her dress, I think, half an hour ago: may be she'll pass through this way, and the gentleman may have a sight of her, since it weighs so much upon his mind. Let me put up the cap too, sir: it's quite the fashion, you may assure the Lincolnshire ladies.—Oh! here's Miss Barton."

Miss Barton made her appearance, with all her most bewitching smiles and graces. Without seeming to notice Wright, she seated herself in a charming attitude; and, leaning pensively on the counter, addressed her conversation to her friend, the milliner: but, at every convenient pause, she cast an inquiring glance at Wright, who stood with his long purse of guineas in his hand, and his open pocket-book of bank-notes before him, as if he had been so much astonished by the lady's appearance, that he could not recover his recollection. Now, Wright was a remarkably well-shaped handsome man, and Miss Barton was in reality as much struck by his appearance as he feigned to be by hers. No forbidding reserve condemned him to silence; and, as if inspired by the hope of pleasing, he soon grew talkative.

"This is the most rare town, this, your town of York." said he: "I do not well know how I shall ever he able to get myself out of it: so many fine sights, my eyes be quite dazzled!" "And pray, sir, which of all the fine sights do you like the best?" said the milliner.

"Oh! the ladies be the finest of all the fine sights: and I know who I think the finest lady I ever beheld—but will never tell—never."

"Never, sir?" said the milliner, whilst Miss Barton modestly cast down her eyes. "Never's a bold word, sir. I've a notion you'll live to break that rash resolution."

Miss Barton sighed, and involuntarily looked at the glass.

"Why, where's the use," pursued Wright, "of being laughed at? Where's the sense of being scoffed at, as a man might be, that would go for to pay a compliment, not well knowing how, to a lady that is used to have court made to her by the first gentlemen in all York?"

"Those that think they don't know how to pay a compliment often pay the best to my fancy," said the milliner. "What says Miss Barton?"

Miss Barton sighed and blushed, or looked as if she meant to blush; and then, raising her well-practised eyes, exclaimed, with theatrical tones and gestures:

"Ye sacred pow'rs, whose gracious providence
Is watchful for our good, guard me from men,
From their deceitful tongues, their vows and flatteries;
Still let me pass neglected by their eyes:
Let my bloom wither and my form decay,
That none may think it worth their while to ruin me,
And fatal love may never be my bane."

Scarcely had she concluded her speech, when Pierce Marvel came breathless into the shop. Wright was standing so as to be completely hidden by the door: and Marvel, not seeing his friend, addressed himself, as soon as he had breath, to his mistress.—The lady's manner changed, and Wright had an opportunity of seeing and admiring her powers of acting. To Marvel, she was coy and disdainful.

"I expect my friend and relation in town every hour," said he to her in a low voice; "and then I shall be able to settle with your brother about the sale of Clover-hill. You half promised that you would walk with me this morning." "Not without my brother: excuse me, sir," said the coy lady, withdrawing with the dignity of a princess. "When your friend arrives, for whose advice I presume you wait, you will be able to decide your heart. Mine cannot be influenced by base lucre, or mercenary considerations—Unhand me, sir."

"I will run immediately to the inn, to see whether my friend is come," cried Marvel. "Believe me, I am as much above mercenary considerations as yourself; but I have promised not to conclude upon the sale till he comes, and he would take it ill to be sent for, and then to be made a fool of.—I'll run to the Green Man again immediately, to see if he is come."

Marvel darted out of the shop. Wright, during this parley, which lasted but a few seconds, had kept himself snug in his hiding-place, and appeared to the milliner to be wholly absorbed in casting up his bill, in which there was a shilling wrong. He came from behind the door as soon as Marvel departed; and, saying that he would call for his purchases in an hour's time, left the milliner's, took a hackney coach, and drove to the Green Man, where he was now sure of meeting his cousin.

"Thank Heaven! you are come at last," cried Marvel, the moment he saw him. "Thank Heaven! you are come! do not let us lose a moment. If you are not tired, if you are not hungry, come along with me, and I'll introduce you to my charming Alicia Barton."

"I am both tired and hungry," replied Wright: "so let us have a hot beef-steak, and let me sit down and rest myself."

It was the utmost stretch of Marvel's patience to wait for the beef-steak; and he could scarcely conceive how any one could prefer eating it to seeing his charming Alicia. He did not eat a morsel himself, but walked up and down the room with quick steps.

"Oh! my dear Wright," cried he, "it is a sign you've never seen her, or you would eat a little faster."

"Does every body eat fast, who has seen Miss Barton?" said Wright; "then to be sure I should; for I have seen her within this half hour."

"Seen her! Seen Alicia! Seen her within this half hour! That's impossible.—How could you see her? Where could you see her?" "I saw her in your company," rejoined Wright, coolly.

"In my company! How could that be, without my seeing you?—You are making a jest of me."

"Not at all; only take care that you do not make a jest of yourself. I assure you that I say nothing but truth: I've seen you and your Miss Barton this very morning: nay, I'll tell you what you said to her; you told her that you could not sell Clover-hill till I came to town."

Marvel stared, and stood in silent astonishment.

"Ay," continued Wright, "you see by this how many things may pass before a man's eyes and ears, when he is in love, without his seeing or hearing them. Why, man, I was in the milliner's shop just now, standing in the corner behind the door; but you could see nothing but your charming Miss Barton."

"I beg your pardon for being so blind," said Marvel, laughing; "but you are too good-natured to take offence; though you don't know what it is to be in love."

"There you are mistaken; for I am as much in love as yourself at this instant."

"Then I'm undone," cried Marvel, turning as pale as death.

"Why so?" said Wright; "will you allow nobody, man, to be in love but yourself? I don't see why I have not as good a right to fall in love as you have."

"To be sure you have," said Marvel, trying to recover himself; "and I can't say but what you deal fairly by me, to tell me so honestly at once. More fool I to send for you. I might have foreseen this, blockhead as I am! but you deal fairly by me, Wright: so I cannot complain, and will not, happen what may. Let him who can win her, wear her. We start fair; for though I have had the advantage of a first acquaintance, you are much the handsomer man of the two; and that goes for a great deal with some ladies, though not perhaps with Alicia Barton."

"There, perhaps, you may find yourself mistaken," replied Wright, with a significant look.

"You don't say so? You don't think so?" cried Marvel, with great emotion. "I say what I think; and, if I may trust a woman's looks, I've some reason for my thoughts."

Marvel took up the tankard which stood on the table, and swallowed down a hasty draught; and then said, though with an altered voice, "Cousin Wright, let him who can win her, wear her, as I said before. I sha'n't quarrel with you if you deal fairly by me; so tell me honestly, did you never see her before this morning?"

"Never, as I am an honest man," said Wright.

"Then, here's my hand for you," said Marvel. "All's fair and handsome on your part. Happen what may, as I said before, I will not quarrel with you. If she was decreed to fall in love with you at first sight, why that's no fault of yours; and if she tells me so fairly, why no great fault of hers. She has encouraged me a little; but still women will change their minds, and I shall not call her a jilt if she speaks handsomely to me. It will go a little to my heart at first, no doubt; but I shall bear it like a man, I hope; and I shall not quarrel with you, cousin Wright, whatever else I do."

Marvel shook Wright's hand heartily; but turned away directly afterwards, to hide his agitation.

"Why now, cousin Marvel, you are a good fellow; that's the truth of it," said Wright. "Trust to me: and, if the girl is what you think her, you shall have her: that I promise you."

"That's more than you can promise, being as you say as much in love as I am."

"I say I'm more in love than you are: but what then, I ask you?"

"What then! why, we cannot both have Alicia Barton."

"Very true. I would not have her if you would give her to me."

"Would not have her!" cried Marvel, with a look of joyous astonishment: "but, did not you tell me you were in love with her?"

"Not I. You told it to yourself. I said I was in love; but cannot a man be in love with any woman in this whole world but Miss Barton?"

Marvel capered about the room with the most lively expressions of delight, shook hands with his cousin, as if he would have pulled his arm off, and then suddenly stopping, said, "But what do you think of my Alicia? Though you are not in love with her, I hope you think well of her?"

"I must see more of her before I am qualified to speak."

"Nay, nay, no drawbacks: out with it. I must know what you think of her at this time being."

"At this time being, then, I think, she is what they call a—coquette."

"Oh, there you are out, indeed, cousin Wright! she's more of what they call a prude than a coquette."

"To you, perhaps; but not to me, cousin. Let every one speak of her as they find," replied Wright.

Marvel grew warm in defence of Miss Barton's prudery; and at last ended by saying, "that he'd stake his life upon it, she was no jilt. If she had taken a fancy to you, Wright, she would honestly tell me so, I'm convinced; and, when she finds you are thinking of another woman, her pride would soon make her think no more of you. 'Tis but little she could have thought in the few minutes you were in her company; and it is my opinion she never thought of you at all—no offence."

"No offence, I promise you," said Wright; "but let us put her to the trial: do you keep your own counsel; go on courting her your own way, and let me go mine. Don't you say one word of my being here in York; but put her off about the sale of Clover-hill, till such time as you are sure of her heart."

To this proposal Marvel joyfully agreed; and, as to the time of trial, Wright asked only one week. His cousin then told him the new scheme, from which he expected to make so much: it had been suggested by Alicia's brother. "I am to sell Clover-hill; and, with the money that I get for it, Barton and I are to build and fit up a theatre in Lincoln, and be the managers ourselves. I assure you, he says, and they all say, I should make a figure on the stage: and Miss Barton whispered, in my hearing, that I should make a capital Lothario," added Marvel, throwing himself into a stage attitude, and reciting, in a voice that made Wright start,"'Earth, Heav'n, and fair Calista, judge the combat.'" "Very fine, no doubt," said Wright; "but I am no judge of these matters; only this I am sure of, that, with respect to selling Clover-hill, you had best go slowly to work, and see what the sister is, before you trust to the brother. It is not for my interest, I very well know, to advise you against this scheme; because, if I wanted to make certain of your not coming in for my uncle's legacy, I could not take a better way than to urge you to follow your fancy. For, say that you lay out all you have in the world on the building of this playhouse, and say that Barton's as honest a man as yourself: observe, your playhouse cannot be built in less than a couple of years, and the interest of your money must be dead all that time; and pray how are you to bring yourself up, by the end of the ten years? Consider, there are but seven years of the time to come."

Marvel gave his cousin hearty thanks for his disinterested advice, but observed that actors and managers of playhouses were, of all men, they who were most likely to grow rich in a trice; that they often cleared many hundreds in one night for their benefits; that even, if he should fail to hit the public taste himself, as an actor, he was sure at least, if he married the charming Alicia, that she would be a source of inexhaustible wealth. "Not," added he, "that I think of her in that light; for my soul is as much superior to mercenary considerations as her own."

"More, perhaps," said Wright; but seeing fire flash in his cousin's eyes at this insinuation, he contented himself for the present with the promise he had obtained, that nothing should be concluded till the end of one week; that no mention should be made to Miss Barton, or her brother, of his arrival in town; and that he should have free liberty to make trial of the lady's truth and constancy, in any way he should think proper. Back to his friend the milliner's he posted directly. Miss Barton was gone out upon the race-ground in Captain Mowbray's curricle: in her absence, Wright was received very graciously by the milliner, who had lodgings to let, and who readily agreed to let them to him for a week, as he offered half a guinea more than she could get from anybody else. She fancied that he was deeply smitten with

Miss Barton's charms, and encouraged his passion, by pretty broad hints that it was reciprocal. Miss Barton drank tea this evening with the milliner: Wright was of the party, and he was made to understand that others had been excluded: "for Miss Barton," her friend observed, "was very nice as to her company."

Many dexterous efforts were made to induce Wright to lay open his heart; for the dyer's lady had been cross-questioned as to his property in Lincolnshire, and she being a lover of the marvellous, had indulged herself in a little exaggeration; so that he was considered as a prize, and Miss Barton's imagination settled the matter so rapidly, that she had actually agreed to make the milliner a handsome present on the wedding-day. Upon this hint, the milliner became anxious to push forward the affair. Marvel, she observed, hung back about the sale of his estate; and, as to Sir Plantagenet Mowbray's son, he was bound hand and foot by his father, so could do nothing genteel: besides, honourable matrimony was out of the question there.

All these things considered, the milliner's decision was, on perfectly prudential and virtuous motives, in favour of Wright. Miss Barton's heart, to use her own misapplied term, spoke warmly in his favour; for he was, without any comparison, the handsomest of her lovers; and his simplicity and apparent ignorance of the world were rather recommendations than objections.

Upon her second interview with him, she had, however, some reason to suspect that his simplicity was not so great as she had imagined. She was surprised to observe, that, notwithstanding all their artful hints, Wright came to nothing like a positive proposal, nor even to any declaration of his passion. The next day she was yet more astonished; for Wright, though he knew she was a full hour in the milliner's shop, never made the slightest attempt to see her; nay, in the evening, he met her on the public walk, and passed without more notice than a formal bow, and without turning his head back to look after her, though she was flirting with a party of gentlemen, expressly for the purpose of exciting his jealousy.

Another consultation was held with her friend the milliner: "These men are terrible creatures to deal with," said her confidant. "Do you know, my dear creature, this man, simple as he looks, has been very near taking us in. Would you believe it? he is absolutely courting a Lincolnshire lady for a wife. He wrote a letter to her, my dear Alicia, this morning, and begged me to let my boy run with it to the post-office. I winded and winded, saying he was mighty anxious about the letter, and so on, till, at the last, out comes the truth. Then I touched him about you; but he said, 'an actress was not fit for a farmer's wife, and that you had too many admirers already.' You see, my dear creature, that he has none of the thoughts we built upon. Depend upon it he is a shrewd man, and knows what he is about; so, as we cannot do better than Marvel, my advice—"

"Your advice!" interrupted Miss Barton: "I shall follow no advice but my own." She walked up and down the small parlour in great agitation.

"Do as you please, my dear; but remember I cannot afford to lay out of my money to all eternity. The account between us has run up to a great sum; the dresses were such as never were made up before in York, and must be paid for accordingly, as you must be sensible, Miss Barton. And when you have an opportunity of establishing yourself so handsomely, and getting all your debts paid; and when your brother, who was here an hour ago, presses the match with Mr. Marvel so much; it is very strange and unaccountable of you to say, 'you will take nobody's advice but your own;' and to fall in love, ma'am, as you are doing, as fast as you can, with a person who has no serious intentions, and is going to be married to another woman. For shame, Miss Barton; is this behaving with proper propriety? Besides,

I've really great regard for that poor young man that you have been making a fool of; I'm sure he is desperately in love with you."

"Then let him show it, and sell Clover-hill," said Miss Barton.

Her mind balanced between avarice and what she called love. She had taken a fancy to Wright, and his present coldness rather increased than diminished her passion: he played his part so well, that she could not tell how to decide. In the mean time, the milliner pressed for her money; and Alicia's brother bullied loudly in favour of Marvel: he had engaged the milliner, whom he was courting, to support his opinion. Marvel, though with much difficulty, stood his ground, and refused to sell Clover-hill, till he should be perfectly sure that Miss Barton would marry him, and till his relation should arrive in town, and give his consent.

CHAPTER III

Mr. Barton and the milliner now agreed, that if fair means would not bring the charming Alicia to reason, others must be used; and it was settled that she should be arrested for her debt to the milliner, which was upwards of fifty pounds. "She knows," said this considerate brother, "that I have neither the power nor the will to pay the money. Sir Plantagenet's son is as poor as Job; so she must have recourse to Marvel; and, if she gives him proper encouragement, he'll pay the money in a trice. As to this man, who lodges with you, let her apply to him if she likes it; she will soon see how he will answer her. By your account he is a shrewd fellow, and not like our friend Marvel."

On Friday morning the charming Alicia was arrested, at the suit of her dear friend and confidant, the milliner. The arrest was made in the milliner's shop. Alicia would doubtless have screamed and fainted, with every becoming spirit and grace, if any spectators had been present: but there was no one in the shop to admire or pity. She rushed with dishevelled hair, and all the stage show of distraction, into Wright's apartment; but, alas! he was not to be found. She then composed herself, and wrote the following note to Marvel:

"TO — MARVEL, ESQ. &C.

"At the Green Man.

"Much as it hurts the delicacy and wounds the pride of Alicia, she is compelled, by the perfidy of a bosom friend of her own sex, to apply for assistance and protection to one who will feel for the indignity that has been shown her. How will his generous nature shudder, when he hears that she is on the point of being dragged to a loathsome dungeon, for want of the paltry sum of fifty pounds! Retrospection may convince the man of her heart, that her soul is superior to mercenary considerations; else, she would not now be reduced so low in the power of her enemies: she scarcely knows what she writes—her heart bleeds—her brain is on fire!

"'Celestial sounds! Peace dawns upon my soul,
And every pain grows less. Oh! gentle Altamont,
Think not too hardly of me when I'm gone,
But pity me. Had I but early known

Thy wond'rous worth, thou excellent young man,
We had been happier both. Now 'tis too late.
And yet my eyes take pleasure to behold thee!
Thou art their last dear object.—Mercy, Heav'n!'
"Your affectionate,
"And (shall I confess it?)
"Too affectionate,
"ALICIA."

Marvel was settling some accounts with Wright when this note was put into his hands: scarcely had he glanced his eye over it, when he started up, seized a parcel of bank notes, which lay on the table, and was rushing out of the room. Wright caught hold of his arm, and stopped him by force.

"Where now? What now, Marvel?" said he.

"Do not stop me, Wright! I will not be stopped! She has been barbarously used. They are dragging her to prison.—They have driven her almost out of her senses. I must go to her this instant."

"Well, well, don't go without your hat, man, for the people in the street will take you for a lunatic. May a friend see this letter that has driven you out of your senses?"

Marvel put it into Wright's hands, who read it with wonderful composure; and when he came to the end of it, only said—"Hum!"

"Hum," repeated Marvel, provoked beyond measure; "you have no humanity. You are most strangely prejudiced. You are worse than Goodenough. Why do you follow me?" continued he, observing that Wright was coming after him across the inn-yard into the street.

"I follow you to take care of you," said Wright, calmly; "and though you do stride on at such a rate, I'll be bound to keep up with you."

He suffered Marvel to walk on at his own pace for the length of two streets, without saying another word; but just as they were turning the corner into the square where the milliner lived, he again caught hold of his cousin's arm, and said to him: "Hark you, Marvel; will you trust me with those bank notes that you have in your pocket? and will you let me step on to the milliner's, and settle this business for you? I see it will cost you fifty pounds, but that I cannot help. You may think yourself well off."

"Fifty pounds! What are fifty pounds?" cried Marvel, hurrying forwards. "You see that my Alicia must be superior to mercenary considerations; for, though she knows I have a good fortune, that could not decide her in my favour."

"No, because she fancies that 1 have a better fortune; and, besides (for there are times when a man must speak plainly), I've a notion she would at this minute sooner be my mistress than your wife, if the thing were fairly tried. She'll take your money as fast as you please; and I may take her as fast as I please."

Incensed at these words, Marvel could scarcely restrain his passion within bounds: but Wright, without being, moved, continued to speak.

"Nay, then, cousin, if you don't believe me, put it to the test!—I'll wait here, at this woollen-draper's, where I am to dine: do you go on to your milliner's, and say what you please, only let me have my turn for half an hour this evening; and, if I am mistaken in the lady, I'll freely own it, and make all due apology."

In the afternoon, Marvel came to Wright with a face full of joy and triumph. "Go to my Alicia now, cousin Wright," said he: "I defy you. She is at her lodging.—She has promised to marry me! I am the happiest man in the world!"

Wright said not a word, but departed. Now he had in his pocket an unanswered billet-doux, which had been laid upon his table the preceding night: the billet-doux had no name to it; but, from all he had remarked of the lady's manners towards him, he could not doubt that it was the charming Alicia's. He was determined to have positive proof, however, to satisfy Marvel's mind completely. The note which he had received was as follows:

"What can be the cause of your cruel and sudden change towards one of whom you lately appeared to think so partially? A certain female friend may deceive you, by false representations: do not trust to her, but learn the real sentiments of a fond heart from one who knows not how to feign. Spare the delicacy of your victim, and guess her name."

To this note, from one "who knew not how to feign," Wright sent the following reply:

"If Miss Barton knows any thing of a letter that was left at Mrs. Stokes's, the milliner's, last night, she may receive an answer to her questions from the bearer; who, being no scholar, hopes she will not take no offence at the shortness of these lines, but satisfy him in the honour of drinking tea with her, who waits below stairs for an answer."

The charming Alicia allowed him the honour of drinking tea with her, and was delighted with the thought that she had at last caught him in her snares. The moment she had hopes of him, she resolved to break her promise to Marvel; and by making a merit of sacrificing to Wright all his rivals, she had no doubt that she should work so successfully upon his vanity, as to induce him to break off his treaty with the Lincolnshire lady.

Wright quickly let her go on with the notion that she had the game in her own hands; at length he assumed a very serious look, like one upon the point of forming some grand resolution; and turning half away from her, said:

"But now, look ye, Miss Barton, I am not a sort of man who would like to be made a fool of. Here I'm told half the gentlemen of York are dying for you; and, as your friend Mrs. Stokes informed—"

"Mrs. Stokes is not my friend, but the basest and most barbarous of enemies," cried Alicia.

"Why, now, this is strange! She was your friend yesterday; and how do I know but a woman may change as quick, and as short, about her lovers, as about her friends?"

"I never can change: fear nothing," said Alicia, tenderly.

"But let me finish what I was saying about Mrs. Stokes; she told me something about one Mr. Marvel, I think they call him; now what is all that?"

"Nothing: he is a foolish young man, who was desperately in love with me, that's all, and offered to marry me; but, as I told him, I am superior to mercenary considerations."

"And is the affair broke off, then?" said Wright, looking her full in the face. "That's in one word what I must be sure of: for I am not a man that would choose to be jilted. Sit you down and pen me a farewell to that same foolish young fellow. I am a plain-spoken man, and now you have my mind."

Miss Barton was now persuaded that all Wright's coldness had proceeded from jealousy: blinded by her passions, and alarmed by the idea that this was the moment in which she must either secure or for ever abandon Wright and his fortune, she consented to his proposal, and wrote the following tender adieu to Marvel:

"TO—MARVEL, ESQ. &C. At the Green Man.

"SIR,

"CIRCUMSTANCES have occurred, since I had last the honour of seeing you, which make it impossible that I should ever think of you more.

"ALICIA BARTON."

Wright said he was perfectly satisfied with this note; and all that he now desired was to be himself the bearer of it to Marvel.

"He is a hot-headed young man," said Alicia; "he will perhaps quarrel with you: let me send the letter by a messenger of my own. You don't know him; you will not be able to find him out. Besides, why will you deprive me of your company? Cannot another carry this note as well as you?"

"None shall carry it but myself," said Wright, holding fast his prize. She was apprehensive of losing him for ever, if she opposed what she thought his jealous humour; so she struggled no longer to hold him, but bade him make haste to return to his Alicia.

He returned no more; but the next morning she received from him the following note:

"TO MISS ALICIA BARTON, &C.

"MADAM,

"Circumstances have occurred, since I had last the honour of seeing you, which make it impossible that I should ever think of you more.

"JOHN WRIGHT.

"P.S. My cousin, Marvel, thanks you for your note. Before you receive this, he will have left York wiser than he came into it by fifty guineas and more."

"Wiser by more than fifty guineas, I hope," said Marvel, as he rode out of town, early in the morning.

"I have been on the point of being finely taken in! I'm sure this will be a lesson to me as long as I live. I shall never forget your good-nature, and steadiness to me, Wright. Now, if it had not been for you, I might have been married to this jade; and have given her and her brother every thing I'm worth in the world. Well, well, this is a lesson I shall remember. I've felt it sharply enough. Now I'll turn my head to my business again, if I can. How Goodenough would laugh at me if he knew this story. But I'll make up for all the foolish things I have done yet before I die; and I hope, before I die, I may be able to show you, cousin Wright, how much I am obliged to you: that would be greater joy to me even than getting by my own ingenuity my uncle Pearson's ten thousand pound legacy. Do, Wright, find out something I can do for you, to make amends for all the trouble I've given you, and all the time I have made you waste: do, there's a good fellow."

"Well, then," said Wright, "I don't want to saddle you with an obligation. You shall pay me in kind directly, since you are so desirous of it. I told you I was in love: you shall come with me and see my mistress, to give me your opinion of her. Every man can be prudent for his neighbour: even you no doubt can," added Wright, laughing. Wright's mistress was a Miss Banks, only daughter to a gentleman who had set up an apparatus for manufacturing woad. Mr. Banks's house was in their way home, and they called there. They knocked several times at the door, before any one answered: at last a boy came to hold their horses, who told them that Mr. Banks was dead, and that nobody could be let into the house. The boy knew nothing of the matter, except that his master died, he believed, of a sort of a fit; and that his young mistress was in great grief: "which I'm mortal sorry for," added he: "for she he's kind hearted and civil spoken, and moreover did give me the very shoes I have on my feet."

"I wish I could see her," said Wright; "I might be some comfort to her."

"Might ye so, master? If that the thing be so," said the boy, looking earnestly in Wright's face, "I'll do my best endeavours."

He ran off at full speed through the back yard, but returned to learn the gentleman's name, which he had forgotten to ask; and presently afterwards he brought his answer. It was written with a pencil, and with a trembling hand:

"My dear Mr. Wright, I cannot see you now: but you shall hear from me as soon as I am able to give an answer to your last.

"S. BANKS."

The words, "My dear," were half rubbed out: but they were visible enough to his eyes. Wright turned his horse's head homewards, and Marvel and he rode away. His heart was so full that he could not speak, and he did not hear what Marvel said to comfort him. As they were thus riding on slowly, they heard a great noise of horsemen behind them; and looking back, they saw a number of farmers, who were riding after them. As they drew near, Wright's attention was roused by hearing the name of Banks frequently repeated. "What news, neighbour?" said Marvel.

"The news is, that Mr. Banks is dead; he died of an apoplectic fit, and has left his daughter a power o' money, they say. Happy the man who gets her! Good morrow to you, gentlemen; we're in haste home."

After receiving this intelligence, Wright read his mistress's note over again, and observed that he was not quite pleased to see the words "My dear" half rubbed out. Marvel exclaimed, "Have nothing more to do with her; that's my advice to you; for I would not marry any woman for her fortune; especially if she thought she was doing me a favour. If she loved you, she would not have rubbed out those words at such a time as this."

"Stay a bit," said Wright; "we shall be better able to judge by and by."

A week passed away, and Wright heard nothing from Miss Banks; nor did he attempt to see her, but waited as patiently as he could for her promised letter. At last it came. The first word was "Sir." That was enough for Marvel, who threw it down with indignation when his cousin showed it to him. "Nay, but read it, at least," said Wright.

"SIR,

"My poor father's affairs have been left in great disorder; and instead of the fortune which you might have expected with me, I shall have little or nothing. The creditors have been very kind to me; and I hope in time to pay all just debts. I have been much hurried with business, or should have written sooner. Indeed it is no pleasant task to me to write at all, on this occasion. I cannot unsay what I have said to you in former times, for I think the same of you as ever I did: but I know that I am not now a fit match for you as to fortune, and would not hold any man to his word, nor could value any man enough to marry him, who would break it. Therefore it will be no grief for me to break off with you if such should be your desire. And no blame shall be thrown upon you by my friends, for I will take the refusal upon myself. I know the terms of your uncle's will, and the great reason you have to wish for a good fortune with your wife; so it is very natural—I mean very likely, you may not choose to be burdened with a woman who has none. Pray speak your mind freely to, sir,

"Your humble servant,
"S. BANKS."

Marvel had no sooner read this letter than he advised his friend Wright to marry Miss Banks directly.

"That is what I have determined to do," said Wright: "for I don't think money the first thing in the world; and I would sooner give up my uncle Pearson's legacy this minute than break my word to any woman, much less to one that I love, as I do Miss Banks, better now than ever. I have just heard from the steward, who brought this letter, how handsomely and prudently she has behaved to other people, as well as to myself: by which I can judge most safely. She has paid all the debts that were justly due, and has sold even the gig, which I know she wished to keep; but, seeing that it was not suited to her present circumstances, her good sense has got the better. Now, to my mind, a prudent wife, even as to money matters, may turn out a greater treasure to a man than what they call a great fortune."

With these sentiments Wright married Miss Banks, who was indeed a very prudent, amiable girl. Goodenough sneered at this match; and observed that he had always foretold Wright would be taken in, sooner or later. Goodenough was now in his thirty-second year, and as he had always determined to marry precisely at this age, he began to look about for a wife. He chose a widow, said to be of a very close saving temper: she was neither young, handsome, nor agreeable; but then she was rich, and it was Goodenough's notion that the main chance should be first considered, in matrimony as in every thing else. Now this notable dame was precisely of his way of thinking; but she had more shrewdness than her lover, and she overreached him in the bargain: her fortune did not turn out to be above one half of what report had represented it; her temper was worse than even her enemies said it was; and the time that was daily wasted in trifling disputes between this well-matched pair was worth more than all the petty savings made by her avaricious habits.

Goodenough cursed himself ten times a day, during the honey-moon; but as he did not like to let the neighbours know how far he had been outwitted, he held his tongue with the fortitude of a martyr; and his partisans all commended him for making so prudent a match. "Ah, ay," said they, "there's Wright, who might have had this very woman, has gone and married a girl without a shilling, with all his prudence; and, as to Marvel, he will surely be bit." There they were mistaken. Marvel was a person capable of learning from experience, and he never forgot the lesson that he had received from the charming Alicia. It seemed to have sobered him completely.

CHAPTER IV

About this time, Mr. James Harrison, an eminent dyer, uncle to Wright's friend of that name at York, came to settle near Clover-hill; and as Marvel was always inclined to be hospitable, he assisted his new neighbour with many of those little conveniences, which money cannot always command at the moment they are wanted. The dyer was grateful; and, in return for Marvel's civilities, let him into many of the mysteries of the dyeing business, which he was anxious to understand. Scarcely a day passed without his calling on Mr. James Harrison. Now, Mr. Harrison had a daughter, Lucy, who was young and pretty, and Marvel thought her more and more agreeable every time he saw her; but, as he told Wright, he was determined not to fall in love with her, until he was quite sure that she was good for something. A few weeks after he had been acquainted with her, he had an opportunity of seeing her tried. Mrs. Isaac Harrison, the dyer of York's lady, came to spend some time; Miss Millicent, or, as she was commonly called, Milly Harrison, accompanied her mother: she, having a more fashionable air than Lucy, and having learned to dance from a London dancing-master, thought herself so much her superior that she ought to direct her in all things. Miss Milly, the Sunday after her arrival, appeared at church in a bonnet that charmed half the congregation; and a crowd of farmers' wives and daughters, the moment church was over, begged the favour of Miss Milly to tell them where and how such a bonnet could be got, and how much it would cost. It was extravagantly dear; and those mothers who had any prudence were frightened at the price: but the daughters were of opinion that it was the cheapest, as well as prettiest thing that ever was seen or heard of; and Miss Milly was commissioned to write immediately to York to bespeak fifteen bonnets exactly like her own. This transaction was settled before they had left the churchyard; and Miss Milly was leaning upon a tombstone to write down the names of those who were most eager to have their bonnets before the next Sunday, when Wright and Marvel came up to the place where the crowd was gathered, and they saw what was going forward.

Miss Barber, Miss Cotton, Miss Lamb, Miss Dishley, Miss Trotter, Miss Hull, Miss Parker, Miss Bury, Miss Oxley, &c. &c. &c. &c. &c. &c. &c. &c. &c. &c. &c., all, in their turn, peeped anxiously over Miss Milly's shoulder, to make themselves sure that their names were in the happy list. Lucy Harrison, alone, stood with a composed countenance in the midst of the agitated group. "Well, cousin Lucy, what say you now? Shall I bespeak a bonnet for you, hey?—Do you know," cried Miss Milly, turning to the admirers of her bonnet, "do you know that I offered to bespeak one yesterday for Lucy; and she was so stingy she would not let me, because it was too dear?" "Too dear! Could ye conceive it?" repeated the young ladies, joining in a scornful titter. All eyes were now fixed upon Lucy, who blushed deeply, but answered, with gentle steadiness, that she really could not afford to lay out so much money upon a bonnet, and that she would rather not have her name put down in the list.

"She's a good prudent girl," whispered Wright to Marvel.

"And very pretty, I am sure; I never saw her look so pretty as at this instant," replied Marvel in a low voice,

"Please yourself, child," said Miss Milly, throwing back her head with much disdain; "but I'm sure you'll please nobody else with such a dowdy thing as that you have on. Lord! I should like to see her walk the streets of York on a Sunday that figure. Lord! how Mrs. Stokes would laugh!"

Here she paused, and several of her fair audience were struck with the terrible idea of being laughed at by a person whom they had never seen, and whom they were never likely to see; and transporting themselves in imagination into the streets of York, felt all the horror of being stared at, in an unfashionable bonnet, by Mrs. Stokes. "Gracious me! Miss Milly, do pray be sure to have mine sent from York afore next Sunday," cried one of the country belles: "and, gracious me! don't forget mine, Miss Mill," was reiterated by every voice but Lucy's, as the crowd followed Miss Harrison out of the churchyard. Great was the contempt felt for her by the company; but she was proof against their ridicule, and calmly ended, as she began, with saying, "I cannot afford it."

"She is a very prudent girl," repeated Wright, in a low voice, to Marvel.

"But I hope this is not stinginess," whispered Marvel. "I would not marry such a stingy animal as Goodenough has taken to wife for all the world. Do you know she has half starved the servant boy that lived with them? There he is, yonder, getting over the stile: did you ever see such a miserable-looking creature?—He can tell you fifty stories of dame Goodenough's stinginess. I would not marry a stingy woman for the whole world. I hope Lucy Harrison is not stingy."

"Pray, Mrs. Wright," said Marvel's friend, turning to his wife, who had been standing beside him, and who had not yet said one word, "what may your opinion be?"

"My opinion is, that she is as generous a girl as any upon earth," said Mrs. Wright, "and I have good reason to say so."

"How? What?" said Marvel, eagerly.

"Her father lent my poor father five hundred pounds; and at the meeting of the creditors after his death, Mr. Harrison was very earnest to have the money paid, because it was his daughter's fortune. When he found that it could not be had immediately, he grew extremely angry; but Lucy pacified him, and told him that she was sure I should pay the money honestly, as soon as I could; and that she would willingly wait to have it paid at a hundred pounds a year, for my convenience. I am more obliged to her for the handsome way in which she trusted to me, than if she had given me half the money. I shall never forget it."

"I hope you forgive her for not buying the bonnet," said Wright to Marvel.

"Forgive her! ay; now I love her for it," said Marvel; "now I know that she is not stingy."

From this day forward, Marvel's attachment to Lucy rapidly increased. One evening he was walking in the fields with Lucy and Miss Milly, who played off her finest York airs to attract his admiration, when the following dialogue passed between them: "La! cousin Lucy," said Miss Millicent, "when shall we get you to York? I long to show you a little of the world, and to introduce you to my friend, Mrs. Stokes, the milliner."

"My father says that he does not wish that I should be acquainted with Mrs. Stokes," said Lucy.

"Your father! Nonsense, child. Your father has lived all his life in the country, the Lord knows where; he has not lived in York, as I have; so how can he know any thing upon earth of the world?—what we call the world, I mean."

"I do not know, cousin Milly, what you call the world; but I think that he knows more of Mrs. Stokes than I do; and I shall trust to his opinion, for I never knew him speak ill of any body without having good reason for it. Besides, it is my duty to obey my father."

"Duty! La! Gracious me! She talks as if she was a baby in leading-strings," cried Miss Milly, laughing; but she was mortified at observing that Marvel did not join, as she had expected, in the laugh: so she added, in a scornful tone, "Perhaps I'm in the wrong box; and that Mr. Marvel is one of them that admires pretty babes in leading-strings."

"I am one of those that admire a good daughter, I confess," said Marvel; "and," said he, lowering his voice, "that love her too."

Miss Milly coloured with anger, and Lucy with an emotion that she had never felt before. As they returned home, they met Mr. Harrison, and the moment Marvel espied him he quitted the ladies.

"I've something to say to you, Mr. Harrison. I should be glad to speak a few words to you in private, if you please," cried he, seizing his arm, and leading him down a by-lane.

Mr. Harrison was all attention; but Marvel began to gather primroses, instead of speaking.

"Well," said Mr. Harrison, "did you bring me here to see you gather primroses?"

After smelling the flowers twenty times, and placing them in twenty different forms, Marvel at last threw them on the bank, and, with a sudden effort, exclaimed, "You have a daughter, Mr. James Harrison."

"I know I have; and I thank God for it."

"So you have reason to do; for a more lovely girl and a better, in my opinion, never existed."

"One must not praise one's own, or I should agree with you," said the proud father.

Again there was silence. And again Marvel picked up his primroses.

"In short," said he, "Mr. Harrison, would you like me for a son-in-law?"

"Would Lucy like you for a husband? I must know that first," said the good father.

"That is what I do not know," replied Marvel; "but, if I was to ask her, she would ask you, I am sure, whether you would like me for a son-in-law."

"At this rate, we shall never get forwards," said Harrison. "Go you back to Miss Milly, and send my Lucy here to me."

We shall not tell how Lucy picked up the flowers, which had been her lover's grand resource; nor how often she blushed upon the occasion: she acknowledged that she thought Mr. Marvel very agreeable, but that she was afraid to marry a person who had so little steadiness. That she had heard of a great number of schemes, undertaken by him, which had failed; or which he had given up as hastily as he had begun them. "Besides," said she, "may be he might change his mind about me as well as about other things; for I've heard from my cousin Milly—I've heard—that—he was in love, not very long since, with an actress in York. Do you think this is all true?"

"Yes, I know it is all true," said Mr. Harrison, "for he told me so himself. He is an honest, open-hearted young man; but I think as you do, child, that we cannot be sure of his steadiness."

When Marvel heard from Mr. Harrison the result of this conversation, he was inspired with the strongest desire to convince Lucy that he was capable of perseverance. To the astonishment of all who knew him, or who thought that they knew him, he settled steadily to business; and, for a whole twelvemonth, no one heard him speak of any new scheme. At the end of this time he renewed his proposal to Lucy; saying that he hoped she would now have some dependence upon his constancy to her, since she had seen the power she had over his mind. Lucy was artless and affectionate, as well as prudent: now that her only real objection to the match was lessened, she did not torment him, to try her power; but acknowledged her attachment to him, and they were married.

Sir Plantagenet Mowbray's agent was much astonished that Lucy did not prefer him, because he was a much richer man than Pierce Marvel; and Miss Milly Harrison was also astonished that Mr. Marvel did not prefer her to such a country girl as Lucy, especially when she had a thousand pounds more to her fortune. But, notwithstanding all this astonishment, Marvel and his wife were perfectly happy.

It was now the fifth year after old Mr. Pearson's death. Wright was at this time the richest of the three nephews; for the money that he had laid out in draining Holland fen began to bring him in twenty per cent. As to Marvel, he had exchanged some of his finest acres for the warren of silver sprigs, the common full of thistles, and the marsh full of reeds: he had lost many guineas by his sheep and their jackets, and many more by his ill-fenced plantations: so that counting all the losses from the failure of his schemes and the waste of his time, he was a thousand pounds poorer than when he first came into possession of Clover-hill.

Goodenough was not, according to the most accurate calculations, one shilling richer or poorer than when he first began the world. "Slow and sure," said his friends: "fair and softly goes far in a day. What he has he'll hold fast; that's more than Marvel ever did, and may be more than Wright will do in the end. He dabbles a little in experiments, as he calls them: this he has learned from his friend Marvel; and this will come to no good."

About this time there was some appearance of a scarcity in England; and many farmers set an unusual quantity of potatoes, in hopes that they would bear a high price the ensuing season. Goodenough, who feared and hated every thing that was called a speculation, declared that, for his part, he would not set a drill more than he used to do. What had always done for him and his should do for him still. With this resolution, he began to set his potatoes: Marvel said to him, whilst he was at work, "Cousin Goodenough, I would advise you not to set the shoots that are at the bottom of these potatoes; for, if you do, they won't be good for any thing. This is a secret I learned last harvest home, from one of my Irish haymakers. I made the experiment last year, and found the poor fellow was quite right. I have given him a guinea for his information; and it will be worth a great deal more to me and my neighbours."

"May be so," said Goodenough; "but I shall set my own potatoes my own way, I thank you, cousin Marvel; for I take it the old way's best, and I'll never follow any other."

Marvel saw that it was in vain to attempt to convince Goodenough: therefore he left him to his old ways. The consequence was, that Goodenongh and his family ate the worst potatoes in the whole country this year; and Marvel cleared above two hundred pounds by twenty acres of potatoes, set according to his friend the Irishman's directions.

This was the first speculation of Marvel's which succeeded; because it was the first which had been begun with prudence, and pursued with steadiness. His information, in the first instance, was good: it came from a person who had actually tried the experiment, and who had seen it made by others; and when he was convinced of the fact, he applied his knowledge at the proper time, boldly extended his experiment, and succeeded. This success raised him in the opinion even of his enemies. His friend, Wright, heartily rejoiced at it; but Goodenough sneered, and said to Wright, "What Marvel has gained this year he'll lose by some scheme the next. I dare to say, now, he has some new scheme or another brewing in his brains at this very moment. Ay—look, here he comes, with two bits of rags in his hand.— Now for it!"

Marvel came up to them with great eagerness in his looks; and showing two freshly-dyed patterns of cloth, said, "Which of these two blues is the brightest?"

"That in your left hand," said Wright; "it is a beautiful blue."

"Marvel rubbed his hands with an air of triumph; but restraining his joy, he addressed himself to Wright in a composed voice.

"My dear Wright, I have many obligations to you; and, if I have any good fortune, you shall be the first to share it with me. As for you, cousin Goodenough, I don't bear malice against you for laughing at me and my herons' feathers, and my silver sprigs, and my sheep's jackets, and my thistles: shake hands, man; you shall have a share in our scheme, if you please."

"I don't please to have no share at all in none of your schemes, cousin Marvel: I thank you kindly," said Goodenough.

"Had not you better hear what it is, before you decide against it?" said Wright.

Marvel explained himself further: "Some time ago," said he, "I was with my father-in-law, who was dyeing some cloth with woad. I observed that one corner of the cloth was of much brighter blue than any of the rest; and upon examining what could be the cause of this, I found that the corner of the cloth had fallen upon the ground, as it was taken out of the dyeing vat, and had trailed through a mixture of colours, which I had accidentally spilled on the floor. I carefully recollected of what this mixture was composed: I found that woad was the principal ingredient; the other—is a secret. I have repeated my experiments several times, and I find that they have always succeeded: I was determined not to speak of my discovery till I was sure of the facts. Now I'm sure of them, my father-in-law tells me that he and his brother at York could ensure to me an advantageous sale for as much blue cloth as I can prepare; and he advised me to take out a patent for the dye."

Goodenough had not patience to listen any longer, but exclaimed:

"Join in a patent! that's more than I would do, I'm sure, cousin Marvel; so don't think to take me in: I'll end as I began, without having any thing to do with any of your new-fangled schemes—Good morning to you."

"I hope, Wright," said Marvel, proudly, "that you do not suspect me of any design to take you in; and that you will have some confidence in this scheme, when you find that my experiments have been accurately tried."

Wright assured Marvel that he had the utmost confidence in his integrity; and that he would carefully go over with him any experiments he chose to show him. "I do not want to worm your secret from you," said he; "but we must make ourselves sure of success before we go to take out a patent, which will be an expensive business."

"You are exactly the sort of man I should wish to have for my partner," cried Marvel, "for you have all the coolness and prudence that I want."

"And you have all the quickness and ingenuity that I want," replied Wright; "so, between us, we should indeed, as you say, make good partners."

A partnership was soon established between Wright and Marvel. The woad apparatus, which belonged to Wright's father-in-law, was given up to the creditors to pay the debts; but none of these creditors understood the management of it, or were willing to engage in it, lest they should ruin themselves. Marvel prevailed upon Wright to keep it in his own hands: and the creditors, who had been well satisfied by his wife's conduct towards them, and who had great confidence in his character for prudence, relinquished their claims upon the property, and trusted to Wright's promise, that they should be gradually paid by instalments.

"See what it is to have chosen a good wife," said Wright. "Good character is often better than good fortune."

The wife returned the husband's compliment; but we must pass over such unfashionable conversation, and proceed with our story.

The reader may recollect our mentioning a little boy, who carried a message from Wright to Miss Banks the day that he called upon her, on his return from York. She had been very good to this boy, and he was of a grateful temper. After he left her father's service, he was hired by a gentleman, who lived near Spalding, and for some time she had heard nothing of him: but, about a year after she was married, his master paid a visit in Lincolnshire, and the lad early one morning came to see his "old young mistress." He came so very early that none of the family were stirring, except Marvel, who had risen by daybreak to finish some repairs that he was making in the woad apparatus. He recognized the boy the moment he saw him, and welcomed him with his usual good-nature.

"Ah, sir!" said the lad, "I be's glad to see things going on here again. I be's main glad to hear how young mistress is happy! But I must be back afore my own present master be's up; so will you be pleased to give my sarvice and duty, and here's a little sort of a tea-chest for her, that I made with the help of a fellow-sarvant of mine. If so be she'll think well of taking it, I should be very proud: it has a lock and key and all."

Marvel was astonished at the workmanship of this tea-chest; and when he expressed his admiration, the boy said, "Oh, sir! all the difficultest parts were done by my fellow-sarvant, who is more handy like than I am, ten to one, though he is a Frenchman. He was one of them French prisoners, and is a curious man. He would have liked of all things to have come here along with me this morning, to get a sight of what's going on here; because that they have woad mills and the like in his own country, he says; but then he would not come spying without leave, being a civil honest man."

Marvel told the boy that his fellow-servant should be heartily welcome to satisfy his curiosity; and the next morning the Frenchman came. He was a native of Languedoc, where woad is cultivated: he had been engaged in the manufacture of it, and Marvel soon found, by his conversation, that he was a well-informed, intelligent man. He told Marvel that there were many natives of Languedoc, at this time, prisoners in England, who understood the business as well as he did, and would be glad to be employed, or to sell their knowledge at a reasonable price. Marvel was not too proud to learn, even from a Frenchman. With Wright's consent, he employed several of these workmen; and he carried, by their means, the manufacture of woad to a high pitch of perfection. How success changes the opinion of men! The Lincolnshire farmers, who had formerly sneered at Marvel as a genius and a projector, began to look up to him as to a very wise and knowing man, when they saw this manufactory continue to thrive; and those who had blamed Wright, for entering into partnership with him, now changed their minds. Neither of them could have done separately what they both effected by their union.

At the end of the ten years, Goodenough was precisely where he was when he began; neither richer nor poorer; neither wiser nor happier; all that he had added to his stock was a cross wife and two cross children. He, to the very last moment, persisted in the belief that he should be the richest of the three, and that Wright and Marvel would finish by being bankrupts. He was in unutterable astonishment, when, upon the appointed day, they produced their account-books to Mr. Constantine, the executor, and it was found that they were many thousand pounds better in the world than himself.

"Now, gentlemen," said Mr. Constantine, "to which of you am I to give your uncle's legacy? I must know which of the partners has the greatest share in the manufactory."

"Wright has the greatest share," cried Marvel; "for without his prudence I should have been ruined."

"Marvel has the greatest share," cried Wright: "for without his ingenuity I should never have succeeded in the business, nor indeed should I have undertaken it."

"Then, gentlemen, you must divide the legacy between you," said Mr. Constantine, "and I give you joy of your happy partnership. What can he more advantageous than a partnership between prudence and justice on the one side, and generosity and abilities on the other?"

OUT OF THE DEBT OF DANGER

CHAPTER I

Leonard Ludgate was the only son and heir of a London haberdasher, who had made some money by constant attendance to his shop. "Out of debt out of danger," was the father's old-fashioned saying. The son's more liberal maxim was, "Spend to-day, and spare to-morrow." Whilst he was under his father's eye, it was not in his power to live up to his principles; and he longed for the time when he should be relieved from his post behind the counter: a situation which he deemed highly unworthy a youth of his parts and spirit. To imprison his elegant person behind a counter in Cranbourne-alley, was, to be sure, in a cruel father's power; but his tyranny could not extend to his mind; and, whilst he was weighing minikin pins, or measuring out penny ribbon, his soul, leaving all these meaner things, was expatiating in Bond-street or Hyde-park. Whilst his fingers mechanically adjusted the scales, or carelessly slipped the yard, his imagination was galloping a fine bay with Tom Lewis, or driving Miss Belle Perkins in a gig.

Now Tom Lewis was a dashing young citizen, whom old Ludgate could not endure; and Miss Belle Perkins a would-be fine lady, whom he advised his son never to think of for a wife. But the happy moment at length arrived, when our hero could safely show how much he despised both the advice and the character of his father; when he could quit his nook behind the counter, throw aside the yard, assume the whip, and affect the fine gentleman. In short, the happy moment came when his father died.

Leonard now shone forth in all the glory which the united powers of tailor, hatter, and hosier, could spread around lug person. Miss Belle Perkins, who had hitherto looked down upon our hero as a reptile of Cranbourne-alley, beheld his metamorphosis with surprise and admiration. And she, who had formerly been heard to say, "she would not touch him with a pair of tongs," now unreluctantly gave him her envied hand at a ball at Bagnigge Wells. Report farther adds that, at tea, Miss Belle whispered loud enough to be heard, that since his queer father's death, Leonard Ludgate had turned out quite a genteeler sort of person than could have been expected.

"Upon this hint he spake." His fair one, after assuming all proper and becoming airs upon the occasion, suffered herself to be prevailed upon to call, with her mother and a friend, at Mr. Ludgate's house in Cranbourne-alley, to see whether it could be possibly inhabited by a lady of her taste and consequence.

As Leonard handed her out of her hackney-coach, she exclaimed, "Bless us, and be we to go up this paved lane, and through the shop, before we can get to the more creditabler apartments?"

"I'm going to cut a passage off the shop, which I've long had in contemplation," replied our hero; "only I can't get light into it cleverly."

"Oh! a lamp in the style of a chandaleer will do vastly well by night, which is the time one wants one's house to put the best foot foremost, for company; and by day we can make a shift, somehow or other, I dare say. Any thing's better than trapesing through a shop; which is a thing I've never been used to, and cannot reconcile myself to by any means."

Leonard immediately acceded to this scheme of the dark passage by day, and the chandaleer by night; and he hurried his fair one through the odious shop to the more creditabler apartments. She was handed above, about, and underneath. She found every particle of the house wanted modernizing immensely, and was altogether smaller than she could ever have conceived beforehand. Our hero, ambitious at once to show his gallantry, spirit, and taste, incessantly protested he would adopt every improvement Miss Belle Perkins could suggest; and he declared that the identical same ideas had occurred to him a hundred and a hundred times, during his poor father's lifetime: but he could never make the old gentleman enter into any thing of the sort, his notions of life being utterly limited, to say no worse. "He had one old saw, for ever grating in my ears, as an answer to everything that bore the stamp of gentility, or carried with it an air of spirit: hey, Allen!" continued our hero, looking over his shoulder at a young man who was casting up accounts; "hey, Allen—you remember the old saw?"

"Yes, sir," replied the young man, "if you mean, 'Out of debt out of danger:' I hope I shall never forget it."

"I hope so too; as you have your fortune to make, it is very proper for you: but for one that has a fortune ready made to spend, I am free to confess I think my principle worth a million of it: and my maxim is, 'Spend to-day, and spare to-morrow:' hey, ladies?" concluded Leonard, appealing with an air secure of approbation to his fair mistress and her young companion.

"Why that suits my notions, I must own candidly," said Belle; "but here's one beside me, or behind me—Where are you, Lucy?" pursued the young lady, addressing herself to her humble companion: "here's one, who is more of your shop-man's way of thinking than yours, I fancy. 'Out of debt out of danger' is just a sober saying to your mind, an't it, Lucy?"

Lucy did not deny the charge. "Well, child," said Miss Perkins, "it's very proper, for you have no fortune of your own to spend."

"It is, indeed," said Lucy, with modest firmness; "for as I have none of my own, if it were my maxim to spend to-day and spare to-morrow, I should be obliged to spend other people's money, which I never will do as long as I can maintain myself independently."

"How proud we are!" cried Miss Perkins, sarcastically. Leonard assented to the sarcasm by his looks; but Allen declared he liked proper pride, and seemed to think that Lucy's was of this species.

An argument might have ensued, if a collation, as Mr. Ludgate called it, had not appeared at this critical moment. Of what it consisted, and how genteelly and gallantly our hero did the honours of his collation, we forbear to relate; but one material circumstance we must not omit, as on this, perhaps more than even on his gentility and gallantry, depended the fortune of the day. In rummaging over a desk to find a corkscrew, young Ludgate took occasion to open and shake a pocket-book, from which fell a shower of bank notes. What effect they produced upon his fair one, and on her mother, can be best judged of by the event. Miss Belle Perkins, after this domiciliary visit, consented to go with our hero on Sunday to Kensington Gardens, Monday to Sadler's Wells, Tuesday on the water, Wednesday to the play, Thursday the Lord knows to what ball, Friday to Vauxhall, and on Saturday to—the altar!

Some people thought the young lady and gentleman rather precipitate; but these were persons who, as the bride justly observed, did not understand any thing in nature of a love match. Those who have more liberal notions, and a more extensive knowledge of the human heart, can readily comprehend how a lady may think a man so odious at one minute, that she could not touch him with a pair of tongs, and so charming the next, that she would die a thousand deaths for him, and him alone. Immediately after the ceremony was performed, Mr. and Mrs. Ludgate went down in the hoy to Margate, to spend their honeymoon in style. Their honeymoon, alas! could not be prolonged beyond the usual bounds. Even the joys of Margate could not be eternal, and the day came too soon when our happy pair were obliged to think of returning home. Home! With what different sensations different people pronounce and hear that word pronounced! Mrs. Leonard Ludgate's home in Cranbourne-alley appeared to her, as she scrupled not to declare, an intolerable low place, after Margate. The stipulated alterations, her husband observed, had been made in the house, but none of them had been executed to her satisfaction. The expedient of the dark passage was not found to succeed: a thorough wind, from the front and back doors, ran along it when either or both were left open to admit light; and this wicked wind, not content with running along the passage, forced its way up and down stairs, made the kitchen chimney smoke, and rendered even the more creditabler apartments scarcely habitable. Chimney doctors were in vain consulted: the favourite dark passage was at length abandoned, and the lady, to her utter discomfiture, was obliged to pass through the shop.

To make herself amends for this mortification, she insisted upon throwing down the partition between the dining-room and her own bedchamber, that she might have one decent apartment at least fit for a rout. It was to no purpose that her friend Lucy, who was called in to assist in making up furniture, represented that this scheme of throwing bedchamber and dining-room into one would be attended with some inconveniences; for instance, that Mr. and Mrs. Ludgate would be obliged, in consequence of this improvement, to sleep in half of the maid's garret, or to sit up all night. This objection was overruled by Mrs. Ludgate, whose genius, fertile in expedients, made every thing easy, by the introduction of a bed in the dining-room, in the shape of a sofa. The newly-enlarged apartment, she observed, would thus answer the double purposes of show and utility; and, as soon as the supper and card tables should be removed, the sofa-bed might be let down. She asserted that the first people in London manage in this way. Leonard could not contradict his lady, because she had a ready method of silencing him, by asking how he could possibly know any thing of life who had lived all his days, except Sundays, in Cranbourne-alley? Then, if any one of his father's old notions of economy by chance twinged his conscience, Belle very judiciously asked how he ever came to think of her for a wife? "Since you have got a genteel wife," said she, "it becomes you to live up to her notions, and to treat her as she and her friends have a right to expect. Before I married you, sir, none of the Perkins's were in trade themselves, either directly or indirectly; and many's the slights and reproaches I've met with from my own relations and former acquaintances, since my marriage, on account of the Ludgates being all tradesfolks; to which I always answer, that my Leonard is going to wash his hands of trade himself, and to make over all concern in the haberdashery line and shop to the young man below stairs, who is much better suited to such things."

By such speeches as these, alternately piquing and soothing the vanity of her Leonard, our accomplished wife worked him to her purposes. She had a rout once a week; and her room was so crowded, that there was scarcely a possibility of breathing. Yet, notwithstanding all this, she one morning declared, with a burst of tears, she was the most miserable woman in the world. And why? Because her friend, Mrs. Pimlico, Miss Coxeater that was, had a house in Weymouth-street; whilst she was forced to keep on being buried in Cranbourne-alley. Mr. Ludgate was moved by his wife's tears, and by his own ambition, and took a house in Weymouth-street. But before they had been there six weeks, the fair one was again found bathed in tears. And why? "Because," said Belle, "because, Mr. Ludgate, the furniture of this house is as old as Methusalem's; and my friend, Mrs. Pimlico, said yesterday that it was a shame to be seen: and so to be sure it is, compared with her own, which is spick and span new. Yet why should she pretend to look down upon me in point of furniture, or any thing? Who was she, before she was married? Little Kitty Coxeater, as we always called her at the dancing school; and nobody ever thought of comparing her, in point of gentility, with Belle Perkins! Why, she is as ugly as sin! though she is my friend, I must acknowledge that; and, if she had all the clothes in the world, she would never know how to put any of them on; that's one comfort. And, as every body says, to be sure she never would have got a husband but for her money. And, after all, what sort of a husband has she got? A perfumer, indeed! a man with a face like one of his own wash-balls, all manner of colours. I declare, I would rather have gone without to the end of my days than have married Mr. Pimlico."

"I cannot blame you there, my dear," said Mr. Ludgate; "for to be sure Mr. Pimlico, much as he thinks of himself and his country house, has as little the air of—the air of fashion as can be well conceived."

Leonard Ludgate made an emphatic pause in this speech; and surveyed himself in a looking-glass with much complacency, whilst he pronounced the word fashion. He, indeed, approved so much of his wife's taste and discernment, in preferring him to Mr. Pimlico, that he could not at this moment help inclining to follow her judgment respecting the furniture. He acceded to her position, that the Ludgates ought to appear at least no shabbier than the Pimlicos. The conclusion was inevitable: Leonard, according to his favourite maxim of "Spend to-day, and spare to-morrow," agreed that they might new furnish the house this year, and pay for it the next. This was immediately done; and the same principle was extended through all their household affairs, as far as the tradesmen concerned would admit of its being carried into practice.

By this means, Mr. and Mrs. Ludgate were not for some time sensible of the difficulties they were preparing for themselves. They went on vying with the Pimlicos, and with all their new acquaintance, who were many of them much richer than themselves; and of this vain competition there was no end. Those who estimate happiness not by the real comforts or luxuries which they enjoy, but by comparison between themselves and their neighbours, must be subject to continual mortification and discontent. Far from being happier than they were formerly, Mr. and Mrs. Ludgate were much more miserable after their removal to Weymouth-street. Was it not better to be the first person in Cranbourne-alley than the last in Weymouth-street? New wants and wishes continually arose in their new situation. They must live like other people. Everybody, that is, everybody in Weymouth-street, did so and so; and, therefore, they must do the same. They must go to such a place, or they must have such a thing, not because it was in itself necessary or desirable, but because everybody, that is, everybody of their acquaintance, did or had the same. Even to be upon a footing with their new neighbours was a matter of some difficulty; and then merely to be upon an equality, merely to be admitted and suffered at parties, is awkward and humiliating. Noble ambition prompted them continually to aim at distinction. The desire to attain il poco piu—the little more, stimulates to excellence, or betrays to ruin, according to the objects of our ambition. No artist ever took more pains to surpass Raphael or Correggio than was taken by Mr. and Mrs. Ludgate to outshine Mr. and Mrs. Pimlico. And still what they had done seemed nothing: what they were to do occupied all their thoughts. No timid economical fears could stop or even startle them in the road to ruin. Faithful to his maxim, our hero denied himself nothing. If, for a moment, the idea that any thing was too expensive suggested itself, his wife banished care by observing, "We need not pay for it now. What signifies it, since we need not think of paying for it till next year?" She had abundance of arguments of similar solidity, adapted to all occasions. Sometimes the thing in question was such a trifle it could not ruin anybody. "'Tis but a guinea! 'Tis but a few shillings!" Sometimes it was a sort of thing that could not ruin anybody, because "'Tis but for once and away!" 'Tis but is a most dangerous thing! How many guineas may be spent upon 'tis but, in the course of one year, in such a city as London!

Bargains! excellent bargains! were also with our heroine admirable pleas for expense. "We positively must buy this, my dear; for it would be a sin to let such a bargain slip through one's fingers. Mrs. Pimlico paid twice as much for what is not half as good. 'Twould be quite a shame to one's good sense to miss such a bargain!" Mrs. Ludgate was one of those ladies who think it is more reasonable to buy a thing because it is a bargain than because they want it: she farther argued, "If we don't want it, we may want it:" and this was a satisfactory plea.

Under the head bargains we must not forget cheap days. Messrs. Run and Raffle advertised a sale of old shop goods, with the catching words—cheap days! Everybody crowded to throw away their money on cheap days; and, amongst the rest, Mrs. Ludgate.

One circumstance was rather disagreeable in these cheap days: ready money was required; and this did not suit those who lived by the favourite maxim of the family. Yet there was a reason that counterbalanced their objection in Mrs. Ludgate's mind: "Mrs. Pimlico was going to Messrs. Run and Raffle's and what would she think, if I wasn't to be there? She'd think, to be sure, that we were as poor as Job." So, to demonstrate that she had ready money to throw away, Mrs. Ludgate must go on the cheap days.

"Belle," said her husband, "ready money's a serious thing."

"Yes, Leonard, but, when nothing else will be taken, you know, one can't do without it."

"But, if one has not it, I tell you, one must do without it," said Leonard peevishly.

"Lord, Mr. Ludgate, if you have not it about you, can't you send to Cranbourne-alley, to Mr. Allen, for some for me? 'Tis but a few guineas I want; and 'twould be a shame to miss such bargains as are to be had for nothing, at Run and Raffle's. And these cheap days are extraordinary things. It can't ruin any body to spend a guinea or two, once and away, like other people."

At the conclusion of her eloquent speech, Mrs. Ludgate rang the bell; and, without waiting for any assent from her husband but silence, bade the footman run to the shop, and desire Allen to send her ten guineas immediately.

Mr. Ludgate looked sullen, whistled, and then posted himself at the parlour window to watch for the ambassador's return. "I wonder," continued Mrs. Ludgate, "I wonder, Leonard, that you let Allen leave you so bare of cash of late! It is very disagreeable to be always sending out of the house, this way, for odd guineas. Allen, I think, uses you very ill; but I am sure I would not let him cheat me, if I was you. Pray, when you gave up the business of the shop to him, was not you to have half the profits for your good-will, and name, and all that!"

"Yes."

"And little enough! But why don't you look after Allen, then, and make him pay us what he owes us?"

"I'll see about it to-morrow, child."

"About how much do you think is owing to us?" pursued Mrs. Ludgate.

"I can't tell, ma'am."

"I wish then you'd settle accounts to-morrow, that I might have some ready money."

The lady seemed to take it for granted that her having ready money would be the necessary and immediate consequence of settling accounts with Allen; her husband could have set her right in this particular, and could have informed her that not a farthing was due to him; that, on the contrary, he had taken up money in advance, on the next half year's expected profits; but Mr. Ludgate was ashamed to let his wife know the real state of his affairs: indeed, he was afraid to look them in the face himself. "Here's the boy coming back!" cried he, after watching for some time in silence at the window.

Leonard went to the street-door to meet him; and Belle followed close, crying, "Well! I hope Allen has sent me the money?"

"I don't know," said the breathless boy. "I have a letter for my master, here, that was written ready, by good luck, afore I got there."

Leonard snatched the letter; and his wife waited to see whether the money was enclosed.

"The rascal has sent me no money, I see, but a letter, and an account as long as my arm."

"No money!" cried Belle; "that's using us very oddly and ill, indeed; and I wonder you submit to such conduct! I declare I won't bear it! Go back, I say, Jack; go, run this minute, and tell Allen he must come up himself; for I, Mrs. Ludgate, wants to speak with him."

"No, my dear, no; nonsense! don't go, Jack. What signifies your sending to speak with Allen? What can you do? How can you settle accounts with him? What should women know of business? I wish women would never meddle with things they don't understand."

"Women can understand well enough when they want money," cried the sharp lady; "and the short and the long of it is, Mr. Ludgate, that I will see and settle accounts with Allen myself; and bring him to reason, if you won't; and this minute, too."

"Bless me! upon my faith, Allen's better than we thought: here's bank-notes within the account," said Mr. Ludgate.

"Ay, I thought he could not be so very impertinent as to refuse when I sent to him myself. But this is only one five pound note: I sent for ten. Where is the other?"

"I want the other myself," said her husband.

The tone was so peremptory, that she dared not tempt him further; and away she went to Messrs. Run and Raffle's, where she had the pleasure of buying a bargain of things that were of no manner of use to her, and for which she paid twice as much as they were worth. These cheap days proved dear days to many.

Whilst Mrs. Ludgate spent the morning at Messrs. Run and Raffle's, her husband was with Tom Lewis, lounging up and down Bond-street. Tom Lewis being just one step above him in gentility, was invited to parties where Ludgate could not gain admittance, was bowed to by people who never bowed to Leonard Ludgate, could tell to whom this livery or that carriage belonged, knew who everybody was, and could point out my lord this, and my lady that, in the park or at the play. All these things made him a personage of prodigious consequence in the eyes of our hero, who looked upon him as the mirror of fashion. Tom knew how to take advantage of this admiration, and borrowed many a guinea from him in their morning walks: in return, he introduced Mr. Ludgate to some of his friends, and to his club.

New occasions, or rather new necessities, for expense occurred every day, in consequence of his connexion with Lewis. Whilst he aimed at being thought a young man of spirit, he could not avoid doing as other people did. He could not think of economy! That would be shabby! On his fortune rested his claims to respect from his present associates; and, therefore, it was his constant aim to raise their opinion of his riches. For some time, extravagance was not immediately checked by the want of money, because he put off the evil day of payment. At last, when bills poured in upon him, and the frequent calls of tradesmen began to be troublesome, he got rid of the present difficulty by referring them to Allen. "Go to Allen; he must settle with you: he does all my business."

Allen sent him account after account, stating the sums he paid by his order. Ludgate thrust the unread accounts into his escritoire, and thought no more of the matter. Allen called upon him, to beg he would come to some settlement, as he was getting more and more, every day, into his debt. Leonard desired to have an account, stated in full, and promised to look over it on Monday: but Monday came, and then it was put off till Tuesday; and so on, day after day.

The more reason he had to know that his affairs were deranged, the more carefully he concealed all knowledge of them from his wife. Her ignorance of the truth not only led her daily into fresh extravagance, but was, at last, the cause of bringing things to a premature explanation. After spending the morning at Messrs. Run and Raffle's, she returned home with a hackney-coach full of bargains. As she came into the parlour, loaded with things that she did not want, she was surprised by the sight of an old friend, whom she had lately treated entirely as a stranger. It was Lucy, who had in former days been her favourite companion. But Lucy had chosen to work, to support herself independently, rather than to be a burden to her friends; and Mrs. Ludgate could not take notice of a person who had degraded herself so far as to become a workwoman at an upholsterer's. She had consequently never seen Lucy since this event took place, except when she went to Mr. Beech the upholsterer's, to order her new furniture. She then was in company with Mrs. Pimlico: and, when she saw Lucy at work in a back parlour with two or three other young women, she pretended not to know her. Lucy could scarcely believe that this was done on purpose; and, at all events, she was not mortified by the insult. She was now come to speak to Mrs. Ludgate about the upholsterer's bill.

"Ha! Lucy, is it you?" said Mrs. Ludgate, as soon as she entered. "I've never seen you in Weymouth-street before! How comes it you never called, if it was only to see our new house? I'm sure I should always be very happy to have you here—when we've nobody with us; and I'm quite sorry as I can't ask you to stay and take a bit of mutton with us to-day, because I'm engaged to dine in Bond-street, with Mrs. Pimlico's cousin, pretty Mrs. Paget, the bride whom you've heard talk of, no doubt. So you'll excuse me if I run away from you, to make myself a little decent; for it's horrid late!"

After running off this speech, with an air and a volubility worthy of her betters, she set before Lucy some of her bargains, and was then retreating to make herself decent; but Lucy stopped her, by saying, "My dear Mrs. Ludgate, I am sorry to detain you, but Mr. Beech, the upholsterer, knowing I have been acquainted with you, has sent me to speak to you about his bill. He is in immediate want of money, because he is fitting out one of his sons for the East Indies."

"Well! but his son's nothing to me! I sha'n't think of paying the bill yet, I can assure him; and you may take it back, and tell him so."

"But," said Lucy, "if I take back such an answer, I am afraid Mr. Beech will send the bill to Mr. Ludgate; and that was what you particularly desired should not be done."

"Why, no; that's what I can't say I should particularly wish, just at present," said Mrs. Ludgate, lowering her tone "because, to tell you a bit of a secret, Lucy, I've run up rather an unconsciable bill, this year, with my milliner and mantua-maker; and I would not have all them bills come upon him all in a lump, and on a sudden, as it were; especially as I laid out more on the furniture than he counts. So, my dear Lucy, I'll tell you what you must do: you must use your influence with Beech to make him wait a little longer. I'm sure he may wait well enough; and he shall be paid next month."

Lucy declared that her influence, on the present occasion, would be of no avail; but she had the good-nature to add, "If you are sure the bill can be paid next month, I will leave my two years' salary in Mr. Beech's hands till then; and this will perhaps satisfy him, if he can get bills from other people paid, to make up the money for his son. He said thirty guineas from you on account would do, for the present; and that sum is due to me."

"Then, my dearest Lucy, for Heaven's sake, do leave it in his hands! You were a good creature to think of it; but you always were a good creature."

"Your mother used to be kind to me, when I was a child; and I am sure I ought not to forget it," said Lucy, the tears starting into her eyes: "and you were once kind to me; I do not forget that," continued Lucy, wiping the tears from her cheeks.—"But do not let me detain you; you are in a hurry to dress to go to Mrs. Pimlico's."

"No—pray—I am not in a hurry now," said Mrs. Ludgate, who had the grace to blush at this instant. "But, if you must go, do take this hat along with you. I assure you it's quite the rage: I got it this morning at Run and Raffle's, and Mrs. Pimlico and Mrs. Paget have got the same."

Lucy declined accepting the hat, notwithstanding this strong and, as Mrs. Ludgate would have thought it, irresistible recommendation. "Now you must have it: it will become you a thousand times better than that you have on," cried Mrs. Ludgate, insisting the more the more Lucy withdrew; "and, besides, you must wear it for my sake. You won't? Then I take it very ill of you that you are so positive; for I assure you, whatever you may think, I wish to be as kind to you now as ever. Only, you know, one can't always, when one lives in another style, be at home as often as one wishes."

Lucy relieved her ci-devant friend from the necessity of making any more awkward apologies, by moving quickly towards the door. "Then you won't forget," continued Mrs. Ludgate, following her into the passage, "you won't forget the job you are to do for me with Beech?"

"Certainly I shall not. I will do what I have promised: but I hope you will be punctual about the payment next month," said Lucy, "because I believe I shall be in want of my money at that time. It is best to tell you exactly the truth."

"Certainly! certainly! you shall have your money before you want it, long and long; and my only reason for borrowing it from you at all is, that I don't like to trouble Mr. Ludgate, till he has settled accounts with Allen, who keeps all our money from us in a strange way; and, in my opinion, uses Leonard exceedingly ill and unfairly."

"Allen!" cried Lucy, stopping short. "Oh, Belle! how can you say so? How can you think so? But you know nothing of him, else you could not suspect him of using any one ill, or unfairly; much less your husband, the son of his old friend."

"Bless me! how she runs on! and how she colours! I am sure I didn't know I was upon such tender ground! I did not know Allen was such a prodigious favourite!"

"I only do him justice in saying that I am certain he could not do an unfair or unhandsome action."

"I know nothing of the matter, I protest; only this—that short accounts, they say, make long friends; and I hope I sha'n't affront any body by saying, it would be very convenient if he could be got to settle with Mr. Ludgate, who, I am sure, is too much the gentleman to ask any thing from him but his own; which, indeed, if it was not for me, he'd be too genteel to mention. But, as I said before, short accounts make long friends; and, as you are so much Allen's friend, you can hint that to him."

"I shall not hint, but say it to him as plainly as possible," replied Lucy; "and you may be certain that he will come to settle accounts with Mr. Ludgate before night." "I am sure I shall be mighty glad of it; and so will Mr. Ludgate," said Belle; and thus they parted.

Mrs. Ludgate with triumph announced to her husband, upon his return home, that she had brought affairs to a crisis with Allen; and that he would come to settle his accounts this evening. The surprise and consternation which appeared in Mr. Ludgate's countenance, convinced the lady that her interference was highly disagreeable.

CHAPTER II

Allen came punctually in the evening to settle his accounts. When he and Leonard were by themselves, he could not help expressing some astonishment, mixed with indignation, at the hints which had been thrown out by Mrs. Ludgate.

"Why, she knows nothing of the matter," said Ludgate. "I've no notion of talking of such things to one's wife; it would only make her uneasy; and we shall be able to go on some way or other. So let us have another bottle of wine, and talk no more of business for this night."

Allen would by no means consent to put off the settlement of accounts, after what had passed. "Short accounts," said he, "as Mrs. Ludgate observed, make long friends."

It appeared, when the statement of affairs was completed, that Allen had advanced above three hundred pounds for Leonard; and bills to a large amount still remained unpaid.

Now it happened that Jack, the footboy, contrived to go in and out of the room several times, whilst Mr. Ludgate and Allen were talking; and he, finding it more for his interest to serve his master's tradesmen than his master, sent immediate notice to all whom it might concern, that Mr. Ludgate's affairs were in a bad way, and that now or never must be the word with his creditors. The next morning bills came showering in upon Leonard whilst he was at breakfast, and amongst them came sundry bills of Mrs. Ludgate's. They could not possibly have come at a more inauspicious moment. People bespeak goods with one species of enthusiasm, and look over their bills with another. We should rather have said people spend with one enthusiasm, and pay with another; but this observation would not apply to our present purpose, for Mr. and Mrs. Ludgate had never yet experienced the pleasure or the pain of paying their debts; they had hitherto been faithful to their maxim of "Spend to-day, and pay to-morrow."

They agreed well in the beginning of their career of extravagance; but the very similarity of their tastes and habits proved ultimately the cause of the most violent quarrels. As they both were expensive, selfish, and self-willed, neither would, from regard to the other, forbear. Comparisons between their different degrees of extravagance commenced; and, once begun, they never ended. It was impossible to settle, to the satisfaction of either party, which of them was most to blame. Recrimination and reproaches were hourly and daily repeated; and the lady usually ended by bursting into tears, and the gentleman by taking his hat and walking out of the house.

In the meantime, the bills must be paid. Mr. Ludgate was obliged to sell the whole of his interest in the shop in Cranbourne-alley; and the ready money he received from Allen was to clear him from all difficulties. Allen came to pay him this sum. "Do not think me impertinent, Mr. Ludgate," said he, "but I cannot for the soul of me help fearing for you. What will you do, when this money is gone? and go it must, at the rate you live, in a very short time."

"You are very good, sir," replied Leonard, coldly, "to interest yourself so much in my concerns; but I shall live at what rate I please. Every man is the best judge of his own affairs."

After this repulse Allen could interfere no further. But when two months had elapsed from the date of Mrs. Ludgate's promised payment of the upholsterer's bill, Lucy resolved to call again upon Mrs. Ludgate. Lucy had now a particular occasion for the money: she was going to be married to Allen, and she wished to put into her husband's hands the little fortune which she had so hardly earned by her own industry. From the time that Allen heard her conversation, when Belle came to view the house in Cranbourne-alley, he had been of opinion that she would make an excellent wife: and the circumstances which sunk Lucy below Mrs. Ludgate's notice raised her in the esteem and affection of this prudent and sensible young man. He did not despise—he admired her for going into a creditable business, to make herself independent, instead of living as an humble companion with Mrs. Ludgate, of whose conduct and character she could not approve.

When Lucy called again upon Mrs. Ludgate to remind her of her promise, she was received with evident confusion. She was employed in directing Mr. Green, a builder, to throw out a bow in her dining-room, and to add a balcony to the windows; for Mrs. Pimlico had a bow and a balcony, and how could Mrs. Ludgate live without them?

"Surely, my dear Mrs. Ludgate," said Lucy, drawing her aside, so that the man who was measuring the windows could not hear what she said, "surely you will think of paying Mr. Beech's bill, as you promised, before you go into any new expense?"

"Hush! hush! don't speak so loud. Leonard is in the next room; and I would not have him hear any thing of Beech's bill, just when the man's here about the balcony, for any thing in the world!"

Lucy, though she was good-natured, was not so weak as to yield to airs and capricious extravagance; and Mrs. Ludgate at last, though with a bad grace, paid her the money which she had intended to lay out in a very different manner. But no sooner had she paid this debt than she considered how she could prevail upon Mr. Green to throw out the bow, and finish the balcony, without paying him for certain alterations he had made in the house in Cranbourne-alley, for which he had never yet received one farthing. It was rather a difficult business, for Mr. Green was a sturdy man, and used to regular payments. He resisted all persuasion, and Mrs. Ludgate was forced again to have recourse to Lucy.

"Do, my dear girl," said she, "lend me only twenty guineas for this positive man; else, you see, I cannot have my balcony." This did not appear to Lucy the greatest of all misfortunes. "But is it not much more disagreeable to be always in debt and danger, than to live in a room without a balcony?" said Lucy.

"Why it is disagreeable, certainly, to be in debt, because of being dunned continually; but the reason I'm so anxious about the balcony, is that Mrs. Pimlico has one, and that's the only thing in which her house is better than mine. Look just over the way: do you see Mrs. Pimlico's beautiful balcony?"

Mrs. Ludgate who had thrust her head far out of the window, pulling Lucy along with her, now suddenly drew back, exclaiming, "Lord, if here is not that odious woman; I hope Jack won't let her in."—She shut the window hastily, ran to the top of the stairs, and called out, "Jack! I say, Jack; don't let nurse in for your life."

"Not if she has the child with her, ma'am?" said Jack.

"No, no, I say!"

"Then that's a sin and a shame," muttered Jack, "to shut the door upon your own child."

Mrs. Ludgate did not hear this reflection, because she had gone back to the man who was waiting for directions about the balcony; but Lucy heard it distinctly. "Ma'am, nurse would come in, for she says she saw you at the window; and here she is, coming up the stairs," cried the footboy.

The nurse came in, with Mrs. Ludgate's child in her arms.

"Indeed, madam," said she, "the truth of the matter is, I can't and won't be denied my own any longer: and it is not for my own sake I speak up so bold, but for the dear babe that I have here in my arms, that can't speak for itself, but only smile in your face, and stretch out its arms to you. I, that am only its nurse, can't bear it; but I have little ones of my own, and can't see them want. I can't do for them all: if I'm not paid my lawful due, how can I? And is it not fit I should think of my own flesh and blood first? So I must give up this one. I must!—I must!"—cried the nurse, kissing the child repeatedly, "I must leave her to her mother."

The poor woman laid the child down on the sofa, then turned her back upon it, and, hiding her face in her apron, sobbed as if her heart would break. Lucy was touched with compassion; the mother stood abashed; shame struggled for a few instants with pride; pride got the victory. "The woman's out of her wits, I believe," cried Mrs. Ludgate. "Mr. Green, if you'll please to call again to-morrow, we'll talk about the balcony. Lucy, give me the child, and don't you fall a crying without knowing why or wherefore. Nurse, I'm surprised at you! Did not I tell you I'd send you your money next week?"

"Oh! yes, madam; but you have said so this many a week; and things are come to such a pass now, that husband says I shall not bring back the child without the money."

"What can I do?" said Mrs. Ludgate.

Lucy immediately took her purse out of her pocket, and whispered, "I will lend you whatever you want to pay the nurse, upon condition that you will give up the scheme of the balcony."

Mrs. Ludgate submitted to this condition; but she was not half so much obliged to Lucy for doing her this real service as she would have been if her friend had assisted in gratifying her vanity and extravagance. Lucy saw what passed in Mrs. Ludgate's mind, and nothing but the sense of the obligations she lay under to Belle's mother could have prevented her from breaking off all connexion with her.

But Mrs. Ludgate was now much inclined to court Lucy's acquaintance, as her approaching marriage with Mr. Allen, who was in good circumstances, made her appear quite a different person. Mrs. Allen would be able, and she hoped willing, to assist her from time to time with money. With this view, Belle showed Lucy a degree of attention and civility which she had disdained to bestow upon her friend whilst she was in an inferior situation. It was in vain, however, that this would-be fine lady endeavoured to draw the prudent Lucy out of her own sphere of life: though Lucy was extremely pretty, she had no desire to be admired; she was perfectly satisfied and happy at home, and she and her husband lived according to old Ludgate's excellent maxim, "Out of debt out of danger."

We shall not weary our readers with the history of all the petty difficulties into which Mr. and Mrs. Ludgate's foolish extravagance led them. The life of the shabby genteel is most miserable. Servants' wages unpaid, duns continually besieging the door, perpetual excuses, falsehoods to be invented, melancholy at home, and forced gaiety abroad! Who would live such a life? Yet all this Mr. and Mrs. Ludgate endured, for the sake of outshining Mr. and Mrs. Pimlico.

It happened that one night, at a party, Mrs. Ludgate caught a violent cold, and her face became inflamed and disfigured by red spots. Being to go to a ball in a few days, she was very impatient to get rid of the eruption; and in this exigency she applied to Mr. Pimlico, the perfumer, who had often supplied her with cosmetics, and who now recommended a beautifying lotion. This quickly cleared her complexion; but she soon felt the effects of her imprudence: she was taken dangerously ill, and the physician who was consulted attributed her disease entirely to the preparation she had applied to her face. Whilst she was ill, an execution was brought against Mr. Ludgate's goods. Threatened with a jail, and incapable of taking any vigorous measures to avoid distress, he went to consult his friend, Tom Lewis. How this Mr. Lewis lived was matter of astonishment to all his acquaintance: he had neither estate, business, or any obvious means of supporting the expense in which he indulged.

"What a happy dog you are, Lewis!" said our hero: "how is it that you live better than I do?"

"You might live as well as I, if you were inclined," said Lewis.

Our hero was all curiosity; and Lewis exacted from him an oath of secrecy. A long pause ensued.

"Have you the courage," said Lewis, "to extricate yourself from all your difficulties at once?"

"To be sure I have; since I must either go to jail this night, or raise two hundred guineas for these cursed fellows!"

"You shall have it in half an hour," said Lewis, "if you will follow my advice."

"Tell me at once what I am to do, and I will do it," cried Leonard. "I will do any thing to save myself from disgrace, and from a jail."

Lewis, who now perceived his friend was worked up to the pitch he wanted, revealed the whole mystery. He was connected with a set of gentlemen, ingenious in the arts of forgery, from whom he purchased counterfeit bank-notes at a very cheap rate. The difficulty and risk of passing them was extreme; therefore the confederates were anxious to throw this part of the business off their hands. Struck with horror at the idea of becoming an accomplice in such a scheme of villany, Leonard stood pale and silent, incapable of even thinking distinctly. Lewis was sorry that he had opened his mind so fully. "Remember your oath of secrecy!" said he.

"I do," replied Ludgate.

"And remember that you must become one of us before night, or go to jail."

Ludgate said he would take an hour to consider of the business, and here they parted; Lewis promising to call at his house before evening, to learn his final decision.

"And am I come to this?" thought the wretched man. "Would to Heaven I had followed my poor father's maxim! but it is now too late."

Mr. Ludgate, when he arrived at home, shut himself up in his own room, and continued walking backwards and forwards, for nearly an hour, in a state of mind more dreadful than can be described. Whilst he was in this situation, some one knocked at the door. He thought it was Lewis, and trembled from head to foot. It was only a servant with a parcel of bills, which several tradesmen, hearing that an execution was in the house, had hastened to present for payment. Among them were those of Mr. Beech, the upholsterer, and Mrs. Ludgate's milliner and mantua-maker, which having been let to run on for above two years and a half, now amounted to a sum that astonished and shocked Mr. Ludgate. He could not remonstrate with his wife, or even vent his anger in reproaches, for she was lying senseless in her bed.

Before he had recovered from this shock, and whilst the tradesmen who brought the bills were still waiting for their money, Lewis and one of his companions arrived. He came to the point immediately. He produced bank-notes sufficient to discharge all his debts, and proposed to lend him this money on condition that he would enter into the confederacy as he had proposed. "All that we ask of you is to pass a certain number of notes for us every week. You will find this to your advantage; for we will allow you a considerable percentage, besides freeing you from your present embarrassments."

The sight of the bank-notes, the pressure of immediate distress, and the hopes of being able to support the style of life in which he had of late appeared, all conspired to tempt Ludgate. When he had, early in life, vaunted to his young companions that he despised his father's old maxim, while he repeated his own, they applauded his spirit. They were not present, at this instant, to pity the wretched state into which that spirit had betrayed him. But our hero has yet much greater misery to endure. It is true his debts were now paid, and he was able to support an external appearance of affluence; but not one day, not one night, could he pass without suffering the horrors of a guilty conscience, and all the terrors which haunt the man who sees himself in hourly danger of detection. He determined to keep his secret cautiously from his wife: he was glad that she was confined to her bed at this time, lest her prying curiosity should discover what was going forward. The species of affection which he had once felt for her had not survived the first six months of their marriage; and their late disputes had rendered this husband and wife absolutely odious to each other. Each believed, and indeed pretty plainly asserted, that they could live more handsomely asunder: but, alas! they were united for better and for worse.

Mrs. Ludgate's illness terminated in another eruption on her face. She was extremely mortified by the loss of her beauty, especially as Mrs. Pimlico frequently contrasted her face with that of Mrs. Paget, who was now acknowledged to be the handsomest woman of Mrs. Pimlico's acquaintance. She endeavoured to make herself of consequence by fresh expense. Mr. Ludgate, to account for the sudden payment of his debts, and the affluence in which he now appeared to live, spread a report of his having had a considerable legacy left to him by a relation, who had died in a distant part of England. The truth of the report was not questioned; and for some time Mr. and Mrs. Ludgate were the envy of their acquaintance. How little the world, as it is called, can judge, by external appearances, of the happiness of those who excite admiration or envy!

"What lucky people the Ludgates are!" cried Mrs. Pimlico. The exclamation was echoed by a crowded card party, assembled at her house. "But then," continued Mrs. Pimlico, "it is a pity poor Belle is so disfigured by that scurvy, or whatever it is, in her face. I remember the time when she was as pretty a woman as you could see: nay, would you believe it, she had once as fine a complexion as young Mrs. Paget!"

These observations circulated quickly, and did not escape Mrs. Ludgate's ear. Her vanity was deeply wounded; and her health appeared to her but a secondary consideration, in comparison with the chance of recovering her lost complexion. Mr. Pimlico, who was an eloquent perfumer, persuaded her that her former illness had nothing to do with the beautifying lotion she had purchased at his shop; and to support his assertions, he quoted examples of innumerable ladies, of high rank and fashion, who were in the constant habit of using this admirable preparation. The vain and foolish woman, notwithstanding the warnings which she had received from the physician who attended her during her illness, listened to the oratory of the perfumer, and bought half a dozen bottles of another kind of beautifying lotion. The eruption vanished from her face, after she had used the cosmetic; and, as she did not feel any immediate bad effects upon her health, she persisted in the practice for some months. The consequence was at last dreadful. She was found one morning speechless in her bed, with one side of her face distorted and motionless. During the night, she had been seized with a paralytic stroke: in a few days she recovered her speech; but her face continued totally disfigured.

This was the severest punishment that could have been inflicted on a woman of her character. She was now ashamed to show herself abroad, and incapable of being contented at home. She had not the friendship of a husband, or the affection of children, to afford her consolation and support. Her eldest child was a boy of about five years old, her youngest four. They were as fretful and troublesome as children usually are, whose education has been totally neglected; and the quarrels between them and Jack the footboy were endless, for Jack was alternately their tutor and their playfellow.

Beside the disorder created in this family by mischievous children, the servants were daily plagues. Nothing was ever done by them well or regularly; and though the master and mistress scolded without mercy, and perpetually threatened to turn Jack or Sukey away, yet no reformation in their manners was produced; for Jack and Sukey's wages were not paid, and they felt that they had the power in their own hands; so that they were rather the tyrants than the servants of the house.

CHAPTER III

Mrs. Ludgate's temper, which never was sweet, was soured to such a degree, by these accumulated evils, that she was insufferable. Her husband kept out of the way as much as possible: he dined and supped at his club, or at the tavern: and, during the evenings and mornings, he was visible at home but for a few minutes. Yet, though his time was passed entirely away from his wife, his children, and his home, he was not happy. His life was a life of perpetual fraud and fear. He was bound by his engagements with Lewis to pass for the confederates a certain number of forged notes every day. This was a perilous task! His utmost exertions and ingenuity were continually necessary to escape detection; and, after all, he was barely able to wrest from the hard hands of his friends a sufficient profit upon his labour to maintain himself. How often did he look back, with regret, to the days when he stood behind the counter, in his father's shop! Then he had in Allen a real friend; but now he had in Lewis only a profligate and unfeeling associate. Lewis cared for no one but himself; and he was as avaricious as he was extravagant; "greedy of what belonged to others, prodigal of his own."

One night, Leonard went to the house where the confederates met, to settle with them for the last parcel of notes that he had passed. Lewis insisted upon being paid for his services before Ludgate should touch a farthing. Words ran high between them: Lewis, having the most influence with his associates, carried his point; and Leonard, who was in want of ready money, could supply himself only by engaging to pass double the usual quantity of forged notes during the ensuing month. Upon this condition, he obtained the supply for which he solicited. Upon his return home, he locked up the forged notes as usual in his escritoir. It happened the very next morning that Mrs. la Mode, the milliner, called upon Mrs. Ludgate. The ruling passion still prevailed, notwithstanding the miserable state to which this lady was reduced. Even palsy could not deaden her personal vanity: her love of dress survived the total loss of her beauty; she became accustomed to the sight of her distorted features, and was still anxious to wear what was most genteel and becoming. Mrs. la Mode had not a more constant visitor.

"How are you, Mrs. Ludgate, this morning?" said she. "But I need not ask, for you look surprising well. I just called to tell you a bit of a secret, that I have told to nobody else; but you being such a friend and a favourite, have a right to know it. You must know, I am going next week to bring out a new spring hat; and I have made one of my girls bring it up, to consult with you before any body else, having a great opinion of your taste and judgment: though it is a thing that must not be mentioned, because it would ruin me with Mrs. Pimlico, who made me swear she should have the first sight."

Flattered by having the first sight of the spring hat, Mrs. Ludgate was prepossessed in its favour; and, when she tried it on, she thought it made her look ten years younger. In short, it was impossible not to take one of the hats, though it cost three guineas, and was not worth ten shillings.

"Positively, ma'am, you must patronize my spring hat," said the milliner.

Mrs. Ludgate was decided by the word patronize: she took the hat, and desired that it should be set down in her bill: but Mrs. la Mode was extremely concerned that she had made a rule, nay a vow, not to take any thing but ready money for the spring hats; and she could not break her vow, even for her favourite Mrs. Ludgate. This was at least a prudent resolution in the milliner, who had lately received notice, from Mr. Ludgate, not to give his wife any goods upon credit, for that he was determined to refuse payment of her bills. The wife, who was now in a weak state of health, was not able as formerly to fight her battles with her husband upon equal terms. To cunning, the refuge of weakness, she had recourse; and she considered that, though she could no longer outscold, she could still outwit her adversary. She could not have the pleasure and honour of patronizing the spring hat, without ready money to pay for it; her husband, she knew, had always bank-notes in his escritoir; and she argued with herself that it was better to act without his consent than against it. She went and tried, with certain keys of her own, to open Leonard's desk; and open it came. She seized from a parcel of bank-notes as many as she wanted, and paid Mrs. la Mode with three of them for the spring hat. When her husband came home the next day, he did not observe that he had lost any of the notes; and, as he went out of the house again without once coming into the parlour where his wife was sitting, she excused herself to her conscience, for not telling him of the freedom she had taken, by thinking—It will do as well to tell him of it to-morrow: a few notes, out of such a parcel as he has in his desk locked up from me, can't signify; and he'll only bluster and bully when I do tell him of it; so let him find it out when he pleases.

The scheme of acting without her husband's consent in all cases, where she was morally certain that if she asked she could not obtain it, Mrs. Ludgate had often pursued with much success. A few days after she had bought the spring hat, she invited Mrs. Pimlico, Mrs. Paget, and all her genteel friends, to tea and cards. Her husband, she knew, would be out of the way, at his club, or at the tavern. Mrs. Pimlico, and Mrs. Paget, and all their genteel friends, did Mrs. Ludgate the honour to wait upon her on the appointed evening, and she had the satisfaction to appear upon this occasion in the new spring hat; while her friend, Mrs. Pimlico, whispered to young Mrs. Paget, "She patronize the new spring hat! What a fool Mrs. la Mode makes of her! A death's head in a wreath of roses! How frightfully ridiculous!"

Unconscious that she was an object of ridicule to the whole company, Mrs. Ludgate sat down to cards in unusually good spirits, firmly believing Mrs. la Mode's comfortable assertion, "that the spring hat made her look ten years younger." She was in the midst of a panegyric upon Mrs. la Mode's taste, when Jack, the footboy, came behind her chair, and whispered that three men were below, who desired to speak to her immediately.

"Men! gentlemen, do you mean?" said Mrs. Ludgate.

"No, ma'am, not gentlemen." "Then send them away about their business, dunce," said the lady. "Some tradesfolk, I suppose; tell them I'm engaged with company."

"But, ma'am, they will not leave the house without seeing you, or Mr. Ludgate."

"Let them wait, then, till Mr. Ludgate comes in. I have nothing to say to them. What's their business, pray?"

"It is something about a note, ma'am, that you gave to Mrs. la Mode, the other day."

"What about it?" said Mrs. Ludgate, putting down her cards.

"They say it is a bad note."

"Well, I'll change it; bid them send it up."

"They won't part with it, ma'am: they would not let it out of their hands, even to let me look at it for an instant."

"What a riot about a pound note," said Mrs. Ludgate, rising from the card-table: "I'll speak to the fellows myself."

She had recourse again to her husband's desk; and, armed with a whole handful of fresh bank-notes, she went to the strangers. They told her that they did not want, and would not receive, any note in exchange for that which they produced; but that, as it was a forgery, they must insist upon knowing from whom she had it. There was an air of mystery and authority about the strangers which alarmed Mrs. Ludgate; and, without attempting any evasion, she said that she took the note from her husband's desk, and that she could not tell from whom he received it. The strangers declared that they must wait till Mr. Ludgate should return home. She offered to give them a guinea to drink, if they would go away quietly; but this they refused. Jack, the footboy, whispered that they had pistols, and that he believed they were Bow-street officers.

They went into the back parlour to wait for Mr. Ludgate; and the lady, in extreme perturbation, returned to her company and her cards. In vain she attempted to resume her conversation about the spring hat, and to conceal the agitation of her spirits. It was observed by all her friends, and especially by Mrs. Pimlico, whose curiosity was strongly excited, to know the cause of her alarm. Mrs. Ludgate looked frequently at her watch, and even yawned without ceremony, more than once, to manifest her desire that the company should depart; but no hints availed. The card players resolutely kept their seats, and even the smell of extinguishing candles had no effect upon their callous senses.

The time appeared insupportably long to the wretched mistress of the house; and the contrast between her fantastic headdress and her agonizing countenance every minute became more striking.

Twelve o'clock struck. "It is growing very late," said Mrs. Ludgate.

"But we must have another rubber," said Mrs. Pimlico.

She began to deal; a knock was heard at the door. "There's Mr. Ludgate, I do suppose," said Mrs. Pimlico, continuing her deal. Mrs. Ludgate left her cards, and went out of the room without speaking. She stopped at the head of the staircase, for she heard a scuffle and loud voices below. Presently all was silent, and she ventured down when she heard the parlour door shut. The footman met her in the passage.

"What is the matter?" said she.

"I don't know; but I must be paid my wages," said he, "or must pay myself."

He passed on rudely. She half opened the parlour door, and looked in: her husband was lying back on the sofa, seemingly stupefied by despair: one of the Bow-street officers was chafing his temples, another was rummaging his desk, and the third was closely examining certain notes, which he had just taken from the prisoner's pockets.

"What is the matter?" cried Mrs. Ludgate, advancing. Her husband lifted up his eyes, saw her, started up, and, stamping furiously, exclaimed, "Cursed, cursed woman! you have brought me to the gallows, and all for this trumpery!" cried he, snatching her gaudy hat from her head, and trampling it under his feet. "For this—for this! you vain, you ugly creature, you have brought your husband to the gallows!"

One of the Bow-street officers caught hold of his uplifted arm, which trembled with rage. His wife sank to the ground; a second paralytic stroke deprived her of the power of speech. As they were carrying her up stairs, Mrs. Pimlico and the rest of the company came out of the dining-room, some of them with cards in their hands, all eagerly asking what was the matter? When they learnt that the Bow-street officers were in the house, and that Mr. Ludgate was taken into custody for uttering forged bank-notes, there was a general uproar. Some declared it was shocking! others protested it was no more than might have been expected! The Ludgates lived so much above their circumstances! Then he was such a coxcomb; and she such a poor vain creature! Better for people to do like their neighbours—to make no show, and live honestly!

In the midst of these effusions of long suppressed envy, some few of the company attempted a slight word or two of apology for their host and hostess; and the most humane went up to the wretched woman's bedchamber, to offer assistance and advice. But the greater number were occupied in tucking up their white gowns, finding their clogs, or calling for hackney coaches. In less than a quarter of an hour the house was clear of all Mrs. Ludgate's friends. And it is to please such friends that whole families ruin themselves by unsuitable expense.

Lucy and Allen were not, however, of this class of friends. A confused report of what had passed the preceding night was spread the next morning in Cranbourne-alley, by a young lady, who had been at Mrs. Ludgate's rout. The moment the news reached Allen's shop, he and Lucy set out immediately to offer their assistance to the unfortunate family. When they got to Weymouth-street, they gave only a single knock at the door, that they might not create any alarm. They were kept waiting a considerable time, and at last the door was opened by a slip-shod cook-maid, who seemed to be just up, though it was near eleven o'clock. She showed them into the parlour, which was quite dark; and, whilst she was opening the shutters, told them that the house had been up all night, what with the Bow-street officers and her mistress's fits. Her master, she added, was carried off to prison, she believed. Lucy asked who was with Mrs. Ludgate, and whether she could go up to her room?

"There's nobody with her, ma'am, but nurse, that called by chance, early this morning, to see the children, and had the good-nature to stay to help, and has been sitting in mistress's room, whilst I went to my bed. I'll step up and see if you can go in, ma'am."

They waited for some time in the parlour, where every thing looked desolate and in disorder. The ashes covered the hearth; the poker lay upon the table, near Mr. Ludgate's desk, the lock of which had been broken open; a brass flat candlestick, covered with tallow, was upon the window-seat, and beside it a broken cruet of vinegar; a cravat, and red silk handkerchief, which had been taken from Mr. Ludgate's neck when he swooned, lay under the table. Lucy and her husband looked at one another for some moments without speaking. At last Allen said, "We had better lock up this press, where there are silver spoons and china, for there is nobody now left to take care of any thing, and the creditors will be here soon to seize all they can." Lucy said that she would go up into the dining-room, and take an inventory of the furniture. In the dining-room she found Jack the footboy collecting shillings from beneath the candlesticks on the card-tables: the two little children were sitting on the floor, the girl playing with a pack of cards, the boy drinking the dregs of a decanter of white wine.—"Poor children! Poor creatures!" said Lucy; "is there nobody to take care of you?"

"No; nobody but Jack," said the boy, "and he's going away. Papa's gone I don't know where; and mama's not up yet, so we have had no breakfast."

The cook-maid came in to say that Mrs. Ludgate was awake, and sensible now, and would be glad to see Mrs. Allen, if she'd be so good as to walk up. Lucy told the children, who clung to her, that she would take them home with her, and give them some breakfast, and then hastened up stairs. She found her wretched friend humbled indeed to the lowest state of imbecile despair. Her speech had returned; but she spoke with difficulty, and scarcely so as to be intelligible. The good-natured nurse supported her in the bed, saying repeatedly, "Keep a good heart, madam; keep a good heart! Don't let your spirits sink so as this, and all may be well yet."

"O Lucy! Lucy! What will become of me now? What a change is here! And nobody to help or advise me! Nobody upon earth! I am forsaken by all the world!"

"Not forsaken by me," said Lucy, in a soothing voice.

"What noise is that below?" cried Mrs. Ludgate.

Lucy went downstairs to inquire, and found that, as Allen had foretold, the creditors were come to seize all they could find. Allen undertook to remain with them, and to bring them to some settlement, whilst Lucy had her unfortunate friend and the two children removed immediately to her own house.

As to Mr. Ludgate, there was no hope for him; the proofs of his guilt were manifest and incontrovertible. The forged note, which his wife had taken from his desk and given to the milliner, was one which had not gone through certain mysterious preparations. It was a bungling forgery. The plate would doubtless have been retouched, had not this bill been prematurely circulated by Mrs. Ludgate: thus her vanity led to a discovery of her husband's guilt. All the associates in Lewis's iniquitous confederacy suffered the just punishment of their crimes. Many applications were made to obtain a pardon for Leonard Ludgate: but the executive power preserved that firmness which has not, upon any similar occasion, ever been relaxed.

Lucy and Allen, those real friends, who would not encourage Mrs. Ludgate in extravagance, now, in the hour of adversity and repentance, treated her with the utmost tenderness and generosity. They were economical, and therefore could afford to be generous. All the wants of this destitute widow were supplied from the profits of their industry: they nursed her with daily humanity, bore with the peevishness of disease, and did all in their power to soothe the anguish of unavailing remorse.

Nothing could be saved from the wreck of Mr. Ludgate's fortune for the widow; but Allen, in looking over old Ludgate's books, had found and recovered some old debts, which Leonard, after his father's death, thought not worth looking after. The sum amounted to about three hundred and twenty pounds. As the whole concern had been made over to him, he could lawfully have appropriated this money to his own use, but he reserved it for his friend's children. He put it out to interest; and in the mean time he and Lucy not only clothed and fed, but educated these orphans, with their own children, in habits of economy and industry. The orphans repaid, by their affection and gratitude, the care that was bestowed upon them; and, when they grew up, they retrieved the credit of their family, by living according to their grandfather's useful maxim—"Out of debt out of danger."

THE LOTTERY

CHAPTER I

Near Derby, on the way towards Darley-grove, there is a cottage which formerly belonged to one Maurice Robinson. The jessamine which now covers the porch was planted by Ellen, his wife: she was an industrious, prudent, young woman; liked by all her neighbours, because she was ready to assist and serve them, and the delight of her husband's heart; for she was sweet-tempered, affectionate, constantly clean and neat, and made his house so cheerful that he was always in haste to come home to her, after his day's work. He was one of the manufacturers employed in the cotton works at Derby; and he was remarkable for his good conduct and regular attendance at his work.

Things went on very well in every respect, till a relation of his, Mrs. Dolly Robinson, came to live with him. Mrs. Dolly had been laundry-maid in a great family, where she learned to love gossiping, and tea-drinkings, and where she acquired some taste for shawls and cherry-brandy. She thought that she did her young relations a great favour by coming to take up her abode with them, because, as she observed, they were young and inexperienced; and she, knowing a great deal of the world, was able and willing to advise them; and besides, she had had a legacy of some hundred pounds left to her, and she had saved some little matters while in service, which might make it worth her relations' while to take her advice with proper respect, and to make her comfortable for the rest of her days.

Ellen treated her with all due deference, and endeavoured to make her as comfortable as possible; but Mrs. Dolly could not be comfortable unless, besides drinking a large spoonful of brandy in every dish of tea, she could make each person in the house do just what she pleased. She began by being dissatisfied because she could not persuade Ellen that brandy was wholesome, in tea, for the nerves; next she was affronted because Ellen did not admire her shawl; and, above all, she was grievously offended because Ellen endeavoured to prevent her from spoiling little George.

George was, at this time, between five and six years old; and his mother took a great deal of pains to bring him up well: she endeavoured to teach him to be honest, to speak the truth, to do whatever she and his father bid him, and to dislike being idle.

Mrs. Dolly, on the contrary, coaxed and flattered him, without caring whether he was obedient or disobedient, honest or dishonest. She was continually telling him that he was the finest little fellow in the world; and that she would do great things for him, some time or another.

What these great things were to be the boy seemed neither to know nor care; and, except at the moments when she was stuffing gingerbread into his mouth, he seemed never to desire to be near her: he preferred being with William Deane, his father's friend, who was a very ingenious man, and whom he liked to see at work.

William gave him a slate, and a slate pencil; and taught him how to make figures, and to cast up sums; and made a little wheel-barrow for him, of which George was very fond, so that George called him in play "King Deane." All these things tended to make Mrs. Dolly dislike William Deane, whom she considered as her rival in power.

One day, it was George's birthday, Mrs. Dolly invited a party, as she called it, to drink tea with her; and, at tea-time, she was entertaining the neighbours with stories of what she had seen in the great world. Amongst others, she had a favourite story of a butler, in the family where she had lived, who bought a ticket in the lottery when he was drunk, which ticket came up a ten thousand pound prize when he was sober; and the butler turned gentleman, and kept his coach directly.

One evening, Maurice Robinson and William came home, after their day's work, just in time to hear the end of this story; and Mrs. Dolly concluded it by turning to Maurice, and assuring him that he must put into the lottery and try his luck: for why should not he be as lucky as another? "Here," said she, "a man is working and drudging all the days of his life to get a decent coat to put on, and a bit of bread to put into his child's mouth; and, after all, may be he can't do it; though all the while, for five guineas, or a guinea, or half-a-guinea even, if he has but the spirit to lay out his money properly, he has the chance of making a fortune without any trouble. Surely a man should try his luck, if not for his own, at least for his children's sake," continued Mrs. Dolly, drawing little George towards her, and hugging him in her arms. "Who knows what might turn up! Make your papa buy a ticket in the lottery, love; there's my darling; and I'll be bound he'll have good luck. Tell him, I'll be bound we shall have a ten thousand pound prize at least; and all for a few guineas. I'm sure I think none but a miser would grudge the money, if he had it to give."

As Mrs. Dolly finished her speech, she looked at William Deane, whose countenance did not seem to please her. Maurice was whistling, and Ellen knitting as fast as possible. Little George was counting William Deane's buttons. "Pray, Mr. Deane," cried Mrs. Dolly, turning full upon him, "what may your advice and opinion be? since nothing's to be done here without your leave and word of command, forsooth. Now, as you know so much and have seen so much of the world, would you be pleased to tell this good company, and myself into the bargain, what harm it can do anybody, but a miser, to lay out a small sum to get a good chance of a round thousand, or five thousand, or ten thousand, or twenty thousand pounds, without more ado?"

As she pronounced the words five thousand, ten thousand, twenty thousand pounds, in a triumphant voice, all the company, except Ellen and William, seemed to feel the force of her oratory.

William coolly answered that he was no miser, but that he thought money might be better laid out than in the lottery; for that there was more chance of a man's getting nothing for his money than of his getting a prize; that when a man worked for fair wages every day, he was sure of getting something for his pains, and with honest industry, and saving, might get rich enough in time, and have to thank himself for it, which would be a pleasant thing: but that if a man, as he had known many, set his heart upon the turning of the lottery wheel, he would leave off putting his hand to any thing the whole year round, and so grow idle, and may be, drunken; "and then," said William, "at the year's end, if he have a blank, what is he to do for his rent, or for his wife and children, that have nothing to depend upon but him and his industry?"

Here Maurice sighed, and so did Ellen, whilst William went on and told many a true story of honest servants, and tradesmen, whom he had known, who had ruined themselves by gaming and lotteries.

"But," said Maurice, who now broke silence, "putting into the lottery, William, is not gaming, like dice or cards, or such things. Putting into the lottery is not gaming, as I take it."

"As I take it, though," replied William, "it is gaming. For what is gaming but trusting one's money, or somewhat, to luck and hap-hazard? And is there not as much hap-hazard in the turning of the wheel as in the coming up of the dice, or the dealing of the cards?"

"True enough; but somebody must get a prize," argued Maurice.

"And somebody must win at dice or cards," said William, "but a many more must lose; and a many more, I take it, must lose by the lottery than by any other game; else how would they that keep the lottery gain by it, as they do? Put a case. If you and I, Maurice, were this minute to play at dice, we stake our money down on the table here, and one or t'other takes all up. But, in the lottery, it is another affair; for the whole of what is put in does never come out."

This statement of the case made some impression upon Maurice, who was no fool; but Mrs. Dolly's desire that he should buy a lottery ticket, was not to be conquered by reason: it grew stronger and stronger the more she was opposed. She was silent and cross during the remainder of the evening; and the next morning, at breakfast, she was so low that even her accustomed dose of brandy, in her tea, had no effect.

Now Maurice, besides his confused hopes that Mrs. Dolly would leave something handsome to him or his family, thought himself obliged to her for having given a helping hand to his father, when he was in distress; and therefore he wished to bear with her humours, and to make her happy in his house. He knew that the lottery ticket was uppermost in her mind, and the moment he touched upon that subject she brightened up. She told him she had had a dream; and she had great faith in dreams: and she had dreamed, three times over, that he had bought number 339 in the lottery, and that it had come up a ten thousand pound prize!

"Well, Ellen," said Maurice, "I've half a mind to try my luck; and it can do us no harm, for I'll only put off buying the cow this year."

"Nay," said Mrs. Dolly, "why so? may be you don't know what I know, that Ellen's as rich as a Jew? She has a cunning little cupboard, in the wall yonder, that I see her putting money into every day of her life, and none goes out."

Ellen immediately went and drew back a small sliding oak door in the wainscot, and took out a glove, in which some money was wrapped; she put it altogether in her husband's hand, saying, with a good-humoured smile, "There is my year's spinning, Maurice: I only thought to have made more of it before I gave it you. Do what you please with it."

Maurice was so much moved by his wife's kindness, that he at the moment determined to give up his lottery scheme, of which, he knew, she did not approve. But, though a good-natured, well-meaning man, he was of an irresolute character; and even when he saw what was best to be done, had not courage to persist. As he was coming home from work, a few days after Ellen had given him the money, he saw, in one of the streets of Derby, a house with large windows finely illuminated, and read the words:

"Lottery-office of Fortunatus, Gould, and Co." At this office was sold the fortunate ticket, which came up on Monday last a twenty thousand pound prize. Ready money paid for prizes immediately on demand. The

  15,000l.
  10,000l.
   5,000l.

still in the wheel. None but the brave deserve a prize."

Whilst Maurice was gazing at this and other similar advertisements, which were exhibited in various bright colours in this tempting window, his desire to try his fortune in the lottery returned; and he was just going into the office to purchase a ticket, when luckily he found that he had not his leathern purse in his pocket. He walked on, and presently brushed by some one; it was William Deane, who was looking very eagerly over some old books, at a bookseller's stall. "I wish I had but money to treat myself with some of these," said William: "but I cannot; they cost such a deal of money, having all these prints in them."

"We can lend you,—no, we can't neither," cried Maurice, stopping himself short; for he recollected that he could not both lend his friend money to buy the books and buy a lottery ticket. He was in great doubt which he should do; and walked on with William, in silence. "So, then," cried he at last, "you would not advise me to put into the lottery?"

"Nay," said William laughing, "it is not for me to advise you about it, now; for I know you are considering whether you had best put it into the lottery or lend me the money to buy these books. Now, I hope you don't think I was looking to my own interest in what I said the other day; for I can assure you, I had no thoughts of meeting with these books at that time, and did not know that you had any money to spare."

"Say no more about it," replied Maurice. "Don't I know you are an honest fellow, and would lend me the money if I wanted it? You shall have it as soon as ever we get home. Only mind and stand by me stoutly, if Mrs. Dolly begins any more about the lottery."

Mrs. Dolly did not fail to renew her attacks; and she was both provoked and astonished when she found that the contents of the leathern purse were put into the hands of William Deane.

"Books, indeed! To buy books forsooth! What business had such a one as he with books?" She had seen a deal of life, she said, and never saw no good come of bookish bodies; and she was sorry to see that her own darling, George, was taking to the bookish line, and that his mother encouraged him in it. She would lay her best shawl, she said, to a gauze handkerchief, that William Deane would, sooner or later, beggar himself, and all that belonged to him, by his books and his gimcracks; "and if George were my son," continued she, raising her voice, "I'd soon cure him of prying and poring into that man's picture-books, and following him up and down with wheels and mechanic machines, which will never come to no good, nor never make a gentleman of him, as a ticket in the lottery might and would."

All mouths were open at once to defend William. Maurice declared he was the most industrious man in the parish; that his books never kept him from his work, but always kept him from the alehouse and bad company; and that, as to his gimcracks and machines, he never laid out a farthing upon them but what he got by working on holidays, and odd times, when other folks were idling or tippling. His master, who understood the like of those things, said, before all the workmen at the mills, that William Deane's machines were main clever, and might come to bring in a deal of money for him and his.

"Why," continued Maurice, "there was Mr. Arkwright, the man that first set a going all our cotton frames here, was no better than William Deane, and yet came at last to make a power of money. It stands to reason, any how, that William Deane is hurting nobody, nor himself neither; and, moreover, he may divert himself his own way, without being taken to task by man, woman, or child. As to children, he's very good to my child; there's one loves him," pointing to George, "and I'm glad of it: for I should be ashamed, so I should, that my flesh and blood should be in any ways disregardful or ungracious to those that be kind and good to them."

Mrs. Dolly, swelling with anger, repeated in a scornful voice, "Disregardful, ungracious! I wonder folks can talk so to me! But this is all the gratitude one meets with, in this world, for all one does. Well, well! I'm an old woman, and shall soon be out of people's way; and then they will be sorry they did not use me better; and then they'll bethink them that it is not so easy to gain a friend as to lose a friend; and then—"

Here Mrs. Dolly's voice was stopped by her sobs; and Maurice, who was a very good-natured man, and much disposed to gratitude, said he begged her pardon a thousand times, if he had done any thing to offend her; and declared his only wish was to please and satisfy her, if she would but tell him how. She continued sobbing, without making any answer, for some time: but at last she cried, "My ad—my ad—my ad-vice is never taken in any thing!"

Maurice declared he was ready to take her advice, if that was the only way to make her easy in her mind. "I know what you mean, now," added he: "you are still harping upon the lottery ticket. Well, I'll buy a ticket this day week, after I've sold the cow I bought at the fair. Will you have done sobbing, now, cousin Dolly?"

"Indeed, cousin Maurice, it is only for your own sake I speak," said she, wiping her eyes. "You know you was always a favourite of mine from your childhood up; I nursed you, and had you on my knee, and foretold often and often you would make a fortune, so I did. And will you buy the ticket I dreamed about, hey?"

Maurice assured her that, if it was to be had, he would. The cow was accordingly sold the following week, and the ticket in the lottery was bought. It was not, however, the number about which Mrs. Dolly had dreamed, for that was already purchased by some other person. The ticket Maurice bought was number 80; and, after he had got it, his cousin Dolly continually deplored that it was not the very number of which she dreamed. It would have been better not to have taken her advice at all than to have taken it when it was too late.

Maurice was an easy-tempered man, and loved quiet; and when he found that he was reproached for something or other whenever he came into his own house, he began to dislike the thought of going home after his day's work, and loitered at public-houses sometimes, but more frequently at the lottery-office. As the lottery was now drawing, his whole thoughts were fixed upon his ticket; and he neglected his work at the manufactory. "What signify a few shillings wages, more or less?" said he to himself. "If my ticket should come up a prize, it makes a rich man of me at once."

His ticket at last was drawn a prize of five thousand pounds! He was almost out of his senses with joy! He ran home to tell the news. "A prize! a prize, Dolly!" cried he, as soon as he had breath to speak.

"That comes of taking my advice!" said Dolly.

"A five thousand pound prize! my dear Ellen," cried he, and down he kicked her spinning-wheel.

"I wish we may be as happy with it as we have been without it, Maurice," said Ellen; and calmly lifted her spinning-wheel up again.

"No more spinning-wheels!" cried Maurice; "no more spinning! no more work! We have nothing to do now but to be as happy as the day is long. Wife, I say, put by that wheel."

"You're a lady now; and ought to look and behave like a lady," added Mrs. Dolly, stretching up her head, "and not stand moping over an old spinning-wheel."

"I don't know how to look and behave like a lady," said Ellen, and sighed: "but I hopes Maurice won't love me the less for that."

Mrs. Dolly was for some time wholly taken up with the pleasure of laying out money, and "preparing," as she said, "to look like somebody." She had many acquaintances at Paddington, she said, and she knew of a very snug house there, where they could all live very genteel.

She was impatient to go thither, for two reasons; that she might make a figure in the eyes of these acquaintances, and that she might get Maurice and little George away from William Deane, who was now become more than ever the object of her aversion and contempt; for he actually advised his friend not to think of living in idleness, though he had five thousand pounds. William moreover recommended it to him to put his money out to interest, or to dispose of a good part of it in stocking a farm, or in fitting out a shop. Ellen, being a farmer's daughter, knew well the management of a dairy; and, when a girl, had also assisted in a haberdasher's shop, that was kept in Derby by her uncle; so she was able and willing, she said, to assist her husband in whichever of these ways of life he should take to.

Maurice, irresolute and desirous of pleasing all parties, at last said, it would be as well, seeing they were now rich enough not to mind such a journey, just to go to Paddington and look about 'em; and if so be they could not settle there in comfort, why still they might see a bit of London town, and take their pleasure for a month or so; and he hoped William Deane would come along with them, and it should not be a farthing out of his pocket.

Little George said every thing he could think of to persuade his King Deane to go with them, and almost pulled him to the coach door, when they were setting off; but William could not leave his master and his business. The child clung with his legs and arms so fast to him that they were forced to drag him into the carriage.

"You'll find plenty of friends at Paddington, who'll give you many pretty things. Dry your eyes, and see! you're in a coach!" said Mrs. Dolly.

George dried his eyes directly, for he was ashamed of crying; but he answered, "I don't care for your pretty things. I shall not find my good dear King Deane any where;" and, leaning upon his mother's lap, he twirled round the wheel of a little cart, which William Deane had given him, and which he carried under his arm as his greatest treasure.

Ellen was delighted to see signs of such a grateful and affectionate disposition in her son, and all her thoughts were bent upon him; whilst Mrs. Dolly chattered on about her acquaintance at Paddington, and her satisfaction at finding herself in a coach once again. Her satisfaction was not, however, of long continuance; for she grew so sick that she was obliged, or thought herself obliged, every quarter of an hour, to have recourse to her cordial bottle. Her spirits were at last raised so much, that she became extremely communicative, and she laid open to Maurice and Ellen all her plans of future pleasure and expense.

"In the first place," said she, "I am heartily glad now I have got you away from that cottage that was not fit to live in; and from certain folks that shall be nameless, that would have one live all one's life like scrubs, like themselves. You must know that when we get to Paddington, the first thing I shall do shall be to buy a handsome coach." "A coach!" exclaimed Maurice and Ellen, with extreme astonishment.

"A coach, to be sure," said Mrs. Dolly. "I say a coach."

"I say we shall be ruined, then," said Maurice; "and laughed at into the bargain."

"La! you don't know what money is," said Mrs. Dolly. "Why haven't you five thousand pounds, man? You don't know what can be done with five thousand pounds, cousin Maurice."

"No, nor you neither, cousin Dolly; or you'd never talk of setting up your coach."

"Why not, pray? I know what a coach costs as well as another. I know we can have a second-hand coach, and we need not tell nobody that it's second-hand, for about a hundred pounds. And what's a hundred pounds out of five thousand?"

"But if we've a coach, we must have horses, must not we?" said Ellen, "and they'll cost a hundred more."

"Oh, we can have job horses, that will cost us little or nothing," said Mrs. Dolly.

"Say £150. a-year," replied Maurice; "for I heard my master's coachman telling that the livery-keeper in London declared as how he made nothing by letting him have job horses for £150. a-year."

"We are to have our own coach," said Dolly, "and that will be cheaper, you know."

"But the coach won't last for ever," said Ellen; "it must be mended, and that will cost something."

"It is time enough to think of that when the coach wants mending," said Mrs. Dolly; who, without giving herself the trouble of calculating, seemed to be convinced that every thing might be done for five thousand pounds. "I must let you know a little secret," continued she. "I have written, that is, got a friend to write, to have the house at Paddington taken for a year; for I know it's quite the thing for us, and we are only to give fifty pounds a-year for it: and you know that one thousand pounds would pay that rent for twenty years to come."

"But then," said Ellen, "you will want to do a great many other things with that thousand pounds. There's the coach you mentioned; and you said we must keep a footboy, and must see a deal of company, and must not grudge to buy clothes, and that we could not follow any trade, nor have a farm, nor do any thing to make money; so we must live on upon what we have. Now let us count, and see how we shall do it. You know, Maurice, that William Deane inquired about what we could get for our five thousand pounds, if we put it out to interest?"

"Ay; two hundred a-year, he said."

"Well, we pay fifty pounds a-year for the rent of the house, and a hundred a-year we three and the boy must have to live upon, and there is but fifty pounds a-year left."

Mrs. Dolly, with some reluctance, gave up the notion of the coach; and Ellen proposed that five hundred pounds should be laid out in furnishing a haberdasher's shop, and that the rest of their money should be put out to interest, till it was wanted. "Maurice and I can take care of the shop very well; and we can live well enough upon what we make by it," said Ellen.

Mrs. Dolly opposed the idea of keeping a shop; and observed that they should not, in that case, be gentlefolks. Besides, she said, she was sure the people of the house she had taken would never let it be turned into a shop.

What Mrs. Dolly had said was indeed true. When they got to Paddington, they found that the house was by no means fit for a shop; and as the bargain was made for a year, and they could not get it off their hands without considerable loss, Ellen was forced to put off her prudent scheme. In the mean time she determined to learn how to keep accounts properly.

There was a small garden belonging to the house, in which George set to work; and though he could do little more than pull up the weeds, yet this kept him out of mischief and idleness; and she sent him to a day-school, where he would learn to read, write, and cast accounts. When he came home in the evenings, he used to show her his copy-book, and read his lesson, and say his spelling to her, while she was at work. His master said it was a pleasure to teach him, he was so eager to learn; and Ellen was glad that she had money enough to pay for having her boy well taught. Mrs. Dolly, all this time, was sitting and gossiping amongst her acquaintance in Paddington. These acquaintance were people whom she had seen when they visited the housekeeper in the great family where she was laundry-maid; and she was very proud to show them that she was now a finer person than even the housekeeper, who was formerly the object of her envy. She had tea-drinking parties, and sometimes dinner parties, two or three in a week; and hired a footboy, and laughed at Ellen for her low notions, and dissuaded Maurice from all industrious schemes; still saying to him, "Oh, you'll have time enough to think of going to work when you have spent all your money."

Maurice, who had been accustomed to be at work for several hours in the day, at first thought it would be a fine thing to walk about, as Mrs. Dolly said, like a gentleman, without having any thing to do; but when he came to try it, he found himself more tired by this way of life than he had ever felt himself in the cotton-mills at Derby. He gaped and gaped, and lounged about every morning, and looked a hundred times at his new watch, and put it to his ear to listen whether it was going, the time seemed to him to pass so slowly. Sometimes he sauntered through the town, came back again, and stood at his own door looking at dogs fighting for a bone; at others, he went into the kitchen, to learn what there was to be for dinner, and to watch the maid cooking, or the boy cleaning knives. It was a great relief for him to go into the room where his wife was at work: but he never would have been able to get through a year in this way without the assistance of a pretty little black horse, for which he paid thirty guineas. During a month he was very happy in riding backwards and forwards on the Edgeware-road: but presently the horse fell lame; it was discovered that he was spavined and broken-winded; and the jockey from whom Maurice bought him was no where to be found. Maurice sold the horse for five guineas, and bought a fine bay for forty, which he was certain would turn out well, seeing he paid such a good price for him; but the bay scarcely proved better than the black. How he managed it we do not know, but it seems he was not so skilful in horses as in cotton-weaving; for at the end of the year he had no horse, and had lost fifty guineas by his bargains.

Another hundred guineas were gone, nobody in the family but himself knew how: but he resolved to waste no more money and began the new year well, by opening a haberdasher's shop in Paddington. The fitting up this shop cost them five hundred pounds; it was tolerably stocked, and Ellen was so active, and so attentive to all customers, that she brought numbers to Maurice Robinson's new shop. They made full twelve per cent, upon all they sold; and, in six months, had turned three hundred pounds twice, and had gained the profit of seventy-two pounds. Maurice, however, had got such a habit of lounging, during his year of idleness, that he could not relish steady attendance in the shop: he was often out, frequently came home late at night, and Ellen observed that he sometimes looked extremely melancholy; but when she asked him whether he was ill, or what ailed him, he always turned away, answering, "Nothing—nothing ails me. Why do ye fancy any thing ails me?"

Alas! it was no fancy. Ellen saw too plainly, that something was going wrong: but as her husband persisted in silence, she could not tell how to assist or comfort him.

Mrs. Dolly in the mean time was going on spending her money in junketing. She was, besides, no longer satisfied with taking her spoonful of brandy in every dish of tea; she found herself uncomfortable, she said, unless she took every morning fasting a full glass of the good cordial recommended to her by her friend, Mrs. Joddrell, the apothecary's wife. Now this good cordial, in plain English, was a strong dram. Ellen, in the gentlest manner she could, represented to Mrs. Dolly that she was hurting her health, and was exposing herself, by this increasing habit of drinking; but she replied with anger, that what she took was for the good of her health; that everybody knew best what agreed with them; that she should trust to her own feelings; and that nobody need talk, when all she took came out of the apothecary's shop, and was paid for honestly with her own money.

Besides what came out of the apothecary's shop, Mrs. Dolly found it agreed with her constantly to drink a pot of porter at dinner, and another at supper; and always when she had a cold, and she had often a cold, she drank large basins full of white wine whey, "to throw off her cold," as she said.

Then by degrees, she lost her appetite, and found she could eat nothing, unless she had a glass of brandy at dinner. Small beer, she discovered, did not agree with her; so at luncheon time she always had a tumbler full of brandy and water. This she carefully mixed herself, and put less and less water in every day, because brandy, she was convinced, was more wholesome for some constitutions than water; and brandy and peppermint, taken together, was an infallible remedy for all complaints, low spirits included.

CHAPTER II

Mrs. Dolly never found herself comfortable, moreover, unless she dined abroad two or three days in the week, at a public-house, near Paddington, where she said she was more at home than she was any where else. There was a bowling-green at this public-house, and it was a place to which tea-drinking parties resorted. Now Mrs. Dolly often wanted to take little George out with her to these parties, and said, "It is a pity and shame to keep the poor thing always mewed up at home, without ever letting him have any pleasure! Would not you like to go with me, George dear, in the one-horse chaise? and would not you be glad to have cakes, and tea, and all the good things that are to be had?"

"I should like to go in the one-horse chaise, to be sure, and to have cakes and tea; but I should not like to go with you, because mother does not choose it," answered George, in his usual plain way of speaking. Ellen, who had often seen Mrs. Dolly offer him wine and punch to drink, by way of a treat, was afraid he might gradually learn to love spirituous liquors; and that if he acquired a habit of drinking such when he was a boy, he would become a drunkard when he should grow to be a man. George was now almost nine years old; and he could understand the reason why his mother desired that he would not drink spirituous liquors. She once pointed out to him a drunken man, who was reeling along the street, and bawling ridiculous nonsense: he had quite lost his senses, and as he did not attend to the noise of a carriage coming fast behind him, he could not get out of the way time enough, and the coachman could not stop his horses; so the drunken man was thrown down, and the wheel of the carriage went over his leg, and broke it in a shocking manner. George saw him carried towards his home, writhing and groaning with pain.

"See what comes of drunkenness!" said Ellen.

She stopped the people, who were carrying the hurt man past her door, and had him brought in and laid upon a bed, whilst a surgeon was sent for. George stood beside the bed in silence; and the words "See what comes of drunkenness!" sounded in his ears.

Another time, his mother pointed out to him a man with terribly swollen legs, and a red face blotched all over, lifted out of a fine coach by two footmen in fine liveries. The man leaned upon a gold-headed cane, after he was lifted from his carriage, and tried with his other hand to take off his hat to a lady, who asked him how he did; but his hand shook so much that, when he had got his hat off, he could not put it rightly upon his head, and his footman put it on for him. The boys in the street laughed at him. "Poor man!" said Ellen; "that is Squire L—, who, as you heard the apothecary say, has drunk harder in his day than any man that ever he knew; and this is what he has brought himself to by drinking! All the physic in the apothecary's shop cannot make him well again! No; nor can his fine coach and fine footmen any more make him easy or happy, poor man!"

George exclaimed, "I wonder how people can be such fools as to be drunkards! I will never be a drunkard, mother; and now I know the reason why you desired me not to drink the wine, when Mrs. Dolly used to say to me, 'Down with it, George dear, it will do ye no harm.'"

These circumstances made such an impression upon George that there was no further occasion to watch him; he always pushed away the glass when Mrs. Dolly filled it for him.

One day his mother said to him, "Now I can trust you to take care of yourself, George, I shall not watch you. Mrs. Dolly is going to a bowling-green tea-party this evening, and has asked you to go with her; and I have told her you shall."

George accordingly went with Mrs. Dolly to the bowling-green. The company drank tea out of doors, in summer-houses. After tea, Mrs. Dolly bid George go and look at the bowling-green; and George was very well entertained with seeing the people playing at bowls; but when it grew late in the evening, and when the company began to go away, George looked about for Mrs. Dolly. She was not in the summer-house, where they had drunk tea, nor was she any where upon the terrace round the bowling-green; so he went to the public-house in search of her, and at last found her standing at the bar with the landlady. Her face was very red, and she had a large glass of brandy in her hand, into which the landlady was pouring some drops, which she said were excellent for the stomach.

Mrs. Dolly started so when she saw George, that she threw down half her glass of brandy. "Bless us, child! I thought you were safe at the bowling-green," said she.

"I saw every body going away," answered George; "so I thought it was time to look for you, and to go home."

"But before you go, my dear little gentleman," said the landlady, "you must eat one of these tarts, for my sake." As she spoke, she gave George a little tart: "and here," added she, "you must drink my health too in something good. Don't be afraid, love; it's nothing that will hurt you: it's very sweet and nice."

"It is wine, or spirits of some sort or other, I know by the smell," said George; "and I will not drink it, thank you, ma'am."

"The boy's a fool!" said Mrs. Dolly; "but it's his mother's fault. She won't let him taste any thing stronger than water. But now your mother's not by, you know," said Mrs. Dolly, winking at the landlady; "now your mother's not by—"

"Yes, and nobody will tell of you," added the landlady; "so do what you like: drink it down, love."

"No!" cried George, pushing away the glass which Mrs. Dolly held to his lips. "No! no! no! I say. I will not do any thing now my mother's not by, that I would not do if she was here in this room."

"Well; hush, hush; and don't bawl so loud though," said Mrs. Dolly, who saw, what George did not see, a gentleman that was standing at the door of the parlour opposite to them, and who could hear every thing that was saying at the bar.

"I say," continued George, in a loud voice, "mother told me she could trust me to take care of myself; and so I will take care of myself; and I am not a fool, no more is mother, I know; for she told me the reasons why it is not good to drink spirituous—." Mrs. Dolly pushed him away, without giving him time to finish his sentence, bidding him go and see whether the gig was ready; for it was time to be going home.

As George was standing in the yard, looking at the mechanism of the one-horse chaise and observing how the horse was put to, somebody tapped him upon the shoulder, and looking up, he saw a gentleman with a very good-natured countenance, who smiled upon him, and asked him whether he was the little boy who had just been talking so loud in the bar?

"Yes, sir," says George. "You seem to be a good little boy," added he; "and I liked what I heard you say very much. So you will not do any thing when your mother is not by, that you would not do if she was here—was not that what you said?"

"Yes, sir; as well as I remember."

"And who is your mother?" continued the gentleman. "Where does she live?"

George told him his mother's name, and where she lived; and the gentleman said, "I will call at your mother's house as I go home, and tell her what I heard you say; and I will ask her to let you come to my house, where you will see a little boy of your own age, whom I should be very glad to have seen behave as well as you did just now."

Mr. Belton, for that was the name of the gentleman who took notice of George, was a rich carpet manufacturer. He had a country-house near Paddington; and the acquaintance which was thus begun became a source of great happiness to George. Mr. Belton lent him several entertaining books, and took him to see many curious things in London. Ellen was rejoiced to hear from him the praises of her son. All the pleasure of Ellen's life had, for some months past, depended upon this boy; for her husband was seldom at home, and the gloom that was spread over his countenance alarmed her, whenever she saw him. As for Mrs. Dolly, she was no companion for Ellen: her love of drinking had increased to such a degree that she could love nothing else; and when she was not half intoxicated, she was in such low spirits that she sat (either on the side of her bed, or in her arm-chair, wrapped in a shawl) sighing and crying, and see-sawing herself; and sometimes she complained to Maurice that Ellen did not care whether she was dead or alive; and at others that George had always something or other to do, and never liked to sit in her room and keep her company. Besides all this, she got into a hundred petty quarrels with the neighbours, who had a knack of remembering what she said when she was drunk, and appealing to her for satisfaction when she was sober. Mrs. Dolly regularly expected that Ellen should, as she called it, stand her friend in these altercations; to which Ellen could not always in justice consent. Ah! said Ellen to herself one night, as she was sitting up late waiting for her husband's return home, it is not the having five thousand pounds that makes people happy! When Maurice loved to come home after his day's work to our little cottage, and when our George was his delight, as he is mine, then I was light of heart; but now it is quite otherwise. However, there is no use in complaining, nor in sitting down to think upon melancholy things; and Ellen started up and went to work, to mend one of her husband's waistcoats.

Whilst she was at this employment, she listened continually for the return of Maurice. The clock struck twelve, and one, and no husband came! She heard no noise in the street when she opened her window, for every body but herself was in bed and asleep. At last she heard the sound of footsteps; but it was so dark that she could not see who the person was, who continued walking backwards and forwards, just underneath the window.

"Is it you, Maurice? Are you there, Maurice?" said Ellen. The noise of the footsteps ceased, and Ellen again said, "Is it you, Maurice? Are you there?"

"Yes," answered Maurice; "it is I. Why are you not abed and asleep, at this time of night?"

"I am waiting for you," replied Ellen. "You need not wait for me; I have the key of the house door in my pocket, and can let myself in whenever I choose it."

"And don't you choose it now?" said Ellen.

"No. Shut down the window."

Ellen shut the window, and went and sat down upon the side of her boy's bed. He was sleeping. Ellen, who could not sleep, took up her work again, and resolved to wait till her husband should come in. At last, the key turned in the house door, and presently she heard her husband's steps coming softly towards the room where she was sitting. He opened the door gently, as if he expected to find her asleep, and was afraid of awakening her. He started when he saw her; and slouching his hat over his face, threw himself into a chair without speaking a single word. Something terrible has happened to him, surely! thought Ellen; and her hand trembled so that she could scarcely hold her needle, when she tried to go on working.

"What are you doing there, Ellen?" said he, suddenly pushing back his hat.

"I'm only mending your waistcoat, love," said Ellen, in a faltering voice.

"I am a wretch! a fool! a miserable wretch!" exclaimed Maurice, starting up and striking his forehead with violence as he walked up and down the room.

"What can be the matter?" said Ellen. "It is worse to me to see you in this way, than to hear whatever misfortune has befallen you. Don't turn away from me, husband! Who in the world loves you so well as I do?"

"Oh, Ellen," said he, letting her take his hand, but still turning away, "you will hate me when you know what I have done."

"I cannot hate you, I believe," said Ellen.

"We have not sixpence left in the world!" continued Maurice, vehemently. "We must leave this house to-morrow; we must sell all we have; I must go to jail, Ellen! You must work all the rest of your days harder than ever you did; and so must that poor boy, who lies sleeping yonder. He little thinks that his father has made a beggar of him; and that, whilst his mother was the best of mothers to him, his father was ruining him, her, and himself, with a pack of rascals at the gaming-table. Ellen, I have lost every shilling of our money!"

"Is that all?" said Ellen. "That's bad; but I am glad that you have done nothing wicked. We can work hard, and be happy again. Only promise me now, dear husband, that you will never game any more."

Maurice threw himself upon his knees, and swore that he never, to the last hour of his life, would go to any gaming-table again, or play at any game of chance. Ellen then said all she could to soothe and console him; she persuaded him to take some rest, of which he was much in need, for his looks were haggard, and he seemed quite exhausted. He declared that he had not had a night's good sleep for many months, since he had got into these difficulties by gaming. His mind had been kept in a continual flurry, and he seemed as if he had been living in a fever. "The worst of it was, Ellen," said he, "I could not bear to see you or the boy when I had been losing; so I went on, gaming deeper and deeper, in hopes of winning back what I had lost; and I now and then won, and they coaxed me and told me I was getting a run of luck, and it would be a sin to turn my back on good fortune. This way I was 'ticed to go on playing, till, when I betted higher and higher, my luck left me; or, as I shrewdly suspect, the rascals did not play fair, and they won stake after stake, till they made me half mad, and I risked all I had left upon one throw, and lost it! And when I found I had lost all, and thought of coming home to you and our boy, I was ready to hang myself. Oh, Ellen, if you knew all I have felt! I would not live over again the last two years for this room full of gold!"

Such are the miserable feelings, and such the life, of a gamester!

Maurice slept for a few hours, or rather dozed, starting now and then, and talking of cards and dice, and sometimes grinding his teeth and clenching his hand, till he wakened himself by the violence with which he struck the side of the bed.

"I have had a terrible dream, wife," said he, when he opened his eyes, and saw Ellen sitting beside him on the bed. At first he did not recollect what had really happened; but as Ellen looked at him with sorrow and compassion in her countenance, he gradually remembered all the truth; and, hiding his head under the bed-clothes, he said he wished he could sleep again, if it could be without dreaming such dreadful things.

It was in vain that he tried to sleep; so he got up, resolving to try whether he could borrow twenty guineas from any of his friends, to pay the most pressing of his gaming companions. The first person he asked was Mrs. Dolly: she fell into an hysteric fit when she heard of his losses; and it was not till after she had swallowed a double dram of brandy that she was able to speak, and to tell him that she was the worst person in the world he could have applied to; for that she was in the greatest distress herself, and all her dependance in this world was upon him.

Maurice stood in silent astonishment. "Why, cousin," said he, "I thought, and always believed, that you had a power of money! You know, when you came to live with us, you told me so."

"No matter what I told you," said Mrs. Dolly. "Folks can't live upon air. Yesterday the landlady of the public-house at the bowling-green, whom I'm sure I looked upon as my friend,—but there's no knowing one's friends,—sent me in a bill as long as my arm; and the apothecary here has another against me worse again; and the man at the livery-stables, for one-horse chays, and jobs that I'm sure I forgot ever having, comes and charges me the Lord knows what! and then the grocer for tea and sugar, which I have been giving to folks from whom I have got no thanks. And then I have an account with the linen-draper of I don't know how much! hut he has over-charged me, I know, scandalously, for my last three shawls. And then I have never paid for my set of tea china; and half of the cups are broke, and the silver spoons, and I can't tell what besides."

In short, Mrs. Dolly, who had never kept any account of what she spent, had no idea how far she was getting into a tradesman's debt till his bill was brought home: and was in great astonishment to find, when all her bills were sent in, that she had spent four hundred and fifty pounds in her private expenses, drinking included, in the course of three years and eight months. She had now nothing left to live upon but one hundred pounds, so that she was more likely to be a burden to Maurice than any assistance. He, however, was determined to go to a friend, who had frequently offered to lend him any sum of money he might want, and who had often been his partner at the gaming-table.

In his absence, Ellen and George began to take a list of all the furniture in the house, that it might be ready for a sale, and Mrs. Dolly sat in her arm-chair, weeping and wailing.

"Oh! laud! laud! that I should live to see all this!" cried she. "Ah, lack-a-daisy! lack-a-daisy! lack-a-day! what will become of me? Oh, la! la! la! la!" Her lamentations were interrupted by a knock at the door. "Hark! a knock, a double knock at the door," cried Mrs. Dolly. "Who is it? Ah, lack-a-day, when people come to know what has happened, it will be long enough before we have any more visitors; long enough before we hear any more double knocks at the door. Oh, laud! laud! See who it is, George."

It was Mr. Belton, who was come to ask George to go with him and his little nephew to see some wild beasts at Exeter-'change: he was much surprised at the sorrowful faces of George and Ellen, whom he had always been used to see so cheerful, and inquired what misfortune had befallen them? Mrs. Dolly thought she could tell the story best, so she detailed the whole, with many piteous ejaculations; but the silent resignation of Ellen's countenance had much more effect upon Mr. Belton. "George," said he, "must stay to finish the inventory he is writing for his mother."

Mr. Belton was inquiring more particularly into the amount of Maurice's debts, and the names of the persons to whom he had lost his money at the gaming-table, when the unfortunate man himself came home. "No hope, Ellen!" cried he. "No hope from any of those rascals that I thought my friends. No hope!"

He stopped short, seeing a stranger in the room, for Mr. Belton was a stranger to him. "My husband can tell you the names of all the people," said Ellen, "who have been the ruin of us." Mr. Belton then wrote them down from Maurice's information; and learned from him that he had lost to these sharpers upwards of three thousand eight hundred pounds in the course of three years; that the last night he played, he had staked the goods in his shop, valued at 350l, and lost them; that afterwards he staked the furniture of his house, valued at 160l.; this also he lost; and so left the gaming-table without a farthing in the world.

"It is not my intention," said Mr. Belton, "to add to your present suffering, Mr. Robinson, by pointing out that it has arisen entirely from your own imprudence. Nor yet can I say that I feel much compassion for you; for I have always considered a gamester as a most selfish being, who should be suffered to feel the terrible consequences of his own avaricious folly, as a warning to others."

"Oh, sir! Oh, Mr. Belton!" cried Ellen, bursting now, for the first time, into tears, "do not speak so harshly to Maurice."

"To you I shall not speak harshly," said Mr. Belton, his voice and looks changing; "for I have the greatest compassion for such an excellent wife and mother. And I shall take care that neither you nor your son, whom you have taken such successful pains to educate, shall suffer by the folly and imprudence in which you had no share. As to the ready money which your husband has lost and paid to these sharpers, it is, I fear, irrecoverable; but the goods in your shop, and the furniture in your house, I will take care shall not be touched. I will go immediately to my attorney, and direct him to inquire into the truth of all I have been told, and to prosecute these villains for keeping a gaming-table, and playing at unlawful games. Finish that inventory which you are making out, George, and give it to me; I will have the furniture in your house, Ellen, valued by an appraiser, and will advance you money to the amount, on which you may continue to live in comfort and credit, trusting to your industry and integrity to repay me in small sums, as you find it convenient, out of the profits of your shop."

"Oh, sir!" cried Maurice, clasping his hands with a strong expression of joy, "thank you! thank you from the bottom of my soul! Save her from misery, save the boy, and let me suffer as I ought for my folly."

Mr. Belton, in spite of his contempt for gamesters, was touched by Maurice's repentance; but, keeping a steady countenance, replied in a firm tone, "Suffering for folly does nobody any good, unless it makes them wiser in future."

CHAPTER III

Mrs. Dolly, who had been unaccountably awed to silence by Mr. Belton's manner of speaking and looking, broke forth the moment he had left the house. "Very genteel, indeed; though he might have taken more notice of me. See what, it is, George, to have the luck of meeting with good friends."

"See what it is to deserve good friends, George," said Ellen.

"You'll all remember, I hope," said Mrs. Dolly, raising her voice, "that it was I who was the first and foremost cause of all this, by taking George along with me to the tea-drinking at the bowling-green, where he first got acquainted with Mr. Belton."

"Mr. Belton would never have troubled his head about such a little boy as George," said Ellen, "if it had not been for—you know what I mean, Mrs. Dolly. All I wish to say is, that George's own good behaviour was the cause of our getting acquainted with this good friend."

"And I am sure you were the cause, mother," said George, "of what you call my good behaviour."

Mrs. Dolly, somewhat vexed at this turn, changed the conversation saying, "Well, 'tis no matter how we made such a good acquaintance; let us make the most of him, and drink his health, as becomes us, after dinner. And now, I suppose, all will go on as usual: none of our acquaintance in Paddington need know any thing of what has happened."

Ellen, who was very little solicitous about what Mrs. Dolly's acquaintance in Paddington might think, observed that, so far from going on as usual, now they were living on borrowed money, it was fit they should retrench all their expenses, and give up the drawing-room and parlour of the house to lodgers.

"So, then, we are to live like shabby wretches for the rest of our days!" cried Mrs. Dolly. "Better live like what we are, poor but industrious people," replied Ellen, "and then we shall never be forced to do any thing shabby."

"Ay, Ellen, you are, as you always are, in the right; and all I desire now, in this world, is to make up for the past, and to fall to work in some way or other; for idleness was what first led me to the gaming-table."

Mrs. Dolly opposed these good resolutions, and urged Maurice to send George to Mr. Belton, to beg him to lend them some more money. "Since he is in the humour to be generous, and since he has taken a fancy to us," said she, "why not take him at his word, and make punch whilst the water's hot?"

But all that Mrs. Dolly said was lost upon Ellen, who declared that she would never be so mean as to encroach upon such a generous friend; and Maurice protested that nothing that man, woman, or devil, could say, should persuade him to live in idleness another year. He sent George the next morning to Mr. Belton with a letter, requesting that he would procure employment for him, and stating what he thought himself fit for. Amongst other things, he mentioned that he could keep accounts. That he could write a good hand was evident, from his letter. Mr. Belton, at this time, wanted a clerk in his manufactory; and, upon Maurice's repeating his promise never more to frequent the gaming-table, Mr. Belton, after a trial, engaged him as his clerk, at a salary of 50l. per annum.

Every thing now went on well for some months. Maurice, on whom his wife's kindness had made a deep impression, became thoroughly intent upon his business, and anxious to make her some amends for his past follies. His heart was now at ease: he came home, after his day's work at the counting-house, with an open, cheerful countenance; and Ellen was perfectly happy. They sold all the furniture that was too fine for their present way of life to the new lodgers, who took the drawing-room and front parlour of their house; and lived on the profits of their shop, which, being well attended, was never in want of customers.

One night, at about ten o'clock, as little George was sitting, reading the history of Sandford and Merton, in which he was much interested, he was roused by a loud knocking at the house door. He ran to open it: but how much was he shocked at the sight he beheld! It was Mrs. Dolly! her leg broken, and her skull fractured!

Ellen had her brought in, and laid upon a bed, and a surgeon was immediately sent for. When Maurice inquired how this terrible accident befel Mrs. Dolly, the account he received was, that she was riding home from the bowling-green public-house, much intoxicated; that she insisted upon stopping to get a glass of peppermint and brandy for her stomach; that, seeing she had drunk too much already, every thing possible was done to prevent her from taking any more; but she would not be advised: she said she knew best what agreed with her constitution; so she alighted and took the brandy and peppermint; and when she was to get upon her horse again, not being in her right senses, she insisted upon climbing up by a gate that was on the road-side, instead of going, as she was advised, to a bank that was a little further on. The gate was not steady, the horse being pushed moved, she fell, broke her leg, and fractured her skull.

She was a most shocking spectacle when she was brought home. At first she was in great agony; but she afterwards fell into a sort of stupor, and lay speechless.

The surgeon arrived: he set her leg; and during this operation, she came to her senses, but it was only the sensibility of pain. She was then trepanned; but all was to no purpose—she died that night; and of all the friends, as she called them, who used to partake in her tea-drinkings and merry-makings, not one said more when they heard of her death than "Ah, poor Mrs. Dolly! she was always fond of a comfortable glass: 'twas a pity it was the death of her at last."

Several tradesmen, to whom she died in debt, were very loud in their complaints; and the landlady at the bowling-green did not spare her memory. She went so far as to say, that it was a shame such a drunken quean should have a Christian burial. What little clothes Mrs. Dolly left at her death were given up to her creditors. She had owed Maurice ten guineas ever since the first month of their coming to Paddington; and when she was on her death-bed, during one of the intervals that she was in her senses, she beckoned to Maurice, and told him, in a voice scarcely intelligible, he would find in her left-hand pocket what she hoped would pay him the ten guineas he had lent to her. However, upon searching this pocket, no money was to be found, except sixpence in halfpence; nor was there any thing of value about her. They turned the pocket inside out, and shook it; they opened every paper that came out of it, but these were all old bills. Ellen at last examined a new shawl which had been thrust into this pocket, and which was all crumpled up: she observed that one of the corners was doubled down, and pinned; and upon taking out the yellow crooked pin, she discovered, under the corner of the shawl, a bit of paper, much soiled with snuff, and stained with liquor. "How it smells of brandy!" said Ellen, as she opened it. "What is it, Maurice?"

"It is not a bank note. It is a lottery ticket, I do believe!" cried Maurice. "Ay, that it is! She put into the lottery without letting us know any thing of the matter. Well, as she said, perhaps this may pay me my ten guineas, and overpay me, who knows? We were lucky with our last ticket; and why should not we be as lucky with this, or luckier, hey, Ellen? We might have ten thousand pounds or twenty thousand pounds this time, instead of five, why not, hey, Ellen?" But Maurice observing that Ellen looked grave, and was not much charmed with the lottery ticket, suddenly changed his tone, and said, "Now don't you, Ellen, go to think that my head will run on nothing but this here lottery ticket. It will make no difference on earth in me: I shall mind my business just as well as if there was no such thing, I promise you. If it come up a prize, well and good: and if it come up a blank, why well and good too. So do you keep the ticket, and I shall never think more about it, Ellen. Only, before you put it by, just let me look at the number. What makes you smile?"

"I smiled only because I think I know you better than you, know yourself. But, perhaps, that should not make me smile," said Ellen: and she gave a deep sigh.

"Now, wife, why will you sigh? I can't bear to hear you sigh," said Maurice, angrily. "I tell you I know myself, and have a right to know myself, I say, a great deal better than you do; and so none of your sighs, wife."

Ellen rejoiced to see that his pride worked upon him in this manner; and mildly told him she was very glad to find he thought so much about her sighs. "Why," said Maurice, "you are not one of those wives that are always taunting and scolding their husbands; and that's the reason, I take it, why a look or a word from you goes so far with me." He paused for a few moments, keeping his eyes fixed upon the lottery ticket; then, snatching it up, he continued: "This lottery ticket may tempt me to game again: for, as William Deane said, putting into the lottery is gaming, and the worst sort of gaming. So, Ellen, I'll show you that though I was a fool once, I'll never be a fool again. All your goodness was not thrown away upon me. I'll go and sell this lottery ticket immediately at the office, for whatever it is worth: and you'll give me a kiss when I come home again, I know, Ellen."

Maurice, pleased with his own resolution, went directly to the lottery office to sell his ticket. He was obliged to wait some time, for the place was crowded with persons who came to inquire after tickets which they had insured.

Many of these ignorant imprudent poor people had hazarded guinea after guinea, till they found themselves overwhelmed with debt; and their liberty, character, and existence, depending on the turning of the wheel. What anxious faces did Maurice behold! How many he heard, as they went out of the office, curse their folly for having put into the lottery!

He pressed forward to sell his ticket. How rejoiced he was when he had parted with this dangerous temptation, and when he had received seventeen guineas in hand, instead of anxious hopes! How different were his feelings at this instant from those of many that were near him! He stood to contemplate the scene. Here he saw a poor maid-servant, with scarcely clothes to cover her, who was stretching her thin neck across the counter, and asking the clerk, in a voice of agony, whether her ticket, number 45, was come up yet.

"Number 45?" answered the clerk, with the most careless air imaginable. "Yes" (turning over the leaves of his book): "Number 45, you say—Yes: it was drawn yesterday—a blank." The wretched woman clasped her hands, and burst into tears, exclaiming, "Then I'm undone!"

Nobody seemed to have time to attend to her. A man servant, in livery, pushed her away, saying, "You have your answer, and have no more business here, stopping the way. Pray, sir, is number 336, the ticket I've insured so high, come up to-day?"

[Footnote: This was written before the act of parliament against insuring in lotteries.]

"Yes, sir—blank." At the word blank, the disappointed footman poured forth a volley of oaths, declaring that he should be in jail before night; to all which the lottery-office keeper only answered, "I can't help it, sir; I can't help it. It is not my fault. Nobody is forced to put into the lottery, sir. Nobody's obliged to insure, sir. 'Twas your own choice, sir. Don't blame me."

Meanwhile, a person behind the footman, repeating the words he had addressed to the poor woman, cried, "You have your answer, sir; don't stop the way."

Maurice was particularly struck with the agitated countenance of one man, who seemed as if the suspense of his mind had entirely bereaved him of all recollection. When he was pressed forward by the crowd, and found himself opposite to the clerk, he was asked twice, "What's your business, sir?" before he could speak; and then could only utter the words—number 7? "Still in the wheel," was the answer. "Our messenger is not yet returned from Guildhall, with news of what has been drawn this last hour. If you will call again at three, we can answer you." The man seemed to feel this as a reprieve; but as he was retiring, there came one with a slip of paper in his hand. This was the messenger from Guildhall, who handed the paper to the clerk. He read aloud, "Number 7. Were you not inquiring for 7, sir?"

"Yes," said the pale trembling man.

"Number 7 is just come up, sir,—a blank."

At the fatal word blank, the man fell flat upon his face in a swoon. Those near him lifted him out into the street, for air.

"Here, sir; you are going without your change, after waiting for it so long," cried the clerk to Maurice; who, touched with compassion for the man who had just fallen, was following those who were carrying him out. When he got into the street, Maurice saw the poor creature sitting on a stone, supported by a hackney-coachman, who held some vinegar to his nose, at the same time asking him if he did not want a coach?

"A coach! Oh, no," said the man, as he opened his eyes. "I have not a farthing of money in the world." The hackney-coachman swore that was a sad case, and ran across the street to offer his services where they could be paid for: "A coach, if you want one, sir. Heavy rain coming on," said he, looking at the silver which he saw through the half-closed fingers of Maurice's hand.

"Yes, I want a coach," said Maurice: and bade the coachman draw up to the stone, where the poor man who had swooned was sitting. Maurice was really a good-natured fellow; and he had peculiar pity for the anguish this man seemed to feel, because he recollected what he had suffered himself, when he had been ruined at the gaming-table.

"You are not able to walk: here is a coach; I will go your way and set you down, sir," said Maurice.

The unfortunate man accepted this offer. As they went along he sighed bitterly, and once said, with great vehemence, "Curse these lotteries! Curse these lotteries!" Maurice now rejoiced, more than ever, at having conquered his propensity to gaming, and at having sold his ticket.

When they came opposite to a hosier's shop, in Oxford-street, the stranger thanked him, and desired to be set down. "This is my home," said he; "or this was my home, I ought to say," pointing to his shop as he let down the coach-glass. "A sad warning example I am! But I am troubling you, sir, with what no way concerns you. I thank you, sir, for your civility," added he, turning away from Maurice, to hide the tears which stood in his eyes: "good day to you."

He then prepared to get out of the coach; but whilst the coachman was letting down the step, a gentleman came out of the hosier's shop to the door, and cried, "Mr. Fulham, I am glad you are come at last. I have been waiting for you this half-hour, and was just going away." Maurice pulled aside the flap of the hosier's coat, as he was getting out, that he might peep at the gentleman who spoke; the voice was so like William Deane's, that he was quite astonished.—"It is—it is William Deane," cried Maurice, jumping out of the coach and shaking hands with his friend.

William Deane, though now higher in the world than Robinson, was heartily glad to see him again, and to renew their old intimacy. "Mr. Fulham," said he, turning to the hosier, "excuse me to-day; I'll come and settle accounts with you to-morrow."

On their way to Paddington, Maurice related to his friend all that had passed since they parted; how his good luck in the lottery tempted him to try his fortune at the gaming-table; how he was cheated by sharpers, and reduced to the brink of utter ruin; how kind Ellen was towards him in this distress; how he was relieved by Mr. Belton, who was induced to assist him from regard to Ellen and little George; how Mrs. Dolly drank herself into ill health, which would soon have killed her if she had not, in a drunken fit, shortened the business by fracturing her skull; and, lastly, how she left him a lottery ticket, which he had just sold, lest it should be the cause of fresh imprudence. "You see," added Maurice, "I do not forget all you said to me about lotteries.—Better take good advice late than never. But now, tell me your history."

"No," replied William Deane; "that I shall keep till we are all at dinner; Ellen and you, I and my friend George, who, I hope, has not forgotten me." He was soon convinced that George had not forgotten him, by the joy he showed at seeing him again.

At dinner, William Deane informed them that he was become a rich man, by having made an improvement in the machinery of the cotton-mills, which, after a great deal of perseverance, he had brought to succeed in practice. "When I say that I am a rich man," continued he, "I mean richer than ever I expected to be. I have a share in the cotton-mill, and am worth about two thousand pounds."

"Ay," said Maurice, "you have trusted to your own sense and industry, and not to gaming and lotteries."

"I am heartily rejoiced you have nothing more to do with them," said William Deane: "but all this time you forget that I am your debtor. You lent me five guineas at a season when I had nothing. The books I bought with your money helped me to knowledge, without which I should never have got forward. Now I have a scheme for my little friend George, that will, I hope, turn out to your liking. You say he is an intelligent, honest, industrious lad; and that he understands book-keeping, and writes a good hand: I am sure he is much obliged to you for giving him a good education."

"To his mother, there, he's obliged for it all," said Maurice.

"Without it," continued William Deane, "I might wish him very well; but I could do little or nothing for him. But, as I was going to tell you, that unfortunate man whom you brought to his own door in the hackney-coach to-day, Maurice, is a hosier, who had as good a business as most in the city; but he has ruined himself entirely by gaming. He is considerably in our debt for cotton, and I am to settle accounts with him to-morrow, when he is to give up all his concerns into my hands, in behalf of his brother, who has commissioned me to manage the business, and dissolve the partnership; as he cannot hazard himself, even out of friendship for a brother, with one that has taken to gaming. Now my friend, the elder Fulham, is a steady man, and is in want of a good lad for an apprentice. With your leave, I will speak to him, and get him to take George; and as to the fee, I will take care and settle that for you. I am glad I have found you all out at last. No thanks, pray. Recollect, I am only paying my old debts."

As William Deane desired to have no thanks, we shall omit the recital of those which he received, both in words and looks. We have only to inform our readers, further, that George was bound apprentice to the hosier; that he behaved as well as might be expected from his excellent education; that Maurice continued, in Mr. Belton's service, to conduct himself so as to secure the confidence and esteem of his master; and that he grew fonder and fonder of home, and of Ellen, who enjoyed the delightful reflection that she had effected the happiness of her husband and her son.

May equal happiness attend every such good wife and mother! And may every man, who, like Maurice, is tempted to be a gamester, reflect that a good character, and domestic happiness, which cannot be won in any lottery, are worth more than the five thousand, or even the ten thousand pounds prize, let any Mrs. Dolly in Christendom say what she will to the contrary.

CHAPTER I

There are two sorts of content: one is connected with exertion, the other with habits of indolence; the first is a virtue, the second a vice. Examples of both may be found in abundance in Ireland. There you may sometimes see a man in sound health submitting day after day to evils which a few hours' labour would remedy; and you are provoked to hear him say, "It will do well enough for me. Didn't it do for my father before me? I can make a shift with things for my time: any how, I'm content."

This kind of content is indeed the bane of industry. But instances of a different sort may be found, in various of the Irish peasantry. Amongst them we may behold men struggling with adversity with all the strongest powers of mind and body; and supporting irremediable evils with a degree of cheerful fortitude which must excite at once our pity and admiration.

In a pleasant village in the province of Leinster there lives a family of the name of Gray. Whether or not they are any way related to Old Robin Gray, history does not determine; but it is very possible that they are, because they came, it is said, originally from the north of Ireland, and one of the sons is actually called Robin. Leaving this point, however, in the obscurity which involves the early history of the most ancient and illustrious families, we proceed to less disputable and perhaps more useful facts. It is well known, that is, by all his neighbours, that farmer Gray began life with no very encouraging prospects: he was the youngest of a large family, and the portion of his father's property that fell to his share was but just sufficient to maintain his wife and three children. At his father's death, he had but 100l. in ready money, and he was obliged to go into a poor mud-walled cabin, facing the door of which there was a green pool of stagnant water; and before the window, of one pane, a dunghill that, reaching to the thatch of the roof, shut out the light, and filled the house with the most noisome smell. The ground sloped towards the house door; so that in rainy weather, when the pond was full, the kitchen was overflowed; and at all times the floor was so damp and soft, that the print of the nails of brogues was left in it wherever the wearer set down his foot. To be sure these nail-marks could scarcely be seen, except just near the door or where the light of the fire immediately shone; because, elsewhere, the smoke was so thick, that the pig might have been within a foot of you without your seeing him. The former inhabitants of this mansion had, it seems, been content without a chimney: and, indeed, almost without a roof; the couples and purlins of the roof having once given way, had never been repaired, and swagged down by the weight of the thatch, so that the ends threatened the wigs of the unwary.

The prospect without doors was scarcely more encouraging to our hero than the scene within: the farm consisted of about forty acres; and the fences of the grazing-land were so bad, that the neighbours' cattle took possession of it frequently by day, and always by night. The tillage-ground had been so ill managed by his predecessor, that the land was what is called quite out of heart.

If farmer Gray had also been out of heart, he and his family might at this hour have been beggars. His situation was thought desperate by many of his neighbours; and a few days after his father's decease, many came to condole with him. Amongst the rest was "easy Simon;" or, as some called him, "soft Simon," on account of his unresisting disposition, and contented, or, as we should rather name it, reckless temper. He was a sort of a half or a half quarter gentleman, had a small patrimony of a hundred or a hundred and fifty pounds a year, a place in the excise worth fifty more, and a mill, which might have been worth another hundred annually, had it not been suffered to stand still for many a year.

"Wheugh! Wheugh! What a bustle we are in! and what a world of trouble is here!" cried Simon, when he came to Gray's house, and found him on the ladder taking off the decayed thatch; whilst one of his sons, a lad of about fourteen, was hard at work filling a cart from the dunghill, which blockaded the window. His youngest son, a boy of twelve, with a face and neck red with heat, was making a drain to carry off the water from the green pond; and Rose, the sister, a girl of ten years old, was collecting the ducks, which her mother was going to carry to her landlord's to sell.

"Wheugh! Wheugh! Wheugh! Why what a world of bustle and trouble is here! Troth, Jemmy Gray, you're in a bad way, sure enough! Poor cratur! Poor cratur!"

"No man," replied Gray, "deserves to be called poor, that has his health, and the use of his limbs. Besides," continued he, "have not I a good wife and good children: and, with those blessings, has not a man sufficient reason to be content?"

"Ay, to be sure: that's the only way to get through this world," said Simon; "whatever comes, just to take it easy, and be content. Content and a warm chimney corner is all in all, according to my notion."

"Yes, Simon," said Gray, laughing; "but your kind of content would never do for me. Content, that sits down in the chimney corner, and does nothing but smoke his pipe, will soon have the house about his ears; and then what will become of Content?"

"Time enough to think of that when it comes," said Simon: "fretting never propped a house yet; and if it did, I would rather see it fall than fret."

"But could not you prop the house," said Gray, "without fretting?"

"Is it by putting my shoulders to it?" said Simon. "My shoulders have never been used to hard work, and don't like it any way. As long as I can eat, drink, and sleep, and have a coat to my back, what matter for the rest? Let the world go as it will, I'm content. Shoo! Shoo! The button is off the neck of this great coat of mine, and how will I keep it on? A pin sure will do as well as a button, and better. Mrs. Gray, or Miss Rose, I'll thank you kindly for a pin."

He stuck the pin in the place of the button, to fasten the great coat round his throat, and walked off: it pricked his chin about a dozen times before the day was over; but he forgot the next day, and the next, and the next, to have the button sewed on. He was content to make shift, as he called it, with the pin. This is precisely the species of content which leads to beggary.

Not such the temper of our friend Gray. Not an inconvenience that he could remedy, by industry or ingenuity, was he content to endure; but necessary evils he bore with unshaken patience and fortitude. His house was soon new roofed and new thatched; the dunghill was removed, and spread over that part of his land which most wanted manure; the putrescent water of the standing pool was drained off, and fertilized a meadow; and the kitchen was never again overflowed in rainy weather, because the labour of half a day made a narrow trench which carried off the water. The prints of the shoe-nails were no longer visible in the floor; for the two boys trod dry mill seeds into the clay, and beat the floor well, till they rendered it quite hard and even. The rooms also were cleared of smoke, for Gray built a chimney; and the kitchen window, which had formerly been stuffed up, when the wind blew too hard, with an old or new hat, was glazed. There was now light in the house. Light! the great friend of cleanliness and order. The pig could now no longer walk in and out, unseen and unreproved; he ceased to be an inmate of the kitchen.

The kitchen was indeed so altered from what it had been during the reign of the last master, that he did not know it again. It was not in the least like a pig-sty. The walls were whitewashed; and shelves were put up, on which clean wooden and pewter utensils were ranged. There were no heaps of forlorn rubbish in the corners of the room; nor even an old basket, or a blanket, or a cloak, or a great coat thrown down, just for a minute, out of the girl's way. No: Rose was a girl who always put every thing in its place; and she found it almost as easy to hang a coat, or a cloak, upon a peg, as to throw it down on the floor. She thought it as convenient to put the basket and turf-kish out of her way, when her brothers had brought in the potatoes and fuel, as to let them lie in the middle of the kitchen, to be stumbled over by herself and her mother, or to be gnawed and clawed by a cat and dog. These may seem trifles unworthy the notice of the historian; but trifles such as these contribute much to the comfort of a poor family, and therefore deserve a place in their simple annals.

It was a matter of surprise and censure to some of farmer Gray's neighbours, that he began by laying out it could not be less than ten pounds (a great sum for him!) on his house and garden at the first setting out; when, to be sure, the land would have paid him better if the money had been laid out there. And why could not he make a shift to live on in the old cabin, for a while, as others had done before his time well enough? A poor man should be contented with a poor house. Where was the use, said they, of laying out the good ready penny in a way that would bring nothing in?

Farmer Gray calculated that he could not have laid out his money to better advantage; for by these ten pounds he had probably saved his wife, his children, and himself, from a putrid fever, or from the rheumatism. The former inhabitants of this house, who had been content to live with the dunghill close to the window, and the green pool overflowing the kitchen, and the sharp wind blowing in through the broken panes, had in the course of a few years lost their health. The father of the family had been crippled by the rheumatism, two children died of the fever, and the mother had such an inflammation in her eyes that she could not see to work, spin, or do anything. Now the whole that was lost by the family sickness, the doctor's bill, and the burying of the two children, all together, came in three years to nearly three times ten pounds. Therefore Mr. Gray was, if we only consider money, a very prudent man. What could he or any body do without health? Money is not the first thing to be thought of in this world; for there are many things that money cannot buy, and health is one of them. "Health can make money, but money cannot make health," said our wise farmer. "And then, for the value of a few shillings, say pounds, we have light to see what we are doing, and shelves, and a press to hold our clothes in. Why now, this will be all so much saved to us, by and by; for the clothes will last the longer, and the things about us will not go to wreck; and when I and the boys can come home after our day's work to a house like this, we may be content."

Having thus ensured, as far as it was in his power, health, cleanliness, and comfort in his house, our hero and his sons turned their attention to the farm. They set about to repair all the fences; for the boys, though they were young, were able to help their father in the farm: they were willing to work, and happy to work with him. John, the eldest lad, could set potatoes, and Robin was able to hold the plough: so that Gray did not hire any servant-boy to help him; nor did Mrs. Gray hire a maid. "Rose and I," said she, "can manage very well to look after the two cows, and milk them, and make the butter, and get something too by our spinning. We must do without servants, and may be happy and content to serve ourselves."

"Times will grow better; that is, we shall make them better every year: we must have the roughest first," said Gray.

The first year, to be sure, it was rough enough; and, do what they could, they could not do more than make the rent of the farm, which rent amounted to forty pounds. The landlord was a Mr. Hopkins, agent to a gentleman who resided in England. Mr. Hopkins insisted upon having the rent paid up to the day, and so it was. Gray contented himself by thinking that this was perhaps for the best. "When the rent is once paid," said he, "it cannot be called for again, and I am in no man's power; that's a great comfort. To be sure, if the half year's rent was left in my hands for a few months, it might have been of service: but it is better not to be under an obligation to such a man as Mr. Hopkins, who would make us pay for it in some shape or other, when we least expected it."

Mr. Hopkins was what is called in Ireland a middle-man; one that takes land from great proprietors, to set it again at an advanced, and often an exorbitant, price, to the poor. Gray had his land at a fair rent, because it was not from Mr. Hopkins his father had taken the lease, but from the gentleman to whom this man was agent. Mr, Hopkins designed to buy the land which Gray farmed, and he therefore wished to make it appear as unprofitable as possible to his landlord, who, living in England, knew but little of his own estate. "If these Grays don't pay the rent," said he to his driver, "pound their cattle, and sell at the end of eight days. If they break and run away, I shall have the land clear, and may make a compliment of it to tenants and friends of my own, after it comes into my hands." He was rather disappointed, when the rent was paid to the day. "But," said he, "it won't be so next year; the man is laying out his money on the ground, on draining and fencing, and that won't pay suddenly. We'll leave the rent in his hands for a year or so, and bring down an ejectment upon him, if he once gets into our power, as he surely will. Then, all that he has done to the house will be so much in my way. What a fool he was to lay out his money so!"

It happened, however, that the money which Gray had laid out in making his house comfortable and neat was of the greatest advantage to him, and at a time and in a way which he least expected. His cottage was within sight of the high road, that led to a town from which it was about a mile distant. A regiment of English arrived, to be quartered in the town; and the wives of some of the soldiers came a few hours after their husbands. One of these women, a sergeant's wife, was taken suddenly in labour, before they reached the town; and the soldier who conducted the baggage-cart in which she was, drew up to the first amongst a row of miserable cabins that were by the road-side, to ask the people if they would give her lodging: but the sick woman was shocked at the sight of the smoke and dirt of this cabin, and begged to be carried on to the neat whitewashed cottage that she saw at a little distance. This was Gray's house.

His wife received the stranger with the greatest kindness and hospitality; she was able to offer her a neat bed, and a room that was perfectly dry and clean. The sergeant's wife was brought to bed soon after her arrival, and remained with Mrs. Gray till she recovered her strength. She was grateful for the kindness that was shown to her by Mrs. Gray; and so was her husband, the sergeant. He came one evening to the cottage, and in his blunt English fashion said, "Mr. Gray, you know I, or my wife, which is the same thing, have cause to be obliged to you, or your wife, which comes also to the same thing: now one good turn deserves another. Our colonel has ordered me, I being quarter-master, to sell off by auction some of the cast horses belonging to the regiment: now I have bought in the best for a trifle, and have brought him here, with me, to beg you'll accept of him, by way some sort of a return for the civilities you and your wife, that being, as I said, the same thing, showed me and mine."

Gray replied he was obliged to him for this offer of the horse, but that he could not think of accepting it; that he was very glad his wife had been able to show any kindness or hospitality to a stranger; but that, as they did not keep a public-house, they could not take any thing in the way of payment.

The sergeant was more and more pleased by farmer Gray's generosity. "Well," said he, "I heard, before I came to Ireland, that the Irish were the most hospitable people on the face of the earth; and so I find it come true, and I shall always say so, wherever I'm quartered hereafter. And now do pray answer me, is there any the least thing I can ever do to oblige you? for, if the truth must be told of me, I don't like to lie. under an obligation, any more than another, where I can help it."

"To show you that I do not want to lay you under one," said Gray, "I'll tell you how you can do as much for me, and ten times as much, as I have done for you; and this without hurting yourself or any of your employers a penny."

"Say how, and it shall be done."

"By letting me have the dung of the barracks, which will make my land and me rich, without making you poorer; for I'll give you the fair price, whatever it is. I don't ask you to wrong your employers of a farthing."

The sergeant promised this should be done, and rejoiced that he had found some means of serving his friend. Gray covered ten acres with the manure brought from the barracks; and the next year these acres were in excellent heart. This was sufficient for the grazing of ten cows: he had three, and he bought seven more; and with what remained of his hundred pounds, after paying for the cows, he built a shed and a cow-house. His wife, and daughter Rose, who was now about fourteen, were excellent managers of the dairy. They made, by butter and butter-milk, about four pounds each cow within the year. The butter they salted and took to market, at the neighbouring town; the butter-milk they sold to the country people, who, according to the custom of the neighbourhood, came to the house for it. Besides this, they reared five calves, which, at a year old, they sold for fifteen guineas and a half. The dairy did not, however, employ all the time of this industrious mother and daughter; they had time for spinning, and by this cleared six guineas. They also made some little matter by poultry; but that was only during the first year: afterwards Mr. Hopkins sent notice that they must pay all the duty-fowl, and duty-geese, and turkeys, charged in the lease, or compound with him by paying two guineas a year. This gentleman had many methods of squeezing money out of poor tenants; and he was not inclined to spare the Grays, whose farm he now more than ever wished to possess, because its value had been considerably increased, by the judicious industry of the farmer and his sons.

[Footnote: See a very curious anecdote in the Statistical Survey of the Queen's County.]

Young as they were, both farmer Gray's sons had a share in these improvements. The eldest had drained a small field, which used to be called the rushy field, from its having been quite covered with rushes. Now there was not a rush to be found upon it, and his father gave him the profits of the field, and said that it should be called by his name. Robin, the youngest son, had, by his father's advice, tried a little experiment, which many of his neighbours ridiculed at first, and admired at last. The spring, which used to supply the duck-pond, that often flooded the house, was at the head of a meadow, that sloped with a fall sufficient to let the water run off. Robin flooded the meadow at the proper season of the year, and it produced afterwards a crop such as never had been seen there before. His father called this meadow Robin's meadow, and gave him the value of the hay that was made upon it.

"Now, my dear boys," said this good father, "you have made a few guineas for yourselves; and here are a few more for you, all that I can spare: let us see what you can do with this money. I shall take a pride in seeing you get forward by your own industry and cleverness; I don't want you to slave for me all your best days; but shall always be ready, as a father should be, to give you a helping hand."

The sons had scarcely a word in answer to this, for their hearts were full; but that night, when they were by themselves, one said to the other, "Brother, did you see Jack Reel's letter to his father? They say he has sent home ten guineas to him. Is there any truth in it, think you?"

"Yes; I saw the letter, and a kinder never was written from son to father. The ten guineas I saw paid into the old man's hand; and, at that same minute, I wished it was I that was doing the same by my own father."

[Footnote: This is fact.]

"That was just what I was thinking of, when I asked you if you saw the letter. Why, Jack Reel had nothing, when he went abroad with the army to Egypt, last year. Well, I never had a liking myself to follow the drum: but it's almost enough to tempt one to it. If I thought I could send home ten guineas to my father, I would 'list to-morrow."

"That would not be well done of you, Robin," said John; "for my father would rather have you, a great deal, than the ten guineas, I am sure: to say nothing of my poor mother, and Rose, and myself, who would be sorry enough to hear of your being knocked on the head, as is the fate, sooner or later, of them that follow the army. I would rather be any of the trades that hurt nobody, and do good to a many along with myself, as father said t'other day. Then, what a man makes so, he makes with a safe conscience, and he can enjoy it."

"You are right, John, and I was wrong to talk of 'listing," said Robin; "but it was only Jack Reel's letter, and the ten guineas sent to his father, that put it into my head. I may make as much for my father by staying at home, and minding my business. So now, good night to you; I'll go to sleep, and we can talk more about it all to-morrow."

The next morning, as these two youths were setting potatoes for the family, and considering to what they should turn their hands when the potatoes were all set, they were interrupted by a little gossoon, who came running up as hard as he could, crying, "Murder! Murder! Simon O'Dougherty wants you. For the love of God, cross the bog in all haste, to help pull out his: horse, that has tumbled into the old tan-pit, there beyond, in the night!"

The two brothers immediately followed the boy, carrying with them a rope and a halter, as they guessed that soft Simon would not have either. They found him wringing his hands beside the tan-pit, in which his horse lay smothering. A little ragged boy was tugging at the horse's head, with a short bit of hay-rope. "Oh, murder! Murder! What will I do for a halter? Sure the horse will be lost, for want of a halter; and where in the wide world will I look for one?" cried Simon, without stirring one inch from the spot. "Oh, the blessing of Heaven be with you, lads," continued he, turning at the sight of the Grays; "you've brought us a halter. But see! It's just over with the poor beast. All the world put together will not get him alive out of that. I must put up with the loss, and be content. He cost me fifteen good guineas, and he could leap better than any horse in the county. Oh, what a pity on him! What a pity! But, take it easy; that's all we have for it! Poor cratur! Poor cratur!"

Without listening to Simon's lamentations, the active lads, by the help of Simon and the two boys, pulled the horse out of the pit. The poor animal was nearly exhausted by struggling: but, after some time, he stretched himself, and, by degrees, recovered sufficiently to stand. One of his legs, however, was so much hurt that he could scarcely walk; and Simon said he would surely go lame for life.

"Who now would ever have thought of his straying into such an ugly place of all others?" continued he. "I know, for my share, the spot is so overgrown with grass and rubbish, of one kind or other, and it's so long since any of the tanning business was going on here, in my uncle O'Haggarty's time, that I quite forgot there were such things as tan-pits, or any manner of pits, in my possession; and I wish these had been far enough off before my own little famous Sir Hyacinth O'Brien had strayed into them, laming himself for life, like a blockhead. For the case was this: I came home late last night, not as sober as a judge, and, finding no one up but the girl, I gave her the horse to put into the stable, and she forgot the door after her, which wants a lock; and there being but a scanty feed of oats, owing to the boy's negligence, and no halter to secure the beast, my poor Sir Hyacinth strayed out here, as ill luck would have it, into the tan-pit. Bad luck to my uncle O'Haggarty, that had the tan-yard here at all! He might have lived as became him, without dirtying his hands with the tanning of dirty hides."

"I was just going," said John Gray, "to comfort you, Simon, for the laming of your horse, by observing that, if you had your tan-yard in order again, you could soon make up the price of another horse."

"Ohoo! I would not be bothered with anything of the kind. There's the mill of Rosanna there, beyond, was the plague of my life, till it stopped; and I was glad to have fairly done with it. Them that come after me may set it a-going again, and welcome. I have enough just to serve my time, and am content any way."

"But, if you could get a fair rent for the tan-yard, would you let it?" said John.

"To that I should make no objection in life; provided I had no trouble with it," replied Simon.

"And if you could get somebody to keep the mill of Rosanna going, without giving you any trouble, you would not object to that, would you?" said Robin.

"Not I, to be sure," replied Simon, laughing. "Whatever God sends, be it more or less, I am content. But I would not have you think me a fool, for all I talk so easy about the matter; I know very well what I might have got for the mill some years ago, when first it stopped, if I would have let it to the man that proposed for it; but though he was as substantial a tenant as you could see, yet he affronted me once, at the last election, by calling a freeholder of mine over the coals; and so I was proud of an opportunity to show him I did not forget. So I refused to let him the mill on any terms; and I made him a speech for his pride to digest at the same time. 'Mr. Hopkins,' said I, 'the lands of Rosanna have been in my family these two hundred years and upwards; and though, now-a-days, many men think that every thing is to be done for money, and though you, Mr. Hopkins, have made as much money as most men could in the same time,—all which I don't envy you,—yet I must make bold to tell you, that the lands of Rosanna, or any part or parcel thereof, is what you'll never have whilst I'm alive, Mr. Hopkins, for love or money.' The spirit of the O'Doughertys was up within me; and though all the world calls me easy Simon, I have my own share of proper spirit. These mushroom money-makers, that start up from the very dirt under one's feet, I can't for my part swallow them. Now I should be happy to give you a lease of the mill of Rosanna, after refusing Hopkins; for you and your father before you, lads, have been always very civil to me. My tan-pits and all I am ready to talk to you about, and thank you for pulling my horse out for me this morning. Will you walk up and look at the mill? I would attend you myself, but must go to the farrier about Sir Hyacinth's leg, instead of standing talking here any longer. Good morning to you kindly. The girl will give you the key of the mill, and show you everything, the same as myself."

Simon gathered his great coat about him, and walked away to the farrier, whilst the two brothers rejoiced that they should see the mill without hearing him talk the whole time. Simon, having nothing to do all day long but to talk, was an indefatigable gossip. When the lands of Rosanna were in question, or when his pride was touched, he was terribly fluent.

CHAPTER II

Upon examining the mill, which was a common oat-mill, John Gray found that the upper mill-stone was lodged upon the lower; and that this was all which prevented the mill from going. No other part of it was damaged or out of repair. As to the tan-yard, it was in great disorder; but it was very conveniently situated; was abundantly supplied with water on one side, and had an oak copse at the back, so that tan could readily be procured. It is true that the bark of these oak trees, which had been planted by his careful uncle O'Haggarty, had been much damaged since Simon came into possession; for he had, with his customary negligence, suffered cattle to get amongst them. He had also, to supply himself with ready money, occasionally cut down a great deal of the best timber before it arrived at its full growth; and at this time the Grays found every tree of tolerable size marked for destruction with the initials of Simon O'Dougherty's name.

Before they said anything more about the mill or the tan-yard to Simon, these prudent brothers consulted their father: he advised them to begin cautiously, by offering to manage the mill and the tan-yard, during the ensuing season, for Simon, for a certain share in the profits; and then, if they should find the business likely to succeed, they might take a lease of the whole. Simon willingly made this agreement; and there was no danger in dealing with him, because, though careless and indolent, he was honest, and would keep his engagements. It was settled that John and Robin should have the power, at the end of the year, either to hold or give up all concern in the mill and tan-yard; and, in the mean time, they were to manage the business for Simon, and to have such a share in the profits as would pay them reasonably for their time and labour.

They succeeded beyond their expectations in the management of the mill and tan-yard during their year of probation; and Simon, at the end of that time, was extremely glad to give them a long lease of the premises, upon their paying him down, by way of fine, the sum of 150l. This sum their father, who had good credit, and who could give excellent security upon his farm, which was now in a flourishing condition, raised for them; and they determined to repay him the money by regular yearly portions out of their profits.

Success did not render these young men presumptuous or negligent: they went on steadily with business, were contented to live frugally and work hard for some years. Many of the sons of neighbouring tradesmen and farmers, who were able perhaps to buy a horse or two, or three good coats in a year, and who set up for gentlemen, and spent their days in hunting, shooting, or cockfighting, thought that the Grays were poor-spirited fellows for sticking so close to business. They prophesied that, even when these brothers should have made a fortune, they would not have the liberality to spend or enjoy it; but this prediction was not verified. The Grays had not been brought up to place their happiness merely in the scraping together pounds, shillings, and pence; they valued money for money's worth, not for money's sake; and, amongst the pleasures it could purchase, they thought that of contributing to the happiness of their parents and friends the greatest. When they had paid their father the hundred and fifty pounds he had advanced, their next object was to build a neat cottage for him, near the wood and mill of Rosanna, on a beautiful spot, upon which they had once heard him say that he should like to have a house.

We mentioned that Mr. Hopkins, the agent, had a view to this farm; and that he was desirous of getting rid of the Grays: but this he found no easy matter to accomplish, because the rent was always punctually paid. There was no pretence for driving, even for the duty-fowls; Mrs. Gray always had them ready at the proper time. Mr. Hopkins was farther provoked by seeing the rich improvements which our farmer made every year on his land: his envy, which could be moved by the meanest objects of gain, was continually excited by his neighbour's successful industry. To-day he envied him his green meadows, and to-morrow the crocks of butter, packed on the car for Dublin. Farmer Gray's ten cows, which regularly passed by Mr. Hopkins's window morning and evening, were a sight that often spoiled his breakfast and supper: but that which grieved this envious man the most was the barrack manure; he would stand at his window, and, with a heavy heart, count the car loads that went by to Gray's farm.

Once he made an attempt to ruin Gray's friend, the sergeant, by accusing him secretly of being bribed to sell the barrack manure to Gray for less than he had been offered for it by others: but the officer to whom Mr. Hopkins made this complaint was fortunately a man who did not like secret informations: he publicly inquired into the truth of the matter, and the sergeant's honesty and Mr. Hopkins's meanness were clearly proved and contrasted. The consequence of this malicious interference was beneficial to Gray; for the officer told the story to the colonel of the regiment which was next quartered in the town, and he to the officer who succeeded him; so that year after year Mr. Hopkins applied in vain for the barrack manure. Farmer Gray had always the preference, and the hatred of Mr. Hopkins knew no bounds; that is, no bounds but the letter of the law, of which he was ever mindful, because lawsuits are expensive.

At length, however, he devised a legal mode of annoying his enemy. Some land belonging to Mr. Hopkins lay between Gray's farm and the only bog in the neighbourhood: now he would not permit Mr. Gray, or any body belonging to him, to draw turf upon his bog-road; and he absolutely forbade his own wretched tenants to sell turf to the object of his envy. By these means, he flattered himself he should literally starve the enemy out of house and home.

Things were in this situation when John and Robin Gray determined to build a house for their father at Rosanna. They made no secret to him of their intentions; for they did not want to surprise but to please him, and to do every thing in the manner that would be most convenient to him and their mother. Their sister, Rose, was in all their counsels; and it had been for the last three years one of her chief delights to go, after her day's work was done, to the mill at Rosanna, to see how her brothers were going on. How happy are those families where there is no envy or jealousy; but in which each individual takes an interest in the prosperity of the whole! Farmer Gray was heartily pleased with the gratitude and generosity of his boys, as he still continued to call them; though, by-the-bye, John was now three-and-twenty, and his brother only two years younger.

"My dear boys," said he, "nothing could be more agreeable to me and your mother than to have a snug cottage near you both, on the very spot which you say I pitched upon two years ago. This cabin that we now live in, after all I have tried to do to prop it up, and notwithstanding all Rose does to keep it neat and clean withinside, is but a crazy sort of a place. We are able now to have a better house, and I shall be glad to be out of the reach of Mr. Hopkins's persecution. Therefore, let us set about and build the new house. You shall contribute your share, my boys; but only a share: mind, I say only a share. And I hope next year to contribute my share towards building a house for each of you: it is time you should think of marrying, and settling: it is no bad thing to have a house ready for a bride. We shall have quite a little colony of our own at Rosanna. Who knows but I may live to see my grand-children, ay, and my great-grand-children, settled there all round me, industrious and contented?"

Good-will is almost as expeditious and effectual as Aladdin's lamp:—the new cottage for farmer Gray was built at Rosanna, and he took possession of it the ensuing spring. They next made a garden, and furnished it with all sorts of useful vegetables and some pretty flowers. Rose had great pleasure in taking care of this garden. Her brothers also laid out a small green lawn before the door; and planted the boundaries with white-thorn, crab-trees, lilacs, and laburnums. The lawn sloped down to the water-side; and the mill and copse behind it were seen from the parlour windows. A prettier cottage, indeed so pretty a one, was never before seen in this county.

But what was better far than the pretty cottage, or the neat garden, or the green lawn, or the white-thorn, the crab-trees, the lilacs, and the laburnums, was the content that smiled amongst them.

Many who have hundreds and thousands are miserable, because they still desire more; or rather because they know not what they would have. For instance, Mr. Hopkins, the rich Mr. Hopkins, who had scraped together in about fifteen years above twenty thousand, some said thirty thousand pounds, had never been happy for a single day, either whilst he was making this fortune or when he had made it; for he was of an avaricious, discontented temper. The more he had, the more he desired. He could not bear the prosperity of his neighbours; and if his envy made him industrious, yet it at the same time rendered him miserable. Though he was what the world calls a remarkably fortunate man, yet the feelings of his own mind prevented him from enjoying his success. He had no wife, no children, to share his wealth. He would not marry, because a wife is expensive; and children are worse than taxes. His whole soul was absorbed in the love of gain. He denied himself not only the comforts but the common necessaries of life. He was alone in the world. He was conscious that no human being loved him. He read his history in the eyes of all his neighbours.

It was known that he had risen upon the ruin of others; and the higher he had risen, the more conspicuous became the faults of his character. Whenever any man grew negligent of his affairs, or by misfortune was reduced to distress, Hopkins was at hand to take advantage of his necessities. His first approaches were always made under the semblance of friendship; but his victims soon repented their imprudent confidence when they felt themselves in his power. Unrestrained by a sense of honour or the feelings of humanity, he felt no scruple in pursuing his interest to the very verge of what the law would call fraud. Even his own relations complained that he duped them without scruple; and none but strangers to his character, or persons compelled by necessity, would have any dealings with this man. Of what advantage to him, or to any one else, were the thousands he had accumulated?

It may be said that such beings are necessary in society; that their industry is productive; and that, therefore, they ought to be preferred to the idle, unproductive members of the community: but wealth and happiness are not the same things. Perhaps, at some future period, enlightened politicians may think the happiness of nations more important than their wealth. In this point of view, they would consider all the members of society, who are productive of happiness, as neither useless nor despicable; and, on the contrary, they would contemn and discourage those who merely accumulate money, without enjoying or dispensing happiness. But some centuries must probably elapse before such a philosophic race of politicians can arise. In the mean time, let us go on with our story.

CHAPTER III

Mr. Hopkins was enraged when he found that his expected victim escaped his snares. He saw the pretty cottage rise, and the mill of Rosanna work, in despite of his malevolence. He long brooded over his malice in silence. As he stood one day on the top of a high mount on his own estate, from which he had a view of the surrounding country, his eyes fixed upon the little paradise in the possession of his enemies. He always called those his enemies of whom he was the enemy: this is no uncommon mistake, in the language of the passions.

"The Rosanna mill shall be stopped before this day twelvemonth, or my name is not Hopkins," said he to himself. "I have sworn vengeance against those Grays; but I will humble them to the dust, before I have done with them. I shall never sleep in peace till I have driven those people from the country."

It was, however, no easy matter to drive from the country such inoffensive inhabitants. The first thing Mr. Hopkins resolved upon was to purchase from Simon O'Dougherty the field adjoining to that in which the mill stood. The brook flowed through this field, and Mr. Hopkins saw, with malicious satisfaction, that he could at a small expense turn the course of the stream, and cut off the water from the mill.

Poor Simon by this time had reduced himself to a situation in which his pride was compelled to yield to pecuniary considerations. Within the last three years, his circumstances had been materially changed. Whilst he was a bachelor, his income had been sufficient to maintain him in idleness. Soft Simon, however, at last, took it into his head to marry; or rather a cunning damsel, who had been his mistress for some years, took it into her head to make him marry. She was skilled in the arts both of wheedling and scolding: to resist these united powers was too much to be expected from a man of Simon's easy temper.

He argued thus with himself:—"She has cost me more as she is than if she had been my wife twice over; for she has no interest in looking after any thing belonging to me, but only just living on from day to day, and making the most for herself and her children. And the children, too, all in the same way, snatching what they could make sure of for themselves. Now, if I make her my lawful wife, as she desires, the property will be hers, as well as mine; and it will be her interest to look after all. She is a stirring, notable woman, and will save me a world of trouble, and make the best of every thing for her children's sake; and they, being then all acknowledged by me, will make my interest their own, as she says; and, besides, this is the only way left me to have peace."

To avoid the cares and plagues of matrimony, and that worst of plagues a wife's tongue, Simon first was induced to keep a mistress, and now to silence his mistress, he made her his wife. She assured him, that, till she was his lawful lady, she never should have peace or quietness; nor could she, in conscience, suffer him to have a moment's rest.

Simon married her, to use his own phrase, out of hand: hut the marriage was only the beginning of new troubles. The bride had hordes and clans of relations, who came pouring in from all quarters to pay their respects to Mrs. O'Dougherty. Her good easy man could not shut his doors against any one: the O'Doughertys were above a hundred years, ay, two hundred years ago, famous for hospitality; and it was incumbent upon Simon O'Dougherty to keep up the honour of the family. His four children were now to be maintained in idleness; for they, like their father, had an insurmountable aversion to business. The public opinion of Simon suddenly changed. Those who were any way related to the O'Doughertys, and who dreaded that he and his children should apply to them for pecuniary assistance, began the cry against him of, "What a shame it is that the man does not do something for himself and his family! How can those expect to be helped who won't help themselves? He is contented, indeed! Yes, and he must soon be contented to sell the lands that have been in the family so long; and then, by and by, he must be content, if he does not bestir himself, to be carried to jail. It is a sin for any one to be content to eat the bread of idleness!"

[Footnote: Essay on Charity Schools.]

These and similar reproaches were uttered often, in our idle hero's presence. They would perhaps have excited him to some sort of exertion, if his friend, Sir Hyacinth O'Brien, had not, in consequence of certain electioneering services, and in consideration of his being one of the best sportsmen in the county, and of Simon's having named a horse after him, procured for him a place of about fifty pounds a year in the revenue. Upon the profits of this place Simon contrived to live, in a shambling sort of way.

How long he might have shuffled on is a problem which must now for ever remain unsolved; for his indolence was not permitted to take its natural course; his ruin was accelerated by the secret operation of an active and malignant power. Mr. Hopkins, who had determined to get that field which joined to Gray's mill, and who well knew that the pride of the O'Doughertys would resist the idea of selling to him any part or parcel of the lands of Rosanna, devised a scheme to reduce Simon to immediate and inextricable distress. Simon was, as it might have been foreseen, negligent in discharging the duties of his office, which was that of a supervisor.

He either did not know, or connived at the practices, of sundry illegal distillers in his neighbourhood. Malicious tongues did not scruple to say that he took money, upon some occasions, from the delinquents; but this he positively denied. Possibly his wife and sons knew more of this matter than he did. They sold certain scraps of paper, called protections, to several petty distillers, whose safest protection would have been Simon's indolence. One of the scraps of paper, to which there was O'Dougherty's signature, fell into the hands of Mr. Hopkins.

That nothing might be omitted to ensure his disgrace, Hopkins sent a person, on whom he could depend, to give Simon notice that there was an illegal still at such a house, naming the house for which the protection was granted. Soft Simon received the information with his customary carelessness, said it was too late to think of going to seize the still that evening, and declared he would have it seized the next day: but the next day he put it off, and the day afterwards he forgot it, and the day after that, he received a letter from the collector of excise, summoning him to answer to an information which had been laid against him for misconduct. In this emergency, he resolved to have recourse to his friend Sir Hyacinth O'Brien, who, he thought, could make interest to screen him from justice. Sir Hyacinth gave him a letter to the collector, who happened to be in the country. Away he went with the letter: he was met on the road by a friend, who advised him to ride as hard after the collector as he could, to overtake him before he should reach Counsellor Quin's, where he was engaged to dine. Counsellor Quin was candidate for the county in opposition to Sir Hyacinth O'Brien; and it was well understood that whomsoever the one favoured the other hated. It behoved Simon, therefore, to overtake the collector before he should be within the enemy's gates. Simon whipped and spurred, and puffed and fretted, but all in vain, for he was mounted upon the horse which, as the reader may remember, fell into the tan-pit. The collector reached Counsellor Quin's long before Simon arrived; and, when he presented Sir Hyacinth's letter, it was received in a manner that showed it came too late. Simon lost his place and his fifty pounds a year: but what he found most trying to his temper were the reproaches of his wife, which were loud, bitter, and unceasing. He knew, from experience, that nothing could silence her but letting her "have all the plea;" so he suffered her to rail till she was quite out of breath, and he very nearly asleep, and then said, "What you have been observing is all very just, no doubt; but since a thing past can't be recalled, and those that are upon the ground, as our proverb says, can go no lower, that's a great comfort; so we may be content."

"Content, in troth! Is it content to live upon potatoes and salt? I, that am your lawful wife! And you, that are an O'Dougherty too, to let your lady be demeaned and looked down upon, as she will be now, even by them that are sprung up from nothing since yesterday. There's Mrs. Gray, over yonder at Rosanna, living on your own land: look at her and look at me! and see what a difference there is!"

"Some difference there surely is," said Simon.

"Some difference there surely is," repeated Mrs. O'Dougherty, raising her voice to the shrillest note of objurgation; for she was provoked by a sigh that escaped Simon, as he pronounced his reply, or rather his acceding sentence. Nothing, in some cases, provokes a female so much as agreeing with her.

"And if there is some difference betwixt me and Mrs. Gray, should be glad to know whose fault that is?"

"So should I, Mrs. O'Dougherty."

"Then I'll tell you, instantly, whose fault it is, Mr. O'Dougherty: the fault is your own, Mr. O'Dougherty. No, the fault is mine, Mr. O'Dougherty, for marrying you, or consorting with you at all. If I had been matched to an active, industrious man, like Mr. Gray, I might have been as well in the world and better than Mrs. Gray; for I should become a fortune better than she, or any of her seed, breed, or generation; and it's a scandal in the face of the world, and all the world says so, it's a scandal to see them Grays flourishing and settling a colony, there at Rosanna, at our expense!"

"Not at our expense, my dear, for you know we made nothing of either tan-yard or mill; and now they pay us 30l. a year, and that punctually too. What should we do without it, now we have lost the place in the revenue? I am sure, I think we were very lucky to get such tenants as the Grays."

"In truth, I think no such thing; for if you had been blessed with the sense of a midge, you might have done all they have done yourself: and then what a different way your lawful wife and family would have been in! I am sure I wish it had pleased the saints above to have married me, when they were about it, to such a man as farmer Gray or his sons."

"As for the sons," said Simon, "they are a little out of the way in point of age, but to farmer Gray I see no objection in life: and if he sees none, and will change wives, I'm sure, Ally, I shall be content."

The sort of composure and dry humour with which Simon made this last speech overcame the small remains of Mrs. O'Dougherty's patience: she burst into a passion of tears; and from this hour, it being now past eleven o'clock at night, from this hour till six in the morning she never ceased weeping, wailing, and upbraiding.

Simon rose from his sleepless bed, saying, "The saints above, as you call them, must take care of you now, Ally, any how; for I'm fairly tired out: so I must go a-hunting or a-shooting with my friend, Sir Hyacinth O'Brien, to recruit my spirits."

The unfortunate Simon found, to his mortification, that his horse was so lame he could scarcely walk. Whilst he was considering where he could borrow a horse, just for the day's hunt, Mr. Hopkins rode into his yard, mounted upon a fine hunter. Though naturally supercilious, this gentleman could stoop to conquer: he was well aware of Simon's dislike to him, but he also knew that Simon was in distress for money. Even the strongest passions of those who involve themselves in pecuniary difficulties must yield to the exigencies of the moment. Easy Simon's indolence had now reduced him to a situation in which his pride was obliged to bend to his interest. Mr. Hopkins had once been repulsed with haughtiness by the representative of the O'Dougherty family, when he offered to purchase some of the family estate; but his proposal was now better timed, and was made with all the address of which he was master. He began by begging Simon to give him his opinion of the horse on which he was mounted, as he knew Mr. O'Dougherty was a particularly good judge of a hunter; and he would not buy it, from Counsellor Quin's groom, without having a skilful friend's advice. Then he asked whether it was true that Simon and the collector had quarrelled, exclaimed against the malice and officiousness of the informer, whoever he might be, and finished by observing that, if the loss of his place put Simon to any inconvenience, there was a ready way of supplying himself with money, by the sale of any of the lands of Rosanna. The immediate want of a horse, and the comparison he made, at this moment, between the lame animal on which he was leaning and the fine hunter upon which Hopkins was mounted, had more effect upon Simon than all the rest. Before they parted, Mr. Hopkins concluded a bargain for the field on which he had set his heart: he obtained it for less than its value by three years' purchase. The hunter was part of the valuable consideration he gave to Simon.

The moment that Hopkins was in possession of this field adjoining to Gray's mill, he began to execute a malignant project which he had long been contriving.

We shall leave him to his operations; matters of higher import claim our attention. One morning, as Rose was on the little lawn before the house door, gathering the first snowdrops of the year, a servant in a handsome livery rode up, and asked if Mr. Gray or any of the family were at home. Her father and brothers were out in the fields, at some distance; but she said she would run and call them. "There is no occasion, Miss," said the servant; "for the business is only to leave these cards for the ladies of the family."

He put two cards into Rose's hand, and galloped off with the air of a man who had a vast deal of business of importance to transact. The cards contained an invitation to an election ball, which Sir Hyacinth O'Brien was going to give to the secondary class of gentry in the county. Rose took the cards to her mother; and whilst they were reading them over for the second time, in came farmer Gray to breakfast. "What have we here, child?" said he, taking up one of the cards. He looked at his wife and daughter with some anxiety for a moment; and then, as if he did not wish to restrain them, turned the conversation to another subject, and nothing was said of the ball till breakfast was over.

Mrs. Gray then bade Rose go and put her flowers into water; and as soon as she was out of the room, said, "My dear, I see you don't like that we should go to this ball; so I am glad I did not say what I thought of it to Rose before you came in: for you must know, I had a mother's foolish vanity about me; and the minute I saw the card, I pictured to myself our Rose dressed like any of the best of the ladies, and looking handsomer than most of them, and every body admiring her! But perhaps the girl is better as she is, having not been bred to be a lady. And yet, now we are as well in the world as many that set up for and are reckoned gentlefolks, why should not our girl take this opportunity of rising a step in life?"

Mrs. Gray spoke with some confusion and hesitation. "My dear," replied farmer Gray, in a gentle yet firm tone, "it is very natural that you, being the mother of such a girl as our Rose, should be proud of her, and eager to show her to the best advantage; but the main point is to make her happy, not to do just what will please our own vanity for the minute. Now I am not at all sure that raising her a step in life, even if we could do it by sending her to this ball, would be for her happiness. Are not we happy as we are—Come in, Rose, love; come in; I should be glad for you to hear what we are saying, and judge for yourself; you are old enough, and wise enough, I am sure. I was going to ask, are not we all happy in the way we live together now?"

"Yes! Oh yes! That we are, indeed," said both the wife and daughter.

"Then should not we be content, and not wish to alter our condition?"

"But to go to only one ball, father, would not alter our condition, would it?" said Rose, timidly.

"If we begin once to set up for gentry, we shall not like to go back again to be what we are now: so, before we begin, we had best consider what we have to gain by a change. We have meat, drink, clothes, and fire: what more could we have, if we were gentry? We have enough to do, and not too much; we are all well pleased with ourselves, and with one another; we have health and good consciences: what more could we have, if we were to set up to be gentry? Or rather, to put the question closer, could we in that case have all these comforts? No, I think not: for, in the first place, we should be straitened for want of money; because a world of baubles, that we don't feel the want of now, would become as necessary to us as our daily bread. We should be ashamed not to have all the things that gentlefolks have; though these don't signify a straw, nor half a straw, in point of any real pleasure they give, still they must be had. Then we should be ashamed of the work by which we must make money to pay for all these nicknacks. John and Robin would blush up to the eyes, then, if they were to be caught by the genteel folks in their mill, heaving up sacks of flour, and covered all over with meal; or if they were to be found, with their arms bare beyond the elbows, in the tan-yard. And you, Rose, would hurry your spinning-wheel out of sight, and be afraid to be caught cooking my dinner. Yet there is no shame in any of these things, and now we are all proud of doing them."

"And long may we be so!" cried Mrs. Gray. "You are right, and I spoke like a foolish woman. Rose, my child, throw these cards into the fire. We are happy, and contented: and if we change, we shall be discontented and unhappy, as so many of what they call our betters are. There! the cards are burnt; now let us think no more about them."

"Rose, I hope, is not disappointed about this ball; are you, my little Rose?" said her father, drawing her towards him, and seating her on his knee.

"There was one reason, father," said Rose, blushing, "there was one reason, and only one, why I wished to have gone to this ball."

"Well, let us hear it. You shall do as you please, I promise you beforehand. But tell us the reason. I believe you have found it somewhere at the bottom of that snow-drop, which you have been examining this last quarter of an hour. Come, let me have a peep," added he, laughing.

"The only reason, papa, is—was, I mean," said Rose.—"But look! Oh, I can't tell you now. See who is coming."

It was Sir Hyacinth O'Brien, in his gig; and with him his English servant, Stafford, whose staid and sober demeanour was a perfect contrast to the dash and bustle of his master's appearance. This was an electioneering visit. Sir Hyacinth was canvassing the county—a business in which he took great delight, and in which he was said to excel. He possessed all the requisite qualifications, and was certainly excited by a sufficiently strong motive; for he knew that, if he should lose his election, he should at the same time lose his liberty, as the privilege of a member of parliament was necessary to protect him from being arrested. He had a large estate, yet he was one of the poorest men in the county; for no matter what a person's fortune may be, if he spend more than his income, he must be poor. Sir Hyacinth O'Brien not only spent more than his income, but desired that his rent-roll should be thought to be at least double what it really was: of course he was obliged to live up to the fortune which he affected to possess; and this idle vanity early in life entangled him in difficulties from which he had never sufficient strength of mind to extricate himself. He was ambitious to be the leading man in his county, studied all the arts of popularity, and found them extremely expensive, and stood a contested election. He succeeded; but his success cost him several thousands. All was to be set to rights by his talents as a public speaker, and these were considerable. He had eloquence, wit, humour, and sufficient assurance to place them all in the fullest light. His speeches in parliament were much admired, and the passion of ambition was now kindled in his mind: he determined to be a leading man in the senate; and whilst he pursued this object with enthusiasm, his private affairs were entirely neglected. Ambition and economy never can agree. Sir Hyacinth, however, found it necessary to the happiness, that is, to the splendour, of his existence, to supply, by some means or other, the want of what he called the paltry, selfish, counterfeit virtue—economy. Nothing less would do than the sacrifice of that which had been once in his estimation the most noble and generous of human virtues,— patriotism. The sacrifice was painful, but he could not avoid making it; because, after living upon five thousand a-year, he could not live upon five hundred. So, from a flaming patriot, he sunk into a pensioned placeman.

He then employed all his powers of wit and sophistry to ridicule the principles which he had abandoned. In short, he affected to glory in a species of political profligacy; and laughed or sneered at public virtue, as if it could only be the madness of enthusiasm, or the meanness of hypocrisy. By the brilliancy of his conversation, and the gaiety of his manners, Sir Hyacinth sometimes succeeded in persuading others that he was in the right; but, alas! there was one person whom he could never deceive, and that was himself. He despised himself, and nothing could make him amends for the self-complacency that he had lost. Without self-approbation, all the luxuries of life are tasteless.

Sir Hyacinth O'Brien, however, was for some years thought, by those who could see only the outward man, to be happy; and it was not till the derangement of his affairs became public that the world began at once to pity and blame him. He had a lucrative place, but he was, or thought himself, obliged to live in a style suited to it; and he was not one shilling the richer for his place. He endeavoured to repair his shattered fortunes by marrying a rich heiress, but the heiress was, or thought herself, obliged to live up to her fortune; and, of course, her husband was not one shilling the richer for his marriage. When Sir Hyacinth was occasionally distressed for money, his agent, who managed all affairs in his absence, borrowed money with as much expedition as possible; and expedition, in matters of business, must, as every body knows, be paid for exorbitantly. There are men who, upon such terms, will be as expeditious in lending money as extravagance and ambition united can desire. Mr. Hopkins was one of these: and he was the money-lender who supplied the baronet's real and imaginary wants. Sir Hyacinth did not know the extreme disorder of his own affairs, till a sudden dissolution of parliament obliged him to prepare for the expense of a new election. When he went into the country, he was at once beset with duns and constituents who claimed from him favours and promises. Miserable is the man who courts popularity, if he be not rich enough to purchase what he covets.

Our baronet endeavoured to laugh off with a good grace his apostasy from the popular party; and whilst he could laugh at the head of a plentiful table, he could not fail to find many who would laugh with him; but there was a strong party formed against him in the county. Two other candidates were his competitors; one of them was Counsellor Quin, a man of vulgar manners and mean abilities, but yet one who could drink and cajole electors full as well as Sir Hyacinth, with all his wit and elegance. The other candidate, Mr. Molyneux, was still more formidable; not as an electioneerer, but as a man of talents and unimpeached integrity, which had been successfully exerted in the service of his country. He was no demagogue, but the friend of justice and of the poor, whom he would not suffer to be oppressed by the hand of power, or persecuted by the malice of party spirit. A large number of grateful independent constituents united to support this gentleman. Sir Hyacinth O'Brien had reason to tremble for his fate; it was to him a desperate game. He canvassed the county with the most keen activity; and took care to engage in his interest all those underlings who delight in galloping round the country to electioneer, and who think themselves paid by the momentary consequence they enjoy, and the bustle they create.

Amongst these busy-bodies was Simon O'Dougherty: indolent in all his own concerns, he was remarkably active in managing the affairs of others. His home being now insufferable to him, he was glad to stroll about the country; and to him Sir Hyacinth O'Brien left all the dirty work of the canvass. Soft Simon had reduced himself to the lowest class of stalkoes or walking gentlemen, as they are termed; men who have nothing to do, and no fortune to support them, but who style themselves esquire; and who, to use their own mode of expression, are jealous of that title, and of their claims to family antiquity. Sir Hyacinth O'Brien knew at once how to flatter Simon's pride, and to lure him on by promises. Soft Simon believed that the baronet, if he gained his election, would procure him some place equivalent to that of which he had been lately deprived. Upon the faith of this promise, Simon worked harder for his patron than he ever was known to do upon any previous occasion; and he was not deficient in that essential characteristic of an electioneerer, boasting. He carried this habit sometimes rather too far, for he not only boasted so as to bully the opposite party, but so as to deceive his friends: over his bottle, he often persuaded his patron that he could command voters, with whom he had no manner of influence. For instance: he told Sir Hyacinth O'Brien that he was certain all the Grays would vote for him; and it was in consequence of this assurance that the cards of invitation to the ball had been sent to Rose and her mother, and that the baronet was now come in person to pay his respects at Rosanna.

We have kept him waiting an unconscionable time at the cottage door; we must now show him in.

CHAPTER IV

The beauty of Rose was the first thing that struck him upon his entrance. The impression was so sudden, and so lively, that, for a few minutes, the election, and all that belonged to it, vanished from his memory. The politeness of a county candidate made him appear, in other houses, charmed with father, mother, son, and daughter; but in this cottage there was no occasion for dissimulation; he was really pleased with each individual of the family. The natural feelings of the heart were touched. The ambitious man forgot all his schemes, and all his cares, in the contemplation of this humble picture of happiness and content; and the baronet conversed a full quarter of an hour with farmer Gray, before he relapsed into himself.

"How much happier," thought he, "are these people than I am, or than I ever have been! They are contented in obscurity; I was discontented even in the full blaze of celebrity. But my fate is fixed. I embarked on the sea of politics as thoughtlessly as if it were only on a party of pleasure: now I am chained to the oar, and a galley-slave cannot be more wretched."

Perhaps the beauty of Rose had some share in exciting Sir Hyacinth's sudden taste for rural felicity. It is certain he at first expressed more disappointment at hearing she would not go to the ball, than at being told her father and brothers could not vote for him. Farmer Gray, who was as independent in his principles as in his circumstances, honestly answered the baronet, that he thought Mr. Molyneux the fittest man to represent the county; and that it was for him he should therefore vote. Sir Hyacinth tried all his powers of persuasion in vain, and he left the cottage mortified and melancholy.

He met Simon O'Dougherty when he had driven a few miles from the door; and, in a tone of much pique and displeasure, reproached him for having deceived him into a belief that the Grays were his friends. Simon was rather embarrassed; but the genius of gossiping had luckily just supplied him with a hint, by which he could extricate himself from this difficulty.

"The fault is all your own, if I may make so free as to tell you so. Sir Hyacinth O'Brien," said he, "as capital an electioneerer as you are, I'll engage I'll find one that shall outdo you here. Send me and Stafford back again this minute to Rosanna, and we'll bring you the three votes as dead as crows in an hour's time, or my name is not O'Dougherty now."

"I protest, Mr. O'Dougherty, I do not understand you."

"Then let me whisper half a word in your ear, Sir Hyacinth, and I'll make you sensible I'm right." Simon winked most significantly, and looked wondrous wise; then stretching himself half off his horse into the gig to gain Sir Hyacinth's ear, he whispered that he knew, from the best authority, Stafford was in love with Gray's pretty daughter, Rose, and that Rose had no dislike to him; that she was all in all to her father and brothers, and of course could and would secure their votes, if properly spoken to.

This intelligence did not immediately produce the pleasing change of countenance which might have been expected. Sir Hyacinth coldly replied, he could not spare Stafford at present, and drove on. The genius of gossiping, according to her usual custom, had exaggerated considerably in her report. Stafford was attached to Rose, but had never yet told her so; and as to Rose, we might perhaps have known all her mind, if Sir Hyacinth's gig had not appeared just as she was seated on her father's knee, and going to tell him her reasons for wishing to go to the ball.

Stafford acted in the capacity of house-steward to the baronet; and had the management of all his master's unmanageable servants. He had brought with him, from England, ideas of order and punctuality, which were somewhat new, and extremely troublesome to the domestics at Hyacinth-hall: consequently he was much disliked by them; and not only by them but by most of the country people in the neighbourhood, who imagined he had a strong predilection in favour of every thing that was English, and an undisguised contempt for all that was Irish. They, however, perceived that this prejudice against the Irish admitted of exceptions: the family of the Grays, Stafford acknowledged, were almost as orderly, punctual, industrious, and agreeable, as if they had been born in England. This was matter of so much surprise to him, that he could not forbear going at every leisure hour to the mill or the cottage of Rosanna, to convince himself that such things could actually be in Ireland. He bought all the flour for the hall at Rosanna-mill; and Rose supplied the housekeeper constantly with poultry; so that his master's business continually obliged Stafford to repeat his visits; and every time he went to Gray's cottage, he thought it more and more like an English farm-house, and imagined Rose every day looked more like an Englishwoman than any thing else. What a pity she was not born the other side of the water; for then his mother and friends, in Warwickshire, could never have made any objection to her. But, she being an Irishwoman, they would for certain never fancy her. He had oftentimes heard them as good as say, that it would break their hearts if he was to marry and settle amongst the bogs and the wild Irish.

This recollection of his friends' prejudices at first deterred Stafford from thinking of marrying Rose; but it sometimes happens that reflection upon the prejudices of others shows us the folly of our own, and so it was in the present instance. Stafford wrote frequently to his friends in Warwickshire, to assure them that they had quite wrong notions of Ireland; that all Ireland was not a bog; that there were several well-grown trees in the parts he had visited; that there were some as pretty villages as you could wish to see any where, only that they called them towns; that the men, though some of them still wear brogues, were more hospitable to strangers than the English; and that the women, when not smoke-dried, were some of the handsomest he had seen, especially one Rose or Rosamond Gray, who was also the best and most agreeable girl he had ever known; though it was almost a sin to say so much of one who was not an Englishwoman born.

Much more in the same strain Stafford wrote to his mother; who, in reply to these letters, "besought him to consider well what he was about, before he suffered himself to begin falling desperately in love with this Rose or Rosamond Gray, or any Irishwoman whatsoever; who, having been bred in a mud-walled cabin, could never be expected to turn out at the long run equal to a true-born Englishwoman, bred in a slated house."

Stafford's notions had been so much enlarged by his travel, that he could not avoid smiling at some passages in his mother's epistle; yet he so far agreed with her in opinion as to think it prudent not to begin falling desperately in love with any woman, whether Irish or English, till he was thoroughly acquainted with her temper and disposition. He therefore prudently forbore, that is to say, as much as he could forbear, to show any signs of his attachment to Rose, till he had full opportunity of forming a decisive judgment of her character.

This he had now in his power. He saw that his master was struck with the fair Rosamond's charms; and he knew that Sir Hyacinth would pursue his purpose with no common perseverance. His heart beat with joy, when the card which brought her refusal arrived. He read it over and over again; and at last put it into his bosom, close to his heart. "Rose is a good daughter," said he to himself; "and that is a sign that she will make a good wife. She is too innocent to see or suspect that master has taken a fancy to her, but she is right to do as her prudent, affectionate father advises. I never loved that farmer Gray so well, in all my whole life, as at this instant."

Stafford was interrupted in his reverie by his master; who, in an angry voice, called for him to inquire why he had not, according to his orders, served out some oats for his horses the preceding day. The truth was, that anxiety about Rose and the ball had made him totally forget the oats. Stafford coloured a good deal, confessed that he had done very wrong to forget the oats, but that he would go to the granary immediately, and serve them out to the groom. Perhaps Stafford's usual exactness might have rendered his omission pardonable to any less irritable and peremptory master than Sir H. O'Brien.

When Sterne once heard a master severely reprimanding a servant for some trifling fault, he said to the gentleman, "My dear sir, we should not expect to have every virtue under the sun for 20l. a-year."

Sir Hyacinth O'Brien expected to have them for merely the promise of 20l. a-year. Though he never punctually paid his servants' wages, he abused them most insolently whenever he was in a passion. Upon the present occasion, his ill-humour was heightened by jealousy.

"I wish, sir," cried he to Stafford, after pouring forth a volley of oaths, "you would mind your business, and not run after objects that are not fit for you. You are become good for nothing of late; careless, insolent, and not fit to be trusted."

Stafford bore all that his master said till he came to the words not fit to be trusted; but the moment those were uttered, he could no longer command himself; he threw down the great key of the granary, which he held in his hand, and exclaimed, "Not fit to be trusted! Is this the reward of all my services? Not fit to be trusted! Then I have no business here."

"The sooner you go the better, sir," cried the angry baronet, who, at this instant, desired nothing more than to get him out of his way. "You had best set off for England directly: I have no farther occasion for your services."

Stafford said not a word more, but retired from his master's presence to conceal his emotion; and, when he was alone, burst into tears, repeating to himself, "So this is the reward of all my services!"

When Sir Hyacinth's passion cooled, he reflected that seven years' wages were due to Stafford; and as it was not convenient to him at this election time to part with so much ready money, he resolved to compromise. It was not from any sense of justice; therefore it must be said he had the meanness to apologize to his steward, and to hint that he was welcome to remain, if he pleased, in his service.

Satisfied by this explanation, and by the condescension with which it was given, Stafford's affection for his master returned with all its wonted force: and he resumed his former occupations about the house with redoubled activity. He waited only till he could be spared for a day to go to Rosanna, and make his proposal for Rose. Her behaviour concerning the ball convinced him that his mother's prejudices against Irishwomen were ill-founded. Whilst his mind was in this state, his master one morning sent for him, and told him that it was absolutely necessary he should go to a neighbouring county, to some persons who were freeholders, and whose votes might turn the election. The business would only occupy a few days, Sir Hyacinth said; and Stafford willingly undertook it.

The gentlemen to whom Stafford had letters were not at home, and he was detained above a fortnight. When he returned, he took a road which led by Rosanna, that he might at least have the pleasure of seeing Rose for a few minutes; but when he called at the cottage, to his utter surprise, he was refused admittance. Being naturally of a warm temper, and not deficient in pride, his first impulse was to turn his horse's head, and gallop off: but, checking his emotion, he determined not to leave the place till he should discover the cause of this change of conduct. He considered that none of this family had formerly treated him with caprice or duplicity; it was therefore improbable they should suddenly alter their conduct towards him, unless they had reason to believe that they had some sufficient cause. He rode immediately to a field where he saw some labourers at work. Farmer Gray was with them. Stafford leaped from his horse, and, with an air of friendly honesty, held out his hand, saying, "I can't believe you mean to affront me: tell me what is the reason I am not to be let into your house, my good friend?"

Gray leaned upon his stick, and, after looking at him for a moment, replied, "We have been too hasty, I see: we have had no cause of quarrel with you, Stafford: you could never look at me with that honest countenance, if you had any hand in this business."

"What business?" cried Stafford.

"Walk home with me, out of the hearing of these people, and you shall know."

As they walked towards his cottage, Gray took out his great leather pocket-book, and searched for a letter. "Pray, Stafford," said he, "did you, about ten days ago, send my girl a melon?"

"Yes; one of my own raising. I left it with the gardener, to be sent to her with my best respects and services; and a message intimating to say that I was sorry my master's business required I should take a journey, and could not see her for a few days, or something that way."

"No such message came; only your services, the melon, and this note. I declare," continued Gray, looking at Stafford whilst he read the letter, "he turns as pale as my wife herself did when I showed it to her!"

Stafford, indeed, grew pale with anger. It was a billet-doux from his master to Rose, which Sir Hyacinth entreated might be kept secret, promising to make her fortune and marry her well, if she would only have compassion upon a man who adored and was dying for her, &c.

"I will never see my master again," exclaimed Stafford. "I could not see him without the danger of doing something that I might not forgive myself. He a gentleman! He a gentleman! I'll gallop off and leave his letters, and his horse, with some of his people. I'll never see him again. If he does not pay me a farthing of my seven years' wages, I don't care; I will not sleep in his house another night. He a gentleman!"

Farmer Gray was delighted by Stafford's generous indignation; which appeared the more striking, as his manner was usually sober, and remarkably civil.

All this happened at two o'clock in the afternoon; and the evening of the same day he returned to Rosanna. Rose was sitting at work, in the seat of the cottage window. When she saw him at the little white gate, her colour gave notice to her brothers who was coming, and they ran out to meet him.

"You ought to shut your doors against me now, instead of running out to meet me," said he; "for I am not clear that I have a farthing in the world, except what is in this portmanteau. I have been fool enough to leave all I have earned in the hands of a gentleman, who can give me only his bond for my wages. But I am glad I am out of his house, at any rate."

"And I am glad you are in mine," said farmer Gray, receiving him with a warmth of hospitality which brought tears of gratitude into Stafford's eyes. Rose smiled upon her father, and said nothing; but set him his arm-chair, and was very busy arranging the tea-table. Mrs. Gray beckoned to her guest, and made him sit down beside her; telling him he should have as good tea at Rosanna as ever he had in Warwickshire; "and out of Staffordshire ware, too," said she, taking her best Wedgwood teacups and saucers out of a cupboard.

Robin, who was naturally gay and fond of rallying his friends, could not forbear affecting to express his surprise at Stafford's preferring an Irishwoman, of all women in the world. "Are you quite sure, Stafford," said he, "that you are not mistaken? Are you sure my sister has not wings on her shoulders?"

"Have you done now, Robin?" said his mother; who saw that Stafford was a good deal abashed, and had no answer ready. "If Mr. Stafford had a prejudice against us Irish, so much the more honourable for my Rose to have conquered it; and, as to wings, they would have been no shame to us natives, supposing we had them; and of course it was no affront to attribute them to us. Have not the angels themselves wings?"

A timely joke is sometimes a real blessing; and so Stafford felt it at this instant: his bashfulness vanished by degrees, and Robin rallied him no more. "I had no idea," said he, "how easy it is to put an Englishman out of countenance in the company of his mistress."

This was a most happy evening at Rosanna. After Rose retired, which she soon did, to see after the household affairs, her father spoke in the kindest manner to Stafford. "Mr. Stafford," said he, "if you tell me that you are able to maintain my girl in the way of life she is in now, you shall have her: this, in my opinion and in hers, is the happiest life for those who have been bred to it. I would rather see Rose matched to an honest, industrious, good-humoured man, like yourself, whom she can love, than see her the wife of a man as grand as Sir Hyacinth O'Brien. For, to the best of my opinion, it is not the being born to a great estate that can make a man content or even rich: I think myself a richer man this minute than Sir Hyacinth; for I owe no man any thing, am my own master, and can give a little matter both to child and stranger. But your head is very naturally running upon Rose, and not upon my moralizing. All I have to say is, win her and wear her; and, as to the rest, even if Sir Hyacinth never pays you your own, that shall not stop your wedding. My sons are good lads, and you and Rose shall never want, whilst the mill of Rosanna is going."

This generosity quite overpowered Stafford. Generosity is one of the characteristics of the Irish. It not only touched but surprised the Englishman; who, amongst the same rank of his own countrymen, had been accustomed to strict honesty in their dealings, but seldom to this warmth of friendship and forgetfulness of all selfish considerations. It was some minutes before he could articulate a syllable; but, after shaking his intended father-in-law's hand with that violence which expresses so much to English feelings, he said, "I thank you heartily; and, if I live to the age of Methusalem, shall never forget this. A friend in need is a friend indeed. But I will not live upon yours or your good sons' earnings; that would not be fair dealing, or like what I've been bred up to think handsome. It is a sad thing for me that this master of mine can give me nothing, for my seven years' service, but this scrap of paper (taking out of his pocket-book a bond of Sir Hyacinth's). But my mother, though she has her prejudices, and is very stiff about them, being an elderly woman, and never going out of England, or even beyond the parish in which she was born, yet she is kind-hearted; and I cannot think will refuse to help me, or that she will cross me in marriage, when she knows the thing is determined; so I shall write to her before I sleep, and wish I could but enclose in the cover of my letter the picture of Rose, which would be better than all I could say. But no picture would do her justice. I don't mean a compliment, like those Sir Hyacinth paid to her face, but only the plain truth. I mean that a picture could never make my mother understand how good, and sweet-tempered, and modest, Rose is. Mother has a world of prejudices; but she is a good woman, and will prove herself so to me, I make no doubt."

Stafford wrote to his mother a long letter, and received, in a fortnight afterwards, this short answer:

"Son George,

I warned you not to fall in love with an Irishwoman, to which I told you I could never give my consent.

"As you bake, so you must brew. Your sister Dolly is marrying too, and setting up a shop in Warwick, by my advice and consent: all the money I can spare I must give, as in reason, to her who is a dutiful child; and mean, with her and grand-children, if God please, to pass my latter days, as fitting, in this parish of Little Sonchy, in Old England, where I was born and bred. Wishing you may not repent, or starve, or so forth, which please to let me know,

"I am your affectionate mother,
"DOROTHY STAFFORD."

All Stafford's hopes were confounded by this letter: he put it into farmer Gray's hands, without saying a word; then drew his chair away from Rose, hid his face in his hands, and never spoke or heard one word that was saying round about him for full half an hour; till, at last, he was roused by his friend Robin, who, clapping him on his back, said, "Come, Stafford, English pride won't do with us; this is all to punish you for refusing to share and share alike with us in the mill of Rosanna, which is what you must and shall do now, for Rose's sake, if not for ours or your own. Come, say done."

Stafford could not help being moved. All the family, except Rose, joined in these generous entreaties; and her silence said even more than their words. Dinner was on the table before this amicable contest was settled, and Robin insisted upon his drinking a toast with him, in Irish ale; which was, "Rose Gray, and Rosanna-mill."

The glass was just filled and the toast pronounced, when in came one of Gray's workmen, in an indescribable perspiration and rage.

"Master Robin, master John! Master," cried he, "we are all ruined! The mill and all—"

"The mill!" exclaimed every body starting up.

"Ay, the mill: it's all over with it, and with us: not a turn more will Rosanna-mill ever take for me or you; not a turn," continued he, wiping his forehead with his arm, and hiding by the same motion his eyes, which ran over with tears.

"It's all that thief Hopkins's doing. May every guinea he touches, and every shilling, and tester, and penny itself, blister his fingers, from this day forward and for evermore!"

"But what has he done to the mill?"

"May every guinea, shilling, tester, and penny he looks upon, from this day forth for evermore, be a blight to his eyes, and a canker to his heart! But I can't wish him a worse canker than what he has there already. Yes, he has a canker at heart! Is not he eaten up with envy? as all who look at him may read in that evil eye. Bad luck to the hour when it fixed on the mill of Rosanna!"

"But what has he done to the mill? Take it patiently, and tell us quietly," said farmer Gray, "and do not curse the man any more."

"Not curse the man! Take it quietly, master! Is it the time to take it quietly, when he is at the present minute carrying off every drop of water from our mill-course? so he is the villain!"

At these words, Stafford seized his oak stick, and sprang towards the door. Robin and John eagerly followed: but, as they passed their father, he laid a hand on each, and called to Stafford to stop. At his respected voice they all paused. "My children," said he, "what are you going to do? No violence. No violence. You shall have justice, boys, depend upon it; we will not let ourselves be oppressed. If Mr. Hopkins were ten times as great, and twenty times as tyrannical as he is, we shall have justice; the law will reach him: but we must take care and do nothing in anger. Therefore, I charge you, let me speak to him, and do you keep your tempers whatever passes. May be, all this is only 8 mistake: perhaps Mr. Hopkins is only making drains for his own meadow; or, may be, is going to flood it, and does not know, till we tell him, that he is emptying our water-course."

"He can't but know it! He can't but know it! He's'cute enough, and too 'cute," muttered Paddy, as he led the way to the mill. Stafford and the two brothers followed their father respectfully; admiring his moderation, and resolving to imitate it if they possibly could.

Mr. Hopkins was stationed cautiously on the boundary of his own land. "There he is, mounted on the back of the ditch, enjoying the mischief all he can!" cried Paddy. "And hark! He is whistling, whilst our stream is running away from us. May I never cross myself again, if I would not, rather than the best shirt ever I had to my back, push him into the mud, as he deserves, this very minute! And, if it wasn't for my master here, it's what I'd do, before I drew breath again."

Farmer Gray restrained Paddy's indignation with some difficulty; and advancing calmly towards Mr. Hopkins, he remonstrated with him in a mild tone. "Surely, Mr. Hopkins," said he, "you cannot mean to do us such an injury as to stop our mill?"

"I have not laid a finger on your mill," replied Hopkins, with a malicious smile. "If your man there," pointing to Paddy, "could prove my having laid a finger upon it, you might have your action of trespass; but I am no trespasser; I stand on my own land, and have a right to water my own meadow; and moreover have witnesses to prove that, for ten years last past, while the mill of Rosanna was in Simon O'Dougherty's hands, the water-course was never full, and the mill was in disuse. The stream runs against you now, and so does the law, gentlemen. I have the best counsel's opinion in Ireland to back me. Take your remedy, when and where you can find it. Good morning to you."

Without listening to one word more, Mr. Hopkins hastily withdrew: for he had no small apprehensions that Paddy, whose threats he had overheard, and whose eyes sparkled with rage, might execute upon him that species of prompt justice which no quibbling can evade.

"Do not be disheartened, my dear boys," said farmer Gray to his sons, who were watching with mournful earnestness the slackened motion of their water-wheel. "Saddle my horse for me, John; and get yourselves ready, both of you, to come with me to Counsellor Molyneux."

"Oh! father," said John, "there is no use in going to him; for he is one of the candidates, you know, and Mr. Hopkins has a great many votes."

"No matter for that," said Gray: "Mr. Molyneux will do justice; that is my opinion of him. If he was another sort of man, I would not trouble myself to go near him, nor stoop to ask his advice: but my opinion of him is, that he is above doing a dirty action, for votes or any thing else; and I am convinced his own interest will not weigh a grain of dust in the balance against justice. Saddle the horses, boy."

His sons saddled the horses; and all the way the farmer was riding he continued trying to keep up the spirits of his sons, by assurances that if Counsellor Molyneux would take their affair in hand, there would be an end of all difficulty.

"He is not one of those justices of the peace," continued he, "who will huddle half a dozen poor fellows into jail without law or equity. He is not a man who goes into parliament, saying one thing, and who comes out saying another. He is not, like, our friend Sir Hyacinth O'Brien, forced to sell tongue, and brains, and conscience, to keep his head above water. In short, he is a man who dares to be the same, and can moreover afford to be the same, at election time as at any other time; for which reason, I dare to go to him now in this our distress, although, I have to complain of a man who has forty-six votes, which is the number, they say, Mr. Hopkins can command."

Whilst farmer Gray was thus pronouncing a panegyric on Counsellor Molyneux, for the comfort of John and Robin, Stafford was trying to console Rose and her mother, who were struck with sorrow and dismay, at the news of the mill's being stopped. Stafford had himself almost as much need of consolation as they; for he foresaw it was impossible he should at present be united to his dear Rose. All that her generous brothers had to offer was a share in the mill. The father had his farm, but this must serve for the support of the whole family; and how could Stafford become a burden to them, now that they would be poor, when he could not bring himself to be dependent upon them, even when they were, comparatively speaking, rich?

CHAPTER V

With anxious hearts the little party at the cottage expected the return of the father and his sons. Rose sat at the window watching for them: her mother laid down her knitting, and sighed: and Stafford was silent, for he had exhausted all his consolatory eloquence, and saw and felt it had no effect.

"Here they come! But they ride so slow, that I am sure they bring us no good news."

No: there was not any good news. Counsellor Molyneux had indeed behaved as well as man could do: he had declared that he would undertake to manage and plead their cause in any court of justice on earth; and had expressed the strongest indignation against the villany of Hopkins; but, at the same time, he had fairly told the Grays that this litigious man, if they commenced a suit, might ruin them, by law, before they could recover their rights.

"So we may go to bed this night melancholy enough," said Robin; "with the certainty that our mill is stopped, and that we have a long lawsuit to go through, before we can see it going again—if ever we do."

Rose and Stafford looked at one another, and sighed.

"We had better not go to law, to lose the little we have left, at any rate," said Mrs. Gray.

"Wife, I am determined my boys shall have justice," said the father, firmly. "I am not fond of law, God knows! I never had a lawsuit in my life; nobody dreads such things more than I do; but I dread nothing in defence of my sons and justice. Whilst I have a penny left in the world, I'll spend it to obtain them justice. The labour of their lives shall not be in vain; they shall not be robbed of all they have: they shall not be trampled upon by any one living, let him be ever so rich, or ever so litigious. I fear neither his money nor his quirks of law. Plain sense is the same for him and for me; and justice my boys shall have. Mr. Molyneux will plead our cause himself—desire no more. If we fail and are ruined, our ruin be upon the head of him who works it! I shall die content, when I have done all I can to obtain justice for my children."

As soon as these facts were known, every body in the neighbourhood felt extreme indignation against Hopkins; and all joined in pitying the two brothers, and applauding the spirit of their father. There was not an individual who did not wish that Hopkins might be punished; but he had been engaged in so many lawsuits, and had been so successful in screening himself from justice, and in ruining his opponents, that every body feared the Grays, though they were so much in the right, would never be able to make this appear, according to the forms of law: many, therefore, advised that it might not be brought to trial. But farmer Gray persisted, and Counsellor Molyneux steadily abided by his word, and declared he would plead the cause himself.

Mr. Hopkins sent the counsellor a private hint, that if he directly or indirectly protected the Grays, he must give up all hopes of the forty-six votes which, as the county was now nearly balanced, must turn the election. Mr. Molyneux paid no attention to this hint; but, the very day on which he received it, visited farmer Gray in his cottage, walked with him to Rosanna-mill, and settled how the suit should be carried on.

Hopkins swore he would spare no expense to humble the pride both of the Grays and their protector: an unexpected circumstance, however, occurred. It had often been prophesied by Mr. Molyneux, who knew the species of bargains which Hopkins drove with all manner of people by whose distresses he could make money, that he would sooner or later overshoot his mark, as cunning persons often do. Mr. Molyneux predicted that, amongst the medley of his fraudulent purchases, he would at length be the dupe of some unsound title; and that, amongst the multitudes whom he ruined, he would at last meet with some one who would ruin him. The person who was the means of accomplishing this prophecy was indeed the last that would have been guessed—soft Simon O'Dougherty! In dealing with him, Mr. Hopkins, who thoroughly despised indolent honesty, was quite off his guard; and, in truth, poor Simon had no design to cheat him: but it happened that the lease, which he made over to Hopkins, as his title to the field that he sold, was a lease renewable for ever; with a strict clause, binding the lessee to renew, within a certain time after the failure of each life, under penalty of forfeiting the lease. From the natural laziness of easy Simon, he had neglected to renew, and had even forgotten that the life was dropped: he assigned his lease over a bottle to Mr. Hopkins, who seized it with avidity, lest he should lose the lucky moment to conclude a bargain in which, he thought, he had at once over-reached Simon, and had secured to himself the means of wreaking his vengeance upon the Grays. This lease was of the field adjoining to Rosanna-mill; and by the testimony of some old people in the neighbourhood, he fancied he could prove that this meadow was anciently flooded, and that the mill-course had gone into disuse. In all his subsequent operations, he had carefully kept himself, as he thought, upon his own lands; but, now that a suit against him was instituted, it was necessary to look to his own title, into which he knew Mr. Molyneux would examine.

Upon reading over the lease assigned to him by Simon, he noticed the strict clause, binding the tenant to renew within a certain time. A qualm came over him! He was astonished at himself for not having more carefully perused the lease before he concluded the bargain. Had it been with any one but soft Simon, this could not have happened. He hastened in search of Simon with the utmost anxiety, to inquire whether all the lives were in being. Simon at first said he had such a mist over his memory that he could not exactly recollect who the lives were; but at last he made out that one of them had been dead beyond the time for renewal. The gentleman, his landlord, he said, was in Dublin; and he had neglected, sure enough, to write to him from post to post.

The rage of Mr. Hopkins was excessive: he grew white with anger! Easy Simon yawned, and begged him not to take the thing so to heart: "for, after all," said he, "you know the loss must be mine. I can't make good the sale of this field to you, as I have lost it by my own carelessness: but that's nothing to you; for you know, as well as I do, that to make good the deficiency, you will, somehow or other, get a better piece of ground out of the small remains of patrimony I have left, God help me!"

"God help you, indeed!" cried Hopkins, with a look and accent of mingled rage and contempt. "I tell you, man, the loss is mine; and no other land you have, to sell or give, can make me any amends. I shall lose my lawsuit."

"Wheugh! wheugh! Why, so much the better. Where's the use of having lawsuits? The loss of such bad things can never be great."

"No trifling, pray," said Hopkins, with impatience, as he walked up and down the room, and repeatedly struck his forehead.

"Ho! ho! ho! I begin to comprehend. I know whereabouts you are now," cried Simon. "Is not it the Grays you are thinking of? Ah, that's the suit you are talking about. But now, Mr. Hopkins, you ought to rejoice, as I do, instead of grieving, that it is out of your power to ruin that family; for, in truth, they are good people, and have the voice of the country with them against you; and if you were to win your suit twenty times over, that would still be the same. You would never be able to show your face; and, for my own part, my conscience would never forgive me for being instrumental, unknown to myself, in giving you the power to do this mischief. And, after all, what put it into your head to stop Rosanna-mill, when its going gave you no trouble in life?"

Hopkins, who had not listened to one syllable Simon was saying, at this instant suddenly stopped walking; and, in a soft insinuating voice, addressed him in these words:

"Mr. O'Dougherty, you know I have a great regard for you."

"May be so," said Simon; "though that is more than I ever knew you to have for any body."

"Pray be serious. I tell you I have, and will prove it."

"That is more and more surprising, Mr. Hopkins."

"And which is more surprising still, I will make your fortune, if you will do a trifling kindness for me."

"Any thing in nature, that won't give me an unreasonable deal of trouble."

"Oh, this will give you no sort of trouble," said Hopkins. "I will get you, before this day se'nnight, that place in the revenue that you have been wishing for so long, and that Sir Hyacinth O'Brien will never get for you. I say I will insure it to you under my hand, this minute, if you will do what I want of you."

"To be sure I will, if it's no trouble. What is it?"

"Only just," said Hopkins, hesitating; "only just—You must remember—you cannot but recollect that you wrote to your landlord, to offer to renew?"

"I remember to recollect no such thing," said Simon, surprised.

"Yes, yes," said Hopkins; "but he gave you no answer, you know."

"But, I tell you, I never wrote to him at all."

"Pshaw! You have a bad memory, Simon; and your letter might have miscarried. There's nothing simpler than that; nothing more easily said."

"If it were but true," said Simon.

"True or not, it may be said, you know."

"Not by Simon O'Dougherty, Mr. Hopkins.",

"Look you, Mr. O'Dougherty, I have a great regard for you," continued Hopkins, holding him fast, and producing a pocket-book full of bank notes. I must, thought he, come up to this scoundrel's price, for he has me now. He is more knave than fool, I see. "Let us understand one another, my good friend Simon. Name your sum, and make me but a short affidavit, purporting that you did apply for this renewal, and you have your place in the revenue snug besides."

"You don't know whom you are speaking to, Mr. Hopkins," said Simon, looking over his shoulder, with cool and easy contempt. "The O'Doughertys are not accustomed to perjuring themselves; and it's a trouble I would not take for any man, if he were my own father even; no, not for all the places in the revenue that ever were created, nor for all the bank notes ever you cheated mankind out of, Mr. Hopkins, into the bargain. No offence. I never talked of cheating, till you named perjury to me; for which I do not kick you down stairs, in the first place, because there are no stairs, I believe, to my house; next, because, if there were ever so many, it would be beneath me to make use of them upon any such occasion; and, lastly, it would be quite too much trouble. Now we comprehend one another perfectly, I hope, Mr. Hopkins."

Cursing himself, and overwhelmed with confusion, Mr. Hopkins withdrew. Proud of himself, and having a story to tell, Simon O'Dougherty hastened to Rosanna, to relate all that had happened to the Grays, and to congratulate them, as he said, upon his own carelessness.

The joy with which they listened to Simon's story was great, and in proportion to the anxiety they had suffered. In less than half an hour's time, they received a mean, supplicating letter from Hopkins, entreating they would not ruin his reputation, and all his prospects in life, by divulging what had passed; and promising that the mill-stream of Rosanna should be returned to its proper channel, without any expense to them, and that he would make a suitable compensation in money, if they would bind themselves to secrecy.

It will easily be guessed that they rejected all his offers with disdain: the whole affair was told by them to Mr. Molyneux, and the next day all the neighbourhood knew it, and triumphed in the detection of a villain, who had long been the oppressor of the poor. The neighbours all joined in restoring the water to the mill-course; and when Rosanna-mill was once more at work, the village houses were illuminated, and even the children showed their sympathy for the family of the Grays, by huge bonfires and loud huzzas.

Simon O'Dougherty's landlord was so much pleased by the honesty he had shown in this affair, that he renewed the lease of the meadow, instead of insisting upon the forfeiture; and farmer Gray delighted poor Simon still more, by promising to overlook for him the management of the land, which still remained in his possession.

In the mean time, Mr. Hopkins, who could not go out of his own house without being insulted, or without fearing to be insulted, prepared to quit the country. "But before I go," said he, "I shall have the pleasure and triumph, at least, of making Mr. Molyneux lose his election."

The Grays feared Mr. Molyneux would indeed be a sufferer for the generous protection he had afforded them in their distress. The votes were nearly balanced in the county, and the forty-six votes which Hopkins could command would decide the contest. There are often in real life instances of what is called poetical justice. The day before the election, Sir Hyacinth was arrested at the suit of Stafford, who chose his opportunity so well, that the sheriff, though he was a fast friend of the baronet's, could not refuse to do his duty. The sheriff had such a number of writs immediately put into his hands, that bail could not be found; and Mr. Molyneux was elected without opposition.

But, let us return, from the misery of arrests and elections, to peace, industry, family union, and love, in the happy cottage of Rosanna. No obstacles now prevented the marriage of Stafford and Rose; it was celebrated with every simple demonstration of rural felicity. The bride had the blessings of her fond father and mother, the congratulations of her beloved brothers, and the applause of her own heart. Are not these better things than even forty fine wedding gowns, or a coach of Hatchett's best workmanship? Rose thought so, and her future life proved she was not much mistaken. Stafford some time after his marriage took his wife to England, to see his mother, who was soon reconciled to him and her Irish daughter-in-law, whose gentle manners and willing obedience overcame her unreasonable dislike. Old Mrs. Stafford declared to her son, when he was returning, that she had so far got the better of what he called her prejudices, that, if she could but travel to Ireland, without crossing the sea, she verily believed she would go and spend a year with him and the Grays at Rosanna.

[Footnote: Having heard, from good judges, that the language used by Farmer Gray in this story appears superior to his condition, we insert a letter which we lately received from him; matter, manner, and orthography his own.

"To R. L. EDGEWORTH, ESQ.

"HON. SIR,

"I have read your valuable present with care, so has also the whole family; its design is excellent, it breathes forth a spirit of virtue and industry and in a word all the social virtues which constitute human happiness—Its other characters are admirably adapted to expose vice in all its hideous forms, and gives us a view of those baneful principles which terminate in certain misery and proves beyond a doubt that many of mankind are the authors of their own calamities and frequently involve others in the same or similar unhappy circumstances—

"Thrice happy are they who in affluence endeavour thus to amend the morals of mankind; it's they only who enjoy true felicity—their example and their precepts have a powerful influence on all around them, and never fail to excite a virtuous emulation, except, among the utterly abandoned and profligate—

"On the contrary, families in elevated situations of life who devote their time to dissipation and its sensual allurements are the pest of society—the vices and crimes of the great are frequently imitated by the lower ranks—they all die, and no memorial is left behind but that of folly and an ill-spent life.

"May that life of virtue so strongly recommended be long the shining ornament of you and your family, and its end be rewarded with a crown of eternal happiness, which is the joint wish of the family of—

"FARMER GRAY."
"July 1st, 1804."]

THE MANUFACTURERS

CHAPTER I

By patient persevering attention to business, Mr. John Darford succeeded in establishing a considerable cotton manufactory, by means of which he secured to himself in his old age what is called, or what he called, a competent fortune. His ideas of a competent fortune were, indeed, rather unfashionable; for they included, as he confessed, only the comforts and conveniences, without any of the vanities of life. He went farther still in his unfashionable singularities of opinion, for he was often heard to declare that he thought a busy manufacturer might be as happy as any idle gentleman.

Mr. Darford had taken his two nephews, Charles and William, into partnership with him: William, who had been educated by him, resembled him in character, habits, and opinions. Always active and cheerful, he seemed to take pride and pleasure in the daily exertions and care which his situation, and the trust reposed in him, required. Far from being ashamed of his occupations, he gloried in them; and the sense of duty was associated in his mind with the idea of happiness. His cousin Charles, on the contrary, felt his duty and his ideas of happiness continually at variance: he had been brought up in an extravagant family, who considered tradesmen and manufacturers as a caste disgraceful to polite society. Nothing but the utter ruin of his father's fortune could have determined him to go into business.

He never applied to the affairs of the manufactory; he affected to think his understanding above such vulgar concerns, and spent his days in regretting that his brilliant merit was buried in obscurity.

He was sensible that he hazarded the loss of his uncle's favour by the avowal of his prejudices; yet such was his habitual conceit, that he could not suppress frequent expressions of contempt for Mr. Darford's liberal notions. Whenever his uncle's opinion differed from his own, he settled the argument, as he fancied, by saying to himself or to his clerk, "My uncle Darford knows nothing of the world: how should he, poor man! shut up as he has been all his life in a counting-house?"

Nearly sixty years' experience, which his uncle sometimes pleaded as an apology for trusting to his own judgment, availed nothing in the opinion of our prejudiced youth. Prejudiced youth, did we presume to say? Charles would have thought this a very improper expression; for he had no idea that any but old men could be prejudiced. Uncles, and fathers, and grandfathers, were, as he thought, the race of beings peculiarly subject to this mental malady; from which all young men, especially those who have their boots made by a fashionable bootmaker, are of course exempt.

At length the time came when Charles was at liberty to follow his own opinions: Mr. Darford died, and his fortune and manufactory were equally divided between his two nephews. "Now," said Charles, "I am no longer chained to the oar. I will leave you, William, to do as you please, and drudge on, day after day, in the manufactory, since that is your taste: for my part, I have no genius for business. I shall take my pleasure; and all I have to do is to pay some poor devil for doing my business for me."

"I am afraid the poor devil will not do your business as well as you would do it yourself," said William: "you know the proverb of the master's eye."

"True! true! Very likely," cried Charles, going to the window to look at a regiment of dragoons galloping through the town; "but I have other employment for my eyes. Do look at those fine fellows who are galloping by! Did you ever see a handsomer uniform than the colonel's? And what a fine horse! 'Gad! I wish I had a commission in the army: I should so like to be in his place this minute."

"This minute? Yes, perhaps, you would; because he has, as you say, a handsome uniform and a fine horse: but all his minutes may not be like this minute."

"Faith, William, that is almost as soberly said as my old uncle himself could have spoken. See what it is to live shut up with old folks! You catch all their ways, and grow old and wise before your time."

"The danger of growing wise before my time does not alarm me much: but perhaps, cousin, you feel that danger more than I do?"

"Not I," said Charles, stretching himself still farther out of the window to watch the dragoons, as they were forming on the parade in the market-place. "I can only say, as I said before, that I wish I had been put into the army instead of into this cursed cotton manufactory. Now the army is a genteel profession, and I own I have spirit enough to make it my first object to look and live like a gentleman."

"And I have spirit enough," replied William, "to make it my first object to look and live like an independent man; and I think a manufacturer, whom you despise so much, may be perfectly independent. I am sure, for my part, I am heartily obliged to my uncle for breeding me up to business; for now I am at no man's orders; no one can say to me, 'Go to the east, or go to the west; march here, or march there; fire upon this man, or run your bayonet into that.' I do not think the honour and pleasure of wearing a red coat, or of having what is called a genteel profession, would make me amends for all that a soldier must suffer, if he does his duty. Unless it were for the defence of my country, for which I hope and believe I should fight as well as another, I cannot say that I should like to be hurried away from my wife and children, to fight a battle against people with whom I have no quarrel, and in a cause which perhaps I might not approve of."

"Well, as you say, William, you that have a wife and children are quite in a different situation from me. You cannot leave them, of course. Thank my stars, I am still at liberty, and I shall take care and keep myself so: my plan is to live for myself, and to have as much pleasure as I possibly can."

Whether this plan of living for himself was compatible with the hopes of having as much pleasure as possible, we leave it to the heads and hearts of our readers to decide. In the mean time we must proceed with his history.

Soon after this conversation had passed between the two partners, another opportunity occurred of showing their characters still more distinctly.

A party of ladies and gentlemen, travellers, came to the town, and wished to see the manufactories there. They had letters of recommendation to the Mr. Darfords; and William, with great good-nature, took them to see their works. He pointed out to them, with honest pride, the healthy countenances of the children whom they employed.

"You see," said he, "that we cannot be reproached with sacrificing the health and happiness of our fellow-creatures to our own selfish and mercenary views. My good uncle took all the means in his power to make every person concerned in this manufactory as happy as possible; and I hope we shall follow his example. I am sure the riches of both the Indies could not satisfy me, if my conscience reproached me with having gained wealth by unjustifiable means. If these children were over-worked, or if they had not fresh air and wholesome food, it would be the greatest misery to me to come into this room and look at them. I could not do it. But, on the contrary, knowing, as I do, that they are well treated and well provided for in every respect, I feel joy and pride in coming amongst them, and in bringing my friends here."

William's eyes sparkled, as he thus spoke the generous sentiments of his heart; but Charles, who had thought himself obliged to attend the ladies of the party to see the manufactory, evidently showed he was ashamed of being considered as a partner. William, with perfect simplicity, went on to explain every part of the machinery, and the whole process of the manufacture; whilst his cousin Charles, who thought he should that way show his superior liberality and politeness, every now and then interposed with, "Cousin, I'm afraid we are keeping the ladies too long standing. Cousin, this noise must certainly annoy the ladies horridly. Cousin, all this sort of thing cannot be very interesting, I apprehend, to the ladies. Besides, they won't have time, at this rate, to see the china-works; which is a style of thing more to their taste, I presume."

The fidgeting impatience of our hero was extreme; till at last he gained his point, and hurried the ladies away to the china-works. Amongst these ladies there was one who claimed particular attention, Miss Maude Germaine, an elderly young lady, who, being descended from a high family, thought herself entitled to be proud. She was yet more vain than proud, and found her vanity in some degree gratified by the officious attention of her new acquaintance, though she affected to ridicule him to her companions, when she could do so unobserved. She asked them, in a whisper, how they liked her new cicerone; and whether he did not show the lions very prettily, considering who and what he was?

It has been well observed "that people are never ridiculous by what they are, but by what they pretend to be."

[Footnote: Rochefoucault]

These ladies, with the best dispositions imaginable for sarcasm, could find nothing to laugh at in Mr. William Darford's plain unassuming manners; as he did not pretend to be a fine gentleman, there was no absurd contrast between his circumstances and his conversation; while almost every word, look, or motion of his cousin was an object of ridicule, because it was affected. His being utterly unconscious of his foibles, and perfectly secure in the belief of his own gentility, increased the amusement of the company. Miss Maude Germaine undertook to play him off, but she took sufficient care to prevent his suspecting her design. As they were examining the beautiful china, she continually appealed to Mr. Charles Darford, as a man of taste; and he, with awkward gallantry, and still more awkward modesty, always began his answers by protesting he was sure Miss Maude Germaine was infinitely better qualified to decide in such matters than he was: he had not the smallest pretensions to taste; but that, in his humble opinion, the articles she pitched upon were evidently the most superior in elegance, and certainly of the newest fashion. "Fashion, you know, ladies, is all in all in these things, as in every thing else."

Miss Germaine, with a degree of address which afforded much amusement to herself and her companions, led him to extol or reprobate whatever she pleased; and she made him pronounce an absurd eulogium on the ugliest thing in the room, by observing it was vastly like what her friend, Lady Mary Crawley, had just bought for her chimney-piece.

Not content with showing she could make our man of taste decide as she thought proper, she was determined to prove that she could make him reverse his own decisions, and contradict himself, as often as she pleased. They were at this instant standing opposite to two vases of beautiful workmanship.

"Now," whispered she to one of her companions, "I will lay you any wager I first make him say that both those vases are frightful; then that they are charming; afterward that he does not know which he likes best; next, that no person of any taste can hesitate betwixt them; and at last, when he has pronounced his decided humble opinion, he shall reverse his judgment, and protest he meant to say quite the contrary."

All this the lady accomplished much to her satisfaction and to that of her friends; and so blind and deaf is self-love, our hero neither heard nor saw that he was the object of derision. William, however, was rather more clear-sighted; and as he could not bear to see his cousin make himself the butt of the company, he interrupted the conversation, by begging the ladies would come into another room to look at the manner in which the china was painted. Charles, with a contemptuous smile, observed that the ladies would probably find the odour of the paint rather too much for their nerves. Full of the sense of his own superior politeness, he followed; since it was determined that they must go, as he said, nolens volens. He did not hear Miss Germaine whisper to her companions as they passed, "Can any thing in nature be much more ridiculous than a vulgar manufacturer, who sets up for a fine gentleman?"

Amongst the persons who were occupied in painting a set of china with flowers, there was one who attracted particular attention, by the ease and quickness with which she worked. An iris of her painting was produced, which won the admiration of all the spectators; and whilst Charles was falling into ecstasies about the merit of the painting, and the perfection to which the arts are now carried in England, William was observing the flushed and unhealthy countenance of the young artist. He stopped to advise her not to overwork herself, to beg she would not sit in a draught of wind where she was placed, and to ask her, with much humanity, several questions concerning her health and her circumstances. Whilst he was speaking to her, he did not perceive that he had set his foot by accident on Miss Germaine's gown; and, as she walked hastily on, it was torn in a deplorable manner. Charles apologized for his cousin's extreme absence of mind and rudeness; and with a candid condescension added, "Ladies, you must not think ill of my cousin William, because he is not quite so much your humble servant as I am: notwithstanding his little rusticities, want of polish, gallantry, and so forth, things that are not in every man's power, I can assure you there is not a better man in the world; except that he is so entirely given up to business, which indeed ruins a man for every thing else."

The apologist little imagined he was at this moment infinitely more awkward and ill-bred than the person whom he affected to pity and to honour with his protection. Our hero continued to be upon the best terms possible with himself and with Miss Maude Germaine, during the remainder of this day. He discovered that this lady intended to pass a fortnight with a relation of hers in the town of —. He waited upon her the next day, to give her an account of the manner in which he had executed some commissions about the choice of china with which she had honoured him.

One visit led to another, and Charles Darford was delighted to find himself admitted into the society of such very genteel persons. At first, he was merely proud of being acquainted with a lady of Miss Maude Germaine's importance, and contented himself with boasting of it to all his acquaintance; by degrees, he became more audacious; he began to fancy himself in love with her, and to flatter himself she would not prove inexorable. The raillery of some of his companions piqued him to make good his boast; and he determined to pay his addresses to a lady, who, they all agreed, could never think of a man in business.

Our hero was not entirely deluded by his vanity: the lady's coquetry contributed to encourage his hopes. Though she always spoke of him to her friends as a person whom it was impossible she could ever think of for a moment, yet as soon as he made a declaration of his love to her, she began to consider that a manufacturer might have common sense, and even some judgment and taste. Her horror of people in business continued in full force; but she began to allow there was no general rule that did not admit of an exception. When her female friends laughed, following the example she had set them, at Charles Darford, her laughter became fainter than theirs; and she was one evening heard to ask a stranger, who saw him for the first time, whether that young gentleman looked as if he was in business?

Sundry matters began to operate in our hero's favour, precedents, opportunely produced by her waiting-maid, of ladies of the first families in England, ladies even of the first fashion, who had married into mercantile houses; a present, too, from her admirer of the beautiful china vase, of which she had so often made him change his opinion, had its due effect; but the preponderating motive was the dread of dying an old maid, if she did not accept of this offer.

After various airs, and graces, and doubts, and disdains, this, fair lady consented to make her lover happy, on the express condition that he should change his name from Darford to Germaine. that he should give up all share in the odious cotton manufactory, and that he should purchase the estate of Germaine-park, in Northamptonshire, to part with which, as it luckily happened, some of her great relations were compelled.

In the folly of his joy, at the prospect of an alliance with the great Germaine family, he promised every thing that was required of him, notwithstanding the remonstrances of his friend William, who represented to him, in the forcible language of common sense, the inconveniences of marrying into a family that would despise him; and of uniting himself to such an old coquette as Miss Germaine, who would make him not only a disagreeable but a most extravagant wife.

"Do you not see," said he, "that she has not the least affection for you? she marries you only because she despairs of getting any other match; and because you are rich, and she is poor. She is seven years older than you, by her own confession, and consequently will be an old woman whilst you are a young man. She is, as you see—I mean as I see—vain and proud in the extreme; and if she honours you with her hand, she will think you can never do enough to make her amends for having married beneath her pretensions. Instead of finding in her, as I find in my wife, the best and most affectionate of friends, you will find her your torment through life; and consider, this is a torment likely to last these thirty or forty years. Is it not worth while to pause—to reflect for as many minutes, or even days?"

Charles paused double the number of seconds, perhaps, and then replied, "You have married to please yourself, cousin William, and I shall marry to please myself. As I don't mean to spend my days in the same style in which you do, the same sort of wife that makes you happy could never content me. I mean to make some figure in the world; I know no other use of fortune; and an alliance with the Germaines brings me at once into fashionable society. Miss Maude Germaine is very proud, I confess; but she has some reason to be proud of her family; and then, you see, her love for me conquers her pride, great as it is."

William sighed when he saw the extent of his cousin's folly. The partnership between the two Darfords was dissolved.

It cost our hero much money but no great trouble to get his name changed from Darford to Germaine; and it was certainly very disadvantageous to his pecuniary interest to purchase Germaine-park, which was sold to him for at least three years' purchase more than its value: but, in the height of his impatience to get into the fashionable world, all prudential motives appeared beneath his consideration. It was, as he fancied, part of the character of a man of spirit, the character he was now to assume and support for life, to treat pecuniary matters as below his notice. He bought Germaine-park, married Miss Germaine, and determined no mortal should ever find out, by his equipages or style of life, that he had not been born the possessor of this estate.

In this laudable resolution, it cannot possibly be doubted but that his bride encouraged him to the utmost of her power. She was eager to leave the county where his former friends and acquaintance resided; for they were people with whom, of course, it could not be expected that she should keep up any manner of intercourse. Charles, in whose mind vanity at this moment smothered every better feeling, was in reality glad of a pretext for breaking off all connexion with those whom he had formerly loved. He went to take leave of William in a fine chariot, on which the Germaine arms were ostentatiously blazoned. That real dignity, which arises from a sense of independence of mind, appeared in William's manners; and quite overawed and abashed our hero, in the midst of all his finery and airs. "I hope, cousin William," said Charles, "when you can spare time, though, to be sure, that is a thing hardly to be expected, as you are situated; but, in case you should be able any ways to make it convenient, I hope you will come and take a look at what we are doing at Germaine-park."

There was much awkward embarrassment in the enunciation of this feeble invitation: for Charles was conscious he did not desire it should be accepted, and that it was made in direct opposition to the wishes of his bride. He was at once relieved from his perplexity, and at the same time mortified, by the calm simplicity with which William replied, "I thank you, cousin, for this invitation; but you know I should be an encumbrance to you at Germaine-park: and I make it a rule neither to go into any company that would be ashamed of me, or of which I should be ashamed."

"Ashamed of you! But—What an idea, my dear William! Surely you don't think—you can't imagine—I should ever consider you as any sort of encumbrance?—I protest—"

"Save yourself the trouble of protesting, my dear Charles," cried William, smiling with much good-nature: "I know why you are so much embarrassed at this instant; and I do not attribute this to any want of affection for me. We are going to lead quite different lives. I wish you all manner of satisfaction. Perhaps the time may come when I shall be able to contribute to your happiness more than I can at present."

Charles uttered some unmeaning phrases, and hurried to his carriage. At the sight of its varnished panels he recovered his self-complacency and courage, and began to talk fluently about chariots and horses, whilst the children of the family followed to take leave of him, saying, "Are you going quite away, Charles? Will you never come back to play with us, as you used to do?" Charles stepped into his carriage with as much dignity as he could assume; which, indeed, was very little. William, who judged of his friends always with the most benevolent indulgence, excused the want of feeling which Charles betrayed during this visit. "My dear," said he to his wife, who expressed some indignation at the slight shown to their children, "we must forgive him; for, you know, a man cannot well think of more than one thing at a time; and the one thing that he is thinking of is his fine chariot. The day will come when he will think more of fine children; at least I hope so, for his own sake."

And now, behold our hero in all his glory; shining upon the Northamptonshire world in the splendour of his new situation! The dress, the equipage, the entertainments, and, above all, the airs of the bride and bridegroom, were the general subject of conversation in the county for ten days. Our hero, not precisely knowing what degree of importance Mr. Germaine, of Germaine-park, was entitled to assume, out-Germained Germaine.

The country gentlemen first stared, then laughed, and at last unanimously agreed, over their bottle, that this new neighbour of theirs was an upstart, who ought to be kept down: and that a vulgar manufacturer should not be allowed to give himself airs merely because he had married a proud lady of good family. It was obvious, they said, he was not born for the situation in which he now appeared. They remarked and ridiculed the ostentation with which he displayed every luxury in his house; his habit of naming the price of every thing, to enforce its claim to admiration; his affected contempt for economy; his anxiety to connect himself with persons of rank, joined to his ignorance of the genealogy of nobility, and the strange mistakes he made between old and new titles.

Certain little defects in his manners, and some habitual vulgarisms in his conversation, exposed him also to the derision of his well-bred neighbours. Mr. Germaine saw that the gentlemen of the county were leagued against him; but he had neither temper nor knowledge of the world sufficient to wage this unequal war. The meanness with which he alternately attempted to court and to bully his adversaries, shewed them, at once, the full extent of their power and of his weakness. Things were in this position when our hero unluckily affronted Mr. Cole, one of the proudest gentlemen in the county, by mistaking him for a merchant of the same name; and, under this mistake, neglecting to return his visit. A few days afterwards at a public dinner, Mr. Cole and Mr. Germaine had some high words, which were repeated by the persons present in various manners; and this dispute became the subject of conversation in the county, particularly amongst the ladies. Each related, according to her fancy, what her husband had told her; and as these husbands had drunk a good deal, they had not a perfectly clear recollection of what had passed, so that the whole and every part of the conversation was exaggerated. The fair judges, averse as they avowed their feelings were to duelling, were clearly of opinion, among themselves, that a real gentleman would certainly have called Mr. Cole to account for the words he uttered, though none of them could agree what those words were.

Mrs. Germaine's female friends, in their coteries, were the first to deplore, with becoming sensibility, that she should be married to a man who had so little the spirit as well as the manners of a man of birth. Their pity became progressively vehement the more they thought of, or at least the more they talked of, the business; till at last one old lady, the declared and intimate friend of Mrs. Germaine, unintentionally, and in the heat of tattle, made use of one phrase that led to another, and another, till she betrayed, in conversation with that lady, the gossiping scandal of these female circles.

Mrs. Germaine, piqued as her pride was, and though she had little affection for her husband, would have shuddered with horror to have imagined him in the act of fighting a duel, and especially at her instigation; yet of this very act she became the cause. In their domestic quarrels, her tongue was ungovernable: and at such moments, the malice of husbands and wives often appears to exceed the hatred of the worst of foes; and, in the ebullition of her vengeance, when his reproaches had stung her beyond the power of her temper to support, unable to stop her tongue, she vehemently told him he was a coward, who durst not so talk to a man! He had proved himself a coward; and was become the by-word and contempt of the whole county! Even women despised his cowardice!

However astonishing it may appear to those who are unacquainted with the nature of quarrels between man and wife, it is but too certain that such quarrels have frequently led to the most fatal consequences. The agitation of mind which Mrs. Germaine suffered the moment she could recollect what she had so rashly said, her vain endeavours to prove to herself that, so provoked, she could not say less, and the sudden effect which she plainly saw her words had produced upon her husband, were but a part of the punishment that always follows conduct and contentions so odious.

Mr. Germaine gazed at her a few moments with wildness in his eyes; his countenance expressed the stupefaction of rage: he spoke not a word; but started at length, and snatched up his hat. She was struck with panic terror, gave a scream, sprang after him, caught him by the coat, and, with the most violent protestations, denied the truth of all she had said. The look he gave her cannot be described; he rudely plucked the skirt from her grasp, and rushed out of the house.

All day and all night she neither saw nor heard of him: in the morning he was brought home, accompanied by a surgeon, in the carriage of a gentleman who had been his second, dangerously wounded.

He was six weeks confined to his bed; and, in the first moment of doubt expressed by the surgeon for his life, she expressed contrition which was really sincere: but, as he recovered, former bickerings were renewed; and the terms on which they lived gradually became what they had been.

Neither did his duel regain that absurd reputation for which he fought; it was malignantly said he had neither the courage to face a man, nor the understanding to govern a wife.

Still, however, Mrs. Germaine consoled herself with the belief that the most shocking circumstance of his having been partner in a manufactory was a profound secret. Alas! the fatal moment arrived when she was to be undeceived in this her last hope. Soon after Mr. Germaine recovered from his wounds she gave a splendid bail, to which the neighbouring nobility and gentry were invited. She made it a point, with all her acquaintance, to come on this grand night.

The more importance the Germaines set upon success, and the more anxiety they betrayed, the more their enemies enjoyed the prospect of their mortification. All the young belles, who had detested Miss Maude Germaine for the airs she used to give herself at county assemblies, now leagued to prevent their admirers from accepting her invitation. All the married ladies whom she had outshone in dress and equipage, protested they were not equal to keep up an acquaintance with such prodigiously fine people; and that, for their part, they must make a rule not to accept of such expensive entertainments, as it was not in their power to return them.

Some persons of consequence in the county kept their determination in doubt, suffered themselves to be besieged daily with notes and messages, and hopes that their imaginary coughs, head-aches, and influenzas, were better, and that they would find themselves able to venture out on the 15th. When the coughs, head-aches, and influenzas, could hold out no longer, these ingenious tormentors devised new pretexts for supposing it would be impossible to do themselves the honour of accepting Mr. and Mrs. Germaine's obliging invitation on the 15th. Some had recourse to the roads, and others to the moon.

Mrs. Germaine, whose pride was now compelled to make all manner of concessions, changed her night from the 15th to the 20th, to insure a full moon to those timorous damsels whom she had known to go home nine miles from a ball the darkest night imaginable, without scruple or complaint. Mr. Germaine, at his own expense, mended some spots in the roads, which were obstacles to the delicacy of other travellers; and when all this was accomplished, the haughty leaders of the county fashions condescended to promise they would do themselves the pleasure to wait upon Mr. and Mrs. Germaine on the 20th.

Their cards of acceptation were shown with triumph by the Germaines; but it was a triumph of short duration. With all the refinement of cruelty, they gave hopes which they never meant to fulfil. On the morning, noon, and night, of the 20th, notes poured in with apologies, or rather with excuses, for not keeping their engagements. Scarcely one was burnt, before another arrived. Mrs. Germaine could not command her temper; and she did not spare her husband in this trying moment.

The arrival of some company for the ball interrupted a warm dispute between the happy pair. The ball was very thinly attended; the guests looked as if they were more inclined to yawn than to dance. The supper table was not half filled; and the profusion with which it was laid out was forlorn and melancholy: every thing was on too grand a scale for the occasion; wreaths of flowers, and pyramids, and triumphal arches, sufficient for ten times as many guests! Even the most inconsiderate could not help comparing the trouble and expense incurred by the entertainment with the small quantity of pleasure it produced. Most of the guests rose from table, whispering to one another, as they looked at the scarcely-tasted dishes, "What a waste! What a pity! Poor Mrs. Germaine! What a melancholy sight this must be to her!"

The next day, a mock heroic epistle, in verse, in the character of Mrs. Germaine, to one of her noble relations, giving an account of her ball and disappointment, was handed about, and innumerable copies were taken. It was written with some humour and great ill-nature. The good old lady who occasioned the duel, thought it but friendly to show Mrs. Germaine a copy of it; and to beg she would keep it out of her husband's way: it might be the cause of another duel! Mrs. Germaine, in spite of all her endeavours to conceal her vexation, was obviously so much hurt by this mock heroic epistle, that the laughers were encouraged to proceed; and the next week a ballad, entitled, "THE MANUFACTURER TURNED GENTLEMAN," was circulated with the same injunctions to secresy, and the same success. Mr. and Mrs. Germaine, perceiving themselves to be the objects of continual enmity and derision, determined to leave the county. Germaine-park was forsaken; a house in London was bought; and, for a season or two, our hero was amused with the gaieties of the town, and gratified by finding himself actually moving in that sphere of life to which he had always aspired. But he soon perceived that the persons whom, at a distance, he had regarded as objects of admiration and envy, upon a nearer view were capable of exciting only contempt or pity. Even in the company of honourable and right honourable men, he was frequently overpowered with ennui; and, amongst all the fine acquaintances with which his fine wife crowded his fine house, he looked in vain for a friend: he looked in vain for a William Darford.

One evening, at Ranelagh, Charles happened to hear the name of Mr. William Darford pronounced by a lady who was walking behind him: he turned eagerly to look at her; but, though he had a confused recollection of having seen her face before, he could not remember when or where he had met with her. He felt a wish to speak to her, that he might hear something of those friends whom he had neglected, but not forgotten. He was not, however, acquainted with any of the persons with whom she was walking, and was obliged to give up his purpose. When she left the room, he followed her, in hopes of learning, from her servants, who she was; but she had no servants—no carriage!

Mrs. Germaine, who clearly inferred she was a person of no consequence, besought her husband not to make any further inquiries. "I beg, Mr. Germaine, you will not gratify your curiosity about the Darfords at my expense. I shall have a whole tribe of vulgar people upon my hands, if you do not take care. The Darfords, you know, are quite out of our line of life; especially in town."

This remonstrance had a momentary effect upon Mr. Germaine's vanity; but a few days afterwards he met the same lady in the park, attended by Mr. William Darford's old servant. Regardless of his lady's representations, he followed the suggestions of his own heart, and eagerly stopped the man to inquire after his friends in the most affectionate manner. The servant, who was pleased to see that Charles was not grown quite so much a fine gentleman as to forget all his friends in the country, became very communicative; he told Mr. Germaine that the lady, whom he was attending, was a Miss Locke, governess to Mr. William Darford's children; and that she was now come to town to spend a few days with a relation, who had been very anxious to see her. This relation was not either rich or genteel; and though our hero used every persuasion to prevail upon his lady to show Miss Locke some civility whilst she was in town, he could not succeed. Mrs. Germaine repeated her former phrase, again and again, "The Darfords are quite out of our line of life;" and this was the only reason she would give.

Charles was disgusted by the obstinacy of his wife's pride, and indulged his better feelings by going frequently to visit Miss Locke. She stayed, however, but a fortnight in town; and the idea of his friends, which had been strongly recalled by his conversations with her, gradually faded away. He continued the course of life into which he had been forced, rather from inability to stop than from inclination to proceed. Their winters were spent in dissipation in town; their summers wasted at watering-places, or in visits to fine relations, who were tired of their company, and who took but little pains to conceal this sentiment. Those who do not live happily at home can seldom contrive to live respectably abroad. Mr. and Mrs. Germaine could not purchase esteem, and never earned it from the world or from one another. Their mutual contempt increased every day. Only those who have lived with bosom friends whom they despise can fully comprehend the extent and intensity of the evil.

We spare our readers the painful detail of domestic grievances and the petty mortifications of vanity: from the specimens we have already given they may form some idea, but certainly not a competent one, of the manner in which this ill-matched pair continued to live together for twelve long years. Twelve long years! The imagination cannot distinctly represent such a period of domestic suffering; though, to the fancy of lovers, the eternal felicity to be ensured by their union is an idea perfectly familiar and intelligible. Perhaps, if we could bring our minds to dwell more upon the hours, and less upon the years of existence, we should make fewer erroneous judgments. Our hero and heroine would never have chained themselves together for life, if they could have formed an adequate picture of the hours contained in the everlasting period of twelve years of wrangling. During this time, scarcely an hour, certainly not a day, passed in which they did not, directly or indirectly, reproach one another; and tacitly form, or explicitly express, the wish that they had never been joined in holy wedlock.

They, however, had a family. Children are either the surest bonds of union between parents, or the most dangerous causes of discord. If parents agree in opinion as to the management of their children, they must be a continually increasing source of pleasure; but where the father counteracts the mother, and the mother the father—where the children cannot obey or caress either of their parents without displeasing the other, what can they become but wretched little hypocrites, or detestable little tyrants?

Mr. and Mrs. Germaine had two children, a boy and a girl. From the moment of their birth, they became subjects of altercation and jealousy. The nurses were obliged to decide whether the infants were most like the father or the mother: two nurses lost their places, by giving what was, in Mr. Germaine's opinion, an erroneous decision upon this important question. Every stranger who came to pay a visit was obliged to submit to a course of interrogations on this subject; and afterwards, to their utter confusion, saw biting of lips, and tossing of heads, either on the paternal or maternal side. At last, it was established that Miss Maude was the most like her mamma, and master Charles the most like his papa. Miss Maude, of course, became the faultless darling of her mother, and master Charles the mutinous favourite of his father. A comparison between their features, gestures, and manners, was daily instituted, and always ended in words of scorn, from one party or the other. Even whilst they were pampering these children with sweetmeats, or inflaming them with wine, the parents had always the same mean and selfish views. The mother, before she would let her Maude taste the sweetmeats, insisted upon the child's lisping out that she loved mamma best; and before the little Charles was permitted to carry the bumper of wine to his lips, he was compelled to say he loved papa best. In all their childish quarrels, Maude ran roaring to her mamma, and Charles sneaked up to his papa.

As the interests of the children were so deeply concerned in the question, it was quickly discovered who ruled in the house with the strongest hand. Mr. Germaine's influence over his son diminished, as soon as the boy was clearly convinced that his sister, by adhering to her mamma, enjoyed a larger share of the good things. He was wearied out by the incessant rebuffs of the nursery-maids, who were all in their lady's interests; and he endeavoured to find grace in their sight, by recanting all the declarations he had made in his father's favour. "I don't like papa best now: I love mamma best to-day."

"Yes, master, but you must love mamma best every day, or it won't do, I promise you."

By such a course of nursery precepts, these unfortunate children were taught equivocation, falsehood, envy, jealousy, and every fault of temper which could render them insupportable to themselves, and odious to others. Those who have lived in the house with spoiled children must have a lively recollection of the degree of torment they can inflict upon all who are within sight or hearing. These domestic plagues became more and more obnoxious; and Mrs. Germaine, in the bitterness of her heart, was heard to protest she wished she had never had a child! Children were pretty things at three years old, but began to be great plagues at six, and were quite intolerable at ten.

Schools, and tutors, and governesses, were tried without number; but those capricious changes served only to render the pupils still more unmanageable. At length Mr. and Mrs. Germaine's children became so notoriously troublesome, that every body dreaded the sight of them.

One summer, when Mrs. Germaine was just setting out on a visit to my Lady Mary Crawley, when the carriage was actually at the door, and the trunks tied on, an express arrived from her ladyship with a letter, stipulating that neither Miss Maude nor Master Charles should be of the party. Lady Mary declared she had suffered so much from their noise, quarrelling, and refractory tempers when they were with her the preceding summer, that she could not undergo such a trial again; that their mother's nerves might support such things, but that hers really could not: besides, she could not, in justice and politeness to the other friends who were to be in her house, suffer them to be exposed to such torments. Lady Mary Crawley did not give herself any trouble to soften her expressions, because she would have been really glad if they had given offence, and if Mrs. Germaine had resented her conduct, by declining to pay that annual visit which was now become, in the worst sense of the word, visitation. To what meanness proud people are often forced to submit! Rather than break her resolution never to spend another summer at her own country seat, Mrs. Germaine submitted to all the haughtiness of her Leicestershire relations, and continued absolutely to force upon them visits which she knew to be unwelcome.

But what was to be done about her children! The first thing, of course, was to reproach her husband. "You see, Mr. Germaine, the effect of the pretty education you have given that boy of yours. I am sure, if he had not gone with us last summer into Leicestershire, my Maude would not have been in the least troublesome to Lady Mary."

"On the contrary, my dear, I have heard Lady Mary herself say, twenty times, that Charles was the best of the two; and I am persuaded, if Maude had been away, the boy would have become quite a favourite."

"There you are utterly mistaken, I can assure you, my dear; for you know you are no great favourite of Lady Mary's yourself; and I have often heard her say that Charles is your image."

"It is very extraordinary that all your great relations show us so little civility, my dear. They do not seem to have much regard for you."

"They have regard enough for me, and showed it formerly; but of late, to be sure, I confess, things are altered. They never have been so cordial since my marriage, and, all things considered, I scarcely know how to blame them."

Mr. Germaine bowed, by way of thanking his lady for this compliment. She besought him not to bow so like a man behind a counter, if he could possibly help it. He replied, it became him to submit to be schooled by a wife, who was often taken for his mother. At length, when every species of reproach, mental and personal, which conjugal antipathy could suggest, had been exhausted, the orators recurred to the business of the day, and to the question, "What is to be done with the children whilst we are at Lady Mary Crawley's?"

CHAPTER II

In this embarrassment we must leave the Germaines for the present, and refresh ourselves with a look at a happy circle—the family of Mr. Darford, where there is no discordance of opinions, of tastes, or of tempers; none of those evils which arise sometimes from the disappointment and sometimes from the gratification of vanity and pride.

Mr. Darford succeeded beyond his most sanguine expectations in the management of his business. Wealth poured in upon him; but he considered wealth, like a true philosopher, only as one of the means of happiness: he did not become prodigal or avaricious; neither did he ever feel the slightest ambition to quit his own station in society. He never attempted to purchase from people of superior rank admission into their circles, by giving luxurious and ostentatious entertainments. He possessed a sturdy sense of his own value, and commanded a species of respect very different from that which is paid to the laced livery or the varnished equipage.

The firmness of his character was, however, free from all severity: he knew how to pardon in others the weakness and follies from which he was himself exempt. Though his cousin was of such a different character, and though, since his marriage, Mr. Germaine had neglected his old friends, William felt more compassion for his unhappiness than resentment for his faults. In the midst of his own family, William would often say, "I wish poor Charles may ever be as happy as we are!" Frequently, in his letters to London correspondents, he desired them to inquire, privately, how Mr. Germaine went on.

For some time he heard of nothing but his extravagance, and of the entertainments given to the fine world by Mrs. Germaine; but in the course of a few years, his correspondents hinted that Mr. Germaine began to be distressed for money, and that this was a secret which had been scrupulously kept from his lady, as scrupulously as she concealed from him her losses at play. Mr. Darford also learned from a correspondent who was intimately acquainted with one of Mrs. Germaine's friends, that this lady lived upon very bad terms with her husband; and that her children were terribly spoiled by the wretched education they received.

These accounts gave William sincere concern: far from triumphing in the accomplishing of his prophecies, he never once recalled them to the memory even of his own family; all his thoughts were intent upon saving his friend from future pain.

One day, as he was sitting with his family round their cheerful tea-table, his youngest boy, who had climbed upon his knees, exclaimed, "Papa! what makes you so very grave to-night? You are not at all like yourself! What can make you sorry?"

"My dear little boy," said his father, "I was thinking of a letter I received to-day from London."

"I wish those letters would never come, for they always make you look sad, and make you sigh! Mamma, why do you not desire the servants not to bring papa any more such letters? What did this letter say to you, papa, to make you so grave?"

"My dear," said his father, smiling at the child's simplicity, "this letter told me that your little cousin Charles is not quite so good a boy as you are."

"Then, papa, I will tell you what to do: send our Miss Locke to cousin Charles, and she will soon make him very good."

"I dare say she would," replied the father, laughing: "but, my dear boy, I cannot send Miss Locke; and I am afraid she would not like to go: besides, we should be rather sorry to part with her."

"Then, papa, suppose you were to send for my cousin; and Miss Locke could take care of him here, without leaving us?"

"Could take care of him—true; but would she? If you can prevail upon her to do so, I will send for your cousin."

The proposal, though playfully made, was seriously accepted by Miss Locke: and the more willingly, as she remembered, with gratitude, the attention Mr. Germaine had paid to her some years before, when with poor relations in London.

Mr. Darford wrote immediately, to invite his cousin's children to his house; and the invitation was most gladly accepted, for it was received the very day when Mr. and Mrs. Germaine were so much embarrassed by Lady Mary Crawley's absolute refusal to admit these children into her house. Mrs. Germaine was not too proud to accept of favours from those whom she had treated as beneath her acquaintance, "quite out of her line of life!" She despatched her children directly to Mr. Darford's; and Miss Locke undertook the care of them. It was not an easy or agreeable task; but she had great obligations to Mrs. Darford, and was rejoiced at finding an opportunity of showing her gratitude.

Miss Locke was the young woman whose painting of an iris had been admired by Charles and by Miss Maude Germaine when they visited the china works, thirteen or fourteen years before this time. She was at that period very ill, and in great distress: her father had been a bankrupt, and to earn bread for herself and her sisters she was obliged to work harder than her health and strength allowed. Probably she would have fallen a sacrifice to her exertions, if she had not been saved by the humanity of Mr.

Darford; and, fortunately for him, he was married to a woman who sympathized in all his generous feelings, and who assisted him in every benevolent action.

Mrs. Darford, after making sufficient inquiries as to the truth of the story, and the character of the girl, was so much pleased with all she heard of her merit, and so much touched by her misfortunes, that she took Miss Locke into her family to teach her daughters to draw. She well knew that a sense of dependence is one of the greatest evils; and she was careful to relieve the person whom she obliged from this painful feeling, by giving her an opportunity of being daily useful to her benefactress. Miss Locke soon recovered her health: she perceived she might be serviceable in teaching the children of the family many things besides drawing; and, with unremitting perseverance, she informed her own mind, that she might be able to instruct her pupils. Year after year she pursued this plan; and was rewarded by the esteem and affection of the happy family in which she lived.

But though Miss Locke was a woman of great abilities, she had not the magical powers attributed to some characters in romance; she could not instantaneously produce a total reformation of manners. The habits of spoiled children are not to be changed by the most skilful preceptress, without the aid of time. Miss Maude Germaine and her brother had tempers which tried Miss Locke's patience to the utmost; but, gradually, she acquired some influence over these wayward spirits. She endeavoured with her utmost skill to eradicate the jealousy which had been implanted in the minds of the brother and sister. They found that they were now treated with strict impartiality, and they began to live together more peaceably.

Time was willingly allowed to Miss Locke by their parents, who were glad to be disencumbered of their children. Eighteen months passed away, and no news were heard of Mr. and Mrs. Germaine, except that they continued the same extravagant, dissipated course of life, and that they began to be much embarrassed in their circumstances. At last Mr. Darford received a letter which informed him that an execution was laid on Mr. Germaine's fine house in town; and that he and his family were all in the greatest distress and affliction.

William hastened immediately to London. He was denied admittance at Mr. Germaine's: the porter, with an air of mystery, said that his master was ill, and did not choose to see any body. William, however, forced his way up stairs.

Charles, at the sight of him, stepped back, exclaiming, "May I believe my eyes? William! Is it you?"

"Yes, it is William; your old friend William," said Mr. Darford, embracing him affectionately. Pride and shame struggled in the mind of Charles; and, turning aside to repress the tears, which in the first instance of emotion had started into his eyes, he went to the farthest end of the room for an arm-chair for his cousin, placed it with awkward ceremony, and said, "Won't you be seated, cousin Darford? I am sure Mrs. Germaine and I are much indebted to you and Mrs. Darford, for your goodness to our children. I was just thinking of writing to you about them;—but we are in sad confusion here, just at this moment. I am quite ashamed—I did not expect—Why did you never honour us with a visit before? I am sure you could not possibly have hit upon a more unlucky moment for a visit—for yourself, I mean." "If it proves lucky to you, my dear Charles," replied William mildly, "I shall think it the most fortunate moment I could possibly have chosen."

Vanquished by the tone of this reply, our hero burst into tears: he squeezed his friend's hand, but could not speak. Recovering himself, after a few minutes, he said, "You are too good, cousin William, and always were! I thought you called in by accident; I had no supposition that you came on purpose to assist me in this moment of distress—embarrassment, I ought to say; for, in fact, it is only a mere temporary embarrassment."

"I am heartily glad to hear it. But, speak to me freely, Charles: do not conceal the real state of your affairs from your best friend. What tendency could this have but to plunge you into irretrievable ruin?"

Charles paused for a minute. "The truth of the matter is, my dear William," continued he, "that there are circumstances in this business which I should be sorry reached Mrs. Germaine's ear, or any of her cursed proud relations; for if once they heard of it, I should have no peace for the rest of my life. Indeed, as to peace, I cannot boast of much as it is: but it might be worse, much worse, if the whole truth came out. To you, however, I can trust it; though in your line of life, it would be counted a shocking thing: but still you are so indulgent—"

William listened without being able to guess where this preamble would end.

"In the first place," continued Charles, "you know—Mrs. Germaine is almost ten years older than I am."

"Six years, I thought you formerly told me?"

"I beg your pardon, ten—ten—within a few months. If I said six, it was before our marriage, when I knew no better. She owns to seven: her own relations say eight; her nurse said nine; and I say ten."

"Well, ten let it be, since you will have it so."

"I should be very glad to have it otherwise, I promise you, if I could: for it is not very pleasant to a man like me, to be quizzed by half the young men of fashion in town, for having married a woman old enough to be my mother."

"Not quite old enough to be your mother," said his cousin, in a conciliatory tone; "these young men of fashion are not the best calculators. Mrs. Germaine could not well have been your mother, since at the worst, by your own account, there is only ten years difference between you."

"Oh, but that is not all; for, what is still worse, Mrs. Germaine, thanks to the raking hours she keeps, and gaming and fretting, looks full ten years older than she is: so that you see, in fact, there are twenty years between us."

"I do not see it, indeed," replied William, smiling; "but I am bound to believe what you assert. Let me ask you, to what does this discussion, concerning poor Mrs. Germaine's age, tend?"

"To justify, or at least to excuse, poor Mr. Germaine for keeping a mistress, who is something younger, something prettier, and, above all, something more good-humoured, than his wife."

"Perhaps the wife would be as good-humoured as the mistress, if she were as happy in possessing her husband's affections."

"Affections! Oh, Lord! Affections are out of the question, Mrs. Germaine does not care a straw about my affections."

"And yet you dread that she should have the least hint of your having a mistress."

"Of course. You don't see my jet. You don't consider what a devil of a handle that would give her against me. She has no more love for me than this table; but she is jealous beyond all credibility, and she knows right well how to turn her jealousy to account. She would go caballing amongst her tribes of relations, and get all the women and all the world on her side, with this hue and cry of a mistress; and then I should be branded as the worst husband upon earth. That indeed I should laugh at, because all the young men in town would keep me in countenance; but Mrs. Germaine would rummage out the history of the sums of money I have given this girl, and then would set those against her play-debts, and I should have no more hold over her; for, you know, if I should begin to reproach her with the one, she would recriminate. She is a devil of a hand at that work! Neither you nor any man on earth, except myself, can form any idea of the temper of Mrs. Germaine! She is—to you, my dear friend, I may have the relief of saying so—she is, without exception, the most proud, peevish, selfish, unreasonable, extravagant, tyrannical, unfeeling woman in Christendom!"

"In Christendom! Oh, you exaggerate, Charles!"

"Exaggerate! Upon my soul, I do not: she is all I have said, and more."

"More! Impossible. Come, I see how it is; she has been unlucky at the card-table; you are angry, and therefore you speak, as angry people always do, worse than you think."

[Footnote: Swift.]

"No, not at all, I promise you. I am as perfectly cool as you are. You do not know Mrs. Germaine as well as I do."

"But I know that she is much to be pitied, if her husband has a worse opinion of her than any body else expresses."

"That is precisely because I am her husband, and know her better than other people do. Will not you give me leave to be the best judge in what relates to my own wife? I never, indeed, expected to hear you, of all people upon earth, cousin William, undertake her defence. I think I remember that she was no great favourite of yours before I married, and you dissuaded me as much as possible from the match: yet now you are quite become her advocate, and take her part to my face against me."

"It is not taking her part against you, my dear Charles," replied his cousin, "to endeavour to make you better satisfied with your wife. I am not so obstinate in self-opinion as to wish, at the expense of your domestic happiness, to prove that I was right in dissuading you from the match; on the contrary, I would do all in my power to make the best of it; and so should you."

"Ah, cousin William, it is easy for you to talk of making the best of a bad match; you who are married to one of the best tempered women alive! I wish you were to live with Mrs. Germaine for one month."

William smiled, as much as to say, "I cannot join in that wish."

"Besides," continued Charles, "if I were to open my whole heart to you, you would pity me on another account. My wife is not my only plague: my mistress is almost as great a torment as my wife."

"What! This mistress of whom you are so fond?"

"Ay! There is the curse! I cannot help being fond of her: and that she knows, and plays me off as she pleases. But I believe the little jilt loves me all the time: because she has offers enough, and from men of the first fashion, if she would leave me. She is certainly a good girl; but then so passionate!"

"I thought you told me she was good-humoured," interrupted his cousin.

"Well, so she is, at times, the best humoured creature in nature; and then she is charming: but when she falls into a passion, she is a little fury! Absolutely a little devil! There is nothing she would not do. Now, do you know, all this terrible business, this execution against me, is her doing?"

"A singular proof of love!" said Mr. William Darford.

"Oh, the fool loves me, notwithstanding; I must do her that justice: but she is quite a child. I put her into a passion, by going down to Leicestershire when she wanted me to stay with her in town. She told me she would be revenged; but I could not believe she would go such lengths. She gave a note of mine, for two hundred guineas, to her uncle; and he got a writ. Now she is in despair about it; I saw her two hours ago all in tears, and tearing her hair, because her uncle won't consent to withdraw the execution. I am sure she is really and truly sorry; and would give her eyes to get me out of this scrape."

"Whether she would give her eyes or not, I will not pretend to determine; but it is plain she would not pay two hundred guineas 'to get you out of this scrape.' Now, where do you intend to get the money?"

"Ah, there's the rub! I have not a farthing, till our next rents come in; and you see these heaps of bills. Then the agent, who manages every thing, Heaven knows how! At Germaine-park, says tenants are breaking; that we are, I do not know how much, in his debt, and that we must sell; but that, if we sell in a hurry, and if our distress be talked of, we shall get nothing for the land, and so shall be ruined outright. Now, this all originates in Mrs. Germaine's pride and positiveness: she never could be prevailed upon to go down to Germaine-park, these ten years past, because some of the Northamptonshire people affronted her: so our affairs have gone on just as the agent pleases; and he is a rascal, I am convinced, for he is always writing to say we are in his debt. But, indeed, my dear William, you are too good to take any interest in this history of my affairs: I am conscious that I have not treated you well."

"Do not talk of that now: do not think of it, Charles," interrupted Mr. Darford. "I am come to town on purpose to be of all the service to you I can. I will discharge this writ upon one, and only upon one, condition."

"Upon any condition you please," cried Charles. "I will give you my bond. I will give you security upon the Germaine estate, if you require it."

"I require no security; I require no bond, Charles; I require only a condition which I believe to be absolutely necessary for your happiness. Promise me you will break off all connexion with this treacherous mistress of yours."

"Treacherous! No, no! I assure you, you mistake the girl."

"Mistake her or not, Charles, without arguing the matter farther, on this one point I must be peremptory; and, positively, the only condition on which I will pay this money is your promise never to see her again."

Charles hesitated. "Upon my soul," cried he, "I believe the girl will break her heart. But then she is so cursedly extravagant, she ruins me! I would have broken with her long ago, if I could have summoned up courage enough. After all, I believe it was more habit, idleness, and fashion, than any thing else, that made me go to see her so often. When I did not know what to do with myself, or when I was put out of humour at home, I went to this girl. Well, let us say no more about it: she is not worth thinking of; I give her up. You may depend upon it, my dear William, I will have nothing more to do with her. I will, since you make that your ultimatum, never see her again."

"Will you write to her then immediately, to let her know your determination?"

"Certainly; immediately."

Charles wrote, to bid adieu to this mistress; to whom, by his own account, habit, idleness, fashion, and the want of a happy home, had attached him; and William gave him a draft for the amount of his debt, by which the execution was taken off.

Mr. Darford seized the moment when his cousin's mind was warmed with gratitude to say a few words, as little in the form of advice as possible, in praise of economy.

"You know, my dear Charles," said he, "that I am, and always was, a very plain man, in my way of living; and I dare say my ideas will appear quite absurd to you, who are used to live with men of taste and fashion; but really these rooms, this furniture, and this house, appear to me fitter for a nobleman than for a man of your fortune."

"It is so. Mrs. Germaine would insist upon my taking it. But I will part with it before next winter. I will advertise it immediately. I will begin a course of economy."

Mr. Germaine's projects of economy were at this moment interrupted by the sudden entrance of his wife. Her eyes flashing with anger, she walked with the proud air of an enraged tragedy queen across the room, seated herself upon a sofa, and, in a voice which trembled with ill-suppressed rage, said, "I am to thank you, Mr. Germaine, for the many obliging things you have said of me this last hour! I have heard them all! You are under a mistake, sir, if you imagine I have been hitherto your dupe. You have never imposed upon me for a moment. I have suspected, this twelvemonth, that you kept a mistress: and now I am happy to have the truth confirmed from your own lips. But I deserve all that has happened! I am justly treated! Weak woman, to marry as I did! No gentleman, sir, would have behaved or would have spoken as you have done! Could not you have been content with ruining yourself and your family, Mr. Germaine, by your profligate low tastes, without insulting me by base reflections upon my temper, and downright falsehoods about my age? No gentleman, sir, would have treated me as you have done. I am the most miserable of women!"

Passion choked her utterance, and she fell back in a violent fit of hysterics. Mr. William Darford was much shocked at this matrimonial scene. The lady had caught hold of his arm, in one of her convulsive motions; and she held it so fast that he could not withdraw. Charles stood in silent dismay. His conscience smote him; and though he could not love his wife, he blamed himself for having rendered her "the most miserable of women." "Leave her to me, Charles," said Mr. Darford, "and I will endeavour to set matters to rights."

Charles shook his head, and left the room. Mrs. Germaine by degrees recovered herself; for a hysteric fit cannot last for ever. She cast her eyes round the room, and exclaimed, "He has done well to leave me! Oh, that it were for ever! Oh, that we had never met! But may I ask why Mr. William Darford is here? My own servant—my own maid, should have been summoned to attend me. We have servants still, sir; and, humbled as I am, I see no necessity for submitting to have cool spectators of our family distresses and family quarrels."

"Believe me, madam," said Mr. Darford, "I am not a cool spectator of either. I do not wish to recal [sic] disagreeable things, but to obtain the right of speaking to you of your affairs as a friend. Permit me to remind you that, when I could not guess you heard me, I defended your interests."

"Really, sir, you spoke so low that I did not distinctly hear what you said; and my feelings were so much hurt, by all I heard from Mr. Germaine, who spoke loud enough, that I attended to nothing else. Upon recollection, I do, however, remember you made some offer to get Mr. Germaine out of his present embarrassments, upon condition that he would break off all connexion with this girl, whom nobody knows; or rather whom every body knows too well."

"And was not this offer of mine some proof, Mrs. Germaine, that I wish your happiness?"

"Why, really, Mr. Darford, having lived in the world as I have done from my childhood, I am not apt to expect much friendship from any one, especially from people in the habits of calculation; and I have been so much deceived where I have unguardedly trusted to the friendship and love of a man brought up in that sort of way, that you must forgive me if I could not bring my mind to think you had any concern for my happiness in the offer you made. I did indeed suppose it would be a mortifying circumstance to you, to see your cousin quite ruined by this infamous creature. I say, I did imagine you would be shocked at seeing your cousin sent to jail. That, you know, is a thing discreditable to a whole family, let it be of what sort it may. From your kindness to our children, I see you consider us as relations. Every human being, I do suppose, has some family pride in their own way."

"I own I have a great deal of family pride, in my own way, madam," replied Mr. Darford, with a calm smile; "I am proud, for instance, of having, and of being able to maintain in perfect independence, a number of good and affectionate children, and a wife, whose good sense and sweetness of temper constitute the happiness of my existence!"

Mrs. Germaine coloured, threw back her head, and strove to conceal the anguish of her conscience. William was sorry he had inflicted pain, but he saw that the only way to make himself understood in this conversation, was to assert that real superiority of character to which, in certain situations, the factitious pretensions of rank or fashion never fail to yield.

"You are at liberty, Mrs. Germaine," continued William, "to interpret my offers and my actions as you think proper; but you will, when you are cool, observe that neither I nor any of my family have any thing to gain from you or yours; not even a curtsy or a bow, in public places; for we do not frequent them. We live retired, and have no connexion with fine people; we preserve our own independence by confining ourselves to our own station in life; and by never desiring to quit it, nor to ape those who are called our betters. From what I have just heard you say, I think it possible you may have formed the idea that we invited your children to our house with the selfish supposition that the connexion, I believe that is the fashionable phrase, might be advantageous to our own. But this is quite a mistake. Our children will live as we do: they have no idea of forming high connexions, because they have been taught not to think them necessary to happiness. I assure you it is not my habit to talk so much of myself and of mine; but I thought it best to explain the truth to you at once, as this was the only way to gain your confidence, and as we have neither of us time to spare."

"Very true," said Mrs. Germaine.

"And now, madam, I have a proposal to make to you, which I hope you will take as it is meant. I understand, from Mr. Germaine, you have some play debts."

"Mr. Germaine does not know their amount," said Mrs. Germaine, lowering her voice, as if she apprehended she might he overheard.

"If you will trust me with that secret, I will not make a bad use of it."

Mrs. Germaine in a whisper named the sum. It was certainly considerable, for the naming of it made Mr. Darford step back with surprise. After a few minutes' thought, he recovered himself, and said, "This is a larger debt than I was aware of, but we will see what can be done. From the time that Charles and I dissolved our partnership, I have never remitted my attention to business; and that very circumstance, for which you must despise me, puts it now in my power to assist you without injuring my own family. I am a man who speak my mind freely, perhaps bluntly. You must solemnly promise me you will never again play at any game of hazard. Upon this condition, I will pay your present debts immediately."

With all the eagerness of a person who wishes to seize an offer which appears too generous to be repeated, Mrs. Germaine promised all that was required. Her debts were paid.

And now her benefactor had hopes that she and her husband would live more prudently; and that they might still enjoy some portion of domestic happiness. Vain hopes! Charles really wished to retrench his expenses; but Mrs. Germaine's pride was an insuperable obstacle to all his plans of economy. She had always been accustomed to such and such things. There was no possibility of living without them. Her relations would be perfectly astonished if she did not appear in the style in which she had always lived before her marriage. Provoked by the insolent absurdity of such arguments, Mr. Germaine insisted with the authoritative voice of a husband who was conscious that he had both reason and power on his side. Hence arose daily altercations, more bitter even than those which jealousy had formerly occasioned. Some wives acknowledge they can more easily forgive a husband's infidelity than his interference in the regulation of their household expenses. Of this class of amiable females was Mrs. Germaine. Though her husband strictly adhered to his promise, never to have any farther connexion with his mistress, yet he was not rewarded by any increase of affection or kindness from his wife; on the contrary, she seemed to be rather vexed that she was deprived of this legitimate subject of complaint. She could not, with so much tragic effect, bewail that her husband would ruin himself and her by his follies.

To loud altercations, silent hatred succeeded. Mrs. Germaine grew sullen, low-spirited, nervous, and hysterical. Among fashionable medical dowagers, she became an interesting personage: but this species of consequence was by no means sufficient to support her self-complacency, and, as she declared, she felt herself incapable of supporting the intolerable burden of ennui.

In various situations, the conduct of many individuals may be predicted with certainty, by those who are acquainted with their previous habits. Habit is, to weak minds, a species of moral predestination, from which they have no power to escape. Their common language expresses their sense of their own inability to struggle against that destiny which their previous folly has prepared. They usually say, "For my part, I cannot help doing so and so. I know it is very wrong. I know it is my ruin; but I own I cannot resist. It is in vain to argue with me: it is my way; it is my fate."

Mrs. Germaine found herself led, "by an irresistible impulse," to the card-table, notwithstanding her solemn promise never more to play at any game of hazard. It was in vain to argue with her. "It was her way; it was her fate; she knew it was very wrong; she knew it was her ruin; but she could not resist!"

In the course of a few months, she was again involved in debt; and she had the meanness and the assurance again to apply to the generosity of Mr. William Darford. Her letter was written in the most abject strain, and was full of all the flattering expressions which she imagined must, from a woman of her birth and consequence in the world, have a magical effect upon one in Mr. William Darford's station. She was surprised when she received a decided refusal. He declined all farther interference, as he perceived it was impossible that he could be of any real utility. He forbore to reproach the lady with her breach of promise: "She will," said he to himself, "be sufficiently punished by the consequences of her own conduct: I would not increase her distress."

A separation from her husband was the immediate consequence. Perhaps it may be thought that, to Mrs. Germaine, this would be no punishment: but the loss of all the pride, pomp, and circumstance of married life, was deeply felt. She was thrown absolutely upon the charity of relations; who had very little charity in any sense of the word. She was disregarded by all her fine acquaintance; she had no friend upon earth to pity her; even her favourite maid gave warning, because she was tired of her mistress's temper, and of receiving no wages.

The detail of poor Mrs. Germaine's mortifications and sufferings cannot be interesting. She was a prey to low spirits, or in other words, to mortified vanity, for some time; and at last died of a nervous fever.

Her husband wrote the following letter to Mr. William Darford, soon after her death:

"MY DEAR WILLIAM,

"You have heard of poor Mrs. Germaine's death, and of the manner of it; no more need be said upon that subject. Whatever were her faults, she has suffered for them; and so have I for mine. Believe me, I am effectually cured of all desire to be a fine gentleman. I shall quit the name of Germaine immediately, and resume that of Darford. You know the state of my affairs. There is yet hope I may set things to rights by my own industry; and I am determined to go into business, and to apply to it in good earnest, for my own sake, and for the sake of my children, whom I have hitherto shamefully neglected. But I had it not always in my power, after my marriage, to do as I wished. No more of that. The blame be upon me for the past; for the future I shall, I hope, be a different man. I dare not ask you to trust so far to these good resolutions as to take me into partnership with you, in your manufactory; but perhaps your good-nature can direct me to some employment suited to my views and capacity. I ask only a fair trial; I think I shall not do as I used to do, and leave all the letters to be written by my partner.

"Give my love to my dear little boy and girl. How can I thank you and Mrs. Darford enough for all you have done for them? There is another person whom I should wish to thank, but scarcely dare to name; feeling, as I do, so unworthy of her goodness.

"Adieu, yours sincerely,
"CHARLES DARFORD, again, thank God."

It is scarcely necessary to inform our readers, that Mr. William Darford received his penitent friend with open arms, took him into partnership, and assisted him in the most kind and judicious manner to re-establish his fortune and his credit. He became remarkable for his steady attention to business; to the great astonishment of those who had seen him only in the character of a dissipated fine gentleman. Few have sufficient strength of mind thus to stop short in the career of folly, and few have the resolution to bear the ridicule thrown upon them even by those whom they despise. Our hero was ridiculed most unmercifully by all his former companions,—by all the Bond-street loungers. But of what consequence was this to him? He did not live among them; he did not hear their witticisms; and well knew that, in less than a twelvemonth, they would forget such a person as Charles Germaine had ever existed. His knowledge of what is called high life had sufficiently convinced him that happiness is not in the gift or in the possession of those who are often, to ignorant mortals, objects of supreme admiration and envy.

Charles Darford looked for happiness, and found it in domestic life.

Belief, founded upon our own experience, is more firm than that which we grant to the hearsay evidence of moralists; but t happy those who, according to the ancient proverb, can profit by the experience of their predecessors!

Feb. 1803.

THE CONTRAST

CHAPTER I

"What a blessing it is to be the father of such a family of children!" said farmer Frankland, as he looked round at the honest affectionate faces of his sons and daughters, who were dining with him on his birthday. "What a blessing it is to have a large family of children!"

"A blessing you may call it, if you will, neighbour," said farmer Bettesworth; "but if I were to speak my mind, I should be apt to call it a curse."

"Why, as to that, we may both be right and both be wrong," replied Frankland; "for children are either a blessing or a curse according as they turn out; and they turn out according as they are brought up. 'Bring up a child in the way it should go;' that has ever been my maxim: show me a better, show me a happier family than my own; and show me a happier father than myself," continued the good old man, with pleasure sparkling in his eyes. Observing, however, that his neighbour Bettesworth looked blank and sighed deeply, he checked himself, and said, in a more humble tone, "To be sure, it is not so mannerly for a man to be praising his own, except it just come from the heart unawares, amongst friends who will excuse it, especially upon such a day as this. This day I am seventy years of age, and never was heartier or happier! So, Fanny, love, fill neighbour Bettesworth a glass of your sister's cider. 'Tis my Patty's making, sir; and better never was drunk. Nay, nay, sit ye still, neighbour; as you happened to call in just as we were all dining, and making merry together, why you cannot do better than to stay and make one of us, seeing that you are heartily welcome." Mr. Bettesworth excused himself, by saying that he was in haste to get home.

No happy home had he, no affectionate children to welcome his return. Yet he had as numerous a family as Mr. Frankland; three sons and two daughters: Idle Isaac, Wild Will, Bullying Bob, Saucy Sally, and Jilting Jessy. Such were the names by which they were called by all who knew them in the town of Monmouth, where they lived. Alliteration had "lent its artful aid" in giving these nicknames; but they were not misapplied.

Mr. Bettesworth was an indolent man, fond of his pipe, and fonder of building castles in the air by his fireside. Mrs. Bettesworth was a vain, foolish vixen; fond of dress, and fonder of her own will. Neither of them took the least care to breed up their children. Whilst they were young, the mother humoured them: when they grew up, she contradicted them in every thing, and then wondered how they could he so ungrateful as not to love her.

The father was also surprised to find that his boys and girls were not as well-mannered, nor as well-tempered, nor as clever, nor as steady, nor as dutiful and affectionate, as his neighbour Frankland's; and he said to himself, "Some folks have the luck of having good children. To be sure, some children are born better than others."

He should rather have said, "To be sure, some children are bred better than others."

Mr. Frankland's wife was a prudent, sensible woman, and had united with him in constant endeavours to educate their family. Whilst they were yet infants, prattling at their mother's knee, she taught them to love and help one another, to conquer their little 154ortin154 humours, and to be obedient and tractable. This saved both them and herself a great deal of trouble afterward; and their father often said, both to the boys and girls, "You may thank your mother, and so may I, for the good tempers you have."

The girls had the misfortune to lose this excellent mother, when one was about seventeen, and the other eighteen; but she was always alive in their memory. Patty, the eldest sister, was homely in her person; but she was so neat in her dress, and she had such a cheerful agreeable temper, that people forgot she was not handsome; particularly as it was observed that she was very fond of her sister Fanny, who was remarkably pretty.

Fanny was neither prudish nor censorious; neither a romp nor a flirt: she was so unaffected and unassuming, that most of her neighbours loved her; and this is saying a great deal in favour of one who had so much the power to excite envy.

Mr. Frankland's eldest son, George, was bred to be a farmer; and he understood country business uncommonly well for a young man of his age. He constantly assisted his father in the management of the farm; and, by this means, acquired much experience with little waste of time or money. His father had always treated him so much as his friend, and had talked to him so openly of his affairs, that he ever looked upon his father's business as his own; and he had no idea of having any separate interest.

James, the second son, was bred to trade. He had been taught whatever was necessary and useful for a man in business; he had habits of punctuality, civil manners, and a thorough love of fair dealing.

Frank, the youngest son, was of a more lively disposition than his brothers; and his father used often to tell him, when he was a boy, that, if he did not take care, his hasty temper would get him into scrapes; and that the brightest parts, as they are called, will be of little use to a man, unless he has also steadiness to go through with whatever he begins. These hints, from a father whom he heartily loved, made so strong an impression upon Frank, that he took great pains to correct the natural violence of his temper, and to learn patience and industry. The three brothers were attached to one another; and their friendship was a source of improvement, as well as of pleasure.

The evening of Mr. Frankland's birthday the whole family retired to an arbour in their garden, and began to talk over their affairs with open hearts.

"Well, Frank, my boy," said the happy father, who was the confidant of his children, "I am sure, if your heart is set upon this match with Jessy Bettesworth, I will do my best to like the girl; and her not being rich shall be no objection to me; we can make that up amongst us, some way or other. But, Frank, it is fair to tell you my opinion of the girl, plainly and fully, beforehand, as I have done. She that has jilted others, I think, would be apt to jilt you, if she met with a better offer."

"Why then, father, I'll not be in a hurry: I'll take time to consider, before I speak to her any more; and I thank you for being so kind, which I hope I shall not forget."

The morning after this conversation passed, Jilting Jessy, accompanied by her sister, Saucy Sally, came to pay Patty and Fanny Frankland a visit. They were full of some piece of news, which they were eager to tell.

"Well, to be sure, I dreamed I had a diamond ring put on my finger by a great lord, not a week ago," cried Jessy; "and who knows but it may come true? You have not heard the news, Fanny Frankland? Hey, Patty?"

"Not they: they never hear any news!" said Sally.

"Well, then, I'll tell you," cried Jessy. "Rich Captain Bettesworth, our relation, who made the great 155ortin abroad, over seas, has just broken his neck out a-hunting; and the 155ortin all comes to us."

"We shall now see whether Mrs. Craddock will push by me again, as she did yesterday in the street! We'll see whether I shan't make as good a fine lady as herself, I warrant it, that's all. It's my turn to push by folk now," said Saucy Sally.

Fanny and Patty Frankland, with sincere good-nature, congratulated their neighbours on this increase of fortune; but they did not think that pushing by Mrs. Craddock could be one of the most useful or agreeable consequences of an increase in fortune.

"Lord, Patty! How you sit moping yourself there at your work," continued Sally; "but some people must work, to be sure, that can't afford to be idle. How you must envy us, Patty!"

Patty assured her she did not in the least envy those who were idle.

"Fine talking! Fine airs, truly, Miss Patty! This is by way of calling me over the coals for being idle, I suppose!" said Sally: "but I've no notion of being taken to task this way. You think you've had a fine education, I suppose, and so are to get a pattern for all Monmouthshire, indeed: but you'll find some people will be as much thought of now as other people, and may hold their heads as high. Edication's a fine thing, no doubt; but fortin's a better, as the world goes, I've a notion: so you may go moping on here as long as you please, being a good child all the days of your life!

   'Come when you're call'd;
   And do as you're bid;
   Shut the door after you;
   And you'll never be chid.'

I'm sure, I would not let my nose be kept to the grindstone, as yours is, for any one living. I've too much spirit, for my part to be made a fool of as some people are; and all for the sake of being called a vastly good daughter, or a vastly good sister, forsooth!"

Nothing but the absolute want of breath could have suspended the remainder of this speech; for she was so provoked to see Patty did not envy her, that she was determined to say every thing she could invent to try her. Patty's temper, however, was proof against the trial; and Saucy Sally, despairing of success against one sister, turned to the other.

"Miss Fanny, I presume," said she, "won't give herself such high and mighty airs, as she used to do, to one of her sweethearts, who shall be nameless."

Fanny blushed, for she knew this speech alluded to Wild Will, who was an admirer of hers, but whom she had never encouraged.

"I hope," said she, "I never gave myself airs to anybody: but, if you mean to speak of your brother William, I assure you that my opinion of him will not be changed by his becoming richer; nor will my father's."

Here the conversation was interrupted by the entrance of Frank, who had just heard, from one of the Bettesworths, of their good fortune. He was impatient to see how Jessy would behave in prosperity. "Now," said he to himself, "I shall judge whether my father's opinion of her or mine is right."

Jilting Jessy had certainly given Frank reason to believe she was very fond of him; but the sudden change in her fortune quite altered her views and opinions. As soon as Frank came in, she pretended to be in great haste to be gone; and, by various petty manoeuvres, avoided giving him an opportunity of speaking to her; though she plainly saw he was anxious to say something to her in private. At length, when she was looking out of the window, to see whether a shower was over, he went behind her and whispered, "Why are you in such haste? Cannot you stay a few minutes with us? You were not always in such a hurry to run away!"

"Lord, nonsense! Mr. Frank. Why will you always plague me with nonsense, Mr. Frank?"

She opened the lattice window as she spoke, put out her beautiful neck as far as possible, and looked up eagerly to the clouds.

"How sweet this jasmine smells!" said Frank, pulling a bit of it which hung over the casement. "This is the jasmine you used to like so much. See, I've nailed it up, and it's finer than ever it was. Won't you have a sprig of it?" offering to put some in her hat, as he had done before; but she now drew back disdainfully, saying:

"Lord! Mr. Frank, it's all wet, and will spoil my new lilac ribbons. How awkward and disagreeable you are always!"

"Always! You did not always think so; at least, you did not say so."

"Well, I think so, and say so now; and that's enough."

"And too much, if you are in earnest; but that I can hardly believe."

"That's your business, and not mine. If you don't choose to believe what I say, how can I help it? But this you'll remember, if you please, sir."

"Sir!!! Oh, Jessy! Is it come to this?".

"To what, sir? For I vow and declare I don't understand you!"

"I have never understood you till now, I am afraid."

"Perhaps not: it's well we understand one another at last Better late than never."

The scornful lady walked off to a looking-glass, to wipe away the insult which her new lilac ribbons had received from Frank's sprig of jasmine.

"One word more, and I have done," said Frank, hastily following her. "Have I done anything to displease you? Or does this change in you proceed from the change in your fortune, Jessy?"

"I'm not obliged, sir, to account for my proceedings to any body; and don't know what right you have to question me, as if you were my lord and judge: which you are not, nor ever will be, thank God!"

Frank's passion struggled with his reason for a few instants. He stood motionless; then, in an altered voice, repeated, "Thank God!" and turned from her with proud composure. From this time forward he paid no more court to Jessy.

"Ah, father!" said he, "you knew her better than I did. I am glad I did not marry her last year, when she would have accepted of me, and when she seemed to love me. I thought you were rather hard upon her then. But you were not in love with her as I was, and now I find you were right."

"My dear Frank," said the good old man, "I hope you will not think me hard another time, when I do not think just the same as you do. I would, as I told you, have done every thing in my power to settle you well in the world, if you had married this girl. I should never have been angry with you; but I should have been bitterly grieved if you had, for the whim of the minute, made yourself unhappy for life. And was it not best to put you upon your guard? What better use can an old man make of his experience than to give it to his children?"

Frank was touched by the kind manner in which his father spoke to him; and Fanny, who was present, immediately put a letter into her father's hand, saying, "I have just received this from Will Bettesworth: what answer do you think I had best give him?"

Now, Fanny, though she did not quite approve of Wild Will's character, felt a little partiality for him, for he seemed to be of a generous temper, and his manners were engaging. She hoped his wildness was only the effect of good spirits, and that he would soon settle to some business. However, she had kept these hopes and this partiality a secret from all but her father, and she had never given Will Bettesworth any encouragement. Her father had not a good opinion of this young man; and she had followed his advice, in keeping him at a distance. His letter was written in so vile a hand, that it was not easy to decipher the meaning:

"MY SWEET PRETTY FANNY,

"Notwithstanding your cruelty, I ham more in love with you than hever; and now I ham come in for a share in a great 158ortin; and shall ask no questions from father nor mother, if you will marry me, having no reason to love or care for either. Mother's as cross as hever, and will never, I am shure, agre to my doing any thing I like myself; which makes me more set upon having my own whay, and I ham more and more in love with you than hever, and would go through fire and water to get you.

"Your true love (in haste),
"WILL BETTESWORTH."

At first reading the letter, Fanny was pleased to find that her lover did not, like Jilting Jessy, change his mind the moment that his situation was altered; but, upon looking over it again, she could not help considering that such an undutiful son was not likely to make a very good husband; and she thought even that Wild Will seemed to be more and more in love with her than ever, from the spirit of opposition; for he had not been much attached to her, till his mother, as he said, set herself against the match. At the end of this letter were the words turn over; but they were so scrawled and blotted, that Fanny thought they were only one of the strange flourishes which he usually made at the end of his name; and consequently she had never turned over, or read the postscript, when she put the epistle into her father's hands. He deciphered the flourish, and read the following addition:

"I know your feather does not like me; but never mind his not being agreuble. As shure as my name's Will, I'd carry you hoff, night or day; and Bob would fight your brothers along with me, if they said a word: for Bob loves fun. I will be at your windor this night, if you are agreuble, like a gurl of spirit."

Fanny was shocked so much that she turned quite pale, and would have sunk to the ground, if she had not been supported by her father. As soon as she recovered herself sufficiently to be able to think, she declared that all the liking she had ever felt for William Bettesworth was completely conquered; and she thanked her father for having early warned her of his character. "Ah! Father," said she, "what a happiness it has been to me that you never made me afraid of you! Else, I never should have dared to tell you my mind; and in what a sad snare might I have been at this instant! If it had not been for you, I should perhaps have encouraged this man; I might not then, may be, have been able to draw back; and what would have become of me?"

It is scarcely necessary to say that Fanny wrote a decided refusal to Wild Will. All connexion between the Bettesworths and Franklands was now broken off. Will was enraged at being rejected by Fanny; and Jessy was equally incensed at finding she was no longer admired by Frank. They, however, affected to despise the Franklands, and to treat them as people beneath their notice. The fortune left by Captain Bettesworth to his relations, was said to be about twenty thousand pounds: with this sum they thought, to use their own expression, they were entitled to live in as great style, and cut as grand a dash, as any of the first families in Monmouthshire. For the present we shall leave them to the enjoyment of their new grandeur, and continue the humble history of farmer Frankland and his family.

By many years of persevering industry, Mr. Frankland had so improved the farm upon which he lived, that he was now affluent, for a man in his station of life. His house, garden, farm-yard, every thing about him, were so neat and comfortable, that travellers, as they passed by, never failed to ask, "Who lives there?" Travellers, however, only saw the outside; and that was not, in this instance, the best part. They would have seen happiness, if they had looked within these farm-house walls: happiness which may be enjoyed as well in the cottage as in the palace; that which arises from family union.

Mr. Frankland was now anxious to settle his sons in the world. George had business enough at home, in taking care of the farm; and James proposed to set up a haberdasher's shop in Monmouth: accordingly, the goods were ordered, and the shop was taken.

There was a part in the roof of the house which let in the wet, and James would not go into it till this was completely repaired; so his packages of goods were sent from London to his father's house, which was only a mile distant from Monmouth. His sisters unpacked them by his desire, to set shop-marks upon each article. Late at night, after all the rest of the family were asleep, Patty was sitting up to finish setting the marks on a box full of ribbons; the only thing that remained to be done. Her candle was just burnt out; and as she was going for another, she went by a passage window that faced the farm-yard, and suddenly saw a great light without. She looked out, and beheld the large hay-rick all in flames. She ran immediately to awaken her brothers and her father. They used every possible exertion to extinguish the fire, and to prevent it from communicating to the dwelling-house; but the wind was high; it blew directly towards the house. George poured buckets of water over the thatch, to prevent its catching fire; but all was in vain: thick flakes of fire fell upon it faster than they could be extinguished, and in an hour's time the dwelling-house was in a blaze.

The first care of the sons had been to get their father and sisters out of danger; then, with great presence of mind, they collected every thing that was most valuable and portable, and laboured hard to save poor James's stock of haberdashery. They were all night hard at work: towards three o'clock the fire was got under, and darkness and silence succeeded. There was one roof of the house saved, under which the whole family rested for a few hours, till the return of daylight renewed the melancholy spectacle of their ruin. Hay, oats, straw, corn-ricks, barn, every thing that the farm-yard contained, was utterly consumed: the walls and some half-burnt beams remained of the dwelling-house, but it was no longer habitable. It was calculated that six hundred pounds would not repair the loss occasioned by this unfortunate accident. How the hay-rick had caught fire nobody knew.

George, who had made up the hay-stack, was most inclined to think that the hay had not been sufficiently dried, and that the rick had heated from this cause. He blamed himself extremely; but his father declared he had seen, felt, and smelt the hay, when the rick was making, and that it was as well saved hay as ever was brought into a farm-yard. This, in some measure, quieted poor George's conscience: and he was yet more comforted by Patty's good-nature, who showed him a bucket of ashes which had been left very near the spot where the hay-rick stood. The servant-girl, who, though careless, was honest, confessed she recollected having accidentally left this bucket in that dangerous place the preceding evening; that she was going with it across the yard to the ash-hole, but she heard her lover whistle to her from the lane, and she set down the bucket in a hurry, ran to meet him, and forgot the ashes. All she could say in her own defence was, that she did not think there was any fire in the bucket.

Her good master forgave her carelessness; he said he was sure she reproached herself enough for it, as indeed she did, and the more so when her master spoke to her so kindly; she cried as if her heart would break; and all that could be done to comfort her, was to set her to work as hard as possible for the family.

They did not, any of them, spend their time in vain lamentations: ready money was wanting to rebuild the house and barns, and James sold to a haberdasher in Monmouth all of his stock which had been saved out of the fire, and brought the money to his father.

"Father," said he, "you gave this to me when you were able to afford it; you want it now, and I can do very well without it. I will go and be shopman in some good shop in Monmouth; and by degrees I shall get on, and do very well in the world. It would be strange if I did not, after the education you have given me."

The father took the money from his son with tears of pleasure. "It is odd enough." Said he, "that I should feel pleasure at such a time; but this is the blessing of having good children. As long as we all are ready to help one another in this manner, we can never be very miserable, happen what may. Now let us think of rebuilding our house," continued the active old man. "Frank, reach me down my hat. I've a twinge of the rheumatism in this arm: I caught a little cold the night of the fire, I believe; but stirring about will do me good, and I must not be lazy: I should be ashamed to be lazy amongst so many active young men." The father and sons were very busy at work, when an ill-looking man rode up to them; and, after asking if their name was Frankland, put a paper into each of their hands. These papers were copies of a notice to quit their farm, before the ensuing first of September, under pain of paying double rent for the same.

"This is some mistake, sir," said old Frankland, mildly.

"No mistake, sir," replied the stranger. "You will find the notice is a good notice, and duly served. Your lease I have seen myself within these few days: it expired last May; and you have held over, contrary to law and justice, eleven months, this being April."

"My father never did anything contrary to law and justice in his whole life," interrupted Frank; whose eyes flashed with indignation.

"Softly, Frank," said his father, putting his hand on his son's shoulder; "softly, my dear boy: let this gentleman and I come to an understanding quietly.—Here is some mistake, sir. It is very true that my lease expired last May; but I had a promise of a renewal from my good landlord."

"I don't know, sir, anything of that," replied the stranger, as he looked over a memorandum-book. "I do not know whom you denominate your good landlord; that being no way of describing a man in the eye of the law: but if you refer to the original grantor, or lessor, Francis Folingsby, of Folingsby-place, Monmouthshire, Esq., I am to inform you that he died at Bath the 17th instant."

"Died! My poor landlord dead! I am very sorry for it."

"And his nephew, Philip Folingsby, Esq., came into possession as heir at law," continued the stranger, in an unvaried tone; "and under his orders I act, having a power of attorney for that purpose."

"But, sir, I am sure Mr. Philip Folingsby cannot know of the promise of renewal, which I had from his uncle."

"Verbal promises, you know, are nothing, sir; mere air, without witnesses: and, if gratuitous on the part of the deceased, are no ways binding, either in common law or equity, on the survivor or heir. In case the promise had been in writing, and on a proper stamp, it would have been something." "It was not in writing, to be sure, sir," said Frankland, "but I thought my good landlord's word was as good as his bond; and I said so."

"Yes," cried Frank; "and I remember when you said so to him, I was by; and he answered, 'You shall have my promise in writing. Such things are of little use between honest men: but who knows what may happen, and who may come after me? Everything about business should be put into writing. I would never let a tenant of mine be at an uncertainty. You have improved your farm, and deserve to enjoy the fruits of your own industry, Mr. Frankland.' Just then company came in, and our landlord put off writing the promise. He next day left the country in a hurry; and I am sure thought, afterwards, he had given us the promise in writing."

"Very clear evidence, no doubt, sir; but not at all to the point at present," said the stranger. "As an agent, I am to know nothing but what is my employer's intent. When we see the writing and stamp, I shall be a better judge," added he with a sneer. "In the mean time, gentlemen, I wish you a good morning: and you will please to observe that you have been duly served with notice to quit, or pay double rent."

"There can be no doubt, however," said Frank, "that Mr. Folingsby will believe you, father. He is a gentleman, I suppose, and not like this new agent, who talks like an attorney. I hate all attorneys."

"All dishonest attorneys, I suppose you mean, Frank," said the benevolent old man; who, even when his temper was most tried, never spoke, or even felt with acrimony.

The new landlord came into the country; and a few days after his arrival, old Frankland went to wait upon him. There was little hope of seeing young Mr. Folingsby; he was a man whose head was at this time entirely full of gigs, and tandems, and unicorns: business was his aversion; pleasure was his business. Money he considered only as the means of pleasure; and tenants only as machines, who make money. He was neither avaricious nor cruel; but thoughtless and extravagant.

Whilst he appeared merely in the character of a young man of fashion, these faults were no offence to his equals, to whom they did no injury: but when he came into possession of a large estate, and when numbers were dependent upon him, they were severely felt by his inferiors.

Mr. Folingsby had just gathered up the reins in hand, and was seated in his unicorn, when farmer Frankland, who had been waiting some hours to see him, came to the side of the carriage. As he took off his hat, the wind blew his grey hair over his face.

"Put on your hat, pray, my good friend; and don't come near these horses, for I can't answer for them. Have you any commands with me?"

"I have been waiting some hours to speak to you, sir; but, if you are not at leisure, I will come again to-morrow morning," said old Frankland.

"Ay, do so; call to-morrow morning; for now I have not one moment to spare," said young Folingsby, as he whipped his horses, and drove off, as if the safety of the nation had depended upon twelve miles an hour.

The next day, and the next, and the next, the old tenant called upon his young landlord, but without obtaining an audience; still he was desired to call to-morrow, and to-morrow, and to-morrow. He wrote several letters to him, but received no answer: at last, after giving half a guinea to his landlord's gentleman, he gained admittance. Mr. Folingsby was drawing on his boots, and his horses were coming to the door. Frankland saw it was necessary to be concise in his story: he slightly touched on the principal circumstances, the length of time he had occupied his farm, the improvements he had made upon the land, and the misfortune which had lately befallen him. The boots were on by the time that he got to the promise of renewal, and the notice to quit.

"Promise of renewal: I know of no such thing. Notice to quit: that's my agent's business; speak to him; he'll do you justice. I really am sorry for you, Mr. Frankland; very sorry, extremely sorry. Damn the rascal who made these boots!—but you see how I'm circumstanced; haven't a moment to myself; only came to the country for a few days; set out for Ascot-races to-morrow; really have not a moment to think of any thing. But speak to Mr. Deal, my agent. He'll do you justice, I'm sure. I leave all these things to him. Jack, that bay horse is coming on—"

"I have spoken to your agent, sir," said the old tenant, following his thoughtless young landlord; "but he said that verbal promises, without a witness present, were nothing but air; and I have nothing to rely on but your justice. I assure you, sir, I have not been an idle tenant: my land will show that I have not."

"Tell Mr. Deal so; make him understand it in this light. I leave every thing of this sort to Mr. Deal. I really have not time for business, but I'm sure Mr. Deal will do you justice."

This was all that could be obtained from the young landlord. His confidence in his agent's sense of justice was somewhat misplaced. Mr. Deal had received a proposal from another tenant for Frankland's farm; and with this proposal a bank note was sent, which spoke more forcibly than all that poor Frankland could urge. The agent took the farm from him; and declared he could not, in justice to his employer, do otherwise; because the new tenant had promised to build upon the land a lodge fit for any gentleman to inhabit, instead of a farm-house.

The transaction was concluded without Mr. Folingsby's knowing any thing more of the matter, except signing the leases, which he did without reading them; and receiving half a year's rent in hand, as a fine, which he did with great satisfaction. He was often distressed for ready money, though he had a large estate; and his agent well knew how to humour him in his hatred of business. No interest could have persuaded Mr. Folingsby deliberately to commit so base an action as that of cheating a deserving old tenant out of a promised renewal; but, in fact, long before the leases were sent to him, he had totally forgotten every syllable that poor Frankland had said to him on the subject.

CHAPTER II

The day on which they left their farm was a melancholy day to this unfortunate family. Mr. Frankland's father and grandfather had been tenants, and excellent tenants, to the Folingsby family: all of them had occupied, and not only occupied, but highly improved, this farm. All the neighbours were struck with compassion, and cried shame upon Mr. Folingsby! But Mr. Folingsby was at Ascot, and did not hear them. He was on the race ground, betting hundreds upon a favourite horse, whilst this old man and his family were slowly passing in their covered cart down the lane which led from their farm, taking a last farewell of the fields they had cultivated, and the harvest they had sown, but which they were never to reap.

Hannah, the servant-girl, who had reproached herself so bitterly for leaving the bucket of ashes near the hay-rick, was extremely active in assisting her poor master. Upon this occasion she seemed to be endowed with double strength; and a degree of cleverness and presence of mind, of which she had never shown any symptoms in her former life: but gratitude awakened all her faculties.

Before she came to this family, she had lived some years with a farmer who, as she now recollected, had a small farm, with a snug cottage upon it, which was to be this very year out of lease. Without saying a word of her intentions, she got up early one morning, walked fifteen miles to her old master's, and offered to pay out of her wages, which she had laid by for six or seven years, the year's rent of this farm before-hand, if the farmer would let it to Mr. Frankland. The farmer would not take the girl's money, for he said he wanted no security from Mr. Frankland, or his son George: they bore the best of characters, he observed, and no people in Monmouthshire could understand the management of land better. He willingly agreed to let him the farm; but it contained only a few acres, and the house was so small that it could scarcely lodge above three people.

Here old Frankland and his eldest son, George, settled. James went to Monmouth, where he became shopman to Mr. Cleghorn, a haberdasher, who took him in preference to three other young men, who applied on the same day. "Shall I tell you the reason why I fixed upon you, James?" said Mr. Cleghorn. "It was not whim; I had my reasons."

"I suppose," said James, "you thought I had been honestly and well brought up; as, I believe, in former times, sir, you knew something of my mother."

"Yes, sir; and in former times I knew something of yourself. You may forget, but I do not, that, when you were a child, not more than nine years old, you came to this shop to pay a bill of your mother's: the bill was cast up a pound too little: you found out the mistake, and paid me the money. I dare say you are as good an accountant, and as honest a fellow, still. I have just been terribly tricked by a lad to whom I trusted foolishly; but this will not make me suspicious towards you, because I know how you have been brought up; and that is the best security a man can have."

[Footnote: This circumstance is a fact.]

Thus, even in childhood, the foundation of a good character may be laid; and thus children inherit the good name of their parents. A rich inheritance! of which they cannot be deprived by the utmost malice of fortune.

The good characters of Fanny and Patty Frankland were well known in the neighbourhood; and when they could no longer afford to live at home, they found no difficulty in getting places. On the contrary, several of the best families in Monmouth were anxious to engage them. Fanny went to live with Mrs. Hungerford, a lady of an ancient family, who was proud, but not insolent, and generous, but not what is commonly called affable. She had several children, and she hired Fanny Frankland for the particular purpose of attending them.

"Pray let me see that you exactly obey my orders, young woman, with respect to my children," said Mrs. Hungerford, "and you shall have no reason to complain of the manner in which you are treated in this house. It is my wish to make every body happy in it, from the highest to the lowest. You have, I understand, received an education above your present station in life; and I hope and trust that you will deserve the high opinion I am, from that circumstance, inclined to form of you."

Fanny was rather intimidated by the haughtiness of Mrs. Hungerford's manner; yet she felt a steady though modest confidence in herself, which was not displeasing to her mistress.

About this time Patty also went into service. Her mistress was a Mrs. Crumpe, a very old rich lady, who was often sick and peevish, and who confessed that she required an uncommonly good-humoured person to wait upon her. She lived a few miles from Monmouth, where she had many relations; but on account of her great age and infirmities, she led an extremely retired life.

Frank was now the only person in the family who was not settled in the world. He determined to apply to a Mr. Barlow, an attorney of an excellent character. He had been much pleased with the candour and generosity Frank showed in a quarrel with the Bettesworths; and he had promised to befriend him, if ever it should be in his power. It happened that, at this time, Mr. Barlow was in want of a clerk; and as he knew Frank's abilities, and had reason to feel confidence in his integrity, he determined to employ him in his office. Frank had once a prejudice against attorneys: he thought that they could not be honest men; but he was convinced of his mistake when he became acquainted with Mr. Barlow. This gentleman never practised any mean pettyfogging arts; on the contrary, he always dissuaded those who consulted him from commencing vexatious suits. Instead of fomenting quarrels, it was his pleasure and pride to bring about reconciliations. It was said of Mr. Barlow that he had lost more suits out of the court, and fewer in them, than any attorney of his standing in England. His reputation was now so great that he was consulted more as a lawyer than as an attorney. With such a master, Frank had a prospect of being extremely happy; and he determined that nothing should be wanting, on his part, to ensure Mr. Barlow's esteem and regard.

James Frankland, in the mean time, went on happily with Mr, Cleghorn, the haberdasher; whose customers all agreed that his shop had never been so well attended as since this young man had been his foreman. His accounts were kept in the most exact manner; and his bills were made out with unrivalled neatness and expedition. His attendance on the shop was so constant that his master began to fear it might hurt his health; especially as he had never, till of late, been used to so confined a life.

"You should go abroad, James, these fine evenings," said Mr. Cleghorn. "Take a walk in the country now and then, in the fresh air. Don't think I want to nail you always to the counter. Come, this is as fine an evening as you can wish: take your hat, and away; I'll mind the shop myself, till you come back. He must be a hard master, indeed, that does not know when he is well served; and that never will be my case, I hope. Good servants make good masters, and good masters good servants. Not that I mean to call you, Mr. James, a servant; that was only a slip of the tongue; and no matter for the tongue, where the heart means well, as mine does towards you."

Towards all the world Mr. Cleghorn was not disposed to be indulgent: he was not a selfish man; but he had a high idea of subordination in life. Having risen himself by slow degrees, he thought that every man in trade should have what he called "the rough as well as the smooth." He saw that his new foreman bore the rough well; and therefore he was now inclined to give him some of the smooth.

James, who was extremely fond of his brother Frank, called upon him and took him to Mrs. Hungerford's, to ask Fanny to accompany them in this walk. They had seldom seen her since they had quitted their father's house and lived in Monmouth; and they were disappointed when they were told, by Mrs. Hungerford's footman, that Fanny was not at home; she was gone to walk out with the children. The man did not know which road they went, so they had no hopes of meeting her; and they took their way through one of the shady lanes near Monmouth. It was late before they thought of returning; for, after several weeks' confinement in close houses, the fresh air, green fields, and sweet-smelling wild flowers in the hedges, were delightful novelties. "Those who see these things every day," said James, "scarcely notice them; I remember I did not when I lived at our farm. So things, as my father used to say, are made equal to people in this world. We, who are hard at work in a close room all day long, have more relish for an evening walk, a hundred to one, than those who saunter about from morning till night."

The philosophic reflections of James were interrupted by the merry voices of a troop of children, who were getting over a stile into the lane, where he and Frank were walking. The children had huge nosegays of honeysuckles, dog-roses, and blue-bells, in their little hands; and they gave their flowers to a young woman who attended them, begging she would hold them whilst they got over the stile. James and Frank went to offer their services to help the children; and then they saw that the young woman, who held the flowers, was their sister Fanny.

"Our own Fanny!" said Frank. "How lucky this is! It seems almost a year since I saw you. We have been all the way to Mrs. Hungerford's to look for you, and have been forced to take half our walk without you; but the other half will make amends. I've a hundred things to say to you: which is your way home? Take the longest way, I entreat you. Here is my arm. What a delightful fine evening it is! But what's the matter?"

"It is a very fine evening," said Fanny, hesitating a little; "and I hope to-morrow will be as fine. I'll ask my mistress to let me walk out with you to-morrow; but this evening I cannot stay with you, because I have the children under my care; and I have promised her that I will never walk with any one when they are with me."

"But your own brother," said Frank, a little angry at this refusal.

"I promised I would not walk with any one; and surely you are somebody: so good night; good bye," replied Fanny, endeavouring to turn off his displeasure with a laugh.

"But what harm, I say, can I do the children, by walking with you?" cried Frank, catching hold of her gown.

"I don't know; but I know what the orders of my mistress are; and you know, dear Frank, that whilst I live with her, I am bound to obey them."

"Oh, Frank, she must obey them," said James.

Frank loosened his hold of Fanny's gown immediately. "You are right, dear Fanny," said he; "you are right, and I was wrong: so good night; good bye. Only remember to ask leave to walk with us to-morrow evening; for I have had a letter from father and brother George, and I want to show it you. Wait five minutes, and I can read it to you now, Fanny."

Fanny, though she was anxious to hear her father's letter, would not wait, but hurried away with the children that were under her care; saying she must keep her promise to her mistress exactly. Frank followed her, and put the letter into her hands. "You are a dear good girl, and deserve all the fine things father says of you in this letter. Take it, child: your mistress does not forbid you receiving a letter from your father, I suppose. I shall wish her hanged, if she does not let you walk with us to-morrow," whispered he.

The children frequently interrupted Fanny, as she was reading her father's letter. "Pray pull that high dog-rose for me, Fanny," said one. "Pray hold me up to that large honeysuckle," said another. "And do, Fanny," said the youngest boy, "let us go home by the common, that I may see the glowworms. Mamma said I might; and whilst we are looking for the glowworms, you can sit on a stone, or a bank, and read your letter in peace."

Fanny, who was always very ready to indulge the children in any thing which her mistress had not forbidden, agreed to this proposal; and when they came to the common, little Gustavus, for that was the name of the eldest boy, found a charming seat for her; and she sat down to read her letter whilst the children ran to hunt for glowworms.

Fanny read her father's letter over three times; and yet few people, except those who have the happiness to love a father as well, and to have a father as deserving to be loved, would think it at all worth reading even once.

"MY DEAR BOYS AND GIRLS,

"It is a strange thing to me to be without you; but, with me or from me, I am sure you are doing well; and that is a great comfort; ay, the best a father can have, especially at my age. I am heartily glad to hear that my Frank has, by his own deserts, got so good a place with that excellent man, Mr. Barlow. He does not hate attorneys now, I am sure. Indeed, it is my belief, he could not hate any body for half an hour together, if he were to do his worst. Thank God, none of my children have been brought up to be revengeful or envious; and they are not fighting with one another, as I hear the poor Bettesworths now all are for the fortune. 'Better is a dinner of herbs, where love is, than a stalled ox, and hatred therewith.' I need not have troubled myself to write this text to any of you; but old men will be talkative. My rheumatism, however, prevents me from being as talkative as I could wish. It has been rather severe or so, owing to the great cold I caught the day that I was obliged to wait so long at squire Folingsby's in my wet clothes. But I hope soon to be stirring again, and to be able to take share of the work about our little farm, with your dear brother George. Poor fellow! he has so much to do, and does so much, that I fear he will overwork himself. He is at this present time out in the little field, opposite my window, digging up the docks, which are very hard to conquer; he has made a brave large heap of them, but I wish to my heart he would not toil so desperately.

"I desire, my dear James and Frank, you will not confine yourselves too much in your shop and at your desk: this is all I have to dread for either of you. Give my love and blessing to my sweet girls. If Fanny was not as prudent as she is pretty, I should be in fear for her; hearing as I do, that Mrs. Hungerford keeps so much fine company. A waiting-maid in such a house is in a dangerous place: but my Fanny, I am sure, will ever keep in mind her mother's precepts and example. I am told that Mrs. Crumpe, Patty's mistress, is (owing, I suppose, to her great age and infirmities) difficult in her humour; but my Patty has so even and pleasant a temper that I defy any one living, that knows her, not to love her. My hand is now quite tired of writing, this being penned with my left, as my right arm is not yet free from rheumatism: I have not James with me to write. God bless and preserve you all, my dear children. With such comforts, I can have nothing to complain of in this world. This I know, I would not exchange any one of you for all my neighbour Bettesworth's fine fortune. Write soon to

"Your affectionate father,
"B. Frankland."

"Look! look at the glowworms!" cried the children, gathering round Fanny, just as she had finished reading her letter. There were prodigious numbers of them on this common; and they shone over the whole ground, in clusters, or singly, like little stars.

Whilst the children were looking with admiration and delight at this spectacle, their attention was suddenly diverted from the glowworms by the sound of a French-horn. They looked round and perceived that it came from the balcony of a house, which was but a few yards distant from the spot where they were standing.

"Oh! let us go nearer to the balcony!" said the children, "that we may hear the music better." A violin, and a clarinet, at this moment began to play.

"Oh! let us go nearer!" said the children, drawing Fanny with all their little force towards the balcony.

"My dears, it is growing late," said she, "and we must make haste home. There is a crowd of company, you see, at the door and at the windows of that house; and if we go near to it, some of them will certainly speak to you, and that, you know, your mamma would not like."

The children paused and looked at one another, as if inclined to submit; but, at this moment, a kettle-drum was heard, and little Gustavus could not resist his curiosity to hear and see more of this instrument: he broke loose from Fanny's hands, and escaped to the house, exclaiming, "I must and will hear it, and see it too!"

Fanny was obliged to pursue him into the midst of the crowd: he made his way up to a young gentleman in regimentals, who took him up in his arms, saying, "By Jove, a fine little fellow! A soldier, every inch of him! By Jove, he shall see the drum, and beat it too; let us see who dares say to the contrary."

As the gallant ensign spoke, he carried Gustavus up a flight of stairs that led to the balcony. Fanny in great anxiety called after him to beg that he would not detain the child, who was trusted to her care: her mistress, she said, would be extremely displeased with her, if she disobeyed her orders.

She was here interrupted in her remonstrance by the shrill voice of a female, who stood on the same stair with the ensign, and whom, notwithstanding the great alteration in her dress, Fanny recognized to be Sally Bettesworth. Jilting Jessy stood beside her.

"Fanny Frankland, I protest! What a pother she keeps about nothing," cried Saucy Sally. "Know your betters, and keep your distance, young woman. Who cares whether your mistress is displeased or not? She can't turn us away, can she, pray? She can't call ensign Bloomington to account, can she, hey?"

An insolent laugh closed this speech; a laugh in which several of the crowd joined: but some gentlemen were interested by Fanny's beautiful and modest countenance, as she looked up to the balcony, and, with tears in her eyes, entreated to be heard. "Oh, for shame, Bloomington! Give her back the boy. It is not fair that she should lose her place," cried they.

Bloomington would have yielded; but Saucy Sally stood before him crying in a threatening tone, "I'll never speak to you again, I promise you, Bloomington, if you give up. A fine thing indeed for a man and a soldier to give up to a woman and a servant-girl! and an impertinent servant-girl! Who cares for her or her place either?"

"I do! I do!" exclaimed little Gustavus, springing from the ensign's arms. "I care for her! She is not an impertinent girl; and I'll give up seeing the kettle-drum, and go home with her directly, with all my heart."

In vain Sally attempted to withhold him; the boy ran down the stairs to Fanny, and marched off with her in all the conscious pride of a hero, whose generosity has fairly vanquished his passions. Little Gustavus was indeed a truly generous child: the first thing he did, when he got home, was to tell his mother all that had passed this evening. Mrs. Hungerford was delighted with her son, and said to him, "I cannot, I am sure, reward you better, my dear, than by rewarding this good young woman. The fidelity with which she has fulfilled my orders, in all that regards my children, places her, in my opinion, above the rank in which she was born. Henceforward she shall hold in my house a station to which her habits of truth, gentleness, and good sense, entitle her."

From this time forward, Fanny, by Mrs. Hungerford's desire, was always present when the children took their lessons from their several masters. Mrs. Hungerford advised her to apply herself to learn all those things which were necessary for a governess to young ladies. "When you speak, your language in general is good, and correct; and no pains shall be wanting, on my part," said this haughty but benevolent lady, "to form your manners, and to develop your talents. This I partly owe you for your care of my children; and I am happy to reward my son Gustavus in a manner which I am certain will be most agreeable to him."

"And, mamma," said the little boy, "may she walk out sometimes with her brothers? for I do believe she loves them as well as I love my sisters."

Mrs. Hungerford permitted Fanny to walk out for an hour, every morning, during the time that her children were with their dancing-master; and at this hour sometimes her brother James, and sometimes her brother Frank, could be spared; and they had many pleasant walks together. What a happiness it was to them to have been thus bred up, from their earliest years, in friendship with one another! This friendship was now the sweetest pleasure of their lives.

Poor Patty! She regretted that she could not join in these pleasant meetings; but, alas! she was so useful, so agreeable, and so necessary to her infirm mistress, that she could never be spared from home. "Where's Patty? why does not Patty do this?" were Mrs. Crumpe's constant questions whenever she was absent. Patty had all the business of the house upon her hands, because nobody could do any thing so well as Patty. Mrs. Crumpe found that no one could dress her but Patty; nobody could make her bed, so that she could sleep on it, but Patty; no one could make jelly, or broth, or whey, that she could taste, but Patty; no one could roast, or boil, or bake, but Patty. Of course, all these things must be done by nobody else. The ironing of Mrs. Crumpe's caps, which had exquisitely nice plaited borders, at last fell to Patty's share; because once, when the laundry-maid was sick, she plaited one so charmingly, that her lady would never afterwards wear any but of her plaiting. Now Mrs. Crumpe changed her cap, or rather had her cap changed, three times a day; and never wore the same cap twice.

The labours of washing, ironing, plaiting, roasting, boiling, baking, making jelly, broth, and whey, were not sufficient: Mrs. Crumpe took it into her head that she could eat no butter but of Patty's churning. But, what was worse than all, not a night passed without Patty's being called up to see "what could be the matter with the dog that was barking, or the cat that was mewing?" And when she was just sinking to sleep again, at daybreak, her lady, in whose room she slept, would call out, "Patty! Patty! There's a dreadful noise in the chicken-yard."

"Oh, ma'am, it is only the cocks crowing."

"Well, do step out, and hinder them from crowing at this terrible rate."

"But, ma'am, I cannot hinder them indeed."

"Oh yes, you could, if you were up. Get up and whip 'em, child. Whip 'em all round, or I shall not sleep a wink more this night."

[Footnote: Taken from life.]

How little poor Patty slept, her lady never considered: not that she was in reality an ill-natured woman, but sickness inclined her to be peevish; and she had so long been used to be humoured and waited upon by relations and servants, who expected she would leave them rich legacies, that she considered herself as a sort of golden idol, to whom all that approached should and would bow as low as she pleased. Perceiving that almost all around her were interested, she became completely selfish. She was from morning till night, from night till morning, nay, from year's end to year's end, so much in the habit of seeing others employed for her, that she absolutely considered this to be the natural and necessary course of things; and she quite forgot to think of the comfort, or even of the well-being, of those creatures who were "born for her use, and live but to oblige her."

From time to time she was so far awakened to feeling, by Patty's exertions and good-humour, that she would say, to quiet her own conscience, "Well! well! I'll make it all up to her in my will! I'll make it all up to her in my will!"

She took it for granted that Patty, like the rest of her dependents, was governed entirely by mercenary considerations; and she was persuaded that the hopes of this legacy would secure Patty her slave for life. In this she was mistaken.

One morning Patty came into her room with a face full of sorrow; a face so unlike her usual countenance, that even her mistress, unaccustomed as she was to attend to the feelings of others, could not help noticing the change.

"Well! What's the matter, child?" said she.

"Oh! sad news, madam!" said Patty, turning aside to hide her tears.

"But what's the matter, child, I say? Can't you speak, whatever it is, hey? What, have you burnt my best cap in the ironing, hey? Is that it?"

"Oh! worse, worse, ma'am!"

"Worse! What can be worse?"

"My brother, ma'am, my brother George, is ill, very ill of a fever; and they don't think he'll live! Here is my father's letter, ma'am!"

"Lord! how can I read it without spectacles? and why should I read it, when you've told me all that's in it? How the child cries!" continued Mrs. Crumpe, raising herself a little on her pillow, and looking at Patty with a sort of astonished curiosity. "Heigho! But I can't stay in bed this way till dinnertime. Get me my cap, child, and dry your eyes; for crying won't do your brother any good."

Patty dried her eyes. "No, crying will not do him any good," said she, "but—"

"But where is my cap? I don't see it on the dressing-table."

"No, ma'am: Martha will bring it in a minute or two: she is plaiting it."

"I will not have it plaited by Martha. Go and do it yourself."

"But, ma'am," said Patty, who, to her mistress's surprise, stood still, notwithstanding she heard this order, "I hope you will be so good as to give me leave to go to my poor brother to-day. All the rest of my brothers and sisters are with him, and he wants to see me; and they have sent a horse for me."

"No matter what they have sent, you sha'n't go; I can't spare you. If you choose to serve me, serve me. If you choose to serve your brother, serve your brother, and leave me."

"Then, madam," said Patty, "I must leave you; for I cannot but choose to serve my brother at such a time as this, if I can serve him; which God grant I mayn't be too late to do!"

"What! You will leave me! Leave me contrary to my orders! Take notice, then: these doors you shall never enter again, if you leave me now," cried Mrs. Crumpe, who, by this unexpected opposition to her orders, was actually worked up to a state unlike her usual peevishness. She started up in her bed, and growing quite red in the face, cried, "Leave me now, and you leave me for ever. Remember that! Remember that!"

"Then, madam, I must leave you for ever," said Patty, moving towards the door. "I wish you your health and happiness, and am sorry to break so short."

"The girl's an idiot!" cried Mrs. Crumpe. "After this you cannot expect that I should remember you in my will."

"No, indeed, madam; I expect no such thing," said Patty. (Her hand was on the lock of the door as she spoke.)

"Then," said Mrs. Crumpe, "perhaps you will think it worth your while to stay with me, when I tell you I have not forgot you in my will? Consider that, child, before you turn the handle of the door. Consider that; and don't disoblige me for ever."

"Oh, madam, consider my poor brother. I am sorry to disoblige you for ever; but I can consider nothing but my poor brother," said Patty. The lock of the door turned quickly in her hand.

"Why! Is your brother rich? What upon earth do you expect from this brother, that can make it worth your while to behave to me in this strange way?" said Mrs. Crumpe.

Patty was silent with astonishment for a few moments, and then answered, "I expect nothing from him, madam; he is as poor as myself; but that does not make me love him the less."

Before Mrs. Crumpe could understand this last speech, Patty had left the room. Her mistress sat up in her bed, in the same attitude, for some minutes after she was gone, looking fixedly at the place where Patty had stood: she could scarcely recover from her surprise; and a multitude of painful thoughts crowded upon her mind.

"If I were dying, and poor, who would come to me? Not a relation I have in the world would come near me! Not a creature on earth loves me as this poor girl loves her brother, who is as poor as herself."

Here her reflections were interrupted by hearing the galloping of Patty's horse, as it passed by the windows. Mrs. Crumpe tried to compose herself again to sleep, but she could not; and in half an hour's time she rang the bell violently, took her purse out of her pocket, counted out twenty bright guineas, and desired that a horse should be saddled immediately, and that her steward should gallop after Patty, and offer her that whole sum in hand, if she would return. "Begin with one guinea, and bid on till you come up to her price," said Mrs. Crumpe. "Have her back again I will, if it were only to convince myself that she is to be had for money as well as other people."

The steward, as he counted the gold in his hand, thought it was a great sum to throw away for such a whim: he had never seen his lady take the whim of giving away ready money before; but it was in vain to remonstrate; she was peremptory, and he obeyed.

In two hours' time he returned, and Mrs. Crumpe saw her gold again with extreme astonishment. The steward said he could not prevail upon Patty even to look at the guineas. Mrs. Crumpe now flew into a violent passion, in which none of our readers will probably sympathize: we shall therefore forbear to describe it.

CHAPTER III

When Patty came within half a mile of the cottage in which her father lived, she met Hannah, the faithful servant, who had never deserted the family in their misfortunes; she had been watching all the morning on the road for the first sight of Patty, but when she saw her, and came quite close up to her, she had no power to speak; and Patty was so much terrified that she could not ask her a single question. She walked her horse a slow pace, and kept silence.

"Won't you go on, ma'am?" said Hannah at last, forcing herself to speak. "Won't you go on a bit faster? He's almost wild to see you."

"He is alive then!" cried Patty. The horse was in full gallop directly, and she was soon at her father's door. James and Frank were there watching for her: they lifted her from the horse; and feeling that she trembled so much as to be scarcely able to stand, they would have detained her a little while in the air; but she passed or rather rushed into the room where her brother lay. He took no notice of her when she came in, for he was insensible. Fanny was supporting his head; she held out her hand to Patty, who went on tiptoe to the side of the bed. "Is he asleep?" whispered she.

"Not asleep, but—He'll come to himself presently," continued Fanny, "and he will be very, very glad you are come; and so will my father."

"Where is my father?" said Patty; "I don't see him."

Fanny pointed to the farthest end of the room, where he was kneeling at his devotion. The shutters being half closed, she could but just see the faint beam which shone upon his grey hairs. He rose, came to his daughter Patty, with an air of resigned grief, and taking her hand between both of his, said, "My love—we must lose him—God's will be done!"

"Oh! there is hope, there is hope still!" said Patty. "See! the colour is coming back to his lips again; his eyes open! Oh! George, dear George, dear brother! It is your own sister Patty: don't you know Patty?"

"Patty!—Yes. Why does she not come to me? I would go to her if I could," said the sufferer, without knowing what he talked of. "Is not she come yet? Send another horse, Frank. Why, it is only six miles. Six miles in three hours, that is—how many miles an hour? ten miles, is it? Don't hurry her—don't tell her I'm so bad; nor my father—don't let him see me, nor James, nor Frank, nor pretty Fanny, nor any body—they are all too good to me: I only wished to see poor Patty once before I die; but don't frighten her—I shall be very well, tell her—quite well, by the time she comes."

After running on in this manner for some time, his eyes closed again, and he lay in a state of stupor. He continued in this condition for some time: at last his sisters, who were watching beside the bed, heard a knocking at the door. It was Frank and James: they had gone for a clergyman, whom George, before he became delirious, had desired to see. The clergyman was come, and with him a benevolent physician, who happened to be at his house, and who insisted upon accompanying him. As soon as the physician saw the poor young man, and felt his pulse, he perceived that the ignorant apothecary, who had been first employed, had entirely mistaken George's disease, and had treated him improperly. His disease was a putrid fever, and the apothecary had bled him repeatedly. The physician thought he could certainly have saved his life, if he had seen him two days sooner; but now it was a hopeless case. All that could be done for him he tried.

Towards evening, the disease seemed to take a favourable turn. George came to his senses, knew his father, his brothers, and Fanny, and spoke to each with his customary kindness, as they stood round his bed: he then asked whether poor Patty was come? When he saw her, he thanked her tenderly for coming to him, but could not recollect he had any thing particular to say to her.

"I only wished to see you all together, to thank you for your good-nature to me ever since I was born, and to take leave of you before I die; for I feel that I am dying. Nay, do not cry so! My father! Oh! my father is most to be pitied; but he will have James and Frank left."

Seeing his father's affliction, which the good old man struggled in vain to subdue, George broke off here: he put his hand to his head, as if fearing it was again growing confused.

"Let me see our good clergyman, now that I am well enough to see him," said he. He then took a hand of each of his brothers and sisters, joined them together, and pressed them to his lips, looking from them to his father, whose back was now turned. "You understand me," whispered George: "he can never come to want, while you are left to work and comfort him. If I should not see you again in this world, farewell! Ask my father to give me his blessing!"

"God bless you, my son! God bless you, my dear good son! God will surely bless so good a son!" said the agonized father, laying his hand upon his son's forehead, which even now was cold with the damp of death.

"What a comfort it is to have a father's blessing!" said George. "May you all have it when you are as I am now!"

"I shall be out of this world long, long before that time, I hope," said the poor old man, as he left the room. "But God's will be done! Send the clergyman to my boy!"

The clergyman remained in the room but a short time: when he returned to the family, they saw by his looks that all was over!

There was a solemn silence.

"Be comforted," said the good clergyman. "Never man left this world with a clearer conscience, or had happier hope of a life to come. Be comforted. Alas! at such a time as this you cannot be comforted by any thing that the tongue of man can say."

All the family attended the funeral. It was on a Sunday, just before morning prayers; and as soon as George was interred, his father, brothers, and sisters, left the churchyard, to avoid being seen by the gay people who were coming to their devotion. As they went home, they passed through the field in which George used to work: there they saw his heap of docks, and his spade upright in the ground beside it, just as he had left it, the last time that he had ever worked.

The whole family stayed for a few days with their poor father. Late one evening, as they were all walking out together in the fields, a heavy dew began to fall; and James urged his father to make haste home, lest he should catch cold, and should have another fit of the rheumatism. They were then at some distance from their cottage; and Frank, who thought he knew a short way home, took them by a new road, which unluckily led them far out of their way; it brought them unexpectedly within sight of their old farm, and of the new house which Mr. Bettesworth had built upon it.

"Oh! my dear father, I am sorry I brought you this way," cried Frank. "Let us turn back."

"No, my son, why should we turn back?" said his father mildly; "we can pass by these fields, and this house, I hope, without coveting our neighbour's goods."

As they came near the house, he stopped at the gate to look at it. "It is a good house," said he; "but I have no need to envy any man a good house; I, that have so much better things—good children!"

Just as he uttered these words, Mr. Bettesworth's house door opened, and three or four men appeared on the stone steps, quarrelling and fighting. The loud voices of Bullying Bob and Wild Will were heard too plainly.

"We have no business here," said old Frankland, turning to his children: "let us go."

The combatants pursued each other with such furious rapidity that they were near to the gate in a few instants.

"Lock the gate, you without there, whoever you are! Lock the gate! or I'll knock you down when I come up, whoever you are;" cried Bullying Bob, who was hindmost in the race.

Wild Will was foremost; he kicked open the gate, but his foot slipped as he was going through: his brother overtook him, and, seizing him by the collar, cried, "Give me back the bank-notes, you rascal! they are mine, and I'll have 'em in spite of you."

"They are mine, and I'll keep 'em in spite of you," retorted Will, who was much intoxicated.

"Oh! what a sight! brothers fighting! Oh! part them, part them! Hold! hold! for Heaven's sake!" cried old Frankland to them.

Frank and James held them asunder, though they continued to abuse one another in the grossest terms. Their father, by this time, came up: he wrung his hands, and wept bitterly.

"Oh! shame, shame to me in my old age!" cried he, "can't you two let me live the few years I have to live in peace? Ah, neighbour Frankland, you are better off! My heart will break soon! These children of mine will be the ruin and the death of me!"

At these words the sons interrupted their father with loud complaints of the manner in which he had treated them. They had quarrelled with one another, and with their father, about money. The father charged them with profligate extravagance; and they accused him of sordid avarice. Mr. Frankland, much shocked at this scene, besought them at least to return to their house, and not to expose themselves in this manner, especially now that they were in the station of gentlemen. Their passions were too loud and brutal to listen to this appeal to their pride; their being raised to the rank of gentlemen could not give them principles or manners; that can only be done by education. Despairing to effect any good, Mr. Frankland retired from this scene, and made the best of his way home to his peaceful cottage.

"My children," said he to his family, as they sat down to their frugal meal, "we are poor, but we are happy in one another. Was not I right to say I need not envy neighbour Bettesworth his fine house? Whatever misfortunes befall me, I have the blessing of good children. It is a blessing I would not exchange for any this world affords. God preserve them in health!"

He sighed, and soon added, "It is a bitter thing to think of a good son, who is dead; but it is worse, perhaps, to think of a bad son, who is alive. That is a misfortune I can never know. But, my dear boys and girls," continued he, changing his tone, "this idle way of life of ours must not last for ever. You are too poor to be idle; and so much the better for you. To-morrow you must all away to your own business."

"But, father," cried they all at once, "which of us may stay with you?"

"None of you, my good children. You are all going on well in the world; and I will not take you from your good masters and mistresses."

Patty now urged that she had the strongest right to remain with her father, because Mrs. Crumpe would certainly refuse to receive her into her service again, after what had passed at their parting: but nothing could prevail upon Frankland; he positively refused to let any of his children stay with him. At last Frank cried, "How can you possibly manage this farm without help? You must let either James or me stay with you, father. Suppose you should be seized with another fit of the rheumatism?"

Frankland paused for a moment, and then answered, "Poor Hannah will nurse me if I fall sick. I am able still to pay her just wages. I will not be a burden to my children. As to this farm, I am going to give it up; for, indeed," said the old man, smiling, "I should not be well able to manage it with the rheumatism in my spade-arm. My landlord, farmer Hewit, is a good-natured friendly man; and he will give me my own time for the rent: nay, he tells me he would let me live in this cottage for nothing: but I cannot do that."
"Then what will you do, dear father?" said his sons.

"The clergyman, who was here yesterday, has made interest for a house for me which will cost me nothing, nor him either; and I shall be very near you both, boys."

"But, father," interrupted Frank, "I know, by your way of speaking, there is something about this house which you do not like."

"That is true," said old Frankland: "but that is the fault of my pride, and of my old prejudices; which are hard to conquer at my time of life. It is certain, I do not much like the thoughts of going into an almshouse."

"An almshouse!" cried all his children at once, in a tone of horror. "Oh! father, you must not, indeed you must not, go into an almshouse!"

The pride which renders the English yeoman averse to live upon public charity is highly advantageous to the industry and virtue of the nation. Even where it is instilled early into families as a prejudice, it is useful, and ought to be respected.

Frankland's children, shocked at the idea of their father's going into an almshouse, eagerly offered to join together the money they had earned, and to pay the rent of the cottage in which he now lived; but Frankland knew that, if he took this money, his children would themselves be in distress. He answered with tears in his eyes,

"My dear children, I thank you all for your goodness; but I cannot accept of your offer. Since I am no longer able to support myself, I will not, from false pride, be the ruin of my children. I will not be a burden to them; and I prefer living upon public charity to accepting of the ostentatious liberality of any one rich man. I am come to a resolution, which nothing shall induce me to break. I am determined to live in the Monmouth almshouse—nay, hear me, my children, patiently—to live in the Monmouth almshouse for one year; and during that time I will not see any of you, unless I am sick. I lay my commands upon you not to attempt to see me till this day twelvemonth. If at that time you are all together able to maintain me, without hurting yourselves, I will most willingly accept of your bounty for the rest of my days."

His children assured him they should be able to earn money sufficient to maintain him, without injury to themselves, long before the end of the year; and they besought him to permit them to do so as soon as it was in their power; but he continued firm in his resolution, and made them solemnly promise they would obey his commands, and not even attempt to see him during the ensuing year. He then took leave of them in a most affectionate manner, saying, "I know, my dearest children, I have now given you the strongest possible motive for industry and good conduct. This day twelvemonth we shall meet again; and I hope it will be as joyful a meeting as this is a sorrowful parting." His children, with some difficulty, obtained permission to accompany him to his new abode.

The almshouses at Monmouth are far superior to common institutions of this kind; they are remarkably neat and comfortable little dwellings, and form a row of pretty cottages, behind each of which there is a garden full of gooseberries, currants, and a variety of useful vegetables. These the old men cultivate themselves. The houses are fitted up conveniently; and each individual is provided with every thing that he wants in his own habitation: so that there is no opportunity or temptation for those petty disputes about property which often occur in charitable institutions that are not prudently conducted. Poor people who have their goods in common must necessarily become quarrelsome.

"You see," said old Frankland, pointing to the shining row of pewter on the clean shelf over the fire-place in his little kitchen; "you see I want for nothing here. I am not much to be pitied."

His children stood silent and dejected, whilst he dressed himself in the uniform belonging to the almshouse. Before they parted, they all agreed to meet at this place that day twelvemonth, and to bring with them the earnings of the year; they had hopes that thus, by their united efforts, a sum might be obtained sufficient to place their father once more in a state of independence. With these hopes they separated, and returned to their masters and mistresses.

CHAPTER IV

Patty went to Mrs. Crumpe's to get her clothes which she had left there, and to receive some months' wages, which were still due for her services. After what had passed, she had no idea that Mrs. Crumpe would wish she should stay with her; and she had heard of another place in Monmouth, which she believed would suit her in every respect.

The first person she saw, when she arrived at the house of her late mistress, was Martha, who, with a hypocritical length of face, said to her, "Sad news! sad news, Mrs. Patty! The passion my lady was thrown into, by your going away so sudden, was of terrible detriment to her. That very night she had a stroke of the palsy, and has scarce spoke since."

"Don't take it to heart, it is none of your fault: don't take it to heart, dear Patty," said Betty, the housemaid, who was fond of Patty. "What could you do but go to your brother? Here, drink this water, and don't blame yourself at all about the matter. Mistress had a stroke sixteen months ago, afore ever you came into the house; and I dare say she'd have had this last whether you had stayed or gone."

Here they were interrupted by the violent ringing of Mrs. Crumpe's bell. They were in the room next to her; and, as she heard voices louder than usual, she was impatient to know what was going on. Patty heard Mrs. Martha answer, as she opened her lady's door, "'Tis only Patty Frankland, ma'am, who is come for her clothes and her wages."

"And she is very sorry to hear you have been so ill; very sorry," said Betty, following to the door.

"Bid her come in," said Mrs. Crumpe, in a voice more distinct than she had ever been heard to speak in since the day of her illness.

"What! are you sorry for me, child?" said Mrs. Crumpe, fixing her eyes upon Patty's. Patty made no answer; but it was plain how much she was shocked.

"Ay, I see you are sorry for me," said her mistress. "And so am I for you," added she, stretching out her hand, and taking hold of Patty's black gown. "You shall have a finer stuff than this for mourning for me. But I know that is not what you are thinking of; and that's the reason I have more value for you than for all the rest of them put together. Stay with me, stay with me, to nurse me; you nurse me to my mind. You cannot leave me in the way I am in now, when I ask you to stay."

Patty could not without inhumanity refuse; she stayed with Mrs. Crumpe, who grew so dotingly fond of her, that she could scarcely bear to have her a moment out of sight. She would take neither food nor medicines but from Patty's hand; and she would not speak, except in answer to Patty's questions. The fatigue and confinement she was now forced to undergo were enough to hurt the constitution of any one who had not very strong health. Patty bore them with the greatest patience and good humour; indeed, the consciousness that she was doing right supported her in exertions which would otherwise have been beyond her power.

She had still more difficult trials to go through: Mrs. Martha was jealous of her favour with her lady, and often threw out hints that some people had much more luck, and more cunning too, than other people; but that some people might perhaps be disappointed at last in their ends.

Patty went on her own straight way, without minding these insinuations at first; but she was soon forced to attend to them. Mrs. Crumpe's relations received intelligence from Mrs. Martha, that her lady was growing worse and worse every hour; and that she was quite shut up under the dominion of an artful servant-girl, who had gained such power over her that there was no knowing what the consequence might be. Mrs. Crumpe's relations were much alarmed by this story: they knew she had made a will in their favour some years before this time, and they dreaded that Patty should prevail upon her to alter it, and should get possession herself of the fortune. They were particularly struck with this idea, because an instance of undue power, acquired by a favourite servant-maid over her doting mistress, happened about this period to be mentioned in an account of a trial in the newspapers of the day. Mrs. Crumpe's nearest relations were two grand-nephews. The eldest was Mr. Josiah Crumpe, a merchant who was settled at Liverpool; the youngest was that ensign Bloomington, whom we formerly mentioned. He had been intended for a merchant, but he would never settle to business; and at last ran away from the counting-house where he had been placed, and went into the army. He was an idle, extravagant young man: his great-aunt was by fits very angry with him, or very fond of him. Sometimes she would supply him with money; at others, she would forbid him her presence, and declare he should never see another shilling of hers. This had been her latest determination; but ensign Bloomington thought he could easily get into favour again, and he resolved to force himself into the house. Mrs. Crumpe positively refused to see him: the day after this refusal he returned with a reinforcement, for which Patty was not in the least prepared: he was accompanied by Miss Sally Bettesworth, in a regimental riding-habit. Jessy had been the original object of this gentleman's gallantry; but she met with a new and richer lover, and of course jilted him. Sally, who was in haste to be married, took undisguised pains to fix the ensign; and she thought she was sure of him. But to proceed with our story.

Patty was told that a lady and gentleman desired to see her in the parlour: she was scarcely in the room when Sally began in a voice capable of intimidating the most courageous of scolds, "Fine doings! Fine doings, here! You think you have the game in your own hands, I warrant, my Lady Paramount; but I'm not one to be bullied, you know of old."

"Nor am I one to be bullied, I hope," replied Patty, in a modest but firm voice. "Will you be pleased to let me know, in a quiet way, what are your commands with me, or my lady?"

"This gentleman here must see your lady, as you call her. To let you into a bit of a secret, this gentleman and I is soon to be one; so no wonder I stir in this affair, and I never stir for nothing; so it is as well for you to do it with fair words as foul. Without more preambling, please to show this gentleman into his aunt's room, which sure he has the best right to see of any one in this world; and if you prevent it in any species, I'll have the law of you; and I take this respectable woman," looking at Mrs. Martha, who came in with a salver of cakes and wine, "I take this here respectable gentlewoman to be my witness, if you choose to refuse my husband (that is to be) admittance to his true and lawful nearest relation upon earth. Only say the doors are locked, and that you won't let him in; that's all we ask of you, Mrs. Patty Paramount. Only say that afore this here witness."

"Indeed, I shall say no such thing, ma'am," replied Patty; "for it is not in the least my wish to prevent the gentleman from seeing my mistress. It was she herself who refused to let him in; and I think, if he forces himself into the room, she will be apt to be very much displeased: but I shall not hinder him, if he chooses to try. There are the stairs, and my lady's room is the first on the right hand. Only, sir, before you go up, let me caution you, lest you should startle her so as to be the death of her. The least surprise or fright might bring on another stroke in an instant."

Ensign Bloomington and Saucy Sally now looked at one another, as if at a loss how to proceed: they retired to a window to consult; and whilst they were whispering, a coach drove up to the door. It was full of Mrs, Crumpe's relations, who came post-haste from Monmouth, in consequence of the alarm given by Mrs. Martha. Mr. Josiah Crumpe was not in the coach: he had been written for, but was not yet arrived from Liverpool.

Now, it must be observed, this coach-full of relations were all enemies to ensign Bloomington; and the moment they put their heads out of the carriage-window, and saw him standing in the parlour, their surprise and indignation were too great for coherent utterance. With all the rashness of prejudice, they decided that he had bribed Patty to let him in and to exclude them. Possessed with this idea, they hurried out of the coach, passed by poor Patty who was standing in the hall, and beckoned to Mrs. Martha, who showed them into the drawing-room, and remained shut up with them there for some minutes. "She is playing us false," cried Saucy Sally, rushing out of the parlour. "I told you not to depend on that Martha; nor on nobody but me: I said I'd force a way for you up to the room, and so I have; and now you have not the spirit to take your advantage. They'll get in all of them before you; and then where will you be, and what will you be?"

Mrs. Crumpe's bell rang violently, and Patty ran up stairs to her room. "I have been ringing for you, Patty, this quarter of an hour! What is all the disturbance I hear below?"

"Your relations, ma'am, who wish to see you. I hope you won't refuse to see them, for they are very anxious."

"Very anxious to have me dead and buried. Not one of them cares a groat for me. I have made my will, tell them; and they will see that in time. I will not see one of them."

By this time, they were all at the bedchamber door, struggling which party should enter first. Saucy Sally's loud voice was heard, maintaining her right to be there, as wife elect to ensign Bloomington.

"Tell them the first who enters this room shall never see a shilling of my money," cried Mrs. Crumpe.

Patty opened the door; the disputants were instantly silent. "Be pleased, before you come in, to hearken to what my mistress says. Ma'am, will you say whatever you think proper yourself," said Patty; "for it is too hard for me to be suspected of putting words into your mouth, and keeping your friends from the sight of you."

"The first of them who comes into this room," cried Mrs. Crumpe, raising her feeble voice to the highest pitch she was able, "the first who enters this room shall never see a shilling of my money; and so on to the next, and the next, and the next. I'll see none of you."

No one ventured to enter. Their infinite solicitude to see how poor Mrs. Crumpe found herself to-day suddenly vanished. The two parties adjourned to the parlour and the drawing-room; and there was nothing in which they agreed, except in abusing Patty. They called for pen, ink, and paper, and each wrote what they wished to say. Their notes were carried up by Patty herself; for Mrs. Martha would not run the risk of losing her own legacy to oblige any of them, though she had been bribed by all. With much difficulty, Mrs. Crumpe was prevailed upon to look at the notes; at last she exclaimed, "Let them all come up! all; this moment tell them, all!"

They were in the room instantly; all, except Saucy Sally: ensign Bloomington persuaded her it was for the best that she should not appear. Patty was retiring, as soon as she had shown them in; but her mistress called to her, and bade her take a key, which she held in her hand, and unlock an escritoir that was in the room. She did so.

"Give me that parcel, which is tied up with red tape, and sealed with three seals," said Mrs. Crumpe.

All eyes were immediately fixed upon it, for it was her will.

She broke the seals deliberately, untied the red string, opened the huge sheet of parchment, and without saying one syllable tore it down the middle; then tore the pieces again, and again, till they were so small that the writing could not be read. The spectators looked upon one another in dismay.

"Ay! you may all look as you please," cried Mrs. Crumpe. "I'm alive, and in my sound senses still; my money's my own; my property's my own; I'll do what I please with it. You were all handsomely provided for in this will; but you could not wait for your legacies till I was under ground. No! you must come hovering over me, like so many ravens. It is not time yet! It is not time yet! The breath is not yet out of my body; and when it is, you shall none of you be the better for it, I promise you. My money's my own; my property's my own; I'll make a new will to-morrow. Good bye to you all. I've told you my mind."

Not the most abject humiliations, not the most artful caresses, not the most taunting reproaches, from any of the company, could extort another word from Mrs. Crumpe. Her disappointed and incensed relations were at last obliged to leave the house; though not without venting their rage upon Patty, whom they believed to be the secret cause of all that had happened. After they had left the house, she went up to a garret, where she thought no one would see her or hear her, sat down on an old bedstead, and burst into tears. She had been much shocked by the scenes that had just passed, and her heart wanted this relief.

"Oh!" thought she, "it is plain enough that it is not riches which make people happy. Here is this poor lady, with heaps of money and fine clothes, without any one in this whole world to love or care for her, but all wishing her dead; worried by her own relations, and abused by them, almost in her hearing, upon her death-bed! Oh! my poor brother! How different it was with you!"

Patty's reflections were here interrupted by the entrance of Martha, who came and sat down on the bedstead beside her, and, with a great deal of hypocritical kindness in her manner, began to talk of what had passed; blaming Mrs. Crumpe's relations for being so hard-hearted and inconsiderate as to force business upon her when she was in such a state. "Indeed, they have no one to thank but themselves, for the new turn things have taken. I hear my mistress has torn her will to atoms, and is going to make a new one! To be sure, you, Mrs. Patty, will be handsomely provided for in this, as is, I am sure, becoming; and I hope, if you have an opportunity, as for certain you will, you won't forget to speak a good word for me!"

Patty, who was disgusted by this interested and deceitful address, answered, she had nothing to do with her mistress's will; and that her mistress was the best judge of what should be done with her own money, which she did not covet.

Mrs. Martha was not mistaken in her opinion that Patty would be handsomely remembered in this new will. Mrs. Crumpe the next morning said to Patty, as she was giving her some medicine, "It is for your interest, child, that I should get through this day, at least; for if I live a few hours longer, you will be the richest single woman in Monmouthshire. I'll show them that all my money's my own; and that I can do what I please with my own. Go yourself to Monmouth, child (as soon as you have plaited my cap), and bring me the attorney your brother lives with, to draw my new will. Don't say one word of your errand to any of my relations, I charge you, for your own sake as well as mine. The harpies would tear you to pieces; but I'll show them that I can do what I please with my own. That's the least satisfaction I can have for my money before I die. God knows, it has been plague enough to me all my life long! But now, before I die—"

"Oh! ma'am," interrupted Patty, "there is no need to talk of your dying now; for I have not heard you speak so strong, or so clear, nor seem so much yourself this long time. You may live yet, and I hope you will, to see many a good day; and to make it up, if I may be so bold to say it, with all your relations: which, I am sure, would be a great ease to your heart; and I am sure they are very sorry to have offended you."

"The girl's a fool!" cried Mrs. Crumpe. "Why, child, don't you understand me yet? I tell you, as plain as I can speak, I mean to leave the whole fortune to you. Well! what makes you look so blank!"

"Because, ma'am, indeed I have no wish to stand in any body's way; and would not for all the world do such an unjust thing as to take advantage of your being a little angry or so with your relations, to get the fortune for myself: for I can do, having done all my life, without fortune well enough; but I could not do without my own good opinion, and that of my father, and brothers, and sister; all which I should lose, if I was to be guilty of a mean thing. So, ma'am," said Patty, "I have made bold to speak the whole troth of my mind to you; and I hope you will not do me an injury, by way of doing me a favour. I am sure I thank you with all my heart for your goodness to me."

Patty turned away as she finished speaking, for she was greatly moved.

"You are a strange girl!" said Mrs. Crumpe. "I would not have believed this, if any one had sworn it to me. Go for the attorney, as I bid you, this minute. I will have my own way."

When Patty arrived at Mr. Barlow's, she asked immediately for her brother Frank, whom she wished to consult; but he was out, and she then desired to speak to Mr. Barlow himself. She was shown into his office, and she told him her business, without any circumlocution, with the plain language and ingenuous countenance of truth.

"Indeed, sir," said she, "I should be glad you would come directly to my mistress and speak to her yourself; for she will mind what you say, and I only hope she may do the just thing by her relations. I don't want her fortune, nor any part of it, but a just recompense for my service. Knowing this, in my own heart, I forgive them for all the ill-will they bear me: it being all founded in a mistaken notion."

There was a gentleman in Mr. Barlow's office who was sitting at a desk writing a letter, when Patty came in: she took him for one of the clerks. Whilst she was speaking, he turned about several times, and looked at her very earnestly. At last he went to a clerk, who was folding up some parchments, and asked who she was? He then sat down again to his writing, without saying a-single word. This gentleman was Mr. Josiah Crumpe, the Liverpool merchant, Mrs. Crumpe's eldest nephew, who had come to Monmouth, in consequence of the account he had heard of his aunt's situation. Mr. Barlow had lately amicably settled a suit between him and one of his relations at Monmouth; and Mr. Crumpe had just been signing the deed relative to this affair. He was struck with the disinterestedness of Patty's conduct; but he kept silence that she might not find out who he was, and that he might have full opportunity of doing her justice hereafter. He was not one of the ravens, as Mrs. Crumpe emphatically called those who were hovering over her, impatient for her death: he had, by his own skill and industry, made himself not only independent, but rich. After Patty was gone, he with the true spirit of a British merchant declared, that he was as independent in his sentiments as in his fortune; that he would not crouch or fawn to man or woman, peer or prince, in his majesty's dominions; no, not even to his own aunt. He wished his old aunt Crumpe, he said, to live and enjoy all she had as long as she could; and if she chose to leave it to him after her death, well and good; he should be much obliged to her: if she did not, why well and good; he should not be obliged to be obliged to her: and that, to his humour, would perhaps be better still.

With these sentiments Mr. Josiah Crumpe found no difficulty in refraining from going to see, or, as he called it, from paying his court to his aunt. "I have some choice West India sweetmeats here for the poor soul," said he to Mr. Barlow: "she gave me sweetmeats when I was a schoolboy; which I don't forget. I know she has a sweet tooth still in her head; for she wrote to me last year, to desire I would get her some: but I did not relish the style of her letter, and I never complied with the order; however, I was to blame: she is an infirm poor creature, and should be humoured now, let her be ever so cross. Take her the sweetmeats; but mind, do not let her have a taste or a sight of them till she has made her will. I do not want to bribe her to leave me her money-bags; I thank my God and myself, I want them not."

Mr. Barlow immediately went to Mrs. Crumpe's. As she had land to dispose of, three witnesses were necessary to the will. Patty said she had two men-servants who could write; but to make sure of a third, Mr. Barlow desired that one of his clerks should accompany him. Frank was out; so the eldest clerk went in his stead.

This clerk's name was Mason; he was Frank's chief friend, and a young man of excellent character. He had never seen Patty till this day; but he had often heard her brother speak of her with so much affection, that he was prepossessed in her favour, even before he saw her. The manner in which she spoke on the subject of Mrs. Crumpe's fortune quite charmed him; for he was of an open and generous temper, and said to himself, "I would rather have this girl for my wife, without sixpence in the world, than any woman I ever saw in my life—if I could but afford it—and if she was but a little prettier. As it is, however, there is no danger of my falling in love with her; so I may just indulge myself in the pleasure of talking to her: besides, it is but civil to lead my horse and walk a part of the way with Frank's sister."

Accordingly, Mason set off to walk a part of the way to Mrs. Crumpe's with Patty; and they fell into conversation, in which they were both so earnestly engaged that they did not perceive how time passed. Instead, however, of part of the way, Mason walked the whole way; and he and Patty were both rather surprised when they found themselves within sight of Mrs. Crumpe's house.

What a fine healthy colour this walking has brought into her face, thought Mason, as he stood looking at her, whilst they were waiting for some one to open the door. Though she has not a single beautiful feature, and though nobody could call her handsome, yet there is so much good-nature in her countenance, that, plain as she certainly is, her looks are more pleasing to my fancy than those of many a beauty I have heard admired.

The door was now opened; and Mr. Barlow, who had arrived some time, summoned Mason to business. They went up to Mrs. Crumpe's room to take her instructions for her new will. Patty showed them in.

"Don't go, child, I will not have you stir," said Mrs. Crumpe. "Now stand there at the foot of my bed, and, without hypocrisy, tell me truly, child, your mind. This gentleman, who understands the law, can assure you that, in spite of all the relations upon earth, I can leave my fortune to whom I please, so do not let fear of my relations prevent you from being happy."

"No, madam," interrupted Patty, "it was not fear that made me say what I did to you this morning; and it is not fear that keeps me in the same mind still. I would not do what I thought wrong myself if nobody else in the whole world was to know it. But, since you desire me to say what I really wish, I have a father, who is in great distress, and I should wish you would leave fifty pounds to him."

"With such principles and feelings," cried Mr. Barlow, "you are happier than ten thousand a year could make you!"

Mason said nothing; but his looks said a great deal: and his master forgave him the innumerable blunders he made in drawing Mrs. Crumpe's will. "Come, Mason, give me up the pen," whispered he at last; "you are not your own man, I see; and I like you the better for being touched with good and generous conduct. But a truce with sentiment, now; I must be a mere man of law. Go you and take a walk, to recover your legal senses."

The contents of Mrs. Crumpe's new will were kept secret: Patty did not in the least know how she had disposed of her fortune; nor did Mason, for he had written only the preamble, when his master compassionately took the pen from his hand. Contrary to expectation, Mrs. Crumpe continued to linger on for some months; and during this time, Patty attended her with the most patient care and humanity. Though long habits of selfishness had rendered this lady in general indifferent to the feelings of her servants and dependants, yet Patty was an exception: she often said to her, "Child, it goes against my conscience to keep you prisoner here the best days of your life, in a sick room: go out and take a walk with your brothers and sister, I desire, whenever they call for you."

These walks with her brothers and sister were very refreshing to Patty, especially when Mason was of the party, as he almost always contrived to be. Every day he grew more and more attached to Patty; for every day he became more and more convinced of the goodness of her disposition and the sweetness of her temper. The affection which he saw her brothers and sister bore her, spoke to his mind most strongly in her favour. They have known her from her childhood, thought he, and cannot be deceived in her character. Tis a good sign that those who know her best love her most; and her loving her pretty sister, Fanny, as she does, is a proof that she is incapable of envy and jealousy.

In consequence of these reflections, Mason determined he would apply diligently to his business, that he might in due time be able to marry and support Patty. She ingenuously told him she had never seen the man she could love so well as himself; but that her first object was to earn some money, to release her father from the almshouse, where she could not bear to see him living upon charity. "When, amongst us all, we have accomplished this," said she, "it will be time enough for me to think of marrying. Duty first and love afterwards."

Mason loved her the better, when he found her so steady in her gratitude to her father; for he was a man of sense, and knew that so good a daughter and sister would, in all probability, make a good wife.

We must now give some account of what Fanny has been doing all this time. Upon her return to Mrs. Hungerford's, after the death of her brother, she was received with the greatest kindness by her mistress, and by all the children, who were really fond of her; though she had never indulged them in anything that was contrary to their mother's wishes.

Mrs. Hungerford had not forgotten the affair of the kettle-drum. One morning she said to her little son, "Gustavus, your curiosity about the kettle-drum and the clarionet shall be satisfied: your cousin Philip will come here in a few days, and he is well acquainted with the colonel of the regiment which is quartered in Monmouth: he shall ask the colonel to let us have the band here, some day. We may have them at the farthest end of the garden; and you and your brothers and sisters shall dine in the arbour, with Fanny, who upon this occasion particularly deserves to have a share in your amusement."

The cousin Philip, of whom Mrs. Hungerford spoke, was no other than Frankland's landlord, young Mr. Folingsby. Besides liking fine horses and fine curricles, this gentleman was a great admirer of fine women.

He was struck with Fanny's beauty the first day he came to Mrs. Hungerford's: every succeeding day he thought her handsomer and handsomer; and every day grew fonder and fonder of playing with his little cousins. Upon some pretence or other, he contrived to be constantly in the room with them when Fanny was there: the modest propriety of her manners, however, kept him at that distance at which it was no easy matter for a pretty girl, in her situation, to keep such a gallant gentleman. His intention, when he came to Mrs. Hungerford's, was to stay but a week; but when that week was at an end, he determined to stay another: he found his aunt Hungerford's house uncommonly agreeable. The moment she mentioned to him her wish of having the band of music in the garden, he was charmed with the scheme, and longed to dine out in the arbour with the children; but he dared not press this point, lest he should excite suspicion.

Amongst other company who dined this day with Mrs. Hungerford was a Mrs. Cheviott, a blind lady, who took the liberty, as she said, to bring with her a young person, who was just come to live with her as a companion. This young person was Jessy Bettesworth; or, as she is henceforth to be called, Miss Jessy Bettesworth. Since her father had "come in for Captain Bettesworth's fortin," her mother had spared no pains to push Jessy forward in the world; having no doubt that "her beauty, when well dressed, would charm some great gentleman; or, may be, some great lord!" Accordingly, Jessy was dizened out in all sorts of finery: her thoughts were wholly bent on fashions and flirting; and her mother's vanity, joined to her own, nearly turned her brain.

Just as this fermentation of folly was gaining force, she happened to meet with Ensign Bloomington at a ball at Monmouth: he fell, or she thought he fell, desperately in love with her; she of course coquetted with him: indeed, she gave him so much encouragement, that every body concluded they were to be married. She and her sister Sally were continually seen walking arm in arm with him in the streets of Monmouth; and morning, noon, and night, she wore the drop-earrings, of which he had made her a present. It chanced, however, that Jilting Jessy heard an officer, in her ensign's regiment, swear she was pretty enough to be the captain's lady instead of the ensign's; and, from that moment, she thought no more of the ensign.

He was enraged to find himself jilted thus by a country girl, and determined to have his revenge: consequently he immediately transferred all his attentions to her sister Sally; judiciously calculating that, from the envy and jealousy he had seen between the sisters, this would be the most effectual mode of mortifying his perfidious fair. Jilting Jessy said her sister was welcome to her cast-off sweethearts: and Saucy Sally replied, her sister was welcome to be her bridemaid; since, with all her beauty, and all her airs, she was not likely to be a bride.

Mrs. Bettesworth had always confessed that Jessy was her favourite: like a wise and kind mother, she took part in all these disputes; and set these amiable sisters yet more at variance, by prophesying that "her Jessy would make the grandest match."

To put her into fortune's way, Mrs. Bettesworth determined to get her into some genteel family, as companion to a lady. Mrs. Cheviott's housekeeper was nearly related to the Bettesworths, and to her Mrs. Bettesworth applied. "But I'm afraid Jessy is something too much of a flirt," said the housekeeper, "for my mistress, who is a very strict, staid lady. You know, or at least we in Monmouth know, that Jessy was greatly talked of about a young officer here in town. I used myself to see her go trailing about, with her muslin and pink, and fine coloured shoes, in the dirt."

"Oh! that's all over now," said Mrs. Bettesworth: "the man was quite beneath her notice—that's all over now: he will do well enough for Sally; but, ma'am, my daughter Jessy has quite laid herself out for goodness now, and only wants to get into some house where she may learn to be a little genteel."

The housekeeper, though she had not the highest possible opinion of the young lady, was in hopes that, since Jessy had now laid herself out for goodness, she might yet turn out well; and, considering that she was her relation, she thought it her duty to speak in favour of Miss Bettesworth. In consequence of her recommendation, Mrs. Cheviott took Jessy into her family; and Jessy was particularly glad to be the companion of a blind lady.

She discovered, the first day she spent with Mrs. Cheviott, that, besides the misfortune of being blind, she had the still greater misfortune of being inordinately fond of flattery. Jessy took advantage of this foible, and imposed so far on the understanding of her patroness, that she persuaded Mrs. Cheviott into a high opinion of her judgment and prudence.

Things were in this situation when Jessy, for the first time, accompanied the blind lady to Mrs. Hungerford's. Without having the appearance or manners of a gentlewoman, Miss Jessy Bettesworth was, notwithstanding, such a pretty, showy girl, that she generally contrived to attract notice. She caught Mr. Folingsby's eye at dinner, as she was playing off her best airs at the side-table; and it was with infinite satisfaction that she heard him ask one of the officers, as they were going out to walk in the garden, "Who is that girl? She has fine eyes, and a most beautiful long neck!" Upon the strength of this whisper, Jessy flattered herself she had made a conquest of Mr. Folingsby; by which idea she was so much intoxicated, that she could scarcely restrain her vanity within decent bounds.

"Lord! Fanny Frankland, is it you? Who expected to meet you sitting here?" said she, when, to her great surprise, she saw Fanny in the arbour with the children. To her yet greater surprise, she soon perceived that Mr. Folingsby's attention was entirely fixed upon Fanny; and that he became so absent he did not know he was walking upon the flower-borders.

Jessy could scarcely believe her senses when she saw that her rival, for as such she now considered her, gave her lover no encouragement. "Is it possible that the girl is such a fool as not to see that this here gentleman is in love with her? No; that is out of the nature of things. Oh! it's all artifice; and I will find out her drift, I warrant, before long!"

Having formed this laudable resolution, she took her measures well for carrying it into effect. Mrs. Cheviott, being blind, had few amusements: she was extremely fond of music, and one of Mrs. Hungerford's daughters played remarkably well on the piano-forte. This evening, as Mrs. Cheviott was listening to the young lady's singing, Jessy exclaimed, "Oh! ma'am, how happy it would make you to hear such singing and music every day."

"If she would come every day, when my sister is practising with the music-master, she might hear enough of it," said little Gustavus. "I'll run and desire mamma to ask her; because," added he, in a low voice, "if I was blind, may be I should like it myself."

Mrs. Hungerford, who was good-natured as well as polite, pressed Mrs. Cheviott to come, whenever it should be agreeable to her. The poor blind lady was delighted with the invitation, and went regularly every morning to Mrs. Hungerford's at the time the music-master attended. Jessy Bettesworth always accompanied her, for she could not go any where without a guide. Jessy had now ample opportunities of gratifying her malicious curiosity; she saw, or thought she saw, that Mr. Folingsby was displeased by the reserve of Fanny's manners; and she renewed all her own coquettish efforts to engage his attention. He amused himself sometimes with her, in hopes of rousing Fanny's jealousy; but he found that this expedient, though an infallible one in ordinary cases, was here totally unavailing. His passion for Fanny was increased so much, by her unaffected modesty, and by the daily proofs he saw of the sweetness of her disposition, that he was no longer master of himself: he plainly told her that he could not live without her.

"That's a pity, sir," said Fanny laughing, and trying to turn off what he said, as if it were only a jest. "It is a great pity, sir, that you cannot live without me; for, you know, I cannot serve my mistress, do my duty, and live with you."

Mr. Folingsby endeavoured to convince, or rather to persuade her, that she was mistaken; and swore that nothing within the power of his fortune should be wanting to make her happy.

"Ah! sir," said she, "your fortune could not make me happy, if I were to do what I know is wrong, what would disgrace me for ever, and what would break my poor father's heart!"

"But your father shall never know any thing of the matter. I will keep your secret from the whole world: trust to my honour."

"Honour! Oh! sir, how can you talk to me of honour! Do you think I do not know what honour is, because I am poor? Or do you think I do not set any value on mine, though you do on yours? Would you not kill any man, if you could, in a duel, for doubting of your honour? And yet you expect me to love you, at the very moment you show me, most plainly, how desirous you are to rob me of mine!"

Mr. Folingsby was silent for some moments; but, when he saw that Fanny was leaving him, he hastily stopped her, and said, laughing, "You have made me a most charming speech about honour; and, what is better still, you looked most charmingly when you spoke it; but now take time to consider what I I have said to you. Let me have your answer to-morrow; and consult this book before you answer me, I conjure you."

Fanny took up the book as soon as Mr Folingsby had left the room; and, without opening it, determined to return it immediately. She instantly wrote a letter to Mr. Folingsby, which she was just wrapping up with the book in a sheet of paper, when Miss Jessy Bettesworth, the blind lady, and the music-master, came into the room. Fanny went to set a chair for the blind lady; and, whilst she was doing so, Miss Jessy Bettesworth, who had observed that Fanny blushed when they came in, slily peeped into the book, which lay on the table. Between the first pages she opened there was a five-pound bank-note; she turned the leaf, and found another, and another, and another at every leaf! Of these notes she counted one-and-twenty! whilst Fanny, unsuspicious of what was doing behind her back, was looking for the children's music-books.

"Philip Folingsby! So, so! Did he give you this book, Fanny Frankland?" said Jessy, in a scornful tone: "it seems truly to be a very valuable performance; and, no doubt, he had good reasons for giving it to you."

Fanny coloured deeply at this unexpected speech; and hesitated, from the fear of betraying Mr. Folingsby. "He did not give me the book: he only lent it to me," said she, "and I am going to return it to him directly."

"Oh! no; pray lend it to me first," replied Jessy, in an ironical tone; "Mr. Folingsby, to be sure, would lend it to me as soon as to you. I'm growing as fond of reading as other folks, lately," continued she, holding the book fast.

"I dare say, Mr. Folingsby would—Mr. Folingsby would lend it to you, I suppose," said Fanny, colouring more and more deeply; "but, as it is trusted to me now, I must return it safe. Pray let me have it, Jessy."

"Oh! yes; return it, madam, safe! I make no manner of doubt you will! I make no manner of doubt you will!" replied Jessy, several times, as she shook the book; whilst the bank-notes fell from between the leaves, and were scattered upon the floor. "It is a thousand pities, Mrs. Cheviott, you can't see what a fine book we have got, full of bank-notes! But Mrs. Hungerford is not blind at any rate, it is to be hoped," continued she, turning to Mrs. Hungerford, who at this instant opened the door.

She stood in dignified amazement. Jessy had an air of malignant triumph. Fanny was covered with blushes; but she looked with all the tranquillity of innocence. The children gathered round her; and blind Mrs. Cheviott cried, "What is going on? What is going on? Will nobody tell me what is going on? Jessy! What is it you are talking about, Jessy?"

"About a very valuable book, ma'am; containing more than I can easily count, in bank-notes, ma'am, that Mr. Folingsby has lent, only lent, ma'am, she says, to Miss Fanny Frankland, ma'am, who was just going to return them to him, ma'am, when I unluckily took up the book, and shook them all out upon the floor, ma'am."

"Pick them up, Gustavus, my dear," said Mrs. Hungerford, coolly. "From what I know of Fanny Frankland, I am inclined to believe that whatever she says is truth. Since she has lived with me, I have never, in the slightest instance, found her deviate from the truth; therefore I must entirely depend upon what she says."

"Oh! yes, mamma," cried the children, all together, "that I am sure you may."

"Come with me, Fanny," resumed Mrs. Hungerford; "it is not necessary that your explanation should be public, though I am persuaded it will be satisfactory."

Fanny was glad to escape from the envious eye of Miss Jessy Bettesworth, and felt much gratitude to Mrs. Hungerford for this kindness and confidence; but, when she was to make her explanation, Fanny was in great confusion. She dreaded to occasion a quarrel between Mr. Folingsby and his aunt; yet she knew not how to exculpate herself, without accusing him.

"Why these blushes and tears, and why this silence, Fanny?" said Mrs. Hungerford, after she had waited some minutes, in expectation she would begin to speak. "Are not you sure of justice from me; and of protection, both from slander and insult? I am fond of my nephew, it is true; but I think myself obliged to you, for the manner in which you have conducted yourself towards my children, since you have had them under your care. Tell me then, freely, if you have any reason to complain of young Mr. Folingsby."

"Oh! madam," said Fanny, "thank you a thousand times for your goodness to me. I do not, indeed, I do not wish to complain of any body; and I would not for the world make mischief between you and your nephew. I would rather leave your family at once; and that," continued the poor girl, sobbing, "that is what I believe I had best; nay, is what I must and will do."

"No, Fanny, do not leave my house, without giving me an explanation of what has passed this morning; for, if you do, your reputation is at the mercy of Miss Jessy Bettesworth's malice."

"Heaven forbid!" said Fanny, with a look of real terror. "I must beg, madam, that you will have the kindness to return this book, and these bank-notes, to Mr. Folingsby; and that you will give him this letter, which I was just going to wrap up in the paper, with the book, when Jessy Bettesworth came in and found the bank-notes, which I had never seen. These can make no difference in my answer to Mr. Folingsby: therefore I shall leave my letter just as it was first written, if you please, madam."

Fanny's letter was as follows:

"SIR,

"I return the book, which you left with me, as nothing it contains can ever alter my opinion on the subject of which you spoke to me this morning. I hope you will never speak to me again, sir, in the same manner. Consider, sir, that I am a poor unprotected girl. If you go on as you have done lately, I shall be obliged to leave good Mrs. Hungerford, who is my only friend. Oh! where shall I find so good a friend? My poor old father is in the almshouse! and there he must remain till his children can earn money sufficient to support him. Do not fancy, sir, that I say this by way of begging from you; I would not, nor would he, accept of any thing that you could offer him, whilst in your present way of thinking. Pray, sir, have some compassion, and do not injure those whom you cannot serve.

"I am, sir,
"Your humble servant,
"FANNY FRANKLAND."

Mr. Folingsby was surprised and confounded, when this letter, and the book containing his bank-notes, were put into his hand by his aunt. Mrs. Hungerford told him by what means the book had been seen by Miss Jessy Bettesworth, and to what imputations it must have exposed Fanny. "Fanny is afraid of making mischief between you and me," continued Mrs. Hungerford "and I cannot prevail upon her to give me an explanation, which I am persuaded would be much to her honour."

"Then you have not seen this letter! Then she has decided without consulting you! She is a charming girl!" cried Mr. Folingsby; "and whatever you may think of me, I am bound, in justice to her, to show you what she has written: that will sufficiently explain how much I have been to blame, and how well she deserves the confidence you place in her."

As he spoke, Mr. Folingsby rang the bell to order his horses. "I will return to town immediately," continued he; "so Fanny need not leave the house of her only friend to avoid me. As to these bank-notes, keep them, dear aunt. She says her father is in great distress. Perhaps, now that I am come 'to a right way of thinking,' she will not disdain my assistance. Give her the money when and how you think proper. I am sure I cannot make a better use of a hundred guineas; and wish I had never thought of making a worse."

Mr. Folingsby returned directly to town; and his aunt thought he had in some measure atoned for his fault by his candour and generosity. Miss Jessy Bettesworth waited all this time, with malicious impatience, to hear the result of Fanny's explanation with Mrs. Hungerford. How painfully was she surprised and disappointed, when Mrs. Hungerford returned to the company, to hear her speak in the highest terms of Fanny! "Oh, mamma," cried little Gustavus, clapping his hands, "I am glad you think her good, because we all think so; and I should be very sorry indeed if she was to go away, especially in disgrace."

"There is no danger of that, my dear," said Mrs. Hungerford. "She shall never leave my house, as long as she desires to stay in it. I do not give, or withdraw, my protection, without good reasons."

Miss Jessy Bettesworth bit her lips. Her face, which nature intended to be beautiful, became almost ugly; envy and malice distorted her features; and, when she departed with Mrs. Cheviott, her humiliated appearance was a strong contrast to the air of triumph with which she had entered.

CHAPTER V

After Jessy and Mrs. Cheviott had left the room, one of the little girls exclaimed, "I don't like that Miss Bettesworth; for she asked me whether I did not wish that Fanny was gone, because she refused to let me have a peach that was not ripe. I am sure I wish Fanny may always stay here."

There was a person in the room who seemed to join most fervently in this wish: this was Mr. Reynolds, the drawing-master. For some time his thoughts had been greatly occupied by Fanny. At first, he was struck with her beauty; but he had discovered that Mr. Folingsby was in love with her, and had carefully attended to her conduct, resolving not to offer himself till he was sure on a point so serious. Her modesty and prudence fixed his affections; and he now became impatient to declare his passion. He was a man of excellent temper and character; and his activity and talents were such as to ensure independence to a wife and family.

Mrs. Hungerford, though a proud, was not a selfish woman: she was glad that Mr. Reynolds was desirous to obtain Fanny, though she was sorry to part with one who was so useful in her family. Fanny had now lived with her nearly two years; and she was much attached to her. A distant relation, about this time, left her five children a small legacy of ten guineas each. Gustavus, though he had some ambition to be master of a watch, was the first to propose that this legacy should be given to Fanny. His brothers and sisters applauded the idea; and Mrs. Hungerford added fifty guineas to their fifty. "I had put by this money," said she, "to purchase a looking-glass for my drawing-room; but it will be much better applied in rewarding one who has been of real service to my children."

Fanny was now mistress of two hundred guineas; a hundred given to her by Mr. Folingsby, fifty by Mrs. Hungerford, and fifty by the children. Her joy and gratitude were extreme: for with this money she knew she could relieve her father; this was the first wish of her heart; and it was a wish in which her lover so eagerly joined that she smiled on him, and said, "Now I am sure you really love me."

"Let us go to your father directly," said Mr. Reynolds. "Let me be present when you give him this money."

"You shall," said Fanny; "but first I must consult my sister Patty and my brothers; for we must all go together; that is our agreement. The first day of next month is my father's birthday; and, on that day, we are all to meet at the almshouse. What a happy day it will be!"

But what has James been about all this time? How has he gone on with his master, Mr. Cleghorn, the haberdasher?

During the eighteen months that James had spent in Mr. Cleghorn's shop, he never gave his master the slightest reason to complain of him; on the contrary, this young man made his employer's interests his own; and, consequently, completely deserved his confidence. It was not, however, always easy to deal with Mr. Cleghorn; for he dreaded to be flattered, yet could not bear to be contradicted. James was very near losing his favour for ever, upon the following occasion.

One evening, when it was nearly dusk, and James was just shutting up shop, a strange-looking man, prodigiously corpulent, and with huge pockets to his coat, came in. He leaned his elbows on the counter, opposite to James, and stared him full in the face without speaking. James swept some loose money off the counter into the till. The stranger smiled, as if purposely to show him this did not escape his quick eye. There was in his countenance an expression of roguery and humour: the humour seemed to be affected, the roguery natural. "What are you pleased to want, sir?" said James.

"A glass of brandy, and your master."

"My master is not at home, sir; and we have no brandy. You will find brandy, I believe, at the house over the way."

"I believe I know where to find brandy a little better than you do; and better brandy than you ever tasted, or the devil's in it," replied the stranger. "I want none of your brandy. I only asked for it to try what sort of a chap you were. So you don't know who I am?"

"No, sir; not in the least."

"No! Never heard of Admiral Tipsey! Where do you come from? Never heard of Admiral Tipsey! whose noble paunch is worth more than a Laplander could reckon," cried he, striking the huge rotundity he praised. "Let me into this back parlour; I'll wait there till your master comes home."

"Sir, you cannot possibly go into that parlour; there is a young lady, Mr. Cleghorn's daughter, sir, at tea in that room: she must not be disturbed," said James, holding the lock of the parlour door. He thought the stranger was either drunk or pretending to be drunk; and contended, with all his force, to prevent him from getting into the parlour.

Whilst they were struggling, Mr. Cleghorn came home. "Heyday! what's the matter? O admiral, is it you?" said Mr. Cleghorn in a voice of familiarity that astonished James. "Let us by, James; you don't know the admiral."

Admiral Tipsey was a smuggler: he had the command of two or three smuggling vessels, and thereupon created himself an admiral: a dignity which few dared to dispute with him, whilst he held his oak stick in his hand. As to the name of Tipsey, no one could be so unjust as to question his claim to it; for he was never known to be perfectly sober, during a whole day, from one year's end to another. To James's great surprise, the admiral, after he had drunk one dish of tea, unbuttoned his waist- coat from top to bottom, and deliberately began to unpack his huge false corpulence! Round him were wound innumerable pieces of lace, and fold after fold of fine cambric. When he was completely unpacked, it was difficult to believe that he was the same person, he looked so thin and shrunk.

He then called for some clean straw, and began to stuff himself out again to what he called a passable size. "Did not I tell you, young man, I carried that under my waistcoat which would make a fool stare? The lace that's on the floor, to say nothing of the cambric, is worth full twice the sum for which you shall have it, Cleghorn. Good night. I'll call again to-morrow, to settle our affairs; but don't let your young man here shut the door, as he did to-day, in the admiral's face. Here is a cravat for you, notwithstanding," continued he, turning to James, and throwing him a piece of very fine cambric. "I must 'list you in Admiral Tipsey's service."

James followed him to the door, and returned the cambric in despite of all his entreaties that he would "wear it, or sell it, for the admiral's sake."

"So, James," said Mr. Cleghorn, when the smuggler was gone, "you do not seem to like our admiral."

"I know nothing of him, sir, except that he is a smuggler; and for that reason I do not wish to have any thing to do with him."

"I am sorry for that," said Mr. Cleghorn, with a mixture of shame and anger in his countenance: "my conscience is as nice as other people's; and yet I have a notion I shall have something to do with him, though he is a smuggler; and, if I am not mistaken, shall make a deal of money by him. I have not had any thing to do with smugglers yet; but I see many in Monmouth who are making large fortunes by their assistance. There is our neighbour, Mr. Raikes; what a rich man he is become! And why should I, or why should you, be more scrupulous than others? Many gentlemen, ay, gentlemen, in the country are connected with them; and why should a shopkeeper be more conscientious than they? Speak; I must have your opinion."

With all the respect due to his master, James gave it as his opinion that it would be best to have nothing to do with Admiral Tipsey, or with any of the smugglers. He observed that men who carried on an illicit trade, and who were in the daily habit of cheating, or of taking false oaths, could not be safe partners. Even putting morality out of the question, he remarked that the smuggling trade was a sort of gaming, by which one year a man might make a deal of money, and another might be ruined.

"Upon my word!" said Mr. Cleghorn, in an ironical tone, "you talk very wisely, for so young a man! Pray, where did you learn all this wisdom?"

"From my father, sir; from whom I learned every thing that I know; every thing that is good, I mean. I had an uncle once, who was ruined by his dealings with smugglers; and who would have died in jail, if it had not been for my father. I was but a young lad at the time this happened; but I remember my father saying to me, the day my uncle was arrested, when my aunt and all the children were crying, 'Take warning by this, my dear James: you are to be in trade, some day or other, yourself: never forget that honesty is the best policy. The fair trader will always have the advantage, at the long run.'"

"Well, well, no more of this," interrupted Mr. Cleghorn. "Good night to you. You may finish the rest of your sermon against smugglers to my daughter there, whom it seems to suit better than it pleases me."

The next day, when Mr. Cleghorn went into the shop, he scarcely spoke to James, except to find fault with him. This he bore with patience, knowing that he meant well, and that his master would recover his temper in time.

"So the parcels were all sent, and the bills made out, as I desired," said Mr. Cleghorn. "You are not in the wrong there. You know what you are about, James, very well; but why should not you deal openly by me, according to your father's maxim, that 'honesty is the best policy?' Why should not you fairly tell me what were your secret views, in the advice you gave me about Admiral Tipsey and the smugglers?"

"I have no secret views, sir," said James, with a look of such sincerity that his master could not help believing him: "nor can I guess what you mean by secret views. If I consulted my own advantage instead of yours, I should certainly use all my influence with you in favour of this smuggler: for here is a letter, which I received from him this morning, 'hoping for my friendship,' and enclosing a ten pound note, which I returned to him."

Mr. Cleghorn was pleased by the openness and simplicity with which James told him all this; and immediately throwing aside the reserve of his manner, said, "James, I beg your pardon; I see I have misunderstood you. I am convinced you were not acting like a double dealer, in the advice you gave me last night. It was my daughter's colouring so much that led me astray. I did, to be sure, think you had an eye to her more than to me, in what you said: but if you had, I am sure you would tell me so fairly."

James was at a loss to comprehend how the advice that he gave concerning Admiral Tipsey and the smugglers could relate to Miss Cleghorn, except so far as it related to her father. He waited in silence for a farther explanation.

"You don't know, then," continued Mr. Cleghorn, "that Admiral Tipsey, as he calls himself, is able to leave his nephew, young Raikes, more than I can leave my daughter? It is his whim to go about dressed in that strange way in which you saw him yesterday; and it is his diversion to carry on the smuggling trade, by which he has made so much; but he is in reality a, rich old fellow, and has proposed that I should marry my daughter to his nephew. Now you begin to understand me, I see. The lad is a smart lad: he is to come here this evening. Don't prejudice my girl against him. Not a word more against smugglers, before her, I beg."

"You shall be obeyed, sir," said James. His voice altered, and he turned pale as he spoke; circumstances which did not escape Mr. Cleghorn's observation.

Young Raikes, and his uncle, the rich smuggler, paid their visit. Miss Cleghorn expressed a decided dislike to both uncle and nephew. Her father was extremely provoked; and in the height of his anger, declared he believed she was in love with James Frankland; that he was a treacherous rascal; and that he should leave the house within three days, if his daughter did not, before that time, consent to marry the man he had chosen for her husband. It was in vain that his daughter endeavoured to soften her father's rage, and to exculpate poor James, by protesting he had never directly or indirectly attempted to engage her affections; neither had he ever said one syllable that could prejudice her against the man whom her father recommended. Mr. Cleghorn's high notions of subordination applied, on this occasion, equally to his daughter and to his foreman: he considered them both as presumptuous and ungrateful; and said to himself, as he walked up and down the room in a rage, "My foreman to preach to me indeed! I thought what he was about all the time! But it sha'n't do—it sha'n't do! My daughter shall do as I bid her, or I'll know why! Have not I been all my life making a fortune for her? and now she won't do as I bid her! She would, if this fellow were out of the house; and out he shall go, in three days, if she does not come to her senses. I was cheated by my last shopman out of my money: I won't be duped by this fellow out of my daughter. No! no! Off he shall trudge! A shopman, indeed, to think of his master's daughter without his consent! What insolence! What the times are come to! Such a thing could not have been done in my days! I never thought of my master's daughter, I'll take my oath! And then the treachery of the rascal! To carry it all on so slily! I could forgive him anything but that: for that he shall go out of this house in three days, as sure as he and I are alive, if this young lady does not give him up before that time."

Passion so completely deafened Mr. Cleghorn that he would not listen to James, who assured him he had never, for one moment, aspired to the honour of marrying his daughter. "Can you deny that you love her? Can you deny," cried Mr. Cleghorn, "that you turned pale yesterday, when you said I should be obeyed?"

James could not deny either of these charges; but he firmly persisted in asserting that he had been guilty of no treachery; that he had never attempted secretly to engage the young lady's affections; and that, on the contrary, he was sure she had no suspicion of his attachment. "It is easy to prove all this to me, by persuading my girl to do as I bid her. Prevail on her to marry Mr. Raikes, and all is well."

"That is out of my power, sir," replied James. "I have no right to interfere, and will not. Indeed, I am sure I should betray myself, if I were to attempt to say a word to Miss Cleghorn in favour of another man: that is a task I could not undertake, even if I had the highest opinion of this Mr. Raikes; but I know nothing concerning him, and therefore should do wrong to speak in his favour merely to please you. I am sorry, very sorry, sir, that you have not the confidence in me which I hoped I had deserved; but the time will come when you will do me justice. The sooner I leave you now, I believe, the better you will be satisfied; and far from wishing to stay three days, I do not desire to stay three minutes in your house, sir, against your will."

Mr. Cleghorn was touched by the feeling and honest pride with which James spoke.

"Do as I bid you, sir," said he; "and neither more nor less,—Stay out your three days; and may be, in that time, this saucy girl may come to reason. If she does not know you love her, you are not so much to blame."

The three days passed away, and the morning came on which James was to leave his master. The young lady persisted in her resolution not to marry Mr. Raikes; and expressed much concern at the injustice with which James was treated on her account. She offered to leave home, and spend some time with an aunt, who lived in the north of England. She did not deny that James appeared to her the most agreeable young man she had seen; but added, she could not possibly have any thoughts of marrying him, because he had never given her the least reason to believe that he was attached to her.

Mr. Cleghorn was agitated, yet positive in his determination that James should quit the house. James went into his master's room to take leave of him. "So then you are really going?" said Mr. Cleghorn. "You have buckled that portmanteau of yours like a blockhead; I'll do it better: stand aside. So you are positively going? Why, this is a sad thing! But then it is a thing, as your own sense and honour tell you— it is a thing—" (Mr. Cleghorn took snuff at every pause of his speech; but even this could not carry him through it;) when he pronounced the words, "It is a thing that must be done," the tears fairly started from his eyes. "Now this is ridiculous!" resumed he. "In my days, in my younger days, I mean, a man could part with his foreman as easily as he could take off his glove. I am sure my master would as soon have thought of turning bankrupt as of shedding a tear at parting with me; and yet I was as good a foreman, in my day, as another. Not so good a one as you are, to be sure. But it is no time now to think of your goodness. Well! what do we stand here for? When a thing is to be done, the sooner it is done the better. Shake hands before you go."

Mr. Cleghorn put into James's hand a fifty pound note, and a letter of recommendation to a Liverpool merchant. James left the house without taking leave of Miss Cleghorn, who did not think the worse of him for his want of gallantry. His master had taken care to recommend him to an excellent house in Liverpool, where his salary would be nearly double that which he had hitherto received; but James was notwithstanding very sorry to leave Monmouth, where his dear brother, sister, and father lived,—to say nothing of Miss Cleghorn.

Late at night, James was going to the inn at which the Liverpool stage set up, where he was to sleep: as he passed through a street that leads down to the river Wye, he heard a great noise of men quarrelling violently. The moon shone bright, and he saw a party of men who appeared to be fighting in a boat that was just come to shore. He asked a person who came out of the public-house, and who seemed to have nothing to do with the fray, what was the matter? "Only some smugglers, who are quarrelling with one another about the division of their booty," said the passenger, who walked on, eager to get out of their way. James also quickened his pace, but presently heard the cry of "Murder! murder! Help! help!" and then all was silence.

A few seconds afterwards he thought that he heard groans. He could not forbear going to the spot whence the groans proceeded, in hopes of being of some service to a fellow-creature. By the time he got thither, the groans had ceased: he looked about, but could only see the men in the boat, who were rowing fast down the river. As he stood on the shore listening, he for some minutes heard no sound but that of their oars; but afterwards a man in the boat exclaimed, with a terrible oath, "There he is! There he is! All alive again! We have not done him business! D—n it, he'll do ours!" The boatmen rowed faster away, and James again heard the groans, though they were now much feebler than before. He searched and found the wounded man; who, having been thrown overboard, had with great difficulty swam to shore, and fainted with the exertion as soon as he reached the land. When he came to his senses, he begged James, for mercy's sake, to carry him into the next public-house, and to send for a surgeon to dress his wounds. The surgeon came, examined them, and declared his fears that the poor man could not live four-and-twenty hours. As soon as he was able to speak intelligibly, he said he had been drinking with a party of smugglers, who had just brought in some fresh brandy, and that they had quarrelled violently about a keg of contraband liquor: he said that he could swear to the man who gave him the mortal wound.

The smugglers were pursued immediately, and taken. When they were brought into the sick man's room, James beheld amongst them three persons whom he little expected to meet in such a situation: Idle Isaac, Wild Will, and Bullying Bob. The wounded man swore positively to their persons. Bullying Bob was the person who gave him the fatal blow; but Wild Will began the assault, and Idle Isaac shoved him overboard; they were all implicated in the guilt; and, instead of expressing any contrition for their crime, began to dispute about which was most to blame: they appealed to James; and, as he would be subpoenaed on their trial, each endeavoured to engage him in his favour. Idle Isaac took him aside, and said to him, "You have no reason to befriend my brothers. I can tell you a secret: they are the greatest enemies your family ever had. It was they who set fire to your father's hay-rick. Will was provoked by your sister Fanny's refusing him; so he determined, as he told me, to carry her off; and he meant to have done so, in the confusion that was caused by the fire; but Bob and he quarrelled the very hour that she was to have been carried off; so that part of the scheme failed. Now I had no hand in all this, being fast asleep in my bed; so I have more claim to your good word, at any rate, than my brothers can have: and so, when we come to trial, I hope you'll speak to my character."

Wild Will next tried his eloquence. As soon as he found that his brother Isaac had betrayed the secret, he went to James, and assured him the mischief that had been done was a mere accident; that it was true he had intended, for the frolic's sake, to raise a cry of fire, in order to draw Fanny out of the house; but that he was shocked when he found how the jest ended.

As to Bullying Bob, he brazened the matter out; declaring he had been affronted by the Franklands, and that he was glad he had taken his revenge of them; that, if the thing was to be done over again, he would do it; that James might give him what character he pleased upon trial, for that a man could be hanged but once.

Such were the absurd, bravadoing speeches he made, while he had an alehouse audience round him, to admire his spirit; but a few hours changed his tone. He and his brothers were taken before a magistrate. Till the committal was actually made out, they had hopes of being bailed: they had despatched a messenger to Admiral Tipsey, whose men they called themselves, and expected he would offer bail for them to any amount; but the bail of their friend Admiral Tipsey was not deemed sufficient by the magistrate.

"In the first place, I could not bail these men; and if I could, do you think it possible," said the magistrate, "I could take the bail of such a man as that?"

"I understood that he was worth a deal of money," whispered James.

"You are mistaken, sir," said the magistrate: "he is what he deserves to be, a ruined man. I have good reasons for knowing this. He has a nephew, a Mr. Raikes, who is a gamester: whilst the uncle has been carrying on the smuggling trade here, at the hazard of his life, the nephew, who was bred up at Oxford to be a fine gentleman, has gamed away all the money his uncle has made during twenty years, by his contraband traffic. At the long run, these fellows never thrive. Tipsey is not worth a groat."

James was much surprised by this information, and resolved to return immediately to Mr. Cleghorn, to tell him what he had heard, and put him on his guard.

Early in the morning he went to his house—"You look as if you were not pleased to see me again," said he to Mr. Cleghorn; "and perhaps you will impute what I am going to say to bad motives; but my regard to you, sir, determines me to acquaint you with what I have heard: you will make what use of the information you please."

James then related what had passed at the magistrate's; and when Mr. Cleghorn had heard all that he had to say, he thanked him in the strongest manner for this instance of his regard; and begged he would remain in Monmouth a few days longer.

Alarmed by the information he received from James, Mr. Cleghorn privately made inquiries concerning young Raikes and his uncle. The distress into which the young man had plunged himself by gambling had been kept a profound secret from his relations. It was easy to deceive them as to his conduct, because his time had been spent at a distance from them: he had but just returned home, after completing his education.

The magistrate from whom James first heard of his extravagance happened to have a son at Oxford, who gave him this intelligence: he confirmed all he had said to Mr. Cleghorn, who trembled at the danger to which he had exposed his daughter. The match with young Raikes was immediately broken off; and all connexion with Admiral Tipsey and the smugglers was for ever dissolved by Mr. Cleghorn.

His gratitude to James was expressed with all the natural warmth of his character. "Come back and live with me," said he. "You have saved me and my daughter from ruin. You shall not be my shopman any longer, you shall be my partner: and, you know, when you are my partner, there can be nothing said against your thinking of my daughter. But all in good time. I would not have seen the girl again if she had married my shopman; but my partner will be quite another thing. You have worked your way up in the world by your own deserts, and I give you joy. I believe, now it's over, it would have gone nigh to break my heart to part with you; but you must be sensible I was right to keep up my authority in my own family. Now things are changed: I give my consent: nobody has a right to say a word. When I am pleased with my daughter's choice, that is enough. There's only one thing that goes against my pride: your father—"

"Oh! sir," interrupted James, "if you are going to say any thing disrespectful of my father, do not say it to me; I beseech you, do not; for I cannot bear it. Indeed I cannot, and will not. He is the best of fathers!"

"I am sure he has the best of children; and a greater blessing there cannot be in this world. I was not going to say any thing disrespectful of him: I was only going to lament that he should be in an almshouse," said Mr. Cleghorn.

"He has determined to remain there," said James, "till his children have earned money enough to support him without hurting themselves. I, my brother, and both my sisters, are to meet at the almshouse on the first day of next month, which is my father's birthday; then we shall join all our earnings together, and see what can be done."

"Remember, you are my partner," said Mr. Cleghorn. "On that day you must take me along with you. My good-will is part of your earnings, and my good-will shall never be shown merely in words."

CHAPTER VI

It is now time to give some account of the Bettesworth family. The history of their indolence, extravagance, quarrels, and ruin, shall be given as shortly as possible.

The fortune left to them by Captain Bettesworth was nearly twenty thousand pounds. When they got possession of this sum, they thought it could never be spent; and each individual of the family had separate plans of extravagance, for which they required separate supplies. Old Bettesworth, in his youth, had seen a house of Squire Somebody, which had struck his imagination, and he resolved he would build just such another. This was his favourite scheme, and he was delighted with the thoughts that it would be realized. His wife and his sons opposed the plan, merely because it was his; and consequently he became more obstinately bent upon having his own way, as he said, for once in his life. He was totally ignorant of building; and no less incapable, from his habitual indolence, of managing workmen: the house might have been finished for one thousand five hundred pounds; it cost him two thousand pounds: and when it was done, the roof let in the rain in sundry places, the new ceilings and cornices were damaged, so that repairs and a new roof, with leaden gutters, and leaden statues, cost him some additional hundreds. The furnishing of the house Mrs. Bettesworth took upon herself; and Sally took upon herself to find fault with every article that her mother bought. The quarrels were loud, bitter, and at last irreconcilable. There was a looking-glass which the mother wanted to have in one room, and the daughter insisted upon putting it into another: the looking-glass was broken between them in the heat of battle. The blame was laid on Sally, who, in a rage, declared she would not and could not live in the house with her mother. Her mother was rejoiced to get rid of her, and she went to live with a lieutenant's lady in the neighbourhood, with whom she had been acquainted three weeks and two days. Half by scolding, half by cajoling her father, she prevailed upon him to give her two thousand pounds for her fortune; promising never to trouble him any more for any thing.

As soon as she was gone, Mrs. Bettesworth gave a house-warming, as she called it, to all her acquaintance; a dinner, a ball, and a supper, in her new house. The house was not half dry, and all the company caught cold. Mrs. Bettesworth's cold was the most severe. It happened at this time to be the fashion to go almost without clothes; and as this lady was extremely vain and fond of dress, she would absolutely appear in the height of fashion. The Sunday after her ball, whilst she had still the remains of a bad cold, she positively would go to church, equipped in one petticoat, and a thin muslin gown, that she might look as young as her daughter Jessy. Every body laughed, and Jessy laughed more than any one else; but, in the end, it was no laughing matter; Mrs. Bettesworth "caught her death of cold." She was confined to her bed on Monday, and was buried the next Sunday.

Jessy, who had a great notion that she should marry a lord, if she could but once get into company with one, went to live with blind Mrs. Cheviott; where, according to her mother's instructions, "she laid herself out for goodness." She also took two thousand pounds with her, upon her promise never to trouble her father more. Her brothers perceived how much was to be gained by tormenting a father, who gave from weakness, and not from a sense of justice, or a feeling of kindness; and they soon rendered themselves so troublesome that he was obliged to buy off their reproaches. Idle Isaac was a sportsman, and would needs have a pack of hounds: they cost him two hundred a year. Then he would have race-horses; and by them he soon lost some thousands. He was arrested for the money, and his father was forced to pay it.

Bob and Will soon afterwards began to think, "it was very hard that so much was to be done for Isaac, and nothing for them!"

Wild Will kept a mistress; and Bullying Bob was a cock-fighter: their demands for money were frequent and unconscionable; and their continual plea was, "Why, Isaac lost a thousand by his race-horses, and why should not we have our share?"

The mistress and the cockpit had their share; and the poor old father, at last, had only one thousand left. He told his sons this, with tears in his eyes: "I shall die in a jail, after all!" said he. They listened not to what he said, for they were intent upon the bank-notes of this last thousand, which were spread upon the table before him. Will, half in jest, half in earnest, snatched up a parcel of the notes; and Bob insisted on dividing the treasure. Will fled out of the house; Bob pursued him, and they fought at the end of their own avenue.

This was on the day that Frankland and his family were returning from poor George's funeral, and saw the battle betwixt the brothers. They were shamed into a temporary reconciliation, and soon afterwards united against their father, whom they represented to all the neighbours as the most cruel and the most avaricious of men, because he would not part with the very means of subsistence to supply their profligacy.

Whilst their minds were in this state, Will happened to become acquainted with a set of smugglers, whose disorderly life struck his fancy. He persuaded his brothers to leave home with him, and to list in the service of Admiral Tipsey. Their manners then became more brutal; and they thought, felt, and lived like men of desperate fortunes. The consequence we have seen. In a quarrel about a keg of brandy, at an alehouse, their passions got the better of them, and, on entering their boat, they committed the offence for which they were now imprisoned.

Mr. Barlow was the attorney to whom they applied, and they endeavoured to engage him to manage their cause on their trial; but he absolutely refused. From the moment he heard from James that Will and Bob Bettesworth were the persons who set fire to Frankland's hay-stack, he urged Frank to prosecute them for this crime. "When you only suspected them, my dear Frank, I strongly dissuaded you from going to law: but now you cannot fail to succeed, and you will recover ample damages."

"That is impossible, my dear sir," replied Frank; "for the Bettesworths, I understand, are ruined."

"I am sorry for that, on your account; but I still think you ought to carry on this prosecution, for the sake of public justice. Such pests of society should not go unpunished."

"They will probably be punished sufficiently for this unfortunate assault, for which they are now to stand their trial. I cannot, in their distress, revenge either my own or my father's wrongs. I am sure he would be sorry if I did; for I have often and often heard him say, 'Never trample upon the fallen.'"

"You are a good, generous young man," cried Mr. Barlow, "and no wonder you love the father who inspired you with such sentiments, and taught you such principles. But what a shame it is that such a father should be in an almshouse! You say he will not consent to be dependent upon any one; and that he will not accept of relief from any but his own children. This is pride; but it is an honourable species of pride; fit for an English yeoman. I cannot blame it. But, my dear Frank, tell your father he must accept of your friend's credit, as well as of yours. Your credit with me is such, that you may draw upon me for five hundred pounds whenever you please. No thanks, my boy. Half the money I owe you for your services as my clerk; and the other half is well secured to me, by the certainty of your future diligence and success in business. You will be able to pay me in a year or two; so I put you under no obligation, remember. I will take your bond for half the money, if that will satisfy you and your proud father."

The manner in which this favour was conferred touched Frank to the heart. He had a heart which could be strongly moved by kindness. He was beginning to express his gratitude, when Mr. Barlow interrupted him with, "Come, come! Why do we waste our time here, talking sentiment, when we ought to be writing law? Here is work to be done, which requires some expedition: a marriage settlement to be drawn. Guess for whom."

Frank guessed all the probable matches amongst his Monmouth acquaintance; but he was rather surprised when told that the bridegroom was to be young Mr. Folingsby; as it was scarcely two months since this gentleman was in love with Fanny Frankland. Frank proceeded to draw the settlement.

Whilst he and Mr. Barlow were writing, they were interrupted by the entrance of Mr. Josiah Crumpe. He came to announce Mrs. Crumpe's death, and to request Mr. Barlow's attendance at the opening of her will. This poor lady had lingered out many months longer than it was thought she could possibly live; and during all her sufferings, Patty, with indefatigable goodness and temper, bore with the caprice and peevishness of disease. Those who thought she acted merely from interested motives expected to find she had used her power over her mistress's mind entirely for her own advantage: they were certain a great part of the fortune would be left to her. Mrs. Crumpe's relations were so persuaded of this, that, when they were assembled to hear her will read by Mr. Barlow, they began to say to one another in whispers, "We'll set the will aside; we'll bring her into the courts: Mrs. Crumpe was not in her right senses when she made this will: she had received two paralytic strokes; we can prove that: we can set aside the will."

Mr. Josiah Crumpe was not one of these whisperers; he set apart from them, leaning on his oaken stick in silence.

Mr. Barlow broke the seals of the will, opened it, and read it to the eager company. They were much astonished when they found that the whole fortune was left to Mr. Josiah Crumpe. The reason for this bequest was given in these words:

"Mr. Josiah Crumpe, being the only one of my relations who did not torment me for my money, even upon my death-bed, I trust that he will provide suitably for that excellent girl, Patty Frankland. On this head he knows my wishes. By her own desire, I have not myself left her any thing; I have only bequeathed fifty pounds for the use of her father."

Mr. Josiah Crumpe was the only person who heard unmoved the bequest that was made to him; the rest of the relations were clamorous in their reproaches, or hypocritical in their congratulations. All thoughts of setting aside the will were, however, abandoned; every legal form had been observed, and with a technical nicety that precluded all hopes of successful litigation.

Mr. Crumpe arose, as soon as the tumult of disappointment had somewhat subsided, and counted with his oaken stick the numbers that were present. "Here are ten of you, I think. Well! you, every soul of you, hate me; but that is nothing to the purpose. I shall keep up to the notion I have of the character of a true British merchant, for my own sake—not for yours. I don't want this woman's money; I have enough of my own, and of my own honest making, without legacy hunting. Why did you torment the dying woman? You would have been better off, if you had behaved better; but that's over now. A thousand pounds a-piece you shall have from me, deducting fifty pounds, which you must each of you give to that excellent girl, Patty Frankland. I am sure you must be all sensible of your injustice to her."

Fully aware that it was their interest to oblige Mr. Crumpe, they now vied with each other in doing justice to Patty. Some even declared they had never had any suspicions of her; and others laid the blame on the false representations and information which they said they had had from the mischief-making Mrs. Martha. They very willingly accepted of a thousand pounds a-piece; and the fifty pounds deduction was paid as a tax by each to Patty's merit.

Mistress now of five hundred pounds, she exclaimed, "Oh! my dear father! You shall no longer live in an almshouse! To-morrow will be the happiest day of my life! I don't know how to thank you as I ought, sir," continued she, turning to her benefactor.

"You have thanked me as you ought, and as I like best," said this plain-spoken merchant, "and now let us say no more about it."

In obedience to Mr. Crumpe's commands, Patty said no more to him; but she was impatient to tell her brother Frank, and her lover, Mr. Mason, of her good fortune: she therefore returned to Monmouth with Mr. Barlow, in hopes of seeing them immediately; but Frank was not at work at the marriage settlement. Soon after Mr. Barlow left him, he was summoned to attend the trial of the Bettesworths.

These unfortunate young men, depending on Frank's good nature, well knowing he had refused to prosecute them for setting fire to his father's hay-rick, thought they might venture to call upon him to give them a good character. "Consider, dear Frank," said Will Bettesworth, "a good word from one of your character might do a great deal for us. You were so many years our neighbour. If you would only just say that we were never counted wild, idle, quarrelsome fellows, to your knowledge. Will you?"

"How can I do that?" said Frank: "or how could I be believed, if I did, when it is so well known in the country—forgive me; at such a time as this I cannot mean to taunt you: but it is well known in the country that you were called Wild Will, Bullying Bob, and Idle Isaac."

"There's the rub!" said the attorney who was employed for the Bettesworths. "This will come out in open court; and the judge and jury will think a great deal of it."

"Oh! Mr. Frank, Mr. Frank," cried old Bettesworth, "have pity upon us! Speak in favour of these boys of mine! Think what a disgrace it is to me in my old age, to have my sons brought this way to a public trial! And if they should be transported! Oh! Mr. Frank, say what you can for them! You were always a good young man, and a good-natured young man."

Frank was moved by the entreaties and tears of the unhappy father; but his good-nature could not make him consent to say what he knew to be false. "Do not call me to speak to their characters upon this trial," said he; "I cannot say any thing that would serve them: I shall do them more harm than good."

Still they had hopes his good-nature would, at the last moment, prevail over his sense of justice, and they summoned him.

"Well, sir," said Bettesworths' counsel, "you appear in favour of the prisoners. You have known them, I understand, from their childhood; and your own character is such that whatever you say in their favour will doubtless make a weighty impression upon the jury."

The court was silent in expectation of what Frank should say. He was so much embarrassed betwixt his wish to serve his old neighbours and playfellows, and his dread of saying what he knew to be false, that he could not utter a syllable. He burst into tears.

[Footnote: This is drawn from real life.]

"This evidence is most strongly against the prisoners," whispered a juryman to his fellows.

The verdict was brought in at last—Guilty!—Sentence—transportation.

As the judge was pronouncing this sentence, old Bettesworth was carried out of the court: he had dropped senseless. Ill as his sons had behaved to him, he could not sustain the sight of their utter disgrace and ruin.

When he recovered his senses, he found himself sitting on the stone bench before the court-house, supported by Frank. Many of the town's-people had gathered round; but regardless of every thing but his own feelings, the wretched father exclaimed, in a voice of despair, "I have no children left me in my old age! My sons are gone! And where are my daughters? At such a time as this, why are not they near their poor old father? Have they no touch of natural affection in them? No! they have none. And why should they have any for me? I took no care of them when they were young; no wonder they take none of me now I am old. Ay! Neighbour Frankland was right: he brought up his children 'in the way they should go.' Now he has the credit and the comfort of them; and see what mine are come to! They bring their father's grey hairs with sorrow to the grave!"

The old man wept bitterly: then looking round him, he again asked for his daughters. "Surely they are in the town, and it cannot be much trouble to them to come to me! Even these strangers, who have never seen me before, pity me. But my own have no feeling; no, not for one another! Do these girls know the sentence that has been passed upon their brothers! Where are they? Where are they? Jessy, at least, might be near me at such a time as this! I was always an indulgent father to Jessy."

There were people present who knew what was become of Jessy; but they would not tell the news to her father at this terrible moment. Two of Mrs. Cheviott's servants were in the crowd; and one of them whispered to Frank, "You had best, sir, prevail on this poor old man to go to his home, and not to ask for his daughter: he will hear the bad news soon enough."

Frank persuaded the father to go home to his lodgings, and did every thing in his power to comfort him. But, alas! the old man said, too truly, "There is no happiness left for me in this world! What a curse it is to have bad children! My children have broken my heart! And it is all my own fault: I took no care of them when they were young; and they take no care of me now I am old. But, tell me, have you found out what is become of my daughter?"

Frank evaded the question, and begged the old man to rest in peace this night. He seemed quite exhausted by grief, and at last sunk into a sort of stupefaction: it could hardly be called sleep. Frank was obliged to return home, to proceed with his business for Mr. Barlow; and he was glad to escape from the sight of misery, which, however he might pity, he could not relieve.

It was happy indeed for Frank that he had taken his father's advice, and had early broken off all connexion with Jilting Jessy. After duping others, she at length had become a greater dupe. She had this morning gone off with a common serjeant, with whom she had fallen suddenly and desperately in love. He cared for nothing but her two thousand pounds; and, to complete her misfortune, was a man of bad character, whose extravagance and profligacy had reduced him to the sad alternative of either marrying for money, or going to jail.

As for Sally, she was at this instant far from all thoughts either of her father or her brothers; she was in the heat of a scolding match, which terminated rather unfortunately for her matrimonial schemes. Ensign Bloomington had reproached her with having forced him into his aunt's room, when she had absolutely refused to see him, and thus being the cause of his losing a handsome legacy. Irritated by this charge, the lady replied in no very gentle terms. Words ran high; and so high at last, that the gentleman finished by swearing that he would sooner marry the devil than such a vixen!

The match was thus broken off, to the great amusement of all Saucy Sally's acquaintance. Her ill-humour had made her hated by all the neighbours; so that her disappointment at the loss of the ensign was embittered by their malicious raillery, and by the prophecy which she heard more than whispered from all sides, that she would never have another admirer, either for "love or money."

Ensign Bloomington was deaf to all overtures of peace: he was rejoiced to escape from this virago; and, as we presume that none of our readers are much interested in her fate, we shall leave her to wear the willow, without following her history farther.

Let us return to Mr. Barlow, whom we left looking over Mr. Folingsby's marriage settlements. When he had seen that they were rightly drawn, he sent Frank with them to Folingsby-hall.

Mr. Folingsby was alone when Frank arrived. "Sit down, if you please, sir," said he. "Though I have never had the pleasure of seeing you before, your name is well known to me. You are a brother of Fanny Frankland's. She is a charming and excellent young woman! You have reason to be proud of your sister, and I have reason to be obliged to her."

He then adverted to what had formerly passed between them at Mrs. Hungerford's; and concluded by saying it would give him real satisfaction to do any service to him or his family. "Speak, and tell me what I can do for you."

Frank looked down, and was silent; for he thought Mr. Folingsby must recollect the injustice that he, or his agent, had shown in turning old Frankland out of his farm. He was too proud to ask favours, where he felt he had a claim to justice.

In fact, Mr. Folingsby had, as he said, "left every thing to his agent;" and so little did he know either of the affairs of his tenants, their persons, or even their names, that he had not at this moment the slightest idea that Frank was the son of one of the oldest and the best of them. He did not know that old

Frankland had been reduced to take refuge in an almshouse, in consequence of his agent's injustice. Surprised by Frank's cold silence, he questioned him more closely, and it was with astonishment and shame that he heard the truth.

"Good heavens!" cried he, "has my negligence been the cause of all this misery to your father—to the father of Fanny Frankland? I remember, now that you recall it to my mind, something of an old man, with fine grey hair, coming to speak to me about some business, just as I was setting off for Ascot races. Was that your father? I recollect I told him I was in a great hurry; and that Mr. Deal, my agent, would certainly do him justice. In this I was grossly mistaken; and I have suffered severely for the confidence I had in that fellow. Thank God, I shall now have my affairs in my own hands. I am determined to look into them immediately. My head is no longer full of horses, and gigs, and curricles. There is a time for every thing: my giddy days are over. I only wish that my thoughtlessness had never hurt any one but myself.

"All I now can do," continued Mr. Folingsby, "is to make amends, as fast as possible, for the past. To begin with your father: most fortunately, I have the means in my power. His farm is come back into my hands; and it shall, to-morrow, be restored to him. Old Bettesworth was with me scarcely an hour ago, to surrender the farm, on which there is a prodigious arrear of rent; but I understand that he has built a good house on the farm; and I am extremely glad of it, for your father's sake. Tell him it shall be his. Tell him I am ready, I am eager, to put him in possession of it; and to repair the injustice I have done, or which, at least, I have permitted to be done, in my name."

Frank was so overjoyed that he could scarcely utter one word of thanks. In his way home he called at Mrs. Hungerford's, to tell the good news to his sister Fanny. This was the eve of their father's birthday; and they agreed to meet at the almshouse in the morning.

The happy morning came. Old Frankland was busy in his little garden, when he heard the voices of his children, who were coming towards him. "Fanny! Patty! James! Frank!. Welcome, my children! Welcome! I knew you would be so kind as to come to see your old father on this day; so I was picking some of my currants for you, to make you as welcome as I can. But I wonder you are not ashamed to come to see me in an almshouse. Such gay lads and lasses! I well know I have reason to be proud of you all. Why, I think, I never saw you, one and all, look so well in my whole life!"

"Perhaps, father," said Frank, "because you never saw us, one and all, so happy! Will you sit down, dear father, here in your arbour; and we will all sit upon the grass, at your feet, and each tell you stories, and all the good news."

"My children," said he, "do what you will with me! It makes my old heart swim with joy to see you all again around me looking so happy."

The father sat down in his arbour, and his children placed themselves at his feet. First his daughter Patty spoke; and then Fanny; then James; and at last Frank. When they had all told their little histories, they offered to their father in one purse their common riches: the rewards of their own good conduct.

"My beloved children!" said Frankland, overpowered with his tears, "this is too much joy for me! this is the happiest moment of my life! None but the father of such children can know what I feel! Your success in the world delights me ten times the more, because I know it is all owing to yourselves."

"Oh! no, dear father!" cried they with one accord; "no, dear, dear father, our success is all owing to you! Every thing we have is owing to you; to the care you took of us, from our infancy upward. If you had not watched for our welfare, and taught us so well, we should not now all be so happy!—Poor Bettesworth!"

Here they were interrupted by Hannah, the faithful maid-servant, who had always lived with old Frankland. She came running down the garden so fast, that, when she reached the arbour, she was so much out of breath she could not speak. "Dear heart! God bless you all!" cried she, as soon as she recovered breath. "But it is no time to be sitting here. Come in, sir, for mercy's sake," said she, addressing herself to her old master. "Come in to be ready; come in all of you to be ready!" "Ready! ready for what?"

"Oh! ready for fine things! Fine doings! Only come in, and I'll tell you as we go along. How I have torn all my hand with this gooseberry-bush! But no matter for that. So then you have not heard a word of what is going on? No, how could you? And you did not miss me, when you first came into the house?"

"Forgive us for that, good Hannah: we were in such a hurry to see my father, we thought of nothing and nobody else."

"Very natural. Well, Miss Fanny, I've been up at the great house, with your lady, Mrs. Hungerford. A better lady cannot be! Do you know she sent for me, on purpose to speak to me; and I know things that you are not to know yet. But this much I may tell you, there's a carriage coming here, to carry my master away to his new house; and there's horses, and side-saddles beside, for you, and you, and you, and I. And Mrs. Hungerford is coming in her own coach; and young Mr. Folingsby is coming in his carriage; and Mr. Barlow in Mr. Jos. Crumpe's carriage; and Mr. Cleghorn, and his pretty daughter, in the gig; and— and—and heaps of carriages besides! friends of Mrs. Hungerford: and there's such crowds gathering in the streets; and I'm going on to get breakfast."

"Oh! my dear father," cried Frank, "make haste, and take off this badge-coat before they come! We have brought proper clothes for you."

Frank pulled off the badge-coat, as he called it, and flung it from him, saying, "My father shall never wear you more."

Fanny had just tied on her father's clean neckcloth, and Patty had smoothed his reverend grey locks, when the sound of the carriages was heard. All that Hannah had told them was true. Mrs. Hungerford had engaged all her friends, and all who were acquainted with the good conduct of the Franklands, to attend her on this joyful occasion.

"Triumphal cavalcades and processions," said she, "are in general foolish things—mere gratifications of vanity; but this is not in honour of vanity, but in honour of virtue. We shall do good in the country, by showing that we respect and admire it, in whatever station it is to be found. Here is a whole family who have conducted themselves uncommonly well; who have exerted themselves to relieve their aged father from a situation to which he was reduced without any fault or imprudence of his own. Their exertions have succeeded. Let us give them, what they will value more than money, SYMPATHY."

Convinced or persuaded by what Mrs. Hungerford said, all her friends and acquaintance attended her this morning to the almshouse. Crowds of people followed; and old Frankland was carried in triumph by his children to his new habitation.

The happy father lived many years to enjoy the increasing prosperity of his family.

[Footnote: It may be necessary to inform some readers, that Patty and Fanny were soon united to their lovers; that James, with Mr. Cleghorn's consent, married Miss Cleghorn; and that Frank did not become an old bachelor: he married an amiable girl, who was ten times prettier than Jilting Jessy, and of whom he was twenty times as fond. Those who wish to know the history of all the wedding-clothes of the parties may have their curiosity gratified by directing a line of inquiry, post-paid, to the editor hereof.]

May every good father have as grateful children!

May, 1801.

THE GRATEFUL NEGRO

In the island of Jamaica there lived two planters, whose methods of managing their slaves were as different as possible. Mr. Jefferies considered the negroes as an inferior species, incapable of gratitude, disposed to treachery, and to be roused from their natural indolence only by force; he treated his slaves, or rather suffered his overseer to treat them, with the greatest severity.

Jefferies was not a man of a cruel, but of a thoughtless and extravagant temper. He was of such a sanguine disposition, that he always calculated upon having a fine season, and fine crops on his plantation; and never had the prudence to make allowance for unfortunate accidents: he required, as he said, from his overseer produce and not excuses.

Durant, the overseer, did not scruple to use the most cruel and barbarous methods of forcing the slaves to exertions beyond their strength.

[Footnote: The Negro Slaves—a fine drama, by Kotzebue. It is to be hoped that such horrible instances of cruelty are not now to be found in nature. Bryan Edwards, in his History of Jamaica, says that most of the planters are humane; but he allows that some facts can be cited in contradiction of this assertion.]

Complaints of his brutality, from time to time, reached his master's ears; but though Mr. Jefferies was moved to momentary compassion, he shut his heart against conviction: he hurried away to the jovial banquet, and drowned all painful reflections in wine.

He was this year much in debt; and, therefore, being more than usually anxious about his crop, he pressed his overseer to exert himself to the utmost.

The wretched slaves upon his plantation thought themselves still more unfortunate when they compared their condition with that of the negroes on the estate of Mr. Edwards. This gentleman treated his slaves with all possible humanity and kindness. He wished that there was no such thing as slavery in the world, but he was convinced, by the arguments of those who have the best means of obtaining information, that the sudden emancipation of the negroes would rather increase than diminish their miseries. His benevolence, therefore, confined itself within the bounds of reason. He adopted those plans for the amelioration of the state of the slaves which appeared to him the most likely to succeed without producing any violent agitation or revolution.

[Footnote: History of the West Indies, from which these ideas are adopted—not stolen.]

For instance, his negroes had reasonable and fixed daily tasks; and when these were finished, they were permitted to employ their time for their own advantage or amusement. If they chose to employ themselves longer for their master, they were paid regular wages for their extra work. This reward, for as such it was considered, operated most powerfully upon the slaves. Those who are animated by hope can perform what would seem impossibilities to those who are under the depressing influence of fear. The wages which Mr. Edwards promised, he took care to see punctually paid.

He had an excellent overseer, of the name of Abraham Bayley, a man of a mild but steady temper, who was attached not only to his master's interests but to his virtues; and who, therefore, was more intent upon seconding his humane views than upon squeezing from the labour of the negroes the utmost produce. Each negro had, near his cottage, a portion of land, called his provision-ground; and one day in the week was allowed for its cultivation.

It is common in Jamaica for the slaves to have provision-grounds, which they cultivate for their own advantage; but it too often happens, that, when a good negro has successfully improved his little spot of ground, when he has built himself a house, and begins to enjoy the fruits of his industry, his acquired property is seized upon by the sheriff's officer for the payment of his master's debts; he is forcibly separated from his wife and children, dragged to public auction, purchased by a stranger, and perhaps sent to terminate his miserable existence in the mines of Mexico; excluded for ever from the light of heaven; and all this without any crime or imprudence on his part, real or pretended. He is punished because his master is unfortunate!

To this barbarous injustice the negroes on Mr. Edwards' plantation were never exposed. He never exceeded his income; he engaged in no wild speculations; he contracted no debts; and his slaves, therefore, were in no danger of being seized by a sheriff's officer: their property was secured to them by the prudence as well as by the generosity of their master.

One morning, as Mr. Edwards was walking in that part of his plantation which joined to Mr. Jefferies' estate, he thought he heard the voice of distress at some distance. The lamentations grew louder and louder as he approached a cottage, which stood upon the borders of Jefferies' plantation.

This cottage belonged to a slave of the name of Caesar, the best negro in Mr. Jefferies' possession. Such had been his industry and exertion, that, notwithstanding the severe tasks imposed by Durant, the overseer, Caesar found means to cultivate his provision-ground to a degree of perfection no where else to be seen on this estate. Mr. Edwards had often admired this poor fellow's industry, and now hastened to inquire what misfortune had befallen him.

When he came to the cottage, he found Caesar standing with his arms folded, and his eyes fixed upon the ground. A young and beautiful female negro was weeping bitterly, as she knelt at the feet of Durant, the overseer, who, regarding her with a sullen aspect, repeated, "He must go. I tell you, woman, he must go. What signifies all this nonsense?"

At the sight of Mr. Edwards, the overseer's countenance suddenly changed, and assumed an air of obsequious civility. The poor woman retired to the farther corner of the cottage, and continued to weep. Caesar never moved. "Nothing is the matter, sir," said Durant, "but that Caesar is going to be sold. That is what the woman is crying for. They were to be married; but we'll find Clara another husband, I tell her; and she'll get the better of her grief, you know, sir, as I tell her, in time." "Never! never!" said Clara.

"To whom is Caesar going to be sold? and for what sum?"

"For what can be got for him," replied Durant, laughing; "and to whoever will buy him. The sheriff's officer is here, who has seized him for debt, and must make the most of him at market."

"Poor fellow!" said Mr. Edwards; "and must he leave this cottage which he has built, and these bananas which has planted?"

Caesar now for the first time looked up, and fixing his eyes upon Mr. Edwards for a moment, advanced with an intrepid rather than an imploring countenance, and said, "Will you be my master? Will you be her master? Buy both of us. You shall not repent of it. Caesar will serve you faithfully."

On hearing these words Clara sprang forward, and clasping her hands together, repeated, "Caesar will serve you faithfully."

Mr. Edwards was moved by their entreaties, but he left them without declaring his intentions. He went immediately to Mr. Jefferies, whom he found stretched on a sofa, drinking coffee. As soon as Mr. Edwards mentioned the occasion of his visit, and expressed his sorrow for Caesar, Jefferies exclaimed, "Yes, poor devil! I pity him from the bottom of my soul. But what can I do? I leave all those things to Durant. He says the sheriff's officer has seized him; and there's an end of the matter. You know, money must be had. Besides, Caesar is not worse off than any other slave sold for debt. What signifies talking about the matter, as if it were something that never happened before! Is not it a case that occurs every day in Jamaica?"

"So much the worse," replied Mr. Edwards.

"The worse for them, to be sure," said Jefferies. "But, after all, they are slaves, and are used to be treated as such; and they tell me the negroes are a thousand times happier here, with us, than they ever were in their own country."

"Did the negroes tell you so themselves?"

"No; but people better informed than negroes have told me so; and, after all, slaves there must be; for indigo, and rum, and sugar, we must have."

"Granting it to be physically impossible that the world should exist without rum, sugar, and indigo, why could they not be produced by freemen as well as by slaves? If we hired negroes for labourers, instead of purchasing them for slaves, do you think they would not work as well as they do now? Does any negro, under the fear of the overseer, work harder than a Birmingham journeyman, or a Newcastle collier, who toil for themselves and their families?"

"Of that I don't pretend to judge. All I know is, that the West India planters would he ruined if they had no slaves; and I am a West India planter."

"So am I; yet I do not think they are the only people whose interests ought to be considered in this business."

"Their interests, luckily, are protected by the laws of the land; and though they are rich men, and white men, and freemen, they have as good a claim to their rights as the poorest black slave on any of our plantations."

"The law, in our case, seems to make the right; and the very reverse ought to be done—the right should make the law."

"Fortunately for us planters, we need not enter into such nice distinctions. You could not, if you would, abolish the trade. Slaves would be smuggled into the islands."

"What! if nobody would buy them? You know that you cannot smuggle slaves into England. The instant a slave touches English ground he becomes free. Glorious privilege! Why should it not be extended to all her dominions? If the future importation of slaves into these islands were forbidden by law, the trade must cease. No man can either sell or possess slaves without its being known: they cannot be smuggled like lace or brandy."

"Well, well!" retorted Jefferies, a little impatiently, "as yet the law is on our side. I can do nothing in this business, nor can you."

"Yes, we can do something; we can endeavour to make our negroes as happy as possible."

"I leave the management of these people to Durant."

"That is the very thing of which they complain; forgive me for speaking to you with the frankness of an old acquaintance."

"Oh! you can't oblige me more: I love frankness of all things! To tell you the truth, I have heard complaints of Durant's severity; but I make it a principle to turn a deaf ear to them, for I know nothing can be done with these fellows without it. You are partial to negroes; but even you must allow they are a race of beings naturally inferior to us. You may in vain think of managing a black as you would a white. Do what you please for a negro, he will cheat you the first opportunity he finds. You know what their maxim is: 'God gives black men what white men forget.'"

To these common-place desultory observations Mr. Edwards made no reply; but recurred to poor Caesar, and offered to purchase both him and Clara, at the highest price the sheriff's officer could obtain for them at market. Mr. Jefferies, with the utmost politeness to his neighbour, but with the most perfect indifference to the happiness of those whom he considered of a different species from himself, acceded to this proposal. Nothing could be more reasonable, he said; and he was happy to have it in his power to oblige a gentleman for whom he had such a high esteem.

The bargain was quickly concluded with the sheriff's officer; for Mr. Edwards willingly paid several dollars more than the market price for the two slaves. When Caesar and Clara heard that they were not to be separated, their joy and gratitude were expressed with all the ardour and tenderness peculiar to their different characters. Clara was an Eboe, Caesar a Koromantyn negro: the Eboes are soft, languishing, and timid; the Koromantyns are frank, fearless, martial, and heroic.

Mr. Edwards took his new slaves home with him, desired Bayley, his overseer, to mark out a provision-ground for Caesar, and to give him a cottage, which happened at this time to be vacant.

"Now, my good friend," said he to Caesar, "you may work for yourself, without fear that what you earn may be taken from you; or that you should ever be sold, to pay your master's debts. If he does not understand what I am saying," continued Mr. Edwards, turning to his overseer, "you will explain it to him."

Caesar perfectly understood all that Mr. Edwards said; but his feelings were at this instant so strong that he could not find expression for his gratitude: he stood like one stupefied! Kindness was new to him; it overpowered his manly heart; and at hearing the words "my good friend," the tears gushed from his eyes: tears which no torture could have extorted! Gratitude swelled in his bosom; and he longed to be alone, that he might freely yield to his emotions.

He was glad when the conch-shell sounded to call the negroes to their daily labour, that he might relieve the sensations of his soul by bodily exertion, He performed his task in silence; and an inattentive observer might have thought him sullen.

In fact, he was impatient for the day to be over, that he might get rid of a heavy load which weighed upon his mind.

The cruelties practised by Durant, the overseer of Jefferies' plantation, had exasperated the slaves under his dominion.

They were all leagued together in a conspiracy, which was kept profoundly secret. Their object was to extirpate every white man, woman, and child, in the island. Their plans were laid with consummate art; and the negroes were urged to execute them by all the courage of despair.

The confederacy extended to all the negroes in the island of Jamaica, excepting those on the plantation of Mr. Edwards. To them no hint of the dreadful secret had yet been given; their countrymen, knowing the attachment they felt to their master, dared not trust them with these projects of vengeance. Hector, the negro who was at the head of the conspirators, was the particular friend of Caesar, and had imparted to him all his designs. These friends were bound to each other by the strongest ties. Their slavery and their sufferings began in the same hour; they were both brought from their own country in the same ship. This circumstance alone forms, amongst the negroes, a bond of connexion not easily to be dissolved. But the friendship of Caesar and Hector commenced even before they were united by the sympathy of misfortune; they were both of the same nation, both Koromantyns. In Africa they had both been accustomed to command; for they had signalized themselves by superior fortitude and courage. They respected each other for excelling in all which they had been taught to consider as virtuous; and with them revenge was a virtue!

Revenge was the ruling passion of Hector: in Caesar's mind it was rather a principle instilled by education. The one considered it as a duty, the other felt it as a pleasure. Hector's sense of injury was acute in the extreme; he knew not how to forgive. Caesar's sensibility was yet more alive to kindness than to insult. Hector would sacrifice his life to extirpate an enemy. Caesar would devote himself for the defence of a friend; and Caesar now considered a white man as his friend.

He was now placed in a painful situation. All his former friendships, all the solemn promises by which he was bound to his companions in misfortune, forbade him to indulge that delightful feeling of gratitude and affection, which, for the first time, he experienced for one of that race of beings whom he had hitherto considered as detestable tyrants—objects of implacable and just revenge!

Caesar was most impatient to have an interview with Hector, that he might communicate his new sentiments, and dissuade him from those schemes of destruction which he meditated. At midnight, when all the slaves except himself were asleep, he left his cottage, and went to Jefferies' plantation, to the hut in which Hector slept. Even in his dreams Hector breathed vengeance. "Spare none! Sons of Africa, spare none!" were the words he uttered in his sleep, as Caesar approached the mat on which he lay. The moon shone full upon him. Caesar contemplated the countenance of his friend, fierce even in sleep. "Spare none! Oh, yes! There is one that must be spared. There is one for whose sake all must be spared."

He wakened Hector by this exclamation. "Of what were you dreaming?" said Caesar.

"Of that which, sleeping or waking, fills my soul—revenge! Why did you waken me from my dream? It was delightful. The whites were weltering in their blood! But silence! we may be overheard."

"No; every one sleeps but ourselves," replied Caesar. "I could not sleep without speaking to you on—a subject that weighs upon my mind. You have seen Mr. Edwards?" "Yes. He that is now your master."

"He that is now my benefactor—my friend!"

"Friend! Can you call a white man friend?" cried Hector, starting up with a look of astonishment and indignation.

"Yes," replied Caesar, with firmness. "And you would speak, ay, and would feel, as I do, Hector, if you knew this white man. Oh, how unlike he is to all of his race, that we have ever seen! Do not turn from me with so much disdain. Hear me with patience, my friend."

"I cannot," replied Hector, "listen with patience to one who between the rising and the setting sun can forget all his resolutions, all his promises; who by a few soft words can be so wrought upon as to forget all the insults, all the injuries he has received from this accursed race; and can even call a white man friend!"

Caesar, unmoved by Hector's anger, continued to speak of Mr. Edwards with the warmest expressions of gratitude; and finished by declaring he would sooner forfeit his life than rebel against such a master. He conjured Hector to desist from executing his designs; but all was in vain. Hector sat with his elbows fixed upon his knees, leaning his head upon his hands, in gloomy silence.

Caesar's mind was divided between love for his friend and gratitude to his master: the conflict was violent and painful. Gratitude at last prevailed: he repeated his declaration, that he would rather die than continue in a conspiracy against his benefactor!

Hector refused to except him from the general doom. "Betray us if you will!" cried he. "Betray our secrets to him whom you call your benefactor! to him whom a few hours have made your friend! To him sacrifice the friend of your youth, the companion of your better days, of your better self! Yes, Caesar, deliver me over to the tormentors: I can endure more than they can inflict. I shall expire without a sigh, without a groan. Why do you linger here, Caesar? Why do you hesitate? Hasten this moment to your master; claim your reward for delivering into his power hundreds of your countrymen! Why do you hesitate? Away! The coward's friendship can be of use to none. Who can value his gratitude? Who can fear his revenge?" Hector raised his voice so high, as he pronounced these words, that he wakened Durant, the overseer, who slept in the next house. They heard him call out suddenly, to inquire who was there: and Caesar had but just time to make his escape, before Durant appeared. He searched Hector's cottage; but finding no one, again retired to rest. This man's tyranny made him constantly suspicious; he dreaded that the slaves should combine against him; and he endeavoured to prevent them, by every threat and every stratagem he could devise, from conversing with each other.

They had, however, taken their measures, hitherto, so secretly, that he had not the slightest idea of the conspiracy which was forming in the island. Their schemes were not yet ripe for execution; but the appointed time approached. Hector, when he coolly reflected on what had passed between him and Caesar, could not help admiring the frankness and courage with which he had avowed his change of sentiments. By this avowal, Caesar had in fact exposed his own life to the most imminent danger, from the vengeance of the conspirators, who might be tempted to assassinate him who had their lives in his power. Notwithstanding the contempt with which, in the first moment of passion, he had treated his friend, he was extremely anxious that he should not break off all connexion with the conspirators. He knew that Caesar possessed both intrepidity and eloquence, and that his opposition to their schemes would perhaps entirely frustrate their whole design. He therefore determined to use every possible means to bend him to their purposes.

The enlightened inhabitants of Europe may, perhaps, smile at the superstitious credulity of the negroes, who regard those ignorant beings called Obeah people with the most profound respect and dread; who believe that they hold in their hands the power of good and evil fortune, of health and sickness, of life and death. The instances which are related of their power over the minds of their countrymen are so wonderful, that none but the most unquestionable authority could make us think them credible. The following passage, from Edwards' History of the West Indies, is inserted, to give an idea of this strange infatuation:

"In the year 1760, when a very formidable insurrection of the Koromantyn or Gold Coast negroes broke out, in the parish of St. Mary, and spread through almost every other district of the island, an old Koromantyn negro, the chief instigator and oracle of the insurgents in that parish, who had administered the fetish, or solemn oath, to the conspirators, and furnished them with a magical preparation, which was to render them invulnerable, was fortunately apprehended, convicted, and hung up with all his feathers and trumperies about him; and his execution struck the insurgents with a general panic, from which they never afterwards recovered. The examinations, which were taken at that period, first opened the eyes of the public to the very dangerous tendency of the Obeah practices; and gave birth to the law, which was then enacted, for their suppression and punishment; but neither the terror of this law, the strict investigation which has since been made after the professors of Obi, nor the many examples of those who, from time to time, have been hanged or transported, have hitherto produced the desired effect. A gentleman, on his returning to Jamaica, in the year 1775, found that a great many of his negroes had died during his absence; and that, of such as remained alive, at least one half were debilitated, bloated, and in a very deplorable condition. The mortality continued after his arrival; and two or three were frequently buried in one day; others were taken ill, and began to decline under the same symptoms. Every means were tried, by medicine and the most careful nursing, to preserve the lives of the feeblest; but in spite of all his endeavours, this depopulation went on for a twelvemonth longer, with more or less intermission, and without his being able to ascertain the real cause, though the Obeah practice was strongly suspected, as well by himself as by the doctor, and other white persons upon the plantation; as it was known to have been very common in that part of the island, and particularly among the negroes of the Popaw or Popo country. Still he was unable to verify his suspicions; because the patients constantly denied their having any thing to do with persons of that order, or any knowledge of them. At length, a negress, who had been ill for some time, came and informed him, that, feeling it was impossible for her to live much longer, she thought herself bound in duty, before she died, to impart a very great secret, and acquaint him with the true cause of her disorder, in hopes that the disclosure might prove the means of stopping that mischief which had already swept away such a number of her fellow slaves. She proceeded to say that her step- mother, a woman of the Popo country, above eighty years old, but still hale and active, had put Obi upon her, as she had upon those who had lately died; and that the old woman had practised Obi for as many years past as she could remember. The other negroes of the plantation no sooner heard of this impeachment than they ran in a body to their master, and confirmed the truth, of it.—Upon this he repaired directly, with six white servants, to the old woman's house; and, forcing open the door, observed the whole inside of the roof, which was of thatch, and every crevice of the wall, stuck with the implements of her trade, consisting of rags, feathers, bones of cats, and a thousand other articles.—The house was instantly pulled down; and, with the whole of its contents, committed to the flames, amidst the general acclamations of all his other negroes.—From the moment of her departure, his negroes seemed all to be animated with new spirits; and the malady spread no farther among them. The total of his losses, in the course of about fifteen years preceding the discovery, and imputable solely to the Obeah practice, he estimates at least, at one hundred negroes."

Esther, an old Koromantyn negress, had obtained by her skill in poisonous herbs, and her knowledge of venomous reptiles, a high reputation amongst her countrymen. She soon taught them to believe her to be possessed of supernatural powers; and she then worked their imagination to what pitch and purpose she pleased.

She was the chief instigator of this intended rebellion. It was she who had stimulated the revengeful temper of Hector almost to frenzy. She now promised him that her arts should be exerted over his friend; and it was not long before he felt their influence. Caesar soon perceived an extraordinary change in the countenance and manner of his beloved Clara. A melancholy hung over her, and she refused to impart to him the cause of her dejection. Caesar was indefatigable in his exertions to cultivate and embellish the ground near his cottage, in hopes of making it an agreeable habitation for her; but she seemed to take no interest in any thing. She would stand beside him immoveable, in a deep reverie; but when he inquired whether she was ill, she would answer no, and endeavour to assume an air of gaiety: but this cheerfulness was transient; she soon relapsed into despondency. At length, she endeavoured to avoid her lover, as if she feared his farther inquiries.

Unable to endure this state of suspense, he one evening resolved to bring her to an explanation. "Clara," said he, "you once loved me: I have done nothing, have I, to forfeit your confidence?"

"I once loved you!" said she, raising her languid eyes, and looking at him with reproachful tenderness; "and can you doubt my constancy? Oh, Caesar, you little know what is passing in my heart! You are the cause of my melancholy!"

She paused and hesitated, as if afraid that she had said too much; but Caesar urged her with so much vehemence, and so much tenderness, to open to him her whole soul, that, at last, she could not resist his eloquence. She reluctantly revealed to him that secret of which she could not think without horror. She informed him, that unless he complied with what was required of him by the sorceress Esther, he was devoted to die. What it was that Esther required of him, Clara knew not: she knew nothing of the conspiracy. The timidity of her character was ill suited to such a project; and every thing relating to it had been concealed from her with the utmost care.

When she explained to Caesar the cause of her dejection, his natural courage resisted these superstitious fears; and he endeavoured to raise Clara's spirits. He endeavoured in vain: she fell at his feet; and with tears, and the most tender supplications, conjured him to avert the wrath of the sorceress, by obeying her commands, whatever they might be!

"Clara," replied he, "you know not what you ask!"

"I ask you to save your life!" said she. "I ask you, for my sake, to save your life, while yet it is in your power!"

"But would you, to save my life, Clara, make me the worst of criminals? Would you make me the murderer of my benefactor?"

Clara started with horror.

"Do you recollect the day, the moment, when we were on the point of being separated for ever, Clara? Do you remember the white man's coming to my cottage? Do you remember his look of benevolence— his voice of compassion? Do you remember his generosity? Oh! Clara, would you make me the murderer of this man?"

"Heaven forbid!" said Clara. "This cannot be the will of the sorceress!"

"It is," said Caesar. "But she shall not succeed, even though she speaks with the voice of Clara. Urge me no further; my resolution is fixed. I should be unworthy of your love if I were capable of treachery and ingratitude."

"But is there no means of averting the wrath of Esther?" said Clara. "Your life—"

"Think, first, of my honour," interrupted Caesar. "Your fears deprive you of reason. Return to this sorceress, and tell her that I dread not her wrath. My hands shall never be imbrued in the blood of my benefactor. Clara! can you forget his look when he told us that we should never more be separated?"

"It went to my heart," said Clara, bursting into tears "Cruel, cruel Esther! Why do you command us to destroy such a generous master?"

The conch sounded to summon the negroes to their morning's work. It happened this day, that Mr. Edwards, who was continually intent upon increasing the comforts and happiness of his slaves, sent his carpenter, while Caesar was absent, to fit up the inside of his cottage; and when Caesar returned from work, he found his master pruning the branches of a tamarind tree that over-hung the thatch. "How comes it, Caesar," said he, "that you have not pruned these branches?"

Caesar had no knife. "Here is mine for you," said Mr. Edwards. "It is very sharp," added he, smiling; "but I am not one of those masters who are afraid to trust their negroes with sharp knives."

These words were spoken with perfect simplicity: Mr. Edwards had no suspicion, at this time, of what was passing in the negro's mind. Caesar received the knife without uttering a syllable; but no sooner was Mr. Edwards out of sight than he knelt down, and, in a transport of gratitude, swore that, with this knife, he would stab himself to the heart sooner than betray his master!

The principle of gratitude conquered every other sensation. The mind of Caesar was not insensible to the charms of freedom: he knew the negro conspirators had so taken their measures that there was the greatest probability of their success. His heart beat high at the idea of recovering his liberty: but he was not to be seduced from his duty, not even by this delightful hope; nor was he to be intimidated by the dreadful certainty that his former friends and countrymen, considering him as a deserter from their cause, would become his bitterest enemies. The loss of Hector's esteem and affection was deeply felt by Caesar. Since the night that the decisive conversation relative to Mr. Edwards passed, Hector and he had never exchanged a syllable.

This visit proved the cause of much suffering to Hector, and to several of the slaves on Jefferies' plantation. We mentioned that Durant had been awakened by the raised voice of Hector. Though he could not find any one in the cottage, yet his suspicions were not dissipated; and an accident nearly brought the whole conspiracy to light. Durant had ordered one of the negroes to watch a boiler of sugar: the slave was overcome by the heat, and fainted. He had scarcely recovered his senses when the overseer came up, and found that the sugar had fermented, by having remained a few minutes too long in the boiler. He flew into a violent passion, and ordered that the negro should receive fifty lashes. His victim bore them without uttering a groan; but, when his punishment was over, and when he thought the overseer was gone, he exclaimed, "It will soon be our turn!"

Durant was not out of hearing. He turned suddenly, and observed that the negro looked at Hector when he pronounced these words, and this confirmed the suspicion that Hector was carrying on some conspiracy. He immediately had recourse to that brutality which he considered as the only means of governing black men: Hector and three other negroes were lashed unmercifully; but no confessions could be extorted.

Mr. Jefferies might perhaps have forbidden such violence to be used, if he had not been at the time carousing with a party of jovial West Indians, who thought of nothing but indulging their appetites in all the luxuries that art and nature could supply. The sufferings which had been endured by many of the wretched negroes to furnish out this magnificent entertainment were never once thought of by these selfish epicures. Yet so false are the general estimates of character, that all these gentlemen passed for men of great feeling and generosity! The human mind, in certain situations, becomes so accustomed to ideas of tyranny and cruelty, that they no longer appear extraordinary or detestable: they rather seem part of the necessary and immutable order of things.

Mr. Jefferies was stopped, as he passed from his dining-room into his drawing-room, by a little negro child, of about five years old, who was crying bitterly. He was the son of one of the slaves who were at this moment under the torturer's hand. "Poor little devil!" said Mr. Jefferies, who was more than half intoxicated. "Take him away; and tell Durant, some of ye, to pardon his father—if he can."

The child ran, eagerly, to announce his father's pardon; but he soon returned, crying more violently than before. Durant would not hear the boy; and it was now no longer possible to appeal to Mr. Jefferies, for he was in the midst of an assembly of fair ladies, and no servant belonging to the house dared to interrupt the festivities of the evening. The three men, who were so severely flogged to extort from them confessions, were perfectly innocent: they knew nothing of the confederacy; but the rebels seized the moment when their minds were exasperated by this cruelty and injustice, and they easily persuaded them to join the league. The hope of revenging themselves upon the overseer was a motive sufficient to make them brave death in any shape.

Another incident, which happened a few days before the time destined for the revolt of the slaves, determined numbers who had been undecided. Mrs. Jefferies was a languid beauty, or rather a languid fine lady who had been a beauty, and who spent all that part of the day which was not devoted to the pleasures of the table, or to reclining on a couch, in dress. She was one day extended on a sofa, fanned by four slaves, two at her head and two at her feet, when news was brought that a large chest, directed to her, was just arrived from London.

This chest contained various articles of dress of the newest fashions. The Jamaica ladies carry their ideas of magnificence to a high pitch: they willingly give a hundred guineas for a gown, which they perhaps wear but once or twice. In the elegance and variety of her ornaments, Mrs. Jefferies was not exceeded by any lady in the island, except by one who had lately received a cargo from England. She now expected to outshine her competitor, and desired that the chest should be unpacked in her presence.

In taking out one of the gowns, it caught on a nail in the lid, and was torn. The lady, roused from her natural indolence by this disappointment to her vanity, instantly ordered that the unfortunate female slave should be severely chastised. The woman was the wife of Hector; and this fresh injury worked up his temper, naturally vindictive, to the highest point. He ardently longed for the moment when he might satiate his vengeance.

The plan the negroes had laid was to set fire to the canes, at one and the same time, on every plantation; and when the white inhabitants of the island should run to put out the fire, the blacks were to seize this moment of confusion and consternation to fall upon them, and make a general massacre. The time when this scheme was to be carried into execution was not known to Caesar; for the conspirators had changed their day, as soon as Hector told them that his friend was no longer one of the confederacy. They dreaded he should betray them; and it was determined that he and Clara should both be destroyed, unless they could be prevailed upon to join the conspiracy.

Hector wished to save his friend, but the desire of vengeance overcame every other feeling. He resolved, however, to make an attempt, for the last time, to change Caesar's resolution.

For this purpose, Esther was the person he employed: she was to work upon his mind by means of Clara. On returning to her cottage one night, she found suspended from the thatch one of those strange fantastic charms with which the Indian sorceresses terrify those whom they have proscribed. Clara, unable to conquer her terror, repaired again to Esther, who received her first in mysterious silence; but, after she had implored her forgiveness for the past, and with all possible humility conjured her to grant her future protection, the sorceress deigned to speak. Her commands were that Clara should prevail upon her lover to meet her, on this awful spot, the ensuing night.

Little suspecting what was going forward on the plantation of Jefferies, Mr. Edwards that evening gave his slaves a holiday. He and his family came out at sunset, when the fresh breeze had sprung up, and seated themselves under a spreading palm-tree, to enjoy the pleasing spectacle of this negro festival. His negroes were all well clad, and in the gayest colours, and their merry countenances suited the gaiety of their dress. While some were dancing, and some playing on the tambourine, others appeared amongst the distant trees, bringing baskets of avocado pears, grapes, and pine-apples, the produce of their own provision-grounds; and others were employed in spreading their clean trenchers, or the calabashes, which served for plates and dishes. The negroes continued to dance and divert themselves till late in, the evening. When they separated and retired to rest, Caesar, recollecting his promise to Clara, repaired secretly to the habitation of this sorceress. It was situated in the recess of a thick wood. When he arrived there, he found the door fastened; and he was obliged to wait some time before it was opened by Esther.

The first object he beheld was his beloved Clara, stretched on the ground, apparently a corpse! The sorceress had thrown her into a trance by a preparation of deadly nightshade. The hag burst into an infernal laugh, when she beheld the despair that was painted in Caesar's countenance. "Wretch!" cried she, "you have defied my power: behold its victim!"

Caesar, in a transport of rage, seized her by the throat: but his fury was soon checked.

"Destroy me," said the fiend, "and you destroy your Clara. She is not dead: but she lies in the sleep of death, into which she has been thrown by magic art, and from which no power but mine can restore her to the light of life. Yes! look at her, pale and motionless! Never will she rise from the earth, unless, within one hour, you obey my commands. I have administered to Hector and his companions the solemn fetish oath, at the sound of which every negro in Africa trembles! You know my object."

"Fiend, I do!" replied Caesar, eyeing her sternly; "but, while I have life, it shall never be accomplished."

"Look yonder!" cried she, pointing to the moon; "in a few minutes that moon will set: at that hour Hector and his friends will appear. They come armed—armed with weapons which I shall steep in poison for their enemies. Themselves I will render invulnerable. Look again!" continued she; "if my dim eyes mistake not, yonder they come. Rash man, you die if they cross my threshold."

"I wish for death," said Caesar. "Clara is dead!"

"But you can restore her to life by a single word." Caesar, at this moment, seemed to hesitate. "Consider! Your heroism is vain," continued Esther. "You will have the knives of fifty of the conspirators in your bosom, if you do not join them; and, after you have fallen, the death of your master is inevitable. Here is the bowl of poison, in which the negro knives are to be steeped. Your friends, your former friends, your countrymen, will be in arms in a few minutes; and they will bear down every thing before them—Victory, Wealth, Freedom, and Revenge, will be theirs."

Caesar appeared to be more and more agitated. His eyes were fixed upon Clara. The conflict in his mind was violent: but his sense of gratitude and duty could not be shaken by hope, fear, or ambition; nor could it be vanquished by love. He determined, however, to appear to yield. As if struck with panic, at the approach of the confederate negroes, he suddenly turned to the sorceress, and said, in a tone of feigned submission, "It is in vain to struggle with fate. Let my knife, too, be dipped in your magic poison."

The sorceress clapped her hands with infernal joy in her countenance. She bade him instantly give her his knife, that she might plunge it to the hilt in the bowl of poison, to which she turned with savage impatience. His knife was left in his cottage, and, under pretence of going in search of it, he escaped. Esther promised to prepare Hector and all his companions to receive him with their ancient cordiality on his return. Caesar ran with the utmost speed along a bye-path out of the wood, met none of the rebels, reached his master's house, scaled the wall of his bedchamber, got in at the window, and wakened him, exclaiming, "Arm—arm yourself, my dear master! Arm all your slaves! They will fight for you, and die for you; as I will the first. The Koromantyn yell of war will be heard in Jefferies plantation this night! Arm—arm yourself, my dear master, and let us surround the rebel leaders while it is yet time. I will lead you to the place where they are all assembled, on condition that their chief, who is my friend, shall be pardoned."

Mr. Edwards armed himself and the negroes on his plantation, as well as the whites; they were all equally attached to him. He followed Caesar into the recesses of the wood.

They proceeded with all possible rapidity, but in perfect silence, till they reached Esther's habitation: which they surrounded completely, before they were perceived by the conspirators.

Mr. Edwards looked through a hole in the wall; and, by the blue flame of a cauldron, over which the sorceress was stretching her shrivelled hands, he saw Hector and five stout negroes standing, intent upon her incantations. These negroes held their knives in their hands, ready to dip them into the bowl of poison. It was proposed, by one of the whites, to set fire immediately to the hut, and thus to force the rebels to surrender. The advice was followed; but Mr. Edwards charged his people to spare their prisoners. The moment the rebels saw that the thatch of the hut was in flames, they set up the Koromantyn yell of war, and rushed out with frantic desperation.

"Yield! You are pardoned, Hector," cried Mr. Edwards, in a loud voice.

"You are pardoned, my friend!" repeated Cæsar.

Hector, incapable at this instant of listening to anything but revenge, sprang forwards, and plunged his knife into the bosom of Cæsar. The faithful servant staggered back a few paces: his master caught him in his arms. "I die content," said he. "Bury me with Clara."

He swooned from loss of blood as they were carrying him home; but when his wound was examined, it was found not to be mortal. As he recovered from his swoon, he stared wildly round him, trying to recollect where he was, and what had happened. He thought that he was still in a dream, when he saw his beloved Clara standing beside him. The opiate, which the pretended sorceress had administered to her, had ceased to operate; she wakened from her trance just at the time the Koromantyn yell commenced. Cæsar's joy!—we must leave that to the imagination.

In the mean time, what became of the rebel negroes, and Mr. Edwards?

The taking the chief conspirators prisoners did not prevent the negroes upon Jefferies' plantation from insurrection. The moment they heard the war-whoop, the signal agreed upon, they rose in a body; and, before they could be prevented, either by the whites on the estate, or by Mr. Edwards' adherents, they had set fire to the overseer's house, and to the canes. The overseer was the principal object of their vengeance—he died in tortures, inflicted by the hands of those who had suffered most by his cruelties. Mr. Edwards, however, quelled the insurgents before rebellion spread to any other estates in the island. The influence of his character, and the effect of his eloquence upon the minds of the people, were astonishing: nothing but his interference could have prevented the total destruction of Mr. Jefferies and his family, who, as it was computed, lost this night upwards of fifty thousand pounds. He was never afterwards able to recover his losses, or to shake off his constant fear of a fresh insurrection among his slaves. At length, he and his lady returned to England, where they were obliged to live in obscurity and indigence. They had no consolation in their misfortunes but that of railing at the treachery of the whole race of slaves. Our readers, we hope, will think that at least one exception may be made, in favour of The Grateful Negro

TO-MORROW

CHAPTER I

It has long been my intention to write my own history, and I am determined to begin it to-day; for half the good intentions of my life have been frustrated by my unfortunate habit of putting things off till to-morrow.

When I was a young man, I used to be told that this was my only fault; I believed it, and my vanity or laziness persuaded me that this fault was but small, and that I should easily cure myself of it in time.

That time, however, has not yet arrived, and at my advanced age I must give up all thoughts of amendment, hoping, however, that sincere repentance may stand instead of reformation.

My father was an eminent London bookseller: he happened to be looking over a new biographical dictionary on the day when I was brought into the world; and at the moment when my birth was announced to him, he had his finger upon the name Basil; he read aloud—"Basil, canonized bishop of Caesarea, a theological, controversial, and moral writer."

"My boy," continued my father, "shall be named after this great man, and I hope and believe that I shall live to see him either a celebrated theological, controversial, and moral author, or a bishop. I am not so sanguine as to expect that he should be both these good things."

I was christened Basil according to my father's wishes, and his hopes of my future celebrity and fortune were confirmed, during my childhood, by instances of wit and memory, which were not perhaps greater than what could have been found in my little contemporaries, but which appeared to the vanity of parental fondness extraordinary, if not supernatural. My father declared that it would be a sin not to give me a learned education, and he went even beyond his means to procure for me all the advantages of the best modes of instruction. I was stimulated, even when a boy, by the idea that I should become a great man, and my masters had for some time reason to be satisfied; but what they called the quickness of my parts continually retarded my progress. The facility with which I learned my lessons encouraged me to put off learning them till the last moment; and this habit of procrastinating, which was begun in presumption, ended in disgrace.

When I was sent to a public school, I found among my companions so many temptations to idleness, that notwithstanding the quickness of my parts, I was generally flogged twice a week. As I grew older, my reason might perhaps have taught me to correct myself, but my vanity was excited to persist in idleness by certain imprudent sayings or whisperings of my father.

When I came home from school at the holidays, and when complaints were preferred against me in letters from my school-master, my father, even while he affected to scold me for my negligence, flattered me in the most dangerous manner by adding—aside to some friend of the family—"My Basil is a strange fellow!—can do any thing he pleases—all his masters say so—but he is a sad idle dog—all your men of genius are so—puts off business always to the last moment—all your men of genius do so. For instance, there is —, whose third edition of odes I have just published—what an idle dog he is! Yet who makes such a noise in the world as he does?—put every thing off till to-morrow, like my Basil—but can do more at the last moment than any man in England—that is, if the fit seizes him—for he does nothing but by fits—has no application—none—says it would 'petrify him to a dunce.' I never knew a man of genius who was not an idle dog."

Not a syllable of such speeches was lost upon me: the idea of a man of genius and of an idle dog were soon so firmly joined together in my imagination, that it was impossible to separate them, either by my own reason or by that of my preceptors. I gloried in the very habits which my tutors laboured to correct; and I never was seriously mortified by the consequences of my own folly till, at a public examination at Eton, I lost a premium by putting off till it was too late the finishing a copy of verses. The lines which I had written were said by all my young and old friends to be beautiful. The prize was gained by one Johnson, a heavy lad, of no sort of genius, but of great perseverance. His verses were finished, however, at the stated time.

"For dulness ever must be regular!"

My fragment, charming as it was, was useless, except to hand about afterward among my friends, to prove what I might have done if I had thought it worth while.

My father was extremely vexed by my missing an opportunity of distinguishing myself at this public exhibition, especially as the king had honoured the assembly with his presence; and as those who had gained premiums were presented to his majesty, it was supposed that their being thus early marked as lads of talents would be highly advantageous to their advancement in life. All this my father felt, and, blaming himself for having encouraged me in the indolence of genius, he determined to counteract his former imprudence, and was resolved, he said, to cure me at once of my habit of procrastination. For this purpose he took down from his shelves Young's Night Thoughts; from which he remembered a line, which has become a stock line among writing-masters' copies:

"Procrastination is the thief of time."

He hunted the book for the words Procrastination, Time, To-day, and To-morrow, and made an extract of seven long pages on the dangers of delay.

"Now, my dear Basil," said he, "this is what will cure you for life, and this you must get perfectly by heart, before I give you one shilling more pocket-money."

The motive was all powerful, and with pains, iteration, and curses, I fixed the heterogeneous quotations so well in my memory that some of them have remained there to this day. For instance—

"Time destroyed
Is suicide, where more than blood is spilt.
Time flies, death urges, knells call, Heav'n invites,
Hell threatens.
We push Time from us, and we wish him back.

Man flies from Time, and Time from man too soon;
In sad divorce this double flight must end;
And then where are we?
Be wise to-day, 'tis madness to defer, &c.
Next day the fatal precedent will plead, &c.

Lorenzo—O for yesterdays to come!
To-day is yesterday return'd; return'd,
Full powered to cancel, expiate, raise, adorn,
And reinstate us on the rock of peace.
Let it not share its predecessor's fate,
Nor, like its elder sisters, die a fool.

Where shall I find him? Angels! tell me where:
You know him; he is near you; point him out;
Shall I see glories beaming from his brow?
Or trace his footsteps by the rising flow'rs?
Your golden wings now hov'ring o'er him shed
Protection: now are wav'ring in applause
To that blest son of foresight! Lord of fate!
That awful independent on to-morrow!
Whose work is done; who triumphs in the past;
Whose yesterdays look backward with a smile."

I spare you the rest of my task, and I earnestly hope, my dear reader, that these citations may have a better effect upon you than they had upon me. With shame I confess, that even with the addition of Shakspeare's eloquent

"To-morrow, and to-morrow, and to-morrow," &c.

which I learnt by heart gratis, not a bit the better was I for all this poetical morality. What I wanted was, not conviction of my folly, but resolution to amend.

When I say that I was not a bit the better for these documentings, I must not omit to observe to you that I was very near four hundred pounds a year the better for them.

Being obliged to learn so much of Young's Night Thoughts by rote, I was rather disgusted, and my attention was roused to criticise the lines which had been forced upon my admiration. Afterward, when I went to college, I delighted to maintain, in opposition to some of my companions, who were enthusiastic admirers of Young, that he was no poet. The more I was ridiculed, the more I persisted. I talked my self into notice; I became acquainted with several of the literary men at Cambridge; I wrote in defence of my opinion, or, as some called it, my heresy. I maintained that what all the world had mistaken for sublimity was bombast; that the Night Thoughts were fuller of witty conceits than of poetical images: I drew a parallel between Young and Cowley; and I finished by pronouncing Young to be the Cowley of the eighteenth century. To do myself justice, there was much ingenuity and some truth in my essay, but it was the declamation of a partisan, who can think only on one side of a question, and who, in the heat of controversy, says more than he thinks, and more than he originally intended.

It is often the fortune of literary partisans to obtain a share of temporary celebrity far beyond their deserts, especially if they attack any writer of established reputation. The success of my essay exceeded my most sanguine expectations, and I began to think that my father was right; that I was born to be a great genius, and a great man. The notice taken of me by a learned prelate, who piqued himself upon being considered as the patron of young men of talents, confirmed me at once in my self-conceit and my hopes of preferment.

I mentioned to you that my father, in honour of my namesake Basil, bishop of Caesarea, and to verify his own presentiments, had educated me for the Church. My present patron, who seemed to like me the better the oftener I dined with him, gave me reason to hope that he would provide for me handsomely. I was not yet ordained, when a living of four hundred per annum fell into his gift: he held it over for some months, as it was thought, on purpose for me.

In the mean time he employed me to write a charity sermon for him, which he was to preach, as it was expected, to a crowded congregation. None but those who are themselves slaves to the habit of procrastination will believe that I could be so foolish as to put off writing this sermon till the Saturday evening before it was wanted. Some of my young companions came unexpectedly to sup with me; we sat late: in the vanity of a young author, who glories in the rapidity of composition, I said to myself that I could finish my sermon in an hour's notice. But, alas! when my companions at length departed, they left me in no condition to complete a sermon. I fell fast asleep, and was wakened in the morning by the bishop's servant. The dismay I felt is indescribable; I started up—it was nine o'clock: I began to write; but my hand and my mind trembled, and my ideas were in such confusion, that I could not, great genius as I was, produce a beginning sentence in a quarter of an hour.

I kept the bishop's servant forty minutes by his watch; wrote and re-wrote two pages, and walked up and down the room; tore my two pages; and at last, when the footman said he could wait no longer, was obliged to let him go with an awkward note, pleading sudden sickness for my apology. It was true that I was sufficiently sick at the time when I penned this note: my head ached terribly; and I kept my room, reflecting upon my own folly, the whole of the day. I foresaw the consequences: the living was given away by my patron the next morning, and all hopes of future favour were absolutely at an end.

My father overwhelmed me with reproaches; and I might perhaps have been reformed by this disappointment, but an unexpected piece of good fortune, or what I then thought good fortune, was my ruin.

Among the multitude of my college-friends was a young gentleman, whose father was just appointed to go out upon the famous embassy to China; he came to our shop to buy Du Halde; and upon hearing me express an enthusiastic desire to visit China, he undertook to apply to his father to take me in the ambassador's suite. His representation of me as a young man of talents and literature, and the view of some botanical drawings, which I executed upon the spur of the occasion with tolerable neatness, procured me the favour which I so ardently desired.

My father objected to my making this voyage. He was vexed to see me quit the profession for which I had been educated; and he could not, without a severe struggle, relinquish his hopes of seeing me a bishop. But I argued that, as I had not yet been ordained, there could be no disgrace or impropriety in my avoiding a mode of life which was not suited to my genius. This word genius had now, as upon all other occasions, a mighty effect upon my father; and, observing this, I declared farther, in a high tone of voice, that from the experience I had already had, I was perfectly certain that the drudgery of sermon-writing would paralyze my genius; and that, to expand and invigorate my intellectual powers, it was absolutely necessary I should, to use a great author's expression, "view in foreign countries varied modes of existence."

My father's hopes that one half of his prophecy would at least be accomplished, and that I should become a great author, revived; and he consented to my going to China, upon condition that I should promise to write a history of my voyage and journey, in two volumes octavo, or one quarto, with a folio of plates. The promise was readily made; for in the plenitude of confidence in my own powers, octavos and quartos shrunk before me, and a folio appeared too small for the various information, and the useful reflections, which a voyage to China must supply.

Full of expectations and projects, I talked from morning till night of my journey: but notwithstanding my father's hourly remonstrances, I deferred my preparations till the last week. Then all was hurry and confusion; tailors and sempstresses, portmanteaus and trunks, portfolios and drawing-boxes, water-colours, crayons, and note-books, wet from the stationer's, crowded my room. I had a dozen small note-books, and a huge commonplace-book, which was to be divided and kept in the manner recommended by the judicious and immortal Locke.

In the midst of the last day's bustle, I sat down at the corner of a table with compass, ruler, and red ink, to divide and rule my best of all possible commonplace-books; but the red ink was too thin, and the paper was not well sized, and it blotted continually, because I was obliged to turn over the pages rapidly; and ink will not dry, nor blotting-paper suck it up, more quickly for a genius than for any other man. Besides, my attention was much distracted by the fear that the sempstress would not send home my dozen of new shirts, and that a vile procrastinating boot-maker would never come with my boots. Every rap at the door I started up to inquire whether that was the shirts, or the boots: thrice I overturned the red, and twice the black ink bottles by these starts; and the execrations which I bestowed upon those tradespeople, who will put off every thing to the last moment, were innumerable. I had orders to set off in the mail-coach for Portsmouth, to join the rest of the ambassador's suite.

The provoking watchman cried "past eleven o'clock" before I had half-finished ruling my commonplace-book; my shirts and my boots were not come: the mail-coach, as you may guess, set off without me. My poor father was in a terrible tremor, and walked from room to room, reproaching me and himself; but I persisted in repeating that Lord M. would not set out the day he had intended: that nobody, since the creation of the world, ever set out upon a long journey the day he first appointed: besides, there were at least a hundred chances in my favour that his lordship would break down on his way to Portsmouth;

that the wind would not be fair when he arrived there; that half the people in his suite would not be more punctual than myself, &c.

By these arguments, or by mere dint of assertion, I quieted my father's apprehensions and my own, and we agreed that, as it was now impossible to go to-day, it was best to stay till to-morrow.

Upon my arrival at Portsmouth, the first thing I heard was that the Lion and Hindostan had sailed some hours before, with the embassy for China. Despair deprived me of utterance. A charitable waiter at the inn, however, seeing my consternation and absolute inability to think or act for myself, ran to make farther inquiries, and brought me back the joyful tidings that the Jackal brig, which was to carry out the remainder of the ambassador's suite, was not yet under weigh; that a gentleman, who was to go in the Jackal, had dined at an hotel in the next street, and that he had gone to the water-side but ten minutes ago.

I hurried after him: the boat was gone. I paid another exorbitantly to take me and my goods to the brig, and reached the Jackal just as she was weighing anchor. Bad education for me! The moment I felt myself safe on board, having recovered breath to speak, I exclaimed, "Here am I, safe and sound! just as well as if I had been here yesterday; better indeed. Oh, after this, I shall always trust to my own good fortune! I knew I should not be too late." When I came to reflect coolly, however, I was rather sorry that I had missed my passage in the Lion, with my friend and protector, and with most of the learned and ingenious men of the ambassador's suite, to whom I had been introduced, and who had seemed favourably disposed towards me. All the advantage I might have derived from their conversation, during this long voyage, was lost by my own negligence. The Jackal lost company of the Lion and Hindostan in the Channel. As my friends afterwards told me, they waited for us five days in Praya Bay; but as no Jackal appeared, they sailed again without her. At length, to our great joy, we descried on the beach of Sumatra a board nailed to a post, which our friends had set up there, with a written notice to inform us that the Lion and Hindostan had touched on this shore on such a day, and to point out to us the course that we should keep in order to join them.

At the sight of this writing my spirits revived: the wind favoured us; but, alas! in passing the Straits of Banka, we were damaged so that we were obliged to return to port to refit, and to take in fresh provision. Not a soul on board but wished it had been their fate to have had a berth in the other ships; and I more loudly than any one else expressed this wish twenty times a-day. When my companions heard that I was to have sailed in the ambassador's ship, if I had been time enough at Spithead, some pitied and some rallied me: but most said I deserved to be punished for my negligence. At length we joined the Lion and Hindostan at North Island. Our friends had quite given up all hopes of ever seeing us again, and had actually bought at Batavia a French brig, to supply the place of the Jackal. To my great satisfaction, I was now received on board the Lion, and had an opportunity of conversing with the men of literature and science, from whom I had been so unluckily separated during the former part of the voyage. Their conversation soon revived and increased my regret, when they told me of all that I had missed seeing at the various places where they had touched: they talked to me with provoking fluency of the culture of manioc; of the root of cassada, of which tapioca is made; of the shrub called the cactus, on which the cochineal insect swarms and feeds; and of the ipecacuanha-plant; all which they had seen at Rio Janeiro, besides eight paintings representing the manner in which the diamond and gold mines in the Brazils are worked. Indeed, upon cross-examination, I found that these pictures were miserably executed, and scarcely worth seeing.

I regretted more the fine pine-apples, which my companions assured me were in such abundance that they cleaned their swords in them, as being the cheapest acid that could be there procured. But, far beyond these vulgar objects of curiosity, I regretted not having learned any thing concerning the celebrated upas-tree. I was persuaded that, if I had been at Batavia, I should have extracted some information more precise than these gentlemen obtained from the keepers of the medical garden.

I confess that my mortification at this disappointment did not arise solely from the pure love of natural history: the upas-tree would have made a conspicuous figure in my quarto volume. I consoled myself, however, by the determination to omit nothing that the vast empire of China could afford to render my work entertaining, instructive, interesting, and sublime. I anticipated the pride with which I should receive the compliments of my friends and the public upon my valuable and incomparable work; I anticipated the pleasure with which my father would exult in the celebrity of his son, and in the accomplishment of his own prophecies; and, with these thoughts full in my mind, we landed at Mettow, in China.

I sat up late at night writing a sketch of my preface and notes for the heads of chapters. I was tired, fell into a profound sleep, dreamed I was teaching the emperor of China to pronounce 'chrononhotonthologos,' and in the morning was wakened by the sound of the gong; the signal that the accommodation junks were ready to sail with the embassy to Pekin. I hurried on my clothes, and was in the junk before the gong had done beating. I gloried in my celerity; but before we had gone two leagues up the country, I found reason to repent of my precipitation: I wanted to note down my first impressions on entering the Chinese territories; but, alas! I felt in vain in my pocket for my pencil and note-book: I had left them both behind me on my bed. Not only one note-book, but my whole dozen; which, on leaving London, I had stuffed into a bag with my night-gown. Bag, night-gown, note-books, all were forgotten! However trifling it may appear, this loss of the little note-books was of material consequence. To be sure, it was easy to procure paper and make others; but, because it was so easy, it was delayed from hour to hour, and from day to day; and I went on writing my most important remarks on scraps of paper, which were always to be copied to-morrow into a note-book that was then to be made.

We arrived at Pekin, and were magnificently lodged in a palace in that city; but here we were so strictly guarded, that we could not stir beyond the courts of the palace. You will say that in this confinement I had leisure sufficient to make a note-book, and to copy my notes: so I had, and it was my firm intention so to have done; but I put it off because I thought it would take up but a few hours' time, and it could be done any day. Besides, the weather was so excessively hot, that for the first week, I could do nothing but unbutton my waistcoat and drink sherbet. Visits of ceremony from mandarins took up much of our time: they spoke and moved like machines; and it was with much difficulty that our interpreter made us understand the meaning of their formal sentences, which were seldom worth the trouble of deciphering. We saw them fan themselves, drink tea, eat sweetmeats and rice, and chew betel; but it was scarcely worth while to come all the way from Europe to see this, especially as any common Chinese paper or screen would give an adequate idea of these figures in their accustomed attitudes.

I spent another week in railing at these abominably stupid or unnecessarily cautious creatures of ceremony, and made memorandums for an eloquent chapter in my work.

One morning we were agreeably surprised by a visit from a mandarin of a very different description. We were astonished to hear a person in the habit of a Chinese, and bearing the title of a mandarin, address us in French: he informed us that he was originally a French Jesuit, and came over to China with several missionaries from Paris; but as they were prohibited from promulgating their doctrines in this country, most of them had returned to France; a few remained, assumed the dress and manners of the country, and had been elevated to the rank of mandarins as a reward for their learning. The conversation of our Chinese Jesuit was extremely entertaining and instructive; he was delighted to hear news from Europe, and we were eager to obtain from him information respecting China. I paid particular attention to him, and I was so fortunate as to win his confidence, as far as the confidence of a Jesuit can be won. He came frequently to visit me, and did me the honour to spend some hours in my apartment.

As he made it understood that these were literary visits, and as his character for propriety was well established with the government, he excited no suspicion, and we spent our time most delightfully between books and conversation. He gave me, by his anecdotes and descriptions, an insight into the characters and domestic lives of the inhabitants of Pekin, which I could not otherwise have obtained: his talent for description was admirable, and his characters were so new to me that I was in continual ecstasy. I called him the Chinese La Bruyere; and, anticipating the figure which his portraits would make in my future work, thought that I could never sufficiently applaud his eloquence. He was glad to lay aside the solemn gravity of a Chinese mandarin, and to indulge the vivacity of a Frenchman; his vanity was gratified by my praises, and he exerted himself to the utmost to enhance my opinion of his talents.

At length we had notice that it was the emperor's pleasure to receive the embassy at his imperial residence in Tartary, at Jehol; the seat of grateful coolness, the garden of innumerable trees. From the very name of this place I augured that it would prove favourable to the inspirations of genius, and determined to date at least one of the chapters or letters of my future work from this delightful retreat, the Sans Souci of China. Full of this intention, I set out upon our expedition into Tartary.

My good friend, the Jesuit, who had a petition to present to the emperor relative to some Chinese manuscripts, determined, to my infinite satisfaction, to accompany us to Jehol; and our conducting mandarin, Van-Tadge, arranged things so upon our journey that I enjoyed as much of my friend's conversation as possible. Never European travelling in these countries had such advantages as mine; I had a companion who was able and willing to instruct me in every minute particular of the manners, and every general principle of the government and policy, of the people. I was in no danger of falling into the ridiculous mistakes of travellers, who, having but a partial view of things and persons, argue absurdly, and grossly misrepresent, while they intend to be accurate. Many people, as my French mandarin observed, reason like Voltaire's famous traveller, who happening to have a drunken landlord and a red-haired landlady at the first inn where he stopped in Alsace, wrote down among his memorandums—"All the men of Alsace drunkards: all the women red-haired."

When we arrived at Jehol, the hurry of preparing for our presentation to the emperor, the want of a convenient writing-table, and perhaps my habit of procrastination, prevented my writing the chapter for my future work, or noting down any of the remarks which the Jesuit had made upon our journey. One morning when I collected my papers and the scraps of memorandums with which the pockets of all my clothes were stuffed, I was quite terrified at the heap of confusion, and thrust all these materials for my quarto into a canvas bag, purposing to lay them smooth in a portfolio the next day. But the next day I could do nothing of this sort, for we had the British presents to unpack, which had arrived from Pekin; the day after was taken up with our presentation to the emperor, and the day after that I had a new scheme in my head. The emperor, with much solemnity, presented with his own hand to our ambassador a casket, which he said was the most valuable present he could make to the king of England: it contained the miniature pictures of the emperor's ancestors, with a few lines of poetry annexed to each, describing the character, and recording the principal events, of each monarch's reign. It occurred to me that a set of similar portraits and poetical histories of the kings of England would be a proper and agreeable offering to the emperor of China: I consulted my friend the French mandarin, and he encouraged me by assurances that, as far as he could pretend to judge, it would be at present peculiarly suited to the emperor's taste; and that in all probability I should be distinguished by some mark of his approbation, or some munificent reward. My friend promised to have the miniatures varnished for me in the Chinese taste; and he undertook to present the work to the emperor when it should be finished. As it was supposed that the embassy would spend the whole winter in Pekin, I thought that I should have time enough to complete the whole series of British sovereigns. It was not necessary to be very scrupulous as to the resemblance of my portraits, as the emperor of China could not easily detect any errors of this nature: fortunately, I had brought from London with me striking likenesses of all the kings of England, with the principal events of their reign, in one large sheet of paper, which belonged to a joining-map of one of my little cousins. In the confusion of my packing up, I had put it into my trunk instead of a sheet almanack, which lay on the same table. In the course of my life, many lucky accidents have happened to me, even in consequence of my own carelessness; yet that carelessness has afterward prevented my reaping any permanent advantage from my good fortune.

Upon this occasion I was, however, determined that no laziness of mine should deprive me of an opportunity of making my fortune: I set to work immediately, and astonished my friend by the facility with which I made verses. It was my custom to retire from the noisy apartments of our palace to a sort of alcove, at the end of a long gallery, in one of the outer courts, where our corps of artillery used to parade. After their parade was over, the place was perfectly quiet and solitary for the remainder of the day and night. I used to sit up late, writing; and one fine moonlight night, I went out of my alcove to walk in the gallery, while I composed some lines on our great queen Elizabeth. I could not finish the last couplet to my fancy: I sat down upon an artificial rock, which was in the middle of the court, leaned my head upon my hand, and as I was searching for an appropriate rhyme to glory, fell fast asleep. A noise like that of a most violent clap of thunder awakened me; I was thrown with my face flat upon the ground.

When I recovered my senses, the court was filled with persons, some European, some Chinese, seemingly just risen from their beds, with lanterns and torches in their hands; all of them with faces of consternation, asking one another what had happened. The ground was covered with scattered fragments of wooden pillars, mats, and bamboo cane-work; I looked and saw that one end of the gallery in which I had been walking, and the alcove, were in ruins. There was a strong smell of gunpowder. I now recollected that I had borrowed a powder-horn from one of the soldiers in the morning; and that I had intended to load my pistols, but I delayed doing so. The horn, full of gunpowder, lay upon the table in the alcove all day, and the pistols, out of which I had shaken the old priming. When I went out to walk in the gallery, I left the candle burning; and I suppose during my sleep a spark fell upon the loose gunpowder, set fire to that in the horn, and blew up the alcove. It was built of light wood and cane, and communicated only with a cane-work gallery; otherwise the mischief would have been more serious. As it was, the explosion had alarmed not only all the ambassador's suite, who lodged in the palace, but many of the Chinese in the neighbourhood, who could not be made to comprehend how the accident had happened.

Reproaches from all our own people were poured upon me without mercy; and, in the midst of my contrition, I had not for some time leisure to lament the loss of all my kings of England: no vestige of them remained; and all the labour that I had bestowed upon their portraits and their poetical histories was lost to the emperor of China and to myself. What was still worse, I could not even utter a syllable of complaint, for nobody would sympathize with me, all my companions were so much provoked by my negligence, and so apprehensive of the bad consequences which might ensue from this accident. The

Chinese, who had been alarmed, and who departed evidently dissatisfied, would certainly mention what had happened to the mandarins of the city, and they would report it to the emperor.

I resolved to apply for advice to my friend, the Jesuit; but he increased instead of diminished our apprehensions; he said that the affair was much talked of and misrepresented at Jehol; and that the Chinese, naturally timid, and suspicious of strangers, could not believe that no injury was intended to them, and that the explosion was accidental. A child had been wounded by the fall of some of the ruins of the alcove, which were thrown with great violence into a neighbouring house: the butt end of one of my pistols was found in the street, and had been carried to the magistrate by the enraged populace, as evidence of our evil designs. My Jesuit observed to me that there was no possibility of reasoning with the prejudices of any nation; and he confessed he expected that this unlucky accident would have the most serious consequences. He had told me in confidence a circumstance that tended much to confirm this opinion: a few days before, when the emperor went to examine the British presents of artillery, and when the brass mortars were tried, though he admired the ingenuity of these instruments of destruction, yet he said that he deprecated the spirit of the people who employed them, and could not reconcile their improvements in the arts of war with the mild precepts of the religion which they professed.

My friend, the mandarin, promised he would do all in his power to make the exact truth known to the emperor; and to prevent the evil impressions, which the prejudices of the populace, and perhaps the designing misrepresentations of the city mandarins, might tend to create. I must suppose that the good offices of my Jesuit were ineffectual, and that he either received a positive order to interfere no more in our affairs, or that he was afraid of being implicated in our disgrace if he continued his intimacy with me, for this was the last visit I ever received from him.

CHAPTER II

In a few days the embassy had orders to return to Pekin. The ambassador's palace was fitted up for his winter's residence; and, after our arrival, he was arranging his establishment, when, by a fresh mandate from the emperor, we were required to prepare with all possible expedition for our departure from the Chinese dominions. On Monday we received an order to leave Pekin the ensuing Wednesday; and all our remonstrances could procure only a delay of two days. Various causes were assigned for this peremptory order, and, among the rest, my unlucky accident was mentioned. However improbable it might seem that such a trifle could have had so great an effect, the idea was credited by many of my companions; and I saw that I was looked upon with an evil eye.

I suffered extremely. I have often observed, that even remorse for my past negligence has tended to increase the original defect of my character. During our whole journey from Pekin to Canton, my sorrow for the late accident was an excuse to myself for neglecting to make either notes or observations. When we arrived at Canton, my time was taken up with certain commissions for my friends at home, which I had delayed to execute while at Pekin, from the idea that we should spend the whole winter there. The trunks were on board before all my commissions were ready, and I was obliged to pack up several toys and other articles in a basket. As to my papers, they still remained in the canvass bag into which I had stuffed them at Jehol: but I was certain of having leisure, during our voyage home, to arrange them, and to post my notes into Locke's commonplace-book.

At the beginning of the voyage, however, I suffered much from sea-sickness: toward the middle of the time I grew better, and indulged myself in the amusement of fishing while the weather was fine; when the weather was not inviting, in idleness. Innumerable other petty causes of delay occurred: there was so much eating and drinking, so much singing and laughing, and such frequent card-playing in the cabin, that, though I produced my canvass bag above a hundred times, I never could accomplish sorting its contents: indeed, I seldom proceeded farther than to untie the strings.

One day I had the state cabin fairly to myself, and had really begun my work, when the steward came to let me know that my Chinese basket was just washed overboard. In this basket were all the presents and commissions which I had bought at Canton for my friends at home. I ran to the cabin window, and had the mortification to see all my beautiful scarlet calibash boxes, the fan for my cousin, Lucy, and the variety of toys, which I had bought for my little cousins, all floating on the sea far out of my reach. I had been warned before that the basket would be washed overboard, and had intended to put it into a safe place; but unluckily I delayed to do so.

I was so much vexed with this accident, that I could not go on with my writing: if it had not been for this interruption, I do believe I should that day have accomplished my long postponed task. I will not, indeed I cannot, record all the minute causes which afterwards prevented my executing my intentions. The papers were still in the same disorder, stuffed into the canvass bag, when I arrived in England. I promised myself that I would sort them the very day after I got home; but visits of congratulation from my friends upon my return, induced me to delay doing any thing for the first week. The succeeding week I had a multiplicity of engagements: all my acquaintance, curious to hear a man converse who was fresh from China, invited me to dinner and tea parties; and I could not possibly refuse these kind invitations, and shut myself up in my room, like a hackney author, to write. My father often urged me to begin my quarto; for he knew that other gentlemen, who went out with the embassy, designed to write the history of the voyage; and he, being a bookseller, and used to the ways of authors, foresaw what would happen. A fortnight after we came home, the following advertisement appeared in the papers: "Now in the press, and speedily will be published, a Narrative of the British Embassy to China, containing the various Circumstances of the Embassy; with Accounts of the Customs and Manners of the Chinese; and a Description of the Country, Towns, Cities, &c."

I never saw my poor father turn so pale or look so angry as when he saw this advertisement: he handed it across the breakfast table to me.

"There, Basil," cried he, "I told you what would happen, and you would not believe me. But this is the way you have served me all your life, and this is the way you will go on to the day of your death, putting things off till to-morrow. This is the way you have lost every opportunity of distinguishing yourself; every chance, and you have had many, of advancing yourself in the world! What signifies all I have done for you, or all you can do for yourself? Your genius and education are of no manner of use! Why, there is that heavy dog, as you used to call him at Eton, Johnson: look how he is getting on in the world, by mere dint of application and sticking steadily to his profession. He will beat you at every thing, as he beat you at Eton in writing verses."

"Only in copying them, sir. My verses, every body said, were far better than his; only, unluckily, I had not mine finished and copied out in time." "Well, sir, and that is the very thing I complain of. I suppose you will tell me that your voyage to China will be far better than this which is advertised this morning."

"To be sure it will, father; for I have had opportunities, and collected materials, which this man, whoever he is, cannot possibly have obtained. I have had such assistance, such information from my friend the missionary—"

"But, what signifies your missionary, your information, your abilities, and your materials?" cried my father, raising his voice. "Your book is not out, your book will never be finished; or it will be done too late, and nobody will read it; and then you may throw it into the fire. Here you have an opportunity of establishing your fame, and making yourself a great author at once; and if you throw it away, Basil, I give you fair notice, I never will pardon you."

I promised my father that I would set about my work to-morrow; and pacified him by repeating that this hasty publication, which had just been advertised, must be a catchpenny, and that it would serve only to stimulate instead of satisfying the public curiosity. My quarto, I said, would appear afterwards with a much better grace, and would be sought for by every person of science, taste, and literature.

Soothed by these assurances, my father recovered his good-humour, and trusted to my promise that I would commence my great work the ensuing day. I was fully in earnest. I went to my canvass bag to prepare my materials. Alas! I found them in a terrible condition. The sea-water, somehow or other, had got to them during the voyage; and many of my most precious documents were absolutely illegible. The notes, written in pencil, were almost effaced, and when I had smoothed the crumpled scraps, I could make nothing of them. It was with the utmost difficulty I could read even those that were written in ink; they were so villainously scrawled and so terribly blotted. When I had made out the words, I was often at a loss for the sense; because I had trusted so much to the excellence of my memory, that my notes were never either sufficiently full or accurate. Ideas which I had thought could never be effaced from my mind were now totally forgotten, and I could not comprehend my own mysterious elliptical hints and memorandums. I remember spending two hours in trying to make out what the following words could mean: Hoy—alla—hoya;—hoya, hoya—hoy—waudihoya.

At last, I recollected that they were merely the sounds of the words used by the Chinese sailors, in towing the junks, and I was much provoked at having wasted my time in trying to remember what was not worth recording. Another day I was puzzled by the following memorandum: "W: C: 30. f. h.—24 b.—120 m—1—mandarin—C. tradition—2000—200 before J. C.—" which, after three quarters of an hour's study, I discovered to mean that the wall of China is 30 feet high, 24 feet broad, and 120 miles long; and that a mandarin told me, that, according to Chinese tradition, this wall had been built above 2000 years, that is, 200 before the birth of our Saviour.

On another scrap of paper, at the very bottom of the bag, I found the words, "Wheazou—Chanchin—Cuaboocow—Caungcimmfoa—Callachottueng— Quanshanglin—Callachotre shansu," &c.; all which I found to be a list of towns and villages through which we had passed, or palaces that we had seen; but how to distinguish these asunder I knew not, for all recollection of them was obliterated from my mind, and no farther notes respecting them were to be found.

After many days' tiresome attempts, I was obliged to give up all hopes of deciphering the most important of my notes, those which I had made from the information of the French missionary. Most of what I had trusted so securely to my memory was defective in some slight circumstances, which rendered the whole useless. My materials for my quarto shrunk into a very small compass. I flattered myself, however, that the elegance of my composition, and the moral and political reflections with which I intended to intersperse the work, would compensate for the paucity of facts in my narrative.

That I might devote my whole attention to the business of writing, I determined to leave London, where I met with so many temptations to idleness, and set off to pay a visit to my uncle Lowe, who lived in the country, in a retired part of England. He was a farmer, a plain, sensible, affectionate man; and as he had often invited me to come and see him, I made no doubt that I should be an agreeable guest. I had intended to have written a few lines the week before I set out, to say that I was coming; but I put it off till at last I thought that it would be useless, because I should get there as soon as my letter.

I had soon reason to regret that I had been so negligent; for my appearance at my uncle's, instead of creating that general joy which I had expected, threw the whole house into confusion. It happened that there was company in the house, and all the beds were occupied: while I was taking off my boots, I had the mortification to hear my aunt Lowe say, in a voice of mingled distress and reproach, "Come! is he?— My goodness! What shall we do for a bed?—How could he think of coming without writing a line beforehand? My goodness! I wish he was a hundred miles off, I'm sure."

My uncle shook hands with me, and welcomed me to old England again, and to his house; which, he said, should always be open to all his relations. I saw that he was not pleased; and, as he was a man who, according to the English phrase, scorned to keep a thing long upon his mind, he let me know, before he had finished his first glass of ale to my good health, that he was inclinable to take it very unkind indeed that, after all he had said about my writing a letter now and then, just to say how I did, and how I was going on, I had never put pen to paper to answer one of his letters since the day I first promised to write, which was the day I went to Eton school, till this present time of speaking. I had no good apology to make for myself, but I attempted all manner of excuses; that I had put off writing from day to day, and from year to year, till I was ashamed to write at all; that it was not from want of affection, &c.

My uncle took up his pipe and puffed away, while I spoke: and when I had said all that I could devise, I sat silent; for I saw by the looks of all present that I had not mended the matter. My aunt pursed up her mouth, and "wondered, if she must tell the plain truth, that so great a scholar as Mr. Basil could not, when it must give him so little trouble to indite a letter, write a few lines to an uncle who had begged it so often, and who had ever been a good friend."

"Say nothing of that," said my uncle: "I scorn to have that put into account. I loved the boy, and all I could do was done, of course: that's nothing to the purpose; but the longest day I have to live I'll never trouble him with begging a letter from him no more. For now I see he does not care a fig for me; and of course I do not care a fig for he. Lucy, hold up your head, girl; and don't look as if you were going to be hanged."

My cousin Lucy was the only person present who seemed to have any compassion for me; and, as I lifted up my eyes to look at her when her father spoke, she appeared to me quite beautiful. I had always thought her a pretty girl, but she never struck me as any thing very extraordinary till this moment. I was very sorry that I had offended my uncle: I saw he was seriously displeased, and that his pride, of which he had a large portion, had conquered his affection for me.

"'Tis easier to lose a friend than gain one, young man," said he; "and take my word for it, as this world goes, 'tis a foolish thing to lose a friend for want of writing a letter or so. Here's seven years I have been begging a letter now and then, and could not get one. Never wrote a line to me before you went to China; should not have known a word about it but for my wife, who met you by mere chance in London, and gave you some little commission for the children, which it seems you forgot till it was too late. Then, after you came back, never wrote to me."

"And even not to write a line to give one notice of his coming here to-night," added my aunt.

"Oh, as to that," replied my uncle, "he can never find our larder at a nonplus; we have no dishes for him dressed Chinese fashion; but as to roast beef of old England, which, I take it, is worth all the foreign meats in the world, he is welcome to it, and to as much of it as he pleases. I shall always be glad to see him as a relation and so forth, as a good Christian ought, but not as the favourite he used to be—that is out of the question; for things cannot be both done and undone, and time that's past cannot come back again, that is clear; and cold water thrown on a warm heart puts it out; and there's an end of the matter. Lucy, bring me my nightcap."

Lucy, I think, sighed once; and I am sure I sighed above a dozen times; but my uncle put on his red nightcap, and heeded us not. I was in hopes that the next morning he would have been better disposed towards me after having slept off his anger. The moment that I appeared in the morning, the children, who had been in bed when I arrived the preceding night, crowded round me, and one cried, "Cousin Basil, have you brought me the tumbler you promised me from China?"

"Cousin Basil, where's my boat?"

"O Basil, did you bring me the calibash box that you promised me?"

"And pray," cried my aunt, "did you bring my Lucy the fan that she commissioned you to get?"

"No, I'll warrant," said my uncle. "He that cannot bring himself to write a letter in the course of seven years to his friends, will not be apt to trouble his head about their foolish commissions, when he is in foreign parts."

Though I was abashed and vexed, I summoned sufficient courage to reply that I had not neglected to execute the commissions of any of my friends; but that, by an unlucky accident, the basket into which I had packed all their things was washed overboard.

"Hum!" said my uncle.

"And pray," said my aunt, "why were they all packed in a basket? Why were not they put into your trunks, where they might have been safe?"

I was obliged to confess that I had delayed to purchase them till after we left Pekin; and that the trunks were put on board before they were all procured at Canton. My vile habit of procrastination! How did I suffer for it at this moment! Lucy began to make excuses for me, which made me blame myself the more: she said that, as to her fan, it would have been of little or no use to her; that she was sure she should have broken it before it had been a week in her possession; and that, therefore, she was glad that she had it not. The children were clamorous in their grief for the loss of the boat, the tumbler, and the calibash boxes; but Lucy contrived to quiet them in time, and to make my peace with all the younger part of the family. To reinstate me in my uncle's good graces was impossible; he would only repeat to her—"The young man has lost my good opinion; he will never do any good. From a child upward he has always put off doing every thing he ought to do. He will never do any good; he will never be any thing."

My aunt was not my friend, because she suspected that Lucy liked me; and she thought her daughter might do much better than marry a man who had quitted the profession to which he was bred, and was, as it seemed, little likely to settle to any other. My pretensions to genius and my literary qualifications were of no advantage to me, either with my uncle or my aunt; the one being only a good farmer, and the other only a good housewife. They contented themselves with asking me, coolly, what I had ever made by being an author? And when I was forced to answer nothing, they smiled upon me in scorn. My pride was roused, and I boasted that I expected to receive at least 600l. for my "Voyage to China," which I hoped to complete in a few weeks. My aunt looked at me with astonishment; and, to prove to her that I was not passing the bounds of truth, I added, that one of my travelling companions had, as I was credibly informed, received 1000l. for his narrative, to which mine would certainly be far superior.

"When it is done, and when you have the money in your hand to show us, I shall believe you," said my aunt; "and then, and not till then, you may begin to think of my Lucy."

"He shall never have her," said my uncle; "he will never come to good. He shall never have her."

The time which I ought to have spent in composing my quarto I now wasted in fruitless endeavours to recover the good graces of my uncle. Love, assisted as usual by the spirit of opposition, took possession of my heart; and how can a man in love write quartos? I became more indolent than ever, for I persuaded myself that no exertions could overcome my uncle's prejudice against me; and, without his approbation, I despaired of ever obtaining Lucy's hand.

During my stay at my uncle's, I received several letters from my father, inquiring how my work went on, and urging me to proceed as rapidly as possible, lest another "Voyage to China," which it was reported a gentleman of high reputation was now composing, should come out, and preclude mine for ever. I cannot account for my folly: the power of habit is imperceptible to those who submit passively to its tyranny. From day to day I continued procrastinating and sighing, till at last the fatal news came that Sir George Staunton's History of the Embassy to China, in two volumes quarto, was actually published.

There was an end of all my hopes. I left my uncle's house in despair; I dreaded to see my father. He overwhelmed me with well-merited reproaches. All his expectations of my success in life were disappointed; he was now convinced that I should never make my talents useful to myself or to my family. A settled melancholy appeared in his countenance; he soon ceased to urge me to any exertion, and I idled away my time, deploring that I could not marry my Lucy, and resolving upon a thousand schemes for advancing myself, but always delaying their execution till to-morrow.

CHAPTER III

Two years passed away in this manner, about the end of which time my poor father died. I cannot describe the mixed sensations of grief and self-reproach which I felt at his death. I knew that I had never fulfilled his sanguine prophecies, and that disappointment had long preyed upon his spirits. This was a severe shock to me: I was roused from a state of stupefaction by the necessity of acting as my father's executor.

Among his bequests was one which touched me particularly, because I was sensible that it was made from kindness to me. "I give and bequeath the full-length picture of my son Basil, taken when a boy (a very promising boy) at Eton school, to my brother Lowe—I should say to my sweet niece, Lucy Lowe, but am afraid of giving offence."

I sent the picture to my uncle Lowe, with a copy of the words of the will, and a letter written in the bitterness of grief. My uncle, who was of an affectionate though positive temper, returned me the following answer:

"DEAR NEPHEW BASIL,

"Taking it for granted you feel as much as I do, it being natural you should, and even more, I shall not refuse to let my Lucy have the picture bequeathed to me by my good brother, who could not offend me dying, never having done so living. As to you, Basil, this is no time for reproaches, which would be cruel; but, without meaning to look back to the past, I must add that I mean nothing by giving the picture to Lucy but respect for my poor brother's memory. My opinions remaining as heretofore, I think it a duty to my girl to be steady in my determination; convinced that no man (not meaning you in particular) of what I call a putting off temper could make her happy, she being too mild to scold and bustle, and do the man's business in a family. This is the whole of my mind without malice; for how could I, if I were malicious, which I am not, bear malice, and at such a time as this, against my own nephew? and as to anger, that is soon over with me; and though I said I never would forgive you, Basil, for not writing to me for seven years, I do now forgive you with all my heart. So let that be off your conscience. And now I hope we shall be very good friends all the rest of our lives; that is to say, putting Lucy out of the question; for, in my opinion, it is a disagreeable thing to have any bickerings between near relations. So, my dear nephew, wishing you all health and happiness, I hope you will now settle to business. My wife tells me she hears you are left in a good way by my poor brother's care and industry; and she sends her love to you, in which all the family unite; and hoping you will write from time to time, I remain, "My dear nephew Basil, "Your affectionate uncle,

"THOMAS LOWE."

My aunt Lowe added a postscript, inquiring more particularly into the state of my affairs. I answered, by return of post, that my good father had left me much richer than I either expected or deserved: his credit in the booksellers' line was extensive and well established; his shop was well furnished, and he had a considerable sum of money in bank; beside many good debts due from authors, to whom he had advanced cash.

My aunt Lowe was governed by her interest, as decidedly as my uncle was swayed by his humour and affection; and, of course, became more favourable toward me, when she found that my fortune was better than she had expected. She wrote to exhort me to attend to my business, and to prove to my uncle that I could cure myself of my negligent habits. She promised to befriend me, and to do every thing to obtain my uncle's consent to my union with Lucy, upon condition that I would for six months steadily persevere, or, as she expressed herself, show that I could come to good.

The motive was powerful, sufficiently powerful to conquer the force of inveterate habit. I applied resolutely to business, and supported the credit which my father's punctuality had obtained from his customers. During the course of six entire months, I am not conscious of having neglected or delayed to do anything of consequence that I ought to have done except whetting my razor. My aunt Lowe faithfully kept her word with me, and took every opportunity of representing, in the most favourable manner to my uncle, the reformation that love had wrought in my character.

I went to the country, full of hope, at the end of my six probationary months. My uncle, however, with a mixture of obstinacy and good sense, replied to my aunt in my presence: "This reformation that you talk of, wife, won't last. 'Twas begun by love, as you say; and will end with love, as I say. You and I know, my dear, love lasts little longer than the honeymoon; and Lucy is not, or ought not to be, such a simpleton as to look only to what a husband will be for one short month of his life, when she is to live with him for twenty, thirty, may be forty long years; and no help for it, let him turn out what he will. I beg your pardon, nephew Basil; but where my Lucy's happiness is at stake, I must speak my mind as a father should. My opinion, Lucy, is, that he is not a whit changed; and so I now let you understand, if you marry the man, it must be without my consent."

Lucy turned exceedingly pale, and I grew extremely angry. My uncle had, as usual, recourse to his pipe; and to all the eloquence which love and indignation could inspire, he would only answer; between the whiffs of his smoking, "If my girl marries you, nephew Basil, I say she must do so without my consent."

Lucy's affection for me struggled for some time with her sense of duty to her father; her mother supported my cause with much warmth; having once declared in my favour, she considered herself as bound to maintain her side of the question. It became a trial of power between my uncle and aunt; and their passions rose so high in the conflict, that Lucy trembled for the consequences.

One day she took an opportunity of speaking to me in private. "My dear Basil," said she, "we must part. You see that I can never be yours with my father's consent; and without it I could never be happy, even in being united to you. I will not be the cause of misery to all those whom I love best in the world. I will not set my father and mother at variance. I cannot bear to hear the altercations, which rise higher and higher between them every day. Let us part, and all will be right again."

It was in vain that I combated her resolution: I alternately resented and deplored the weakness which induced Lucy to sacrifice her own happiness and mine to the obstinate prejudices of a father; yet I could not avoid respecting her the more for her adhering to what she believed to be her duty. The sweetness of temper, gentleness of disposition, and filial piety, which she showed on this trying occasion, endeared her to me beyond expression.

Her father, notwithstanding his determination to be as immoveable as a rock, began to manifest symptoms of internal agitation; and one night, after breaking his pipe, and throwing down the tongs and poker twice, which Lucy twice replaced, he exclaimed, "Lucy, girl, you are a fool! and, what is worse, you are grown into a mere shadow. You are breaking my heart Why, I know this man, this Basil, this cursed nephew of mine, will never come to good. But cannot you marry him without my consent?"

Upon this hint, Lucy's scruples vanished; and, a few days afterward, we were married. Prudence, virtue, pride, love, every strong motive which can act upon the human mind, stimulated me to exert myself to prove that I was worthy of this most amiable woman. A year passed away, and my Lucy said that she had no reason to repent of her choice. She took the most affectionate pains to convince her father that she was perfectly happy, and that he had judged of me too harshly. His delight at seeing his daughter happy, vanquished his reluctance to acknowledge that he had changed his opinion. I never shall forget the pleasure I felt at hearing him confess that he had been too positive, and that his Lucy had made a good match for herself.

Alas! when I had obtained this testimony in my favour, when I had established a character for exertion and punctuality, I began to relax in my efforts to deserve it: I indulged myself in my old habits of procrastination. My customers and country correspondents began to complain that their letters were unanswered, and that their orders were neglected. Their remonstrances became more and more urgent in process of time, and nothing but actually seeing the dates of their letters could convince me that they were in the right, and that I was in the wrong. An old friend of my father's, a rich gentleman, who loved books, and bought all that were worth buying, sent me, in March, an order for books to a considerable amount. In April, he wrote to remind me of his first letter.

April 3.

"MY DEAR SIR,

"Last month I wrote to request that you would send me the following books:—I have been much disappointed by not receiving them; and I request you will be so good as to forward them immediately.

"I am, my dear sir,
"Yours sincerely,
"J. C."

In May he wrote to me again:

"DEAR SIR,

"I am much surprised at not having yet received the books I wrote for last March—beg to know the cause of this delay; and am,

"Dear sir,
"Yours, &c.
"J. C."

A fortnight afterward, as I was packing up the books for this gentleman, I received the following:

"SIR,

"As it is now above a quarter of a year since I wrote to you for books, which you have not yet sent to me, I have been obliged to apply to another bookseller.

"I am much concerned at being compelled to this: I had a great regard for your father, and would not willingly break off my connexion with his son; but really you have tried my patience too far. Last year I never had from you any one new publication, until it was in the hands of all my neighbours; and I have often been under the necessity of borrowing books which I had bespoken from you months before. I hope you will take this as a warning, and that you will not use any of your other friends as you have used,

"Sir,
"Your humble servant,
"J. C."

This reprimand had little effect upon me, because, at the time when I received it, I was intent upon an object, in comparison with which the trade of a bookseller appeared absolutely below my consideration. I was inventing a set of new taxes for the minister, for which I expected to be liberally rewarded. I was ever searching for some short cut to the temple of Fame, instead of following the beaten road.

I was much encouraged by persons intimately connected with those high in power to hope that my new taxes would be adopted; and I spent my time in attendance upon my patrons, leaving the care of my business to my foreman, a young man whose head the whole week was intent upon riding out on Sunday. With such a master and such a foreman affairs could not go on well.

My Lucy, notwithstanding her great respect for my abilities, and her confidence in my promises, often hinted that she feared ministers might not at last make me amends for the time I devoted to my system of taxation; but I persisted. The file of unanswered letters was filled even to the top of the wire; the drawer of unsettled accounts made me sigh profoundly, whenever it was accidentally opened. I soon acquired a horror of business, and practised all the arts of apology, evasion, and invisibility, to which procrastinators must sooner or later be reduced. My conscience gradually became callous; and I could, without compunction, promise, with a face of truth, to settle an account to-morrow, without having the slightest hope of keeping my word.

I was a publisher as well as a bookseller, and was assailed by a tribe of rich and poor authors. The rich complained continually of delays that affected their fame; the poor of delays that concerned their interest, and sometimes their very existence. I was cursed with a compassionate as well as with a procrastinating temper; and I frequently advanced money to my poor authors, to compensate for my neglect to settle their accounts, and to free myself from the torment of their reproaches.

They soon learned to take a double advantage of my virtues and my vices. The list of my poor authors increased, for I was an encourager of genius. I trusted to my own judgment concerning every performance that was offered to me; and I was often obliged to pay for having neglected to read, or to send to press, these multifarious manuscripts. After having kept a poor devil of an author upon the tenterhooks of expectation for an unconscionable time, I could not say to him, "Sir, I have never opened your manuscript; there it is, in that heap of rubbish: take it away, for Heaven's sake." No, hardened as I was, I never failed to make some compliment, or some retribution; and my compliments were often in the end the most expensive species of retribution.

My rich authors soon deserted me, and hurt my credit in the circles of literary fashion by their clamours. I had ample experience, yet I have never been able to decide whether I would rather meet the "desperate misery" of a famishing pamphleteer, or the exasperated vanity of a rich amateur. Every one of my authors seemed convinced that the fate of Europe or the salvation of the world depended upon the publication of their book on some particular day; while I all the time was equally persuaded that their works were mere trash, in comparison with my new system of taxation; consequently I postponed their business, and pursued my favourite tax scheme.

I have the pride and pleasure to say that all my taxes were approved and adopted, and brought in an immense increase of revenue to the state; but I have the mortification to be obliged to add, that I never, directly or indirectly, received the slightest pecuniary reward; and the credit of all I had proposed was snatched from me by a rogue, who had no other merit than that of being shaved sooner than I was one frosty morning. If I had not put off whetting my razor the preceding day, this would not have happened.

To such a trifling instance of my unfortunate habit of procrastination, must I attribute one of the most severe disappointments of my life. A rival financier, who laid claim to the prior invention and suggestion of my principal taxes, was appointed to meet me at the house of my great man at ten o'clock in the morning. My opponent was punctual; I was half an hour too late: his claims were established; mine were rejected, because I was not present to produce my proofs. When I arrived at my patron's, the insolent porter shut the door in my face; and so ended all hopes from my grand system of taxation.

I went home and shut myself up in my room, to give vent to my grief at leisure; but I was not permitted to indulge my sorrow long in peace. I was summoned by my foreman to come down stairs to one of my enraged authors, who positively refused to quit the shop without seeing me. Of the whole irritable race, the man who was now waiting to see me was the most violent. He was a man of some genius and learning, with great pretensions, and a vindictive spirit. He was poor, yet lived among the rich; and his arrogance could be equalled only by his susceptibility. He was known in our house by the name of Thaumaturgos, the retailer of wonders, because he had sent me a manuscript with this title; and once or twice a week we received a letter or message from him, to inquire when it would be published. I had unfortunately mislaid this precious manuscript. Under this circumstance, to meet the author was almost as dreadful as to stand the shot of a pistol. Down stairs I went, unprovided with any apology.

"Sir," cried my angry man, suppressing his passion, "as you do not find it worth your while to publish Thaumaturges, you will be so obliging as to let me have my manuscript."

"Pardon me, my dear sir," interrupted I; "it shall certainly appear this spring." "Spring! Zounds, sir, don't talk to me of spring. Why, you told me it should be out at Christmas; you said it should be out last June; you promised to send it to press before last Easter. Is this the way I am to be treated?"

"Pardon me, my dear sir. I confess I have used you and the world very ill; but the pressure of business must plead my apology."

"Look you, Mr. Basil Lowe, I am not come here to listen to commonplace excuses. I have been ill used, and know it; and the world shall know it. I am not ignorant of the designs of my enemies; but no cabal shall succeed against me. Thaumaturgos shall not be suppressed! Thaumaturgos shall see the light! Thaumaturgos shall have justice, in spite of all the machinations of malice. Sir, I demand my manuscript."

"Sir, it shall be sent to you to-morrow."

"To-morrow, sir, will not do for me. I have heard of to-morrow from you this twelvemonth past. I will have my manuscript to-day. I do not leave this spot without Thaumaturgos."

Thus driven to extremities, I was compelled to confess that I could not immediately lay my hand upon it; but I added that the whole house should be searched for it instantly. It is impossible to describe the indignation which my author expressed. I ran away to search the house. He followed me, and stood by while I rummaged in drawers and boxes full of papers, and tossed over heaps of manuscripts. No Thaumaturges could be found. The author declared that he had no copy of the manuscript; that he had been offered 500l. for it by another bookseller; and that, for his own part, he would not lose it for twice that sum. Lost, however, it evidently was. He stalked out of my house, bidding me prepare to abide by the consequences. I racked my memory in vain, to discover what I had done with this bundle of wonders. I could recollect only that I carried it a week in my great-coat pocket, resolving every day to lock it up; and that I went to the Mount Coffee-house in this coat several times. These recollections were of little use.

A suit was instituted against me for the value of Thaumaturgos; and the damages were modestly laid by the author at eight hundred guineas. The cause was highly interesting to all the tribe of London booksellers and authors. The court was crowded at an early hour; several people of fashion, who were partisans of the plaintiff, appeared in the gallery; many more, who were his enemies, attended on purpose to hear my counsel ridicule and abuse the pompous Thaumaturgos. I had great hopes, myself, that we might win the day, especially as the lawyer on the opposite side was my old competitor at Eton, that Johnson, whom I had always considered as a mere laborious drudge, and a very heavy fellow. How this heavy fellow got up in the world, and how he contrived to supply, by dint of study, the want of natural talents, I cannot tell; but this I know, to my cost, that he managed his client's cause so ably, and made a speech so full of sound law and clear sense, as effectually to decide the cause against me. I was condemned to pay 500l. damages, and costs of suit. Five hundred pounds lost, by delaying to lock up a bundle of papers! Every body pitied me, because the punishment seemed so disproportioned to the offence. The pity of every body, however, did not console me for the loss of my money.

CHAPTER IV

The trial was published in the papers: my uncle Lowe read it, and all my credit with him was lost for ever. Lucy did not utter a syllable of reproach or complaint; but she used all her gentle influence to prevail upon me to lay aside the various schemes which I had formed for making a rapid fortune, and urged me to devote my whole attention to my business.

The loss which I had sustained, though great, was not irremediable. I was moved more by my wife's kindness than I could have been by the most outrageous invective. But what is kindness, what is affection, what are the best resolutions, opposed to all-powerful habit? I put off settling my affairs till I had finished a pamphlet against government, which my friends and the critics assured me would make my fortune, by attaching to my shop all the opposition members.

My pamphlet succeeded, was highly praised, and loudly abused: answers appeared, and I was called upon to provide rejoinders. Time thus passed away, and while I was gaining fame, I every hour lost money. I was threatened with bankruptcy. I threw aside my pamphlets, and in the utmost terror and confusion, began, too late, to look into my affairs. I now attempted too much: I expected to repair by bustle the effects of procrastination. The nervous anxiety of my mind prevented me from doing any thing well; whatever I was employed about appeared to me of less consequence than a hundred other things which ought to be done. The letter that I was writing, or the account that I was settling, was but one of a multitude, which had all equal claims to be expedited immediately. My courage failed; I abandoned my business in despair. A commission of bankruptcy was taken out against me; all my goods were seized, and I became a prisoner in the King's Bench.

My wife's relations refused to give me any assistance; but her father offered to receive her and her little boy, on condition that she would part from me, and spend the remainder of her days with them. This she positively refused; and I never shall forget the manner of her refusal. Her character rose in adversity. With the utmost feminine gentleness and delicacy, she had a degree of courage and fortitude which I have seldom seen equalled in any of my own sex. She followed me to prison, and supported my spirits by a thousand daily instances of kindness. During eighteen months that she passed with me in a prison, which we then thought must be my abode for life, she never, by word or look, reminded me that I was the cause of our misfortunes: on the contrary, she drove this idea from my thoughts with all the address of female affection. I cannot even, at this distance of time, recall these things to memory without tears.

What a woman, what a wife had I reduced to distress! I never saw her, even in the first months of our marriage, so cheerful and so tender as at this period. She seemed to have no existence but in me and in our little boy, of whom she was dotingly fond. He was at this time just able to run about and talk; his playful caresses, his thoughtless gaiety, and at times a certain tone of compassion for poor papa, were very touching. Alas! he little foresaw.... But let me go on with my history, if I can, without anticipation.

Among my creditors was a Mr. Nun, a paper-maker, who, from his frequent dealings with me, had occasion to see something of my character and of my wife's; he admired her, and pitied me. He was in easy circumstances, and delighted in doing all the good in his power. One morning my Lucy came into my room with a face radiant with joy.

"My love," said she, "here is Mr. Nun below, waiting to see you; but he says he will not see you till I have told you the good news. He has got all our creditors to enter into a compromise, and to set you at liberty."

I was transported with joy and gratitude; our benevolent friend was waiting in a hackney-coach to carry us away from prison. When I began to thank him, he stopped me with a blunt declaration that I was not a bit obliged to him; for that, if I had been a man of straw, he would have done just the same for the sake of my wife, whom he looked upon to be one or other the best woman he had ever seen, Mrs. Nun always excepted.

He proceeded to inform me how he had settled my affairs, and how he had obtained from my creditors a small allowance for the immediate support of myself and family. He had given up the third part of a considerable sum due to himself. As my own house was shut up, he insisted upon taking us home with him: "Mrs. Nun," he said, "had provided a good dinner; and he must not have her ducks and green peas upon the table, and no friends to eat them."

Never were ducks and green peas more acceptable; never was a dinner eaten with more appetite, or given with more good-will. I have often thought of this dinner, and compared the hospitality of this simple-hearted man with the ostentation of great folks, who give splendid entertainments to those who do not want them. In trifles and in matters of consequence this Mr. Nun was one of the most liberal and unaffectedly generous men I ever knew; but the generous actions of men in middle life are lost in obscurity. No matter: they do not act from a love of fame; they act from a better motive, and they have their reward in their own hearts.

As I was passing through Mr. Nun's warehouse, I was thinking of writing something on this subject; but whether it should be a poetic effusion, in the form of "An Ode to him who least expects it," or a prose work, under the title of "Modern Parallels," in the manner of Plutarch, I had not decided, when I was roused from my reverie by my wife, who, pointing to a large bale of paper that was directed to "Ezekiel Croft, merchant, Philadelphia," asked me if I knew that this gentleman was a very near relation of her mother? "Is he, indeed?" said Mr. Nun. "Then I can assure you that you have a relation of whom you have no occasion to be ashamed: he is one of the most respectable merchants in Philadelphia."

"He was not very rich when he left this country about six years ago," said Lucy.

"He has a very good fortune now," answered Mr. Nun.

"And has he made this very good fortune in six years?" cried I. "My dear Lucy, I did not know that you had any relations in America. I have a great mind to go over there myself."

"Away from all our friends!" said Lucy.

"I shall be ashamed," replied I, "to see them after all that has happened. A bankrupt cannot have many friends. The best thing that I can possibly do is to go over to a new world, where I may establish a new character, and make a new fortune."

"But we must not forget," said Mr. Nun, "that in the new world, as in the old one, a character and a fortune must be made by much the same means; and forgive me if I add, the same bad habits that are against a man in one country will be as much against him in another."

True, thought I, as I recollected at this instant my unfortunate voyage to China. But now that the idea of going to America had come into my mind, I saw so many chances of success in my favour, and I felt so much convinced I should not relapse into my former faults, that I could not abandon the scheme. My Lucy consented to accompany me. She spent a week in the country with her father and friends, by my particular desire; and they did all they could to prevail upon her to stay with them, promising to take the best possible care of her and her little boy during my absence; but she steadily persisted in her determination to accompany her husband. I was not too late in going on ship-board this time; and, during the whole voyage, I did not lose any of my goods; for, in the first place, I had very few goods to lose, and, in the next, my wife took the entire charge of those few.

And now behold me safely landed at Philadelphia, with one hundred pounds in my pocket—a small sum of money; but many, from yet more trifling beginnings, had grown rich in America. My wife's relation, Mr. Croft, had not so much, as I was told, when he left England. Many passengers, who came over in the same ship with me, had not half so much. Several of them were, indeed, wretchedly poor.

Among others, there was an Irishman who was known by the name of Barny, a contraction, I believe, for Barnaby. As to his surname he could not undertake to spell it; but he assured me there was no better. This man, with many of his relatives, had come to England, according to their custom, during harvest-time, to assist in reaping, because they gain higher wages than in their own country. Barny heard that he should get still higher wages for labour in America, and accordingly he and his two sons, lads of eighteen and twenty, took their passage for Philadelphia. A merrier mortal I never saw. We used to hear him upon deck, continually singing or whistling his Irish tunes; and I should never have guessed that this man's life had been a series of hardships and misfortunes.

When we were leaving the ship, I saw him, to my great surprise, crying bitterly; and upon inquiring what was the matter, he answered that it was not for himself, but for his sons, he was grieving, because they were to be made redemption-men, that is, they were to be bound to work, during a certain time, for the captain, or for whomever he pleased, till the money due for their passage should be paid. Though I was somewhat surprised at any one's thinking of coming on board a vessel without having one farthing in his pocket, yet I could not forbear paying the money for this poor fellow. He dropped down on the deck upon both his knees as suddenly as if he had been shot, and, holding up his hands to heaven, prayed, first in Irish, and then in English, with fervent fluency, that "I and mine might never want; that I might live long to reign over him; that success might attend my honour wherever I went; and that I might enjoy for evermore all sorts of blessings and crowns of glory."

As I had an English prejudice in favour of silent gratitude, I was rather disgusted by all this eloquence; I turned away abruptly, and got into the boat which waited to carry me to shore.

As we rowed away I looked at my wife and child, and reproached myself with having indulged in the luxury of generosity, perhaps at their expense.

My wife's relation, Mr. Croft, received us better than she expected, and worse than I hoped. He had the face of an acute money-making man; his manners were methodical; caution was in his eye, and prudence in all his motions. In our first half hour's conversation he convinced me that he deserved the character he had obtained, of being upright and exact in all his dealings. His ideas were just and clear, but confined to the objects immediately relating to his business; as to his heart, he seemed to have no notion of general philanthropy, but to have perfectly learned by rote his duty to his neighbour. He appeared disposed to do charitable and good-natured actions from reason, and not from feeling; because they were proper, not merely because they were agreeable. I felt that I should respect, but never love him; and that he would never either love or respect me, because the virtue which he held in the highest veneration was that in which I was most deficient—punctuality. But I will give, as nearly as I can, my first conversation with him; and from that a better idea of his character may be formed than I can afford by any description.

I presented to him Mr. Nun's letter of introduction, and mentioned that my wife had the honour of being related to him. He perused Mr. Nun's letter very slowly. I was determined not to leave him in any doubt, respecting who and what I was; and I briefly told him the particulars of my history. He listened with immoveable attention: and when I had finished, he said, "You have not yet told me what your views are in coming to America."

I replied, "that my plans were not yet fixed."

"But of course," said he, "you cannot have left home without forming some plan for the future. May I ask what line of life you mean to pursue?"

I answered, "that I was undetermined, and meant to be guided by circumstances."

"Circumstances!" said he. "May I request you to explain yourself more fully? for I do not precisely understand to what circumstances you allude."

I was provoked with the man for being so slow of apprehension; but, when driven to the necessity of explaining, I found that I did not myself understand what I meant.

I changed my ground; and, lowering my tone of confidence, said, that as I was totally ignorant of the country, I should wish to be guided by the advice of better informed persons; and that I begged leave to address myself to him, as having had the most successful experience.

After a considerable pause, he replied, it was a hazardous thing to give advice; but that, as my wife was his relation, and as he held it a duty to assist his relations, he should not decline giving me—all the advice in his power.

I bowed, and felt chilled all over by his manner.

"And not only my advice," continued he, "but my assistance—in reason."

I said, "I was much obliged to him."

"Not in the least, young man; you are not in the least obliged to me yet, for I have done nothing for you."

This was true, and not knowing what to say, I was silent.

"And that which I may be able to do for you in future must depend as much upon yourself as upon me. In the first place, before I can give any advice, I must know what you are worth in the world?"

My worth in money, I told him, with a forced smile, was but very trifling indeed. With some hesitation, I named the sum.

"And you have a wife and child to support!" said he, shaking his head. "And your child is too young and your wife too delicate to work. They will be sad burdens upon your hands; these are not the things for America. Why did you bring them with you? But, as that is done, and cannot be mended," continued he, "we must make the best of it, and support them. You say you are ignorant of the country. I must explain to you then how money is to be made here, and by whom. The class of labourers make money readily, if they are industrious, because they have high wages and constant employment; artificers and mechanics, carpenters, shipwrights, wheelwrights, smiths, brick-layers, masons, get rich here, without difficulty, from the same causes; but all these things are out of the question for you. You have head, not hands, I perceive. Now mere head, in the line of bookmaking or bookselling, brings in but poor profit in this country. The sale for imported books is extensive; and our printers are doing something by subscription here, in Philadelphia, and in New York, they tell me. But London is the place for a good bookseller to thrive; and you come from London, where you tell me you were a bankrupt. I would not advise you to have any thing more to do with bookselling or bookmaking. Then, as to becoming a planter: our planters, if they are skilful and laborious, thrive well; but you have not capital sufficient to clear land and build a house; or hire servants to do the work, for which you are not yourself sufficiently robust. Besides, I do not imagine you know much of agricultural concerns, or country business; and even to oversee and guide others, experience is necessary. The life of a back settler I do not advise, because you and your wife are not equal to it. You are not accustomed to live in a log-house, or to feed upon racoons and squirrels: not to omit the constant dread, if not imminent danger, of being burnt in your beds, or scalped, by the Indians with whom you would be surrounded. Upon the whole, I see no line of life that promises well for you but that of a merchant; and I see no means of your getting into this line without property and without credit, except by going into some established house as a clerk. You are a good penman, and ready accountant, I think you tell me; and I presume you have a sufficient knowledge of book-keeping. With sobriety, diligence, and honesty, you may do well in this way; and may look forward to being a partner, and in a lucrative situation, some years hence. This is the way I managed, and I raised myself by degrees to what you see. It is true, I was not at first encumbered with a wife and young child. In due time I married my master's daughter, which was a great furtherance to me; but then, on the other hand, your wife is my relation; and to be married to the relation of a rich merchant is next best to not being married at all in your situation. I told you I thought it my duty to proffer assistance as well as advice: so take up your abode with me for a fortnight; in that time I shall be able to judge whether you are capable of being a clerk; and, if you and I should suit, we will talk farther. You understand that I enter into no engagement, and make no promise; but shall be glad to lodge you, and your wife, and little boy, for a fortnight; and it will be your own fault, and must be your own loss, if the visit turns out waste of time.—I cannot stay to talk to you any longer at present," added he, pulling out his watch, "for I have business, and business waits for no man. Go back to your inn for my relation, and her little one. We dine at two precisely."

I left Mr. Croft's house with a vague indescribable feeling of dissatisfaction and disappointment; but when I arrived at my inn, and repeated all that had passed to my wife, she seemed quite surprised and delighted by the civil and friendly manner in which this gentleman had behaved. She tried to reason the matter with me; but there is no reasoning with imagination.

The fact was, Mr. Croft had destroyed certain vague and visionary ideas, that I had indulged, of making, by some unknown means, a rapid fortune in America; and to be reduced to real life, and sink into a clerk in a merchant's counting-house, was mortification and misery. Lucy in vain dwelt upon the advantage of having found, immediately upon my arrival in Philadelphia, a certain mode of employment, and a probability of rising to be a partner in one of the first mercantile houses, if I went on steadily for a few years. I was forced to acknowledge that her relation was very good; that I was certainly very fortunate; and that I ought to think myself very much obliged to Mr. Croft. But, after avowing all this, I walked up and down the room in melancholy reverie for a considerable length of time. My wife reminded me repeatedly that Mr. Croft said he dined precisely at two o'clock; that he was a very punctual man; that it was a long walk, as I had found it, from the inn to his house; that I had better dress myself for dinner; and that my clean shirt and cravat were ready for me. I still walked up and down the room in reverie till my wife was completely ready, had dressed the child, and held up my watch before my eyes to show me that it wanted but ten minutes of two. I then began to dress in the greatest hurry imaginable: and, unluckily, as I was pulling on my silk stocking, I tore a hole in the leg, or as my wife expressed it, a stitch dropped, and I was forced to wait while she repaired the evil. Certainly this operation of taking up a stitch, as I am instructed to call it, is one of the slowest operations in nature; or, rather, one of the most tedious and teazing manoeuvres of art. Though the most willing and the most dexterous fingers that ever touched a needle were employed in my service, I thought the work would never be finished.

At last, I was hosed and shod, and out we set. It struck a quarter past two as we left the house; we came to Mr. Croft's in the middle of dinner. He had a large company at table; every body was disturbed; my Lucy was a stranger to Mrs. Croft, and was to be introduced; and nothing could be more awkward and embarrassing than our entrée and introduction. There were such compliments and apologies, such changing of places, such shuffling of chairs, and running about of servants, that I thought we should never be seated.

In the midst of the bustle my little chap began to roar most horribly, and to struggle to get away from a black servant, who was helping him up on his chair. The child's terror at the sudden approach of the negro could not be conquered, nor could he by any means be quieted. Mrs, Croft, at last, ordered the negro out of the room, the roaring ceased, and nothing but the child's sobs were heard for some instants.

The guests were all silent, and had ceased eating; Mrs. Croft was vexed because every thing was cold; Mr. Croft was much discomfited, and said not a syllable more than was absolutely necessary, as master of the house. I never ate, or rather I was never at a more disagreeable dinner. I was in pain for Lucy, as well as for myself; her colour rose up to her temples. I cursed myself a hundred times for not having gone to dress in time.

At length, to my great relief, the cloth was taken away; but even when we came to the wine after dinner, the cold formality of my host continued unabated, and I began to fear that he had taken an insurmountable dislike to me, and that I should lose all the advantages of his protection and assistance: advantages which rose considerably in my estimation, when I apprehended I was upon the point of losing them.

Soon after dinner, a young gentleman of the name of Hudson joined the company; his manners and appearance were prepossessing; he was frank and well-bred; and the effect of his politeness was soon felt, as if by magic, for every body became at their ease; his countenance was full of life and fire; and though he said nothing that showed remarkable abilities, everything he said pleased. As soon as he found that I was a stranger, he addressed his conversation principally to me. I recovered my spirits, exerted myself to entertain him, and succeeded. He was delighted to hear news from England, and especially from London; a city which he said he had an ardent desire to visit. When he took leave of me in the evening, he expressed very warmly the wish to cultivate my acquaintance, and I was the more flattered and obliged by this civility, because I was certain that he knew exactly my situation and circumstances, Mrs. Croft having explained them to him very fully even in my hearing.

CHAPTER V

In the course of the ensuing week, young Mr. Hudson and I saw one another almost every day, and our mutual liking for each other's company increased. He introduced me to his father, who had been a planter; and, having made a large fortune, came to reside at Philadelphia, to enjoy himself, as he said, for the remainder of his days. He lived in what the sober Americans called a most luxurious and magnificent style. The best company in Philadelphia met at his house: and he delighted particularly in seeing those who had convivial talents, and who would supply him with wit and gaiety, in which he was naturally rather deficient.

On my first visit, I perceived that his son had boasted of me as one of the best companions in the world; and I determined to support the character that had been given of me; I told two or three good stories, and sang two or three good songs. The company were charmed with me; old Mr. Hudson was particularly delighted; he gave me a pressing general invitation to his house, and most of the principal guests followed his example. I was not a little elated with this success. Mr. Croft was with me at this entertainment; and I own I was peculiarly gratified by feeling that I at once became conspicuous, by my talents, in a company where he was apparently of no consequence, notwithstanding all his wealth and prudence.

As we went home together, he said to me very gravely, "I would not advise you, Mr. Basil Lowe, to accept of all these invitations, nor to connect yourself intimately with young Hudson. The society at Mr. Hudson's is very well for those who have made a fortune, and want to spend it; but for those who have a fortune to make, in my opinion, it is not only useless but dangerous."

I was in no humour, at this moment, to profit by this sober advice; especially as I fancied it might be dictated, in some degree, by envy of my superior talents and accomplishments. My wife, however, supported his advice by many excellent and kind arguments. She observed that these people, who invited me to their houses as a good companion, followed merely their own pleasure, and would never be of any real advantage to me; that Mr. Croft, on the contrary, showed, from the first hour when I applied to him, a desire to serve me; that he had pointed out the means of establishing myself; and that, in the advice he gave me, he could be actuated only by a wish to be of use to me; that it was more reasonable to suspect him of despising than of envying talents which were not directed to the grand object of gaining money.

Good sense, from the lips of a woman whom a man loves, has a mighty effect upon his understanding, especially if he sincerely believe that the woman has no desire to rule. This was my singular case. I promised Lucy I would refuse all invitations for the ensuing fortnight, and devote myself to whatever business Mr. Croft might devise. No one could be more assiduous than I was for ten days; and I perceived that Mr. Croft, though it was not his custom to praise, was well satisfied with my diligence. Unluckily, on the eleventh day I put off in the morning making out an invoice, which he left for me to do, and I was persuaded in the evening to go out with young Mr. Hudson. I had expressed, in conversation with him, some curiosity about the American frog-concerts, of which I had read, in modern books of travels, extraordinary accounts.

Mr. Hudson persuaded me to accompany him to a swamp, at some miles' distance from Philadelphia, to hear one of these concerts. The performance lasted some time, and it was late before we returned to town: I went to bed tired, and waked in the morning with a cold, which I had caught by standing so long in the swamp. I lay an hour after I was called, in hopes of getting rid of my cold: when I was at last up and dressed, I recollected my invoice, and resolved to do it the first thing after breakfast; but, unluckily, I put it off till I had looked for some lines in Homer's "Battle of the Frogs and Mice." There was no Homer, as you may guess, in Mr. Croft's house, and I went to a bookseller's to borrow one: he had Pope's Iliad and Odyssey, but no Battle of the Frogs and Mice. I walked over half the town in search of it; at length I found it, and was returning in triumph, with Homer in each pocket, when at the door of Mr. Croft's house I found half a dozen porters, with heavy loads upon their backs.

"Where are you going, my good fellows?" said I.

"To the quay, sir, with the cargo for the Betsy."

"My God!" cried I. "Stop. Can't you stop a minute? I thought the Betsy was not to sail till to-morrow. Stop one minute."

"No, sir," said they, "that we can't; for the captain bade us make what haste we could to the quay to load her."

I ran into the house; the captain of the Betsy was bawling in the hall, with his hat on the back of his head; Mr. Croft on the landing-place of the warehouse-stairs with open letters in his hand, and two or three of the under-clerks were running different ways with pens in their mouths.

"Mr. Basil! the invoice!" exclaimed all the clerks at once, the moment I made my appearance.

"Mr. Basil Lowe, the invoice and the copy, if you please," repeated Mr. Croft. "We have sent three messengers after you. Very extraordinary to go out at this time of day, and not even to leave word where you were to be found. Here's the captain of the Betsy has been waiting this half hour for the invoice. Well, sir! Will you go for it now? And at the same time bring me the copy, to enclose in this letter to our correspondent by post."

I stood petrified. "Sir, the invoice, sir!—Good Heavens! I forgot it entirely."

"You remember it now, sir, I suppose. Keep your apologies till we have leisure. The invoices, if you please."

"The invoices! My God, sir! I beg ten thousand pardons! They are not drawn out."

"Not drawn out. Impossible!" said Mr. Croft.

"Then I'm off," cried the captain, with a tremendous oath. "I can't wait another tide for any clerk breathing."

"Send back the porters, captain, if you please," said Mr, Croft, coolly. "The whole cargo must be unpacked. I took it for granted, Mr. Basil, that you had drawn the invoice, according to order, yesterday morning; and of course the goods were packed in the evening. I was certainly wrong in taking it for granted that you would be punctual. A man of business should take nothing for granted. This is a thing that will not occur to me again as long as I live."

I poured forth expressions of contrition; but apparently unmoved by them, and without anger or impatience in his manner, he turned from me as soon as the porters came back with the goods, and ordered them all to be unpacked and replaced in the warehouse. I was truly concerned.

"I believe you spent your evening yesterday with young Mr. Hudson?" said he, turning to me.

"Yes, sir,—I am sincerely sorry—"

"Sorrow, in these cases, does no good, sir," interrupted he. "I thought I had sufficiently warned you of the danger of forming that intimacy. Midnight carousing will not do for men of business."

"Carousing, sir!" said I. "Give me leave to assure you that we were not carousing. We were only at a frog-concert."

Mr. Croft, who had at least suppressed his displeasure till now, looked absolutely angry; he thought I was making a joke of him. When I convinced him that I was in earnest, he changed from anger to astonishment, with a large mixture of contempt in his nasal muscles.

"A frog-concert!" repeated he. "And is it possible that any man could neglect an invoice merely to go to hear a parcel of frogs croaking in a swamp? Sir, you will never do in a mercantile house." He walked off to the warehouse, and left me half mortified and half provoked.

From this time forward all hopes from Mr. Croft's friendship were at an end. He was coldly civil to me during the few remaining days of the fortnight that we stayed at his house, He took the trouble, however, of looking out for a cheap and tolerably comfortable lodging for my wife and boy; the rent of which he desired to pay for his relation, he said, as long as I should remain in Philadelphia, or till I should find myself in some eligible situation. He seemed pleased with Lucy, and said she was a very properly conducted, well disposed, prudent young woman, whom he was not ashamed to own for a cousin. He repeated, at parting, that he should be happy to afford me every assistance in reason, towards pursuing any feasible plan of advancing myself; but it was his decided opinion that I could never succeed in a mercantile line.

I never liked Mr. Croft; he was much too punctual, too much of an automaton, for me; but I should have felt more regret at leaving him, and losing his friendship, and should have expressed more gratitude for his kindness to Lucy and my boy, if my head had not at the time been full of young Hudson. He professed the warmest regard for me, congratulated me on getting free from old Croft's mercantile clutches, and assured me that such a man as I was could not fail to succeed in the world by my own talents and the assistance of friends and good connexions.

I was now almost every day at his father's house in company with numbers of rich and gay people, who were all my friends. I was the life of society, was invited every where, and accepted every invitation, because I could not offend Mr. Hudson's intimate acquaintance.

From day to day, from week to week, from month to month, I went on in this style. I was old Hudson's grand favourite, and every body told me he could do any thing he pleased for me. I had formed a scheme, a bold scheme, of obtaining from government a large tract of territory in the ceded lands of Louisiana, and of collecting a subscription in Philadelphia among my friends, to make a settlement there: the subscribers to be paid by instalments, so much the first year, so much the second, and so onward, till the whole should be liquidated. I was to collect hands from the next ships, which were expected to be full of emigrants from Ireland and Scotland. I had soon a long list of subscribers, who gave me their names always after dinner, or after supper. Old Hudson wrote his name at the head of the list, with an ostentatiously large sum opposite to it.

As nothing could be done until the ensuing spring, when the ships were expected, I spent my time in the same convivial manner. The spring came, but there was no answer obtained from government respecting the ceded territory; and a delay of a few months was necessary. Mr. Hudson, the father, was the person who had undertaken to apply for the grant; and he spoke always of the scheme, and of his own powers of carrying it into effect, in the most confident manner. From his conversation any body would have supposed that the mines of Peru were upon his plantation; and that in comparison with his the influence of the President of the United States was nothing. I was a full twelvemonth before I was convinced that he was a boaster and a fabulist; and I was another twelvemonth before I could persuade myself that he was one of the most selfish, indolent, and obstinate of human beings. He was delighted to have me always at his table to entertain him and his guests, but he had not the slightest real regard for me, or care for my interests. He would talk to me as long as I pleased of his possessions, and his improvements, and his wonderful crops; but the moment I touched upon any of my own affairs, he would begin to yawn, throw himself on a sofa, and seem going to sleep. Whenever I mentioned his subscription, he would say with a frown—"We will talk of that, Basil, to-morrow."

Of my whole list of subscribers, not above four ever paid a shilling into my hands: their excuse always was, "When government has given an answer about the ceded territory, we will pay the subscriptions;" and the answer of government always was—"When the subscriptions are paid, we will make out a grant of the land." I was disgusted, and out of spirits; but I thought all my chance was to persevere, and to keep my friends in good-humour: so that I was continually under the necessity of appearing the same jovial companion, laughing, singing, and drinking, when, Heaven knows, my heart was heavy enough.

At the end of the second year of promises, delays, and disappointments, my Lucy, who had always foretold how things would turn out, urged me to withdraw myself from this idle society, to give up my scheme, and to take the management of a small plantation in conjunction with the brother of Mr. Croft. His regard for my wife, who had won much upon this family by her excellent conduct, induced him to make me this offer; but I considered so long, and hesitated so much, whether I should accept of this proposal, that the time for accepting it passed away.

I had still hopes that my friend, young Hudson, would enable me to carry my grand project into execution; he had a considerable plantation in Jamaica, left to him by his grandfather on the mother's side; he was to be of age, and to take possession of it the ensuing year, and he proposed to sell it, and to apply some of the purchase-money to our scheme, of the success of which he had as sanguine expectations as I had myself. He was of a most enthusiastic, generous temper. I had obtained the greatest influence over him, and I am convinced, at this time, there was nothing in the world he would not have sacrificed for my sake. All that he required from me was to be his constant companion. He was extravagantly fond of field sports; and, though a Londoner, I was a good shot, and a good angler; for, during the time I was courting Lucy, I found it necessary to make myself a sportsman to win the favour of her brothers. With these accomplishments, my hold upon the esteem and affections of my friend was all-powerful. Every day in the season we went out shooting or fishing together: then, in the winter-time, we had various employments, I mean, various excuses for idleness. Hudson was a great skaiter, and he had infinite diversion in teaching me to skait at the hazard of my skull. He was also to initiate me in the American pastime of sleighing, or sledging. Many a desperately cold winter's day I have submitted to be driven in his sledge, when I would much rather, I own, have been safe and snug by my own fireside, with my wife.

Poor Lucy spent her time in a disagreeable and melancholy way during these three years: for, while I was out almost every day and all day long, she was alone in her lodging for numberless hours. She never repined, but always received me with a good-humoured countenance when I came home, even after sitting up half the night to wait for my return from Hudson's suppers. It grieved me to the heart to see her thus seemingly deserted, but I comforted myself with the reflection that this way of life would last but for a short time; that my friend would soon be of age, and able to fulfil all his promises; and that we should then all live together in happiness. I assured Lucy that the present idle, if not dissipated, manner in which I spent my days was not agreeable to my taste; that I was often extremely melancholy, even when I was forced to appear in the highest spirits; and that I often longed to be quietly with her, when I was obliged to sacrifice my time to friendship.

It would have been impossible that she and my child could have subsisted all this time independently, but for her steadiness and exertions. She would not accept of any pecuniary assistance except from her relation, Mr. Croft, who regularly paid the rent of her lodgings. She undertook to teach some young ladies, whom Mrs, Croft introduced to her, various kinds of fine needlework, in which she excelled; and for this she was well paid. I know that she never cost me one farthing, during the three years and three months that we lived in Philadelphia. But even for this I do not give her so much credit as for her sweet temper during these trials, and her great forbearance in never reproaching or disputing with me. Many wives, who are called excellent managers, make their husbands pay tenfold in suffering what they save in money. This was not my Lucy's way; and, therefore, with my esteem and respect, she ever had my fondest affections. I was in hopes that the hour was just coming when I should be able to prove this to her, and when we should no longer be doomed to spend our days asunder. But, alas! her judgment was better than mine.

My friend Hudson was now within six weeks of being of age, when, unfortunately, there arrived in Philadelphia a company of players from England. Hudson, who was eager for every thing that had the name of pleasure, insisted upon my going with him to their first representation. Among the actresses there was a girl of the name of Marion, who seemed to be ordinary enough, just fit for a company of strolling players, but she danced passably well, and danced a great deal between the acts that night. Hudson clapped his hands till I was quite out of patience. He was in raptures, and the more I depreciated, the more he extolled the girl. I wished her in Nova Zembla, for I saw he was falling in love with her, and had a kind of presentiment of all that was to follow. To tell the matter briefly, (for what signifies dwelling upon past misfortunes?) the more young Hudson's passion increased for this dancing girl, the more his friendship for me declined; for I had frequent arguments with him upon the subject, and did all I could to open his eyes. I saw that the damsel had art, that she knew the extent of her power, and that she would draw her infatuated lover in to marry her. He was headstrong and violent in all his passions; he quarrelled with me, carried the girl off to Jamaica, married her the day he was of age, and settled upon his plantation. There was an end of all my hopes about the ceded territory.

Lucy, who was always my resource in misfortune, comforted me by saying I had done my duty in combating my friend's folly at the expense of my own interest; and that, though he had quarrelled with me, she loved me the better for it.

Reflecting upon my own history and character, I have often thought it a pity that, with certain good qualities, and I will add talents, which deserved a better fate, I should have never succeeded in any thing I attempted, because I could not conquer one seemingly slight defect in my disposition, which had grown into a habit. Thoroughly determined by Lucy's advice to write to Mr. Croft, to request he would give me another trial, I put off sending the letter till the next day; and that very morning Mr. Croft set off on a journey to a distant part of the country, to see a daughter who was newly married.

I was vexed, and from a want of something better to do, went out a-shooting, to get rid of disagreeable thoughts. I shot several pheasants, and when I came home, carried them, as was my custom, to old Mr. Hudson's kitchen, and gave them to the cook. I happened to stay in the kitchen to feed a favourite dog, while the cook was preparing the birds I had brought. I observed, in the crop of one of the pheasants, some bright green leaves, and some buds, which I suspected to be the leaves and buds of the kalmia latifolia, a poisonous shrub. I was not quite certain, for I had almost forgotten the little botany which I knew before I went to China. I took the leaves home with me, to examine them at leisure, and to compare them with the botanical description; and I begged that the cook would not dress the birds till she saw or heard from me again. I promised to see her, or send to her the next day. But the next day, when I went to the library, to look into a book of botany, my attention was caught by some new reviews, which were just arrived from London. I put off the examination of the kalmia latifolia till the day after. To-morrow, said I, will do just as well, for I know the cook will not dress the pheasants to-day: old Hudson does not like them till they have been kept a day or two.

To-morrow came, and the leaves were forgotten till evening, when I saw them lying on my table, and put them out of the way; lest my little boy should find and eat them. I was sorry that I had not examined them this day, but I satisfied myself in the same way as I had done before: to-morrow will do as well; the cook will not dress the pheasants to-day; old Hudson thinks them the, better for being kept two or three days.

To-morrow came; but, as the leaves of the kalmia latifolia were out of my sight, they went out of my mind. I was invited to an entertainment this day at the mayor's: there was a large company, and after dinner I was called upon, as usual, for a song; the favourite song of

"Dance and sing, Time's on the wing,
Life never knows return of spring;"

when a gentleman came in, pale and breathless, to tell us that Mr. Hudson and three gentlemen, who had been dining with him, were suddenly seized with convulsions after eating of a pheasant, and that they were not expected to live. My blood ran cold: I exclaimed, "My God! I am answerable for this." On my making this exclamation, there was immediate silence in the room; and every eye turned upon me with astonishment and horror. I fell back in my chair, and what passed afterward I know not; but when I came to myself, I found two men in the room with me, who were set to guard me. The bottles and glasses were still upon the table, but the company were all dispersed; and the mayor, as my guards informed me, was gone to Mr. Hudson's to take his dying deposition.

In this instance, as in all cases of sudden alarm, report had exaggerated the evil: Mr. Hudson, though extremely ill, was not dying; his three guests, after some hours' illness, were perfectly recovered. Mr. Hudson, who had eaten the most plentifully of the pheasant, was not himself, as he said, for two days; the third day he was able to see company at dinner as usual, and my mind was relieved from an insupportable state of anxiety.

Upon examination, the mayor was convinced that I was perfectly innocent: the cook told the exact truth, blamed herself for not sending to me before she dressed the birds; but said that she concluded I had found the leaves I took home were harmless, as I never came to tell her the contrary.

I was liberated, and went home to my wife. She clasped me in her arms, but could not articulate a syllable. By her joy at seeing me again, she left me to judge of what she must have suffered during this terrible interval.

For some time after this unfortunate accident happened, it continued to be the subject of general conversation in Philadelphia. The story was told a thousand different ways, and the comments upon it were in various ways injurious to me. Some blamed me, for what indeed I deserved to be most severely blamed, my delaying one hour to examine the leaves found in the crop of the pheasant; others affected to think it absolutely impossible that any human being could be so dilatory and negligent, where the lives of fellow-creatures and friends, and friends by whom I had been treated with the utmost hospitality for years, were concerned. Others, still more malicious, hinted that, though I had been favoured by the mayor, and perhaps by the goodness of poor Mr. Hudson, there must be something more than had come to light in the business; and some boldly pronounced that the story of the leaves of the kalmia latifolia was a mere blind, for that the pheasant could not have been rendered poisonous by such means.

[Footnote: "In the severe winter of the years 1790 and 1791, there appeared to be such unequivocal reasons for believing that several persons in Philadelphia had died in consequence of their eating pheasants, in whose crops the leaves and buds of the kalmia latifolia were found, that the mayor of the city thought it prudent and his duty to warn the people against the use of this bird, by a public proclamation. I know that by many persons, especially by some lovers of pheasants' flesh, the *circumstance just mentioned was supposed to be destitute of foundation: but the foundation was a solid one."*

Vide a paper by B. Smith Barton, M.D., American Transactions, vol. li.]

That a motive might not be wanting for the crime, it was whispered that old Mr. Hudson had talked of leaving me a considerable legacy, which I was impatient to touch, that I might carry my adventuring schemes into execution. I was astonished as much as shocked at the sudden alteration in the manners of all my acquaintants. The tide of popularity changed, and I was deserted. That those who had lived with me so long in convivial intimacy, that those who had courted, admired, flattered me, those who had so often professed themselves my friends, could suddenly, without the slightest probability, believe me capable of the most horrible crime, appeared to me scarcely credible. In reality, many would not give themselves the trouble to think about the matter, but were glad of a pretence to shake off the acquaintance of a man of whose stories and songs they began to be weary, and who had put their names to a subscription, which they did not wish to be called upon to pay. Such is the world! Such is the fate of all good fellows, and excellent bottle companions! Certain to be deserted, by their dear friends, at the least reverse of fortune.

CHAPTER VI

My situation in Philadelphia was now so disagreeable, and my disgust and indignation were so great, that I determined to quit the country. My real friend, Mr. Croft, was absent all this time from town. I am sure, if he had been at home, he would have done me justice; for, though he never liked me, he was a just, slow-judging man, who would not have been run away with by the hurry of popular prejudice: I had other reasons for regretting his absence: I could not conveniently quit America without money, and he was the only person to whom I could or would apply for assistance. We had not many debts, for which I must thank my excellent wife; but, when every thing to the last farthing was paid, I was obliged to sell my watch and some trinkets, to get money for our voyage. I was not accustomed to such things, and I was ashamed to go to the pawnbroker's, lest I should be met and recognized by some of my friends. I wrapped myself up in an old surtout, and slouched my hat over my face.

As I was crossing the quay, I met a party of gentlemen walking arm in arm. I squeezed past them, but one stopped to look after me; and, though I turned down another street to escape him, he dogged me unperceived. Just as I came out of the pawnbroker's shop, I saw him posted opposite to me: I brushed by; I could with pleasure have knocked him down for his impertinence. By the time that I had reached the corner of the street, I heard a child calling after me. I stopped, and a little boy put into my hands my watch, saying, "Sir, the gentleman says you left your watch and these thingumbobs by mistake."

"What gentleman?"

"I don't know, but he was one that said I looked like an honest chap, and he'd trust me to run and give you the watch. He is dressed in a blue coat. He went toward the quay. That's all I know."

On opening the paper of trinkets I found a card with these words: "Barny—with kind thanks."

Barny! Poor Barny! The Irishman whose passage I paid coming to America three years ago. Is it possible?

I ran after him the way which the child directed, and was so fortunate as just to catch a glimpse of the skirt of his coat, as he went into a neat, good-looking house. I walked up and down some time, expecting him to come out again; for I could not suppose that it belonged to Barny. I asked a grocer, who was leaning over his hatch door, if he knew who lived in the next house?

"An Irish gentleman, of the name of O'Grady."

"And his Christian name?"

"Here it is in my books, sir—Barnaby O'Grady."

I knocked at Mr. O'Grady's door, and made my way into the parlour; where I found him, his two sons and his wife, sitting very sociably at tea. He and the two young men rose immediately to set me a chair.

"You are welcome, kindly welcome, sir," said he. "This is an honour I never expected any way. Be pleased to take the seat near the fire. 'Twould be hard indeed if you should not have the best seat that's to be had in this house, where we none of us never should have sat, nor had seats to sit upon, but for you."

The sons pulled off my shabby great coat, and took away my hat, and the wife made up the fire. There was something in their manner altogether which touched me so much, that it was with difficulty I could keep myself from bursting into tears. They saw this, and Barny, (for I shall never call him any thing else,) as he thought that I should like better to hear of public affairs than to speak of my own, began to ask his sons if they had seen the day's papers, and what news there were?

As soon as I could command my voice, I congratulated his family upon the happy situation in which I found them; and asked by what lucky accidents they had succeeded so well?

"The luckiest accident ever happened me before or since I came to America," said Barny, "was being on board the same vessel with such a man as you. If you had not given me the first lift, I had been down for good and all, and trampled under foot long and long ago. But after that first lift, all was as easy as life. My two sons here were not taken from me—God bless you! for I never can bless you enough for that. The lads were left to work for me and with me; and we never parted, hand or heart, but just kept working on together, and put all our earnings as fast as we got them, into the hands of that good woman, and lived hard at first, as we were bred and born to do, thanks be to Heaven! Then we swore against drink of all sorts entirely. And, as I had occasionally served the masons, when I lived a labouring man in the county of Dublin, and knew something of that business, why, whatever I knew I made the most of, and a trowel felt no ways strange to me; so I went to work, and had higher wages at first than I deserved. The same with the two boys: one was as much of a blacksmith as would shoe a horse; and t'other a bit of a carpenter; and the one got plenty of work in the forges, and t'other in the dockyards, as a ship carpenter. So early and late, morning and evening, we were all at the work, and just went this way struggling on even for a twelvemonth, and found, with the high wages and constant employ we had met, that we were getting greatly better in the world. Besides, the wife was not idle. When a girl, she had seen baking, and had always a good notion of it, and just tried her hand upon it now, and found the loaves went down with the customers, and the customers coming faster and faster for them; and this was a great help. Then I grew master mason, and had my men under me, and took a house to build by the job, and that did; and then on to another and another; and after building many for the neighbours, 'twas fit and my turn, I thought, to build one for myself, which I did out of theirs, without wronging them of a penny. And the boys grew master-men in their line; and when they got good coats, nobody could say against them, for they had come fairly by them, and became them well perhaps for that reason. So, not to be tiring you too much, we went on from good to better, and better to best; and if it pleased God to question me how it was we got on so well in the world, I should answer, Upon my conscience, myself does not know; except it be that we never made Saint Monday, nor never put off till the morrow what we could do the day." I believe I sighed deeply at this observation, notwithstanding the comic phraseology in which it was expressed.

[Footnote: Saint Monday, or Saint Crispin. It is a custom in Ireland, among shoemakers, if they intoxicate themselves on Sunday, to do no work on Monday; and this they call making a Saint Monday, or keeping Saint Crispin's day. Many have adopted this good custom from the example of the shoemakers.]

"But all this is no rule for a gentleman born," pursued the good-natured Barny, in answer, I suppose, to the sigh which I uttered; "nor is it any disparagement to him if he has not done as well in a place like America, where he had not the means; not being used to bricklaying and slaving with his hands, and striving as we did. Would it be too much liberty to ask you to drink a cup of tea, and to taste a slice of my good woman's bread and butter? And happy the day we see you eating it, and only wish we could serve you in any way whatsoever."

I verily believe the generous fellow forgot, at this instant, that he had redeemed my watch and wife's trinkets. He would not let me thank him as much as I wished, but kept pressing upon me fresh offers of service. When he found I was going to leave America, he asked what vessel we should go in? I was really afraid to tell him, lest he should attempt to pay for my passage. But for this he had, as I afterwards found, too much delicacy of sentiment. He discovered, by questioning the captains, in what ship we were to sail; and, when we went on board, we found him and his sons there to take leave of us, which they did in the most affectionate manner; and, after they were gone, we found in the state cabin, directed to me, every thing that could be useful or agreeable to us, as sea-stores, for a long voyage.

How I wronged this man, when I thought his expressions of gratitude were not sincere, because they were not made exactly in the mode and with the accent of my own countrymen! I little thought that Barny and his sons would be the only persons who would bid us a friendly adieu when we were to leave America.

We had not exhausted our bountiful provision of sea-stores when we were set ashore in England. We landed at Liverpool; and I cannot describe the melancholy feelings with which I sat down, in the little back parlour of the inn, to count my money, and to calculate whether we had enough to carry us to London. Is this, thought I, as I looked at the few guineas and shillings spread on the table, is this all I have in this world? I, my wife, and child! And is this the end of three years' absence from my native country? As the negroes say of a fool who takes a voyage in vain, I am come back "with little more than the hair upon my head." Is this the end of all my hopes, and all my talents? What will become of my wife and child? I ought to insist upon her going home to her friends, that she may at least have the necessaries and comforts of life, till I am able to maintain her.

The tears started from my eyes; they fell upon an old newspaper, which lay upon the table under my elbow. I took it up to hide my face from Lucy and my child, who just then came into the room: and, as I read without well knowing what, I came among the advertisements to my own name.

"If Mr. Basil Lowe, or his heir, will apply to Mr. Gregory, attorney, No. 34, Cecil-street, he will hear of something to his advantage."

I started up with an exclamation of joy, wiped my tears from the newspaper, put it into Lucy's hand, pointed to the advertisement, and ran to take places in the London coach for the next morning. Upon this occasion I certainly did not delay. Nor did I, when we arrived in London, put off one moment going to Mr. Gregory's, No. 34, Cecil-street.

Upon application to him I was informed that a very distant relation of mine, a rich miser, had just died, and had left his accumulated treasures to me, "because I was the only one of his relations who had never cost him a single farthing." Other men have to complain of their ill fortune, perhaps with justice; and this is a great satisfaction, which I have never enjoyed; for I must acknowledge that all my disasters have arisen from my own folly. Fortune has been uncommonly favourable to me. Without any merit of my own, or rather, as it appeared, in consequence of my negligent habits, which prevented me from visiting a rich relation, I was suddenly raised from the lowest state of pecuniary distress to the height of affluent prosperity.

I took possession of a handsome house in an agreeable part of the town, and enjoyed the delight of sharing all the comforts and luxuries which wealth could procure, with the excellent woman who had been my support in adversity. I must do myself the justice to observe that I did not become dissipated or extravagant; affection and gratitude to my Lucy filled my whole mind, and preserved me from the faults incident to those who rise suddenly from poverty to wealth. I did not forget my good friend, Mr. Nun, who had relieved me formerly from prison; of course I paid the debt which he had forgiven, and lost no opportunity of showing him kindness and gratitude.

I was now placed in a situation where the best parts of my character appeared to advantage, and where the grand defect of my disposition was not apparently of any consequence. I was not now obliged, like a man of business, to be punctual; and delay, in mere engagements of pleasure, was a trifling offence, and a matter of raillery among my acquaintance. My talents in conversation were admired, and, if I postponed letter-writing, my correspondents only tormented me a little with polite remonstrances. I was conscious that I was not cured of my faults; but I rejoiced that I was not now obliged to reform, or in any danger of involving those I loved in distress, by my negligence.

For one year I was happy, and flattered myself that I did not waste my time; for, at my leisure, I read with attention all the ancient and modern works upon education. I resolved to select from them what appeared most judicious and practicable; and so to form, from the beauties of each, a perfect system for the advantage of my son. He was my only child; he had lived with me eighteen months in prison: he was the darling of his mother, whom I adored, and he was thought to be in mind and person a striking resemblance of myself. How many reasons had I to love him!—I doted upon the child. He certainly showed great quickness of intellect, and gave as fair a promise of talents as could be expected at his age. I formed hopes of his future excellence and success in the world, as sanguine as those which my poor father had early formed of mine. I determined to watch carefully over his temper, and to guard him particularly against that habit of procrastination which had been the bane of my life.

One day, while I was alone in my study, leaning on my elbow, and meditating upon the system of education which I designed for my son, my wife came to me and said, "My dear, I have just heard from our friend, Mr. Nun, a circumstance that alarms me a good deal. You know little Harry Nun was inoculated at the same time with our Basil, and by the same person. Mrs. Nun, and all the family, thought he had several spots, just as much as our boy had, and that that was enough; but two years afterwards, while we were in America, Harry Nun caught the small-pox in the natural way, and died. Now it seems the man who inoculated him was quite ignorant; for two or three other children, whom he attended, have caught the disease since, though he was positive that they were safe. Don't you think we had better have our boy inoculated again immediately, by some proper person?"

"Undoubtedly, my dear; undoubtedly. But I think we had better have him vaccined. I am not sure, however; but I will ask Dr. —'s opinion this day, and be guided by that; I shall see him at dinner: he has promised to dine with us."

Some accident prevented him from coming, and I thought of writing to him the next day, but afterward put it off. Lucy came again into my study, where she was sure to find me in the morning. "My dear," said she, "do you recollect that you desired me to defer inoculating our little boy till you could decide whether it be best to inoculate him in the common way or the vaccine?"

"Yes, my dear, I recollect it perfectly well. I am much inclined to the vaccine. My friend, Mr. L—, has had all his children vaccined, and I just wait to see the effect."

"Oh, my love!" said Lucy, "do not wait any longer; for you know we run a terrible risk of his catching the small-pox, every day, every hour."

"We have run that risk, and escaped for these three years past," said I; "and, in my opinion, the boy has had the small-pox."

"So Mr. and Mrs. Nun thought, and you see what has happened. Remember our boy was inoculated by the same man. I am sure, ever since Mr. Nun mentioned this, I never take little Basil out to walk, I never see him in a shop, I never have him in the carriage with me, without being in terror. Yesterday a woman came to the coach-door with a child in her arms, who had a breaking out on his face. I thought it was the small-pox, and was so terrified that I had scarcely strength or presence of mind enough to draw up the glass. Our little boy was leaning out of the door to give a halfpenny to the child. My God! if that child had the small-pox!"

"My love," said I, "do not alarm yourself so terribly; the boy shall be inoculated to-morrow."

"To-morrow! Oh, my dearest love, do not put it off till to-morrow," said Lucy; "let him be inoculated to-day."

"Well, my dear, only keep your mind easy, and he shall be inoculated to-day, if possible; surely you must know I love the boy as well as you do, and am as anxious about him as you can be."

"I am sure of it, my love," said Lucy; "I meant no reproach. But since you have decided that the boy shall be vaccined, let us send directly for the surgeon, and have it done, and then he will be safe."

She caught hold of the bell-cord to ring for a servant: I stopped her.

"No, my dear, don't ring," said I; "for the men are both out. I have sent one to the library for the new Letters on Education, and the other to the rational toy-shop for some things I want for the child."

"Then if the servants are out, I had better walk to the surgeon's, and bring him back with me."

"No, my dear," said I; "I must see Mr. L—'s children first. I am going out immediately; I will call upon them: they are healthy children; we can have the vaccine infection from them, and I will inoculate the boy myself."

Lucy submitted. I take a melancholy pleasure in doing her justice, by recording every argument that she used, and every persuasive word that she said to me, upon this occasion. I am anxious to show that she was not in the least to blame. I alone am guilty! I alone ought to have been the sufferer! It will scarcely be believed—I can hardly believe it myself, that, after all Lucy said to me, I delayed two hours, and stayed to finish making an extract from Rousseau's Emilius before I set out. When I arrived at Mr. L—'s, the children were just gone out to take an airing, and I could not see them. A few hours may sometimes make all the difference between health and sickness, happiness and misery: I put off till the next day the inoculation of my child.

In the mean time a coachman came to me to be hired: my boy was playing about the room, and, as I afterward collected, went close up to the man, and, while I was talking, stood examining a greyhound upon his buttons. I asked the coachman many questions, and kept him for some time in the room. Just as I agreed to take him into my service, he said he could not come to live with me till the next week, because one of his children was ill of the small-pox.

These words struck me to the heart. I had a dreadful presentiment of what was to follow. I remember starting from my seat, and driving the man out of the house with violent menaces. My boy, poor innocent victim! followed, trying to pacify me, and holding me back by the skirts of my coat. I caught him up in my arms. I could not kiss him; I felt as if I was his murderer. I set him down again; indeed I trembled so violently that I could not hold him. The child ran for his mother.

I cannot dwell on these things. Our boy sickened the next week; and the week afterward died in his mother's arms! Her health had suffered much by the trials which she had gone through since our marriage. The disapprobation of her father, the separation from all her friends, who were at variance with me, my imprisonment, and then the death of her only child, were too much for her fortitude. She endeavoured to conceal this from me; but I saw that her health was rapidly declining. She was always fond of the country; and, as my sole object now in life was to do whatsoever I could to console and please her, I proposed to sell our house in town, and to settle somewhere in the country. In the neighbourhood of her father and mother there was a pretty place to be let, which I had often heard her mention with delight; I determined to take it: I had secret hopes that her friends would be gratified by this measure, and that they would live upon good terms with us. Her mother had seemed, by her letters, to be better disposed towards me since my rich relation had left me his fortune. Lucy expressed great pleasure at the idea of going to live in the country, near her parents; and I was rejoiced to see her smile once more. Being naturally of a sanguine disposition, hope revived in my heart; I flattered myself that we might yet be happy, that my Lucy would recover her peace of mind and her health, and that perhaps Heaven might bless us with another child.

I lost no time in entering into treaty for the estate in the country, and I soon found a purchaser for my excellent house in town. But my evil genius prevailed. I had neglected to renew the insurance of my house; the policy was out but nine days, when a fire broke out in one of my servants' rooms at midnight, and, in spite of all the assistance we could procure, the house was burnt to the ground. I carried my wife out senseless in my arms; and, when I had deposited her in a place of safety, returned to search for a portfolio, in which was the purchase-money of the country estate, all in bank-notes. But whether this portfolio was carried off by some of the crowd, which had assembled round the ruins of my house, or whether it was consumed in the flames, I cannot determine. A more miserable wretch than I was could now scarcely be found in the world; and, to complete my misfortunes, I felt the consciousness that they were all occasioned by my own folly.

[Footnote: Founded on fact.]

I am now coming to the most extraordinary and the most interesting part of my history. A new and surprising accident happened.

[Note by the Editor.—What this accident was can never now be known; for Basil put off finishing his history till TO-MORROW.

This fragment was found in an old escritoir, in an obscure lodging in Swallow-street.

August, 1803.]

Maria Edgeworth – A Short Biography

Maria Edgeworth was born at Black Bourton, Oxfordshire on January 1st 1768, the second child of Richard Lovell Edgeworth and Anna Maria Edgeworth (née Elers).

Her early years were with her mother's family in England. Sadly, her mother died when Maria was only five. When her father married his second wife, Honora Sneyd, in 1773, the family went to live at his estate, Edgeworthstown, in County Longford, Ireland.

Maria was later sent to Mrs. Lattafière's school in Derby after Honora fell ill in 1775. There she studied dancing, French and other subjects. After Honora died in 1780 Maria's father married Honora's sister, Elizabeth, causing much social disapproved.

Maria transferred to Mrs. Devis's school in Upper Wimpole Street, London. Her father began to focus more attention on Maria in 1781 when she nearly lost her sight to an eye infection.

She returned home to Ireland at 14, and took charge of her younger siblings. She herself was home-tutored by her father in Irish economics and politics, science, literature and law. Despite her youth literature was in her blood.

She became her father's assistant in managing the Edgeworthstown estate, which had become run-down during the family's absence. Maria would now live and write there for the rest of her life.

With her father she began a lifelong academic collaboration. She meticulously detailed daily Irish life; a valuable lodestone of references for later use in her novels. Maria mixed with the Anglo-Irish gentry, and her aunt, Margaret Ruxton of Blackcastle, supplied her with the novels of Anne Radcliffe and William Godwin and encouraged her ambition to write.

Edgeworth's first published work in 1795 was 'Letters for Literary Ladies'. That same year 'An Essay on the Noble Science of Self-Justification', written for a female audience, states that the fair sex is endowed with an art of self-justification and women should use their gifts to continually challenge the force and power of men, especially their husbands, with wit and intelligence.

In 1796 her first children's book, 'The Parent's Assistant', which included the much loved short story 'The Purple Jar' was published.

In 1798 her father married for the fourth and last time, this time to Frances Beaufort. Frances was a year younger than Maria and they quickly became close.

'Practical Education' (1798) is a progressive work on education that combines the ideas of Locke and Rousseau with scientific inquiry. Edgeworth believed that "learning should be a positive experience and that the discipline of education is more important during the formative years than the acquisition of knowledge." The ultimate goal of Edgeworth's system was to create an independent thinker who understands the consequences of his or her actions.

Her first novel, 'Castle Rackrent' (1800) was published anonymously without her father's knowledge. It was an immediate success and firmly established Maria's appeal to the public.

'Belinda' (1801), was her first full-length novel. It dealt with love, courtship, and marriage, and she examined these as conflicts within her "own personality and environment; conflicts between reason and feeling, restraint and individual freedom, and society and free spirit." Startlingly, 'Belinda' also included a depiction of interracial marriage between an African servant and an English farm-girl. Later editions of the novel, in line with unforgiving times, removed these sections.

Frances also pushed the family to travel more first London (1800), the Midlands (1802) and later the continent; first to Brussels and then to France. They met all the notables, with Maria even receiving a proposal of marriage from a Swedish courtier.

'Tales of Fashionable Life' (1809 and 1812) is a 2-series collection of short stories that often had its focus on the life of women. The second series was so successful that she was now the most commercially successful novelist of her age and ranked alongside her contemporaries Jane Austen and Sir Walter Scott.

On a visit to London in 1813, she met many notables including Lord Byron. She entered into a long correspondence with Sir Walter Scott after the publication of 'Waverley' in 1814, in which he acknowledged her influence, and they formed a lasting friendship. She visited him in Scotland at Abbotsford House in 1823 and the following year he visited Edgeworthstown.

After debating the issue with the economist David Ricardo, Maria came to believe that better management and the further use of science in agriculture would raise food production and help to lower prices. They were both in favour of Catholic Emancipation, enfranchisement for Catholics without property restrictions, agricultural reform and increased educational opportunities for women.

She worked particularly hard to improve the living standards of the poor in Edgeworthstown and to provide schools for the local children whatever their denomination.

After her father's death in 1817 she edited his memoirs, and extended them with her biographical addenda. Her father had married 4 times and sired 22 children. At the height of her creative endeavours, Maria had written, "Seriously it was to please my Father I first exerted myself to write, to please him I continued."

Maria worked for the relief of the famine-stricken Irish peasants during the Irish Potato Famine. She wrote 'Orlandino' and gave the proceeds to the Relieve Fund. However, during the famine her 'business head' insisted that only those tenants who had paid their full rent would receive any relief. She also punished any tenants who voted against her Tory preferences.

'Helen' (1834) is Maria Edgeworth's final novel, the only one she wrote after her father's death. Here the focus was on characters and situation and not moral lessons.

William Rowan Hamilton was elected president of the Royal Irish Academy and Maria's advice was constantly sought especially regarding literature in Ireland. She suggested that women should be allowed to participate in Academy events. Hamilton made Maria an honorary member in 1837.

After a visit to see her relations Maria was struck with severe chest pains and died suddenly of a heart attack in Edgeworthstown on 22nd May 1849. She was 81.

Maria Edgeworth is buried in the family tomb at St. John's Church, Edgeworthstown, Longford, Ireland.

Maria Edgeworth – A Concise Bibliography

Letters for Literary Ladies (1795) Second Edition (1798)
An Essay on the Noble Science of Self-Justification (1795)
The Parent's Assistant (1796)
Practical Education (1798) (2 Vols; collaborated with her father and step-mother)
Castle Rackrent (1800) Novel
Early Lessons (1801)
Moral Tales (1801)
Belinda (1801) Novel
The Mental Thermometer (1801)
Essay on Irish Bulls (1802)
Popular Tales (1804)
The Modern Griselda (1804)
Moral Tales for Young People (1805) (6 Vols)
Leonora (1806)
Essays in Professional Education (1809)
Tales of Fashionable Life (1809)
Ennui (1809) Novel
The Absentee (1812) Novel
Patronage (1814) Novel
Harrington (1817) Novel
Ormond (1817) Novel
Comic Dramas (1817)

Memoirs of Richard Lovell Edgeworth (1820) Editor
Rosamond: A Sequel to Early Lessons (1821)
Frank: A Sequel to Frank in Early Lessons (1822)
Tomorrow (1823) Novel
Helen (1834) novel
Orlandino (1848) Temperance novel